SHAW

AND THE NINETEENTH-CENTURY

THEATER

For Joseph and Sally Meisel

SHAW

AND THE

NINETEENTH-CENTURY

THEATER

BY MARTIN MEISEL

LIMELIGHT EDITIONS

NEW YORK

First Limelight Edition, August 1984
Copyright © 1963, © 1968 by Princeton University Press
All rights reserved under International and Pan-American Copyright
Conventions. Published in the United States by Proscenium Publishers
Inc., New York, and simultaneously in Canada by Fitzhenry & Whiteside
Limited, Toronto.
Originally published by Princeton University Press.

Manufactured in the United States of America

Publication of this book has been aided by
Dartmouth College and by
the Ford Foundation program
to support publication, through university presses,
of work in the humanities and social sciences

Library of Congress Cataloging in Publication Data
Meisel, Martin.
Shaw and the nineteenth-century theater.
Reprint. Originally published: Princeton, N.J.:
Princeton University Press, 1963.
Bibliography: p.
Includes index.
1. Shaw, Bernard, 1856–1950—Criticism and interpretation. 2. English
drama—19th century—History and criticism. I. Title. II. Title: Shaw
and the 19th-century theatre.
PR5367.M38   1984   822'.912   84-4449
ISBN 0-87910-017-6

PREFACE

U N L E S S otherwise indicated, references to Shaw's writings are to Constable's Standard Edition of the Works of Bernard Shaw (London, 1930-1950), and dates in parentheses accompanying titles of nineteenth-century plays are for the first London production. Most nineteenth-century plays reached print in the form of "acting editions." These are identified in the text by the following abbreviations:

Baker—Baker's Edition of Plays
Cumberland—Cumberland's British Theatre
DeWitt—DeWitt's Acting Plays
French A. E.—French's Acting Edition
French S. D.—French's Standard Drama
Lacy—Lacy's Acting Edition
Sergel—Sergel's Acting Drama (The Dramatic Publishing Company)
Spencer—Spencer's Boston Theatre

Two abbreviations are used with a frequency which justifies their excessive compression. These are *OTN* for the three volumes of Shaw's dramatic criticism from the *Saturday Review*, collected in the Standard Edition as *Our Theatres in the Nineties*, and *D.E.M.* for the nineteenth-century files of the *Dublin Evening Mail*.

The idiosyncrasies of Shaw's spelling and punctuation are preserved throughout, though no attempt is made to undo the work of intermediate editorial hands.

I am indebted to The Public Trustee and The Society of Authors, representing the Bernard Shaw Estate, for permission to quote from Shaw's writings, published and unpublished; to G. W. Nash of the Gabrielle Enthoven Theatre Collection and to the Victoria & Albert Museum, to Dr. John D. Gordan of the Henry W. and Albert A. Berg Collection and The New York Public Library, to Miss Helen D. Willard of the Harvard

College Library Theatre Collection, to the Department of Manuscripts of The British Museum, and to Professor Alan Downer, for access to and permission to use manuscript and graphic material; to Mrs. Marguerite McAneny of the William Seymour Theatre Collection, Princeton University, to Miss Audrey Hosford of the Harvard Theatre Collection, and to the staff of the Dartmouth College Library, for their unfailing readiness to help.

I am indebted to Dartmouth College for grants that assisted in the preparation and publication of this study.

I am grateful to those who helped in the conception and shaping of the study, above all to Professors Alan Downer and G. E. Bentley of Princeton University; and to those who advised and criticized, namely Charles A. Carpenter, Jr., of the University of Delaware, Lewis Lockwood of Princeton University, Alex Zwerdling of the University of California at Berkeley, William Crawford, Philip Handler, Lawrence Harvey, Robert Hunter, and Noel Perrin of Dartmouth College, and R. Miriam Brokaw and Gail Filion of Princeton University Press. I am grateful to Mrs. Jennie Wells for her precision and heroism in grappling with several stages of the manuscript. I am at a loss to express my immense debt to my wife, Martha, whose forbearance and generosity do not extend to attempts to enumerate her virtues.

A NOTE TO THE SECOND PRINTING

"AND if I do not clearly express what I mean by that, it is either for the reason that having no conversational powers, I cannot express what I mean, or that having no meaning, I do not mean what I fail to express. Which, to the best of my belief, is not the case."—Mr. Grewgious in *The Mystery of Edwin Drood.*

Time has given me a little perspective on this book—enough to want to register some changes of mind and to declare what I have learned about its scope, intentions, and limitations. Some of this new learning has come from the book's readers; for example, it has not been clear to all readers that my ultimate concern is not to identify sources or even conventions and departures, but to help illuminate how the plays worked or were intended to work.

Most of what I have learned about the book, however, has been an indirect result of that continuing accumulation of evidence and materials and heretofore-unperceived-bearings with which the writer of a study of this sort always plagues himself. Probably the book is healthier for not being now forced to reckon with this accumulation. Yet, the accumulation does offer evidence for some very bare assertions in the book as well as evidence that would have cut through a deal of tortuous argument. For example, I should have liked to have been able to say originally, as I can say now, that Shaw was familiar with the chief theoretical and "practical" works that bore on acting in rhetorical drama of the passions.[1] And it would have saved me trouble on several counts had I been able to put my hands on Shaw's remark to William Archer: "I have finished the first act of my new play [*Mrs. Warren's Pro-*

[1] See Shaw's "Qualifications of the Complete Actor," *The Dramatic Review* (19 Sept. 1885), and his review of Francis Warner's *Physical Expression, The Pall Mall Gazette* (17 Sept. 1885).

fession], in which I have skilfully blended the plot of The Second Mrs Tanqueray with that of The Cenci."[2]

Much of the new accumulation bears on the non-Shavian nineteenth-century drama, one end of that definition of scope offered in the title of the book. I have learned something about the limitations of this book with respect to that title definition. The lines of my original investigation were set when preliminary exploration convinced me of the special relevance of the theater of Shaw's boyhood to his later art. That Shaw several times proclaimed this relevance was a notable comfort. Accordingly my exploration of what Shaw could have brought with him from the Dublin theater of the sixties and seventies was quite exhaustive; whereas my exploration of the London theater between 1876 (when Shaw left Dublin) and the early nineties (when he began to emerge as a man of the theater) was both more general and more selective. Furthermore I took the term "Nineteenth-Century" fairly literally, justified (I thought) beyond mere periodization by the knowledge that Shaw had sharply curtailed his theatergoing after leaving *The Saturday Review* in May 1898.

The evidence makes it plain, however, that the popular theater of Shaw's early London years and the commercial theater before 1914 had more to do than I thought with Shaw's playwriting, with his exploitation of familiar expectations, and his response to current fads and popularities. The earlier period, for example, produced W. S. Gilbert's farcical comedy *On Bail* (1877), whose arrest scene strikingly anticipates that in *The Devil's Disciple* in situation (the mistake of visitor for husband), in dramatic detail (the forced kiss, the exchange of garments, the put-aside handcuffs, the wife's terminal swoon), and even in some of its language. What Gilbert renders as melodramatic farce, however, Shaw restores to the key of ironic melodrama. Similarly, the situations of *Mrs. Warren's Profes-*

[2] *Collected Letters, 1874-1897*, ed. Dan H. Laurence (New York, 1965), p. 403.

sion have a fuller conventional reference than that provided by the contemporary Courtesan Play. The Drury Lane melodrama *Youth* (1881) by Paul Merritt and Augustus Harris, for example, contains a respectable elderly clergyman, father of the hero, who (in Dutton Cook's account) "had it seems gone sadly astray as a young man, and is now punished for his transgressions by the reappearance, after a lapse of thirty years, of a vindictive widow—one *Mrs. Walsingham* . . . who deals much in irony and makes money by usury, and . . . hasten[s] the ruin of the Vicar's son *Frank*."[3] Also relevant (especially in the light of the incest motif Shaw thought so important in *Mrs. Warren*) is the centennial revival, late in 1891, of Thomas Holcroft's *Road to Ruin*.

The later period also offers its evidence of a continuing connection between Shaw and the conventional theater. *Pygmalion*, for example, Shaw's response to the Cinderella romance, seems to have found some of its provocation in Israel Zangwill's *Merely Mary Ann* (1904), a play in which a boardinghouse slavey, "a slim, pretty, almost poetic figure, despite the smut or two on her face," is taken up and partly educated by an irascible artist-composer with blue blood and no money. Naturally she falls in love with him, skirts sexual ruin, and eventually—transformed into an heiress and lady—does marry him. It was in this play Eleanor Robson made her English debut, so impressing Shaw that he wooed her for his *Major Barbara*; and it seems clear that a later Eleanor Robson vehicle, Paul Armstrong's *Salomy Jane* (1907), based on a Bret Harte story, had something to do with *The Shewing-Up of Blanco Posnet*.

Though I would probably trim a number of earlier opinions if I had the chance, I have changed my mind—that is, reversed my opinion—at only two points. The National Theatre's transcendent production of *Uncle Vanya* has changed my mind

[3] *Nights at the Play* (London, 1883), p. 465.

—·[**xi**]·—

about trying to limit the Chekhovian character of *Heartbreak House* to thematic concerns, and I wonder at my curious original persuasion. A more drastic change of mind, since it affects my entire conception of Shaw's dramatic evolution, relates to his use of drawing-room drama, that mode Shaw associated with the once-revolutionary plays and stagecraft of T. W. Robertson and on which he heaped such scorn in the columns of *The Saturday Review*. I argue below that Shaw had no use at all for drawing-room drama; but I now am convinced that the full-blown Discussion Play, as embodied in *Getting Married*, *Misalliance*, and *Heartbreak House*, is the apotheosis of the fashionable drawing-room play, the assimilation of the drawing-room play to the drama of ideas. I argue below that the Discussion Play is a kind of cerebral farce, and there is a good deal in that; but more is to be learned from seeing it as Shaw's permeation of drawing-room drama, his victorious conversion of his old enemy significantly into what his contemporaries saw as the outrageous extreme of Shavian non-drama.

CONTENTS

ILLUSTRATIONS

(following page 208)

SHAW

AND THE NINETEENTH-CENTURY

THEATER

INTRODUCTION

T H E nineteenth century, a period of huge audiences and massive productivity in English drama, is strewn with the calamitously wrecked hopes of good, even great, poets and men of letters to create a drama that would be not simply popular but elevating, literary, endowed with high seriousness, and immortal like the tragedies of Shakespeare. In 1886, six years before he completed *Widowers' Houses*, Shaw reviewed the earliest presentation of Shelley's unlicensable tragedy, *The Cenci*. The play was a failure, Shaw wrote, in the sense of being a great experiment with negative results.

". . . Shelley, groping for the scientific drama which is yet in the future, and which alone could have reconciled his philosophic craving for truth to the unrealities of the stage, certainly got hold of the wrong vehicle when he chose the five-act tragedy in blank verse which had sufficed for Otway and Nicholas Rowe. The obligations imposed on him by this form and its traditions were that he should imitate Shakspere in an un-Shaksperean fashion by attempting to write constantly as Shakspere only wrote at the extreme emotional crises in his plays. . . ."[1]

When Shaw set about producing that drama of the future which reconciled philosophy and the stage, he profited from the common mistake of nineteenth-century men of letters who were not also men of the theater. There is no question that Shaw was as eager to achieve high truth in his work as Shelley, and that he wished to create plays which were Art in its most capitalized sense, which were indeed not only drama but literature. But instead of adopting, like his predecessors, the literary five-act tragedy in blank verse as a vehicle for his seriousness, Shaw chose the conventions, modes, techniques, and genres of the nineteenth-century popular theater.

[1] "Art Corner" in Mrs. Annie Besant's *Our Corner*, VII (June 1886), 371.

The relationship of Shaw, the playwright, to the nineteenth-century popular theater is the subject of this study. The object is to show that this relationship was of the greatest importance in his dramaturgy; that, far from being an exotic transplant or a biological sport in a theater whose strengths were neither literary nor intellectual, Shaw's drama of ideas was a legitimate child of that theater and belongs in the main stream of English dramatic history. Of course what is finally important is not the mere detail of Shaw's connections with the nineteenth-century theater, but what he made of them. The sagacious critic who would simply equate the Shavian drama with its antecedents is a figure of fun, as Shaw cheerfully points out in the epilogue to *Fanny's First Play*. There, as a quartet of critics try to guess the authorship, "Gilbert Gunn" (a burlesque of Gilbert Cannan) asks wearily:

> Well, who do you think? Here you have a rotten old-fashioned domestic melodrama acted by the usual stage puppets. The hero's a naval lieutenant. All melodramatic heroes are naval lieutenants. The heroine gets into trouble by defying the law (if she didnt get into trouble, thered be no drama) and plays for sympathy all the time as hard as she can. Her good old pious mother turns on her cruel father when he's going to put her out of the house, and says she'll go too. Then theres the comic relief: the comic shopkeeper, the comic shopkeeper's wife, the comic footman who turns out to be a duke in disguise, and the young scapegrace who gives the author his excuse for dragging in a fast young woman. All as old and stale as a fried fish shop on a winter morning.

Gunn is quick to acknowledge that there have been certain changes. The lieutenant is a Frenchman who praises the Eng-

lish and disparages the French: "the hackneyed old Shaw
touch." The characters are not elegant, but second-rate middle class. There is no plot, but instead a "feeble air of intellectual pretentiousness" designed to excuse the badness of
the play. "All the old stage conventions and puppets," is
what it comes down to, "without the old ingenuity and the
old enjoyment" (*Fanny's First Play*, pp. 321-22).

Though Shaw took the trouble to compromise a study of
his plays in terms of nineteenth-century dramatic conventions,
it was Shaw himself who, throughout his career, persistently
called attention to his relationship to the theater of his boyhood. It is true that none of his plays can be reduced to the
dramatic commonplaces of any period, particularly those of
the eighties and nineties when Shaw first took up playwriting;
but it is also true that his plays and the dramatic interpretation of his plays are illuminated by the conventions of the
theater of his youth: the provincial stock-company theater as
it existed in Dublin in the sixties and seventies. Furthermore,
the entire theater of his own and his audience's experience
is relevant to an understanding of some of Shaw's intentions
and much of his artistry. (I here assume that intention and
artistry are reciprocally effective and are equally deserving of
study.) Only by recovering Shaw's relation to his antecedents
can his accomplishment, actual and historical, be fairly appreciated.

The new creation of a drama of ideas out of antecedent conventions and materials is the other face of Shaw's relation
to the nineteenth-century theater. However, the ideas themselves—that is, Shaw's social, psychological, and spiritual
vision—are in the present study of only secondary concern.
It is impossible to talk about the embodiment of ideas in
drama without suggesting their nature; but such suggestion
has here a subsidiary place, illustrative and explanatory. On
the other hand, the shaping of conventional materials into a

dramatic vehicle for ideas is the point toward which all discussion tends.

There is a rough chronology in the three major parts of this study. The first part, "Dublin Roots," takes up the provincial theater of the sixties and seventies when Shaw sat in the audience as a spectator. (The Dublin theater of the eighteen-seventies is in some respects an "earlier" theater than its London contemporary.) The second part, "London: Currents and Crosscurrents," takes up the metropolitan theater of the eighties and nineties when Shaw sat in the audience as a critic. The third part, "Dramatic Genre and the Drama of Ideas," takes up the drama Shaw created from the nineteenth-century theater and its kinds when he came upon the scene as a playwright.

Considered more closely, "Dublin Roots" is concerned, not with biography or general theatrical history, but with Shaw's specific artistic heritage from the Dublin theater as manifested in his playwriting. The first chapter, "Theatre Royal and the Theatrical Stereotype," explores the range of dramatic performance available in Dublin (within the limits of Shaw's theater-going), and the stock-company system as a direct and indirect influence on Shaw's work. The second chapter, "Opera and Drama," establishes the kinship between musical and verbal forms in the nineteenth-century theater and examines the workings of the musical branch of Shaw's heritage in his dramaturgy.

"London: Currents and Crosscurrents" examines active and declining traditions in the schizophrenic London theater of the nineties and establishes Shaw's relation both to the immediate climate of his early playwriting and to the theater of his entire experience. First explored, in "Drama," is Shaw's relation to currents of the drama as written; second, in "Acting," to currents of the drama as performed. The scope and subject matter of these two chapters are defined not only retrospectively by Shaw's playwriting but also contemporaneously by his criticism. Continuously from the mid-eighties to the late nineties Shaw wrote weekly reviews of literature, painting, music, and drama, and the categories Shaw established as the basis of his criticism provided the foundations of his personal artistic program. Consequently, the approach to the complexities of the London theater in this section is made as much as possible in terms of Shaw's own critical categories. Shaw, after all, was the first to insist that his criticism was strategic; that is, calculated to advance the influence and prestige of one kind of art at the expense of another.

"Dramatic Genre and the Drama of Ideas" is the heart of the study, and it explores the most fruitful aspect of Shaw's relationship to the nineteenth-century theater. Shaw's plays are not developments of single nineteenth-century sources, but they have class resemblances to groups of nineteenth-century plays where a certain subject matter is characteristically combined with a certain tone and with certain conventions of character, action, and setting. There is no particular melodrama, for example, which forms the basis of *Captain Brassbound's Conversion*; but there is a class of Melodrama, exotic in setting and imperialistic in tone, which Shaw exploits and ridicules in *Captain Brassbound*, using the conventions as a vehicle for his ideas. A characteristic association of convention, tone, and subject matter established a nineteenth-century "genre" as it proved useful to Shaw; and consequently this section of the study attempts to define a series of such genres, many of which have passed out of contemporary knowledge, in order to show their fundamental significance in Shaw's work.

Shaw's exploitation of nineteenth-century genres, which took place over a period of some sixty years, falls into a number of artistically significant patterns. Regarded chronologically, particular genres dominated successive periods. Accordingly, I have compromised with rigid chronology and treated nineteenth-century genres (and within the chapters, sub-genres) by and large in the chronology of their significant exploitation. Another pattern given its proper importance by the compromise between group treatment and rigid chronology is the distinct evolution throughout Shaw's playwriting career from a more or less doctrinaire "realism" to a more or less spontaneous fantasy, from the plays grouped as "Unpleasant" to the final "Extravaganzas."

In "Rhetorical Drama and the Drama of Ideas," the concluding section of this study, it becomes possible to establish Shaw's relation to the poetic and rhetorical vein of *The Cenci*, that is, to the drama which attempted before Shaw to reconcile the literary and the theatrical, the elevated and the popular, the philosophical and the dramatic. We have seen that Shaw had already decided in 1886 that the attempt to write plays wholly in the vein of Shakespeare at his most elevated was absurd and un-Shakespearean. But in the course of exploring Shaw's relation to the nineteenth-century theater as a whole, it becomes evident that he conceived of himself as a writer in the rhetorical mode. His demands on acting, his musical and operatic methodology, his exploitation of Melodrama and the heroic History Play, are consistent parts of Shaw's attempt to embody elements of the old rhetorical tradition in his new drama of ideas. The rhetorical drama of ideas, however, escapes the unmitigated sublimity and unrelieved literary pretentiousness imposed by the tradition of the five-act blank-verse tragedy of the passions; for the rhetoric of ideas involves wit, irony, and argument, *reductio ad absurdum* and farcical anticlimax, as well as passionate declamation. Having discarded the vehicle of the five-act blank-verse tragedy, Shaw embedded rhetorical flights and poetic techniques in the verbal substance of an argumentative comedy. In perspective, it will be seen that Shaw found the solution which, in Shaw's view, Shelley magnificently failed to find, first by turning to popular drama for the conventions and materials of his serious dramatic art, and second by converting an inherited dramatic rhetoric of the passions to a rhetorical drama of ideas.

I

DUBLIN ROOTS

1

THEATRE ROYAL

AND THE THEATRICAL

STEREOTYPE

"... Shaw played the part of the Earl of Horsham in the copy-right performance of Harley Granville-Barker's *Waste*, in a modified version, at the Savoy Theatre, London, January 28, 1908. On the amusing playbill, which was probably prepared jointly by Shaw and Barker, Shaw is banteringly described as 'late of the Theatre Royal, Dublin.' "[1]

IN THE introduction to the Ellen Terry-Bernard Shaw correspondence, which he provided to explain the tone of the letters, but which emerged as an admirable historical portrait of the nineteenth-century theater, Shaw writes of the theater of his childhood:

"From my birth in 1856 to my Hegira to London in 1876, I lived in Dublin, where the theatre had hardly altered, except for its illumination by coal gas, since the eighteenth century. ... As nobody nowadays has the least notion of what the old stock companies were like, and as my own plays are written largely for the feats of acting they aimed at, and as moreover both Ellen Terry and Irving were rooted like myself in that phase of the evolution of the theatre, I may as well say a word or two about them."[2]

During Shaw's first twenty years in London, he discovered that most of what he had to say required extravagant repe-

---

[1] Archibald Henderson, *George Bernard Shaw: Man of the Century* (New York, 1956), p. 669. For convenience, all subsequent reference to the three Henderson biographies shall be by subtitle.

[2] *Ellen Terry and Bernard Shaw: A Correspondence*, ed. Christopher St. John (New York, 1931), p. xv.

tition, and the habit persisted through a lifetime. And throughout his lifetime Shaw declared that his theatrical roots were in the Theatre Royal, Dublin, and it was from there that he had taken his growth. If he claimed descent on one side from Shakespeare, Molière, Bunyan, Mozart, Dickens, Ibsen, and Wagner, he was no less candid in proclaiming his rise from the nineteenth-century stock-company theater, from the stage tricks, conventions, and dramatic genres which haunted its boards, from the theater of Salvini, Ristori, and Barry Sullivan.[3]

There is no direct evidence that Shaw spent an unseemly proportion of his adolescence at the theater. Nevertheless, in his scattered recollections of the Dublin stage he writes not only with his customary air of authority but with an impressive command of illustrative detail. His three volumes of practical theater criticism, *Our Theatres in the Nineties,* contain substantial references to the plays and playing Shaw would have witnessed in Dublin in the seventies; and in his ninety-first year Shaw could recollect not only the great touring stars but also minor favorites in the Theatre Royal's stock company and even a particular stock scene.[4]

Shaw's first theatrical venture was in the week of January

[3] For example, see *Three Plays for Puritans*, p. xxxv. Also, typescript letter to Alan S. Downer, 12 Nov. 1947: ". . . Sullivan was the stage hero of my boyhood and may be said to have formed my theatrical mind. I had also studied Ristori and Salvini at first hand. I had 20 years experience as a playgoer before Barker [Harley Granville-Barker] began as a boy actor." Also, "My Way with a Play," in *Shaw on Theatre,* ed. E. J. West, pp. 272-73: ". . . from my boyish visits to the theatre . . . I had acquired that theatre sense which, when I am writing a play, keeps my imagination unconsciously within the conditions and limits of the stage, the performers, the audience, and even the salary list. . . ."

[4] See "What George Bernard Shaw Looks Forward To," *Bristol Evening Post,* 3 Dec. 1946, p. 2. Of the stock company: "A few of them were favourites, especially the comedians Mrs. Huntley and Sam Johnson; and there was one first-rate actor, Peter Granby, whose Kent in King Lear I have never seen approached, nor his Polonius surpassed." Of the stock scenes: "One in particular, with Big Ben as its centre, was quite cosmopolitan, and served for all places and periods. . . ."

18, 1864. He saw Tom Taylor's *Plot and Passion,* an expert, intrigue-ridden melodrama with secret agents, impenetrable disguise, and a historical (Napoleonic) interest. "I have no idea who acted in it, because it was all real to me. It was followed by 'Puss in Boots,' a full length Christmas panto- mime; and in it, too, the fairy queen was a real fairy, and the policeman a real policeman deliciously shot into several pieces by the clown. . . . I believe the performance began and ended with a farce; for that was the length of entertain- ment the public expected in those days at the old Theatre Royal, Dublin."[5]

Shaw's next visit to the theater, exclusive of opera-going, was four or five years later. "When I next went, I went by myself and saw T. C. King in 'The Corsican Brothers'" (one of the several theatrically great and dramatically sophisticated melodramas of the century).[6] Thereafter Shaw's theatrical education was precipitous. In April 1870, Barry Sullivan appeared in Dublin for the first time as "the leading legiti- mate Actor of the British Stage."[7] He returned for a second two weeks in December and almost every season thereafter. Shaw was powerfully impressed. "Of the English speaking

[5] "The Theatre Today and Yesterday," *Manchester Evening News,* 6 Dec. 1938. Compare the similar account in *Ellen Terry and Bernard Shaw,* p. xvi. The date of Shaw's visit is easily determined. The pantomime of 1863-64 was the only *Harlequin Puss in Boots* at the Theatre Royal be- tween 1833 and the fire which destroyed the theater in 1880. (See R. M. Levey and J. O'Rorke, *Annals of the Theatre Royal, Dublin* [Dublin, 1880], pp. 70-71). During its run, *Puss in Boots* was coupled with Tom Taylor's *Plot and Passion* for only four performances: January 18 (Mon- day), 20, 21, and 22. (Consult the daily advertisements in the *Dublin Evening Mail* [hereafter *D.E.M.*] for the period.)

[6] "The Theatre Today and Yesterday." See *D.E.M.,* advertisement of 25 March 1868, announcing *The Corsican Brothers* for March 28, "in which Mr. T. C. KING/ Will sustain, for the first time these ten years at this Theatre/ the parts of Louis and Fabien de Franchi." King re- turned in November and December of 1869.

March 1868 and March 1876 (Shaw's last month in Dublin) are, there- fore, effective terminal dates for the study of Shaw's experience of the Dublin stage.

[7] *Annals of the Theatre Royal, Dublin,* p. 53.

stars incomparably the greatest was Barry Sullivan, who was in his prime when I was in my teens, the last of the race of heroic figures which had dominated the stage since the palmy Siddons-Kemble days. . . . Had I passed my boyhood in London I should have seen nothing of the very important side of stage art represented by Barry Sullivan's acting."[8]

In 1871, the London production of Albery's *Two Roses* came to Dublin, and Shaw had his first sight of Henry Irving in the character-part of Digby Grant. Before leaving Dublin, he saw Ada Cavendish in Wilkie Collins' *New Magdalen* and Adelaide Ristori in *Maria Stuart*. He saw Charles Mathews in *Cool as a Cucumber* and as Affable Hawk in G. H. Lewes' *Game of Speculation*. He saw Sullivan as Hamlet, Daniel Bandmann as Hamlet, and Miss Marriott as Hamlet. He saw Tom Taylor's *Joan of Arc* and Charles Reade's *It's Never Too Late to Mend*. He saw Madame Céleste in *The Woman in Red* and in *Green Bushes* as "Miami."[9] "The highlights of the season were the Christmas pantomime, the opera with the pit at 4 s., [normally 2 s.] . . . and the visits of Barry Sullivan. . . ."[10] The range of theatrical performance in any given year was enormous. There were the touring stars (Sullivan, Bateman, Bandmann, Charles Mathews, the Boucicaults, Sothern, Toole, Beatrice, Shiel Barry) supported by the stock company and eked out by farce. There were several companies touring with repertory. There was an occasional company with a single London production (Albery's *Two Roses*; Wilkie Collins' *Woman in White*). There was stock fill-in between the touring attractions. There were amateur societies to take the theater for a night (The Strollers; G. J. Lee's

---

[8] *Ellen Terry and Bernard Shaw*, pp. xvii, xviii.

[9] See *Ibid.*, pp. xx, xvi, xix; Shaw, "The Religion of the Pianoforte," *Fortnightly Review*, 61 (1894), 255; preface to *Immaturity*, p. xliv; *OTN*, I, 138, 160, and II, 108; and J. T. Grein's edition of *Widowers' Houses* (London, 1893), p. 113.

[10] "What George Bernard Shaw Looks Forward To," *Bristol Evening Post*, 3 Dec. 1946, p. 2.

amateur opera). There were seasons of opera, presenting the great continental stars. And there was the pantomime.[11]

Actually the stock company system was in the process of dissolution during Shaw's time in Dublin. The company at the Theatre Royal was traditionally the best paid of provincial stock companies, and in an earlier period its manager had been able to fight, strenuously but unsuccessfully, against the systematic engagement of touring stars who would lend their glamour for a share rather than a salary.[12] But even as Shaw was revelling in the splendors of Barry Sullivan, the starring system itself was giving way to fully cast companies, carrying their own sets, and touring the provinces with the latest London hits.

When Shaw began his theater-going, there was one other important theater in Dublin besides the Theatre Royal: the Queen's in Brunswick Street. Shaw remembered it, not quite accurately, "not only as a theatre for crude melodrama, but as a market for ladies who lived by selling themselves," and as a theater he had visited "at most, twice, perhaps only once."[13] However, in 1871, the brothers John and Michael Gunn opened a new theater, the Gaiety, on revolutionary principles. "The starting of the Gaiety Theatre was a distinct parting of the ways. The old-fashioned system of 'the Stock Company' was discarded."[14] To trumpet the revolution, the

[11] Based on the advertisements and notices in the *D.E.M.*, 1868-1876.

[12] See Leman Rede, *Road to the Stage* (London, 1827), p. 11, where provincial salaries are listed comparatively. Later, speaking of the "line" of Walking Gentlemen, Rede says (p. 16) , ". . . the salary is generally low; in Dublin even, not exceeding two guineas per week, and in many respectable companies not more than one." For John Harris's resistance to the starring system, see *Annals of the Theatre Royal, Dublin*, pp. 43-44.

[13] *Bristol Evening Post*, 3 Dec. 1946, p. 2, and *Ellen Terry and Bernard Shaw*, p. xv. Peter Kavanagh, *The Irish Theatre* (Tralee, 1946), reports (p. 390): "During the period when Henry Webb was manager of the Queen's (1854-1874) the standard of the productions was reasonably high . . . In 1874, Arthur Lloyd became manager and from that date onwards the Queen's descended to the production of music hall entertainments and melodrama."

[14] *Souvenir of the Twenty Fifth Anniversary of the Opening of the*

theater opened with "MRS. JOHN WOOD/ Directress of the
ST. JAMES'S THEATRE, LONDON,/ ('Queen of Burlesque'—*Standard*,)/ And the Celebrated ST. JAMES'S [C]OMPANY . . ."
(*D.E.M.*, 27 Nov. 1871) straight from London for a three
weeks' engagement. They opened with *She Stoops to Conquer*
and Brougham's "Great Indian Burlesque," *La Belle Sau-
vage*.[15]

Complete touring companies had not been unknown at the
Theatre Royal. Buckstone's Haymarket Company and Richard Younge's London Comedy Company presenting plays of
T. W. Robertson had visited a number of times in recent
years, and in 1870 the uncertain political situation brought
Mlle. Schneider and a French Offenbach company. When
Irving appeared in 1871, it was with "the entire Company of
London Artistes," who did nothing but Albery's *Two Roses*
(and a farce) for twelve nights.[16] But that the Gaiety, an important provincial theater, should venture to exist without
any stock company at all set the seal upon a radical change
in the times. Fifty years later Shaw wrote of this period, with
retrospective compression: "The stock company was hard
enough to bear when there was no alternative; but when the
London successes began touring through the provinces and
the Irish and Scottish capitals, and were performed there
not as now by secondrate companies giving a mechanical imitation of the original London production, but by the London
cast which had created the success, the stock companies fell
dead at their impact."[17]

Traces of Shaw's provincial experience first appeared, not
in his plays, but in the novels he began writing almost as

Gaiety Theatre 27th November, 1871 (Dublin, 1896), p. 11; cf. *Bristol
Evening Post*, 3 Dec. 1946, p. 2.

[15] For the nature of 19th-century Burlesque (an integral dramatic piece
full of song and dance rather than a music-hall potpourri) see Chapter
15 below.

[16] *D.E.M.*, 15 May 1871; *Annals of the Theatre Royal, Dublin*, p. 49
(1865), pp. 52, 53 (1870), p. 54 (1871).

[17] *Ellen Terry and Bernard Shaw*, p. xix.

soon as he came to London. Several of his heroines are actresses, and in *Love Among the Artists* (written 1881), he
presents a sketch (Chapter VIII) of the life of an actress in
the provinces. Its details—a violent and exacting tragedian,
based on Barry Sullivan; a disastrous Ophelia; the routines
of rehearsal and the week by week progress of the bills—come
straight from Shaw's knowledge of the Theatre Royal, Dublin.
The focus of interest in the chapter is less on its central character than on the already quaint and unfamiliar world in
which she finds herself, and in which she develops as an artist.
Shaw summarizes for us. In four months, we are told, Madge
was "second in skill only to the low comedian and the old
woman, and decidedly superior to the rest of the company."

"Madge's artistic experience thenceforth was varied, though
her daily course was monotonous. Other tragedians came to
Nottingham, but none nearly so terrible, nor, she reluctantly
confessed, nearly so gifted, as he who had taught her the
scene from Hamlet. Some of them, indeed, objected to the
trouble of rehearsing, and sent substitutes who imitated them
in every movement and so drilled the company to act with
them. Occasionally a part in a comedy of contemporary life
enabled Madge to profit by her knowledge of fashionable
society and her taste in modern dress. The next week, perhaps,
she would have to act in a sensational melodrama, and, in a
white muslin robe, to struggle in the arms of a pickpocket in
corduroys, with his clothes and hands elaborately begrimed.
Once she had to play with the wreck of a celebrated actress,
who was never free from the effects of brandy, and who as-
tonished Madge by walking steadily on the stage when she
could hardly stand off it. Then Shakespeare, sensation drama,
Irish melodrama, comic opera or pantomime, new comedy
from London over again, with farce constantly." (pp. 119-20)

"This was the reality," Shaw declares in the last sentence of the chapter, "which took the place of Madge's visions of the life of an actress" (p. 125).

Even if Shaw had been born a cockney full of scorn for provincial theater, he would have been deeply marked as a playgoer and as a playwright by the Permanent Company Playing Repertory. This ubiquitous theatrical organization impressed itself more forcefully on the writing of nineteenth-century English drama than any other condition short of the nature of the audience itself. In such a company, explained Shaw to his German translator, parts were distributed according to a strict etiquette. The rules divided the company into Juvenile Lead and Ingénue, first and second Light Comedians and Singing Chambermaids (or Soubrettes), first and second Low Comedians, Heavies of both sexes, "for villainy, tragedy, blood & thunder &c," aristocratic father and bourgeois father (or first and second Old Man and Old Woman), Walking Gentlemen, Walking Ladies, and Utilities. "These are the names which survive here from the traditions of the XVIII century; but the divisions, under whatever names, always exist in a stock company."[18]

The classification by type, and the particular "lines" (to use the technical term) developed in the theater, provided an eminently judicious and practical solution to the problem of presenting the infinite possibilities of human nature with a finite number of actors. The nineteenth-century solution was by no means unique or independent of earlier solutions. "For stage purposes," wrote Shaw, "there are not many types of character available; and all the playwrights use them over and over again. Idiosyncrasies are useful on the stage only to give an air of infinite variety to the standard types. Shakespear's crude Gratiano is Benedick, Berowne, and Mercutio,

[18] MS letter to Siegfried Trebitsch, 16 Sept. 1920 (all letters to Trebitsch cited in the present study may be found in the Berg Collection, New York Public Library).

finally evolving through Jacques into Hamlet. He is also my Smilash, my Philanderer, my John Tanner.

"Take Falstaff's discourse on honor; and how far are you from Alfred Doolittle's disquisition on middle-class morality?"[19]

Nevertheless, the general adoption of the particular nineteenth-century stock-company solution, and the careful etiquette of its application, wrought strange mutations on the classics of the repertory. For example, while advising aspiring players on securing costume according to "line," Leman Rede writes: "Seconds in Tragedy; or, Juvenile Tragedy, (which frequently goes with the light comedy) . . . A person professing juvenile tragedy should have a dress for Norval [in Home's *Douglas*], which will also serve for Macduff, and other parts; a black bugled one for Romeo's second dress, and which will also do for Laertes in the last act." Again, he reminds the aspirant in another line that "in the most respectable provincial theatres, the low comedian is expected to go on for the Lord Mayor, in 'Richard the Third,' and other characters of minor importance in tragedy."[20] "The low comedian was traditionally cast for Roderigo," wrote Shaw; "and Roderigo consequently was presented, not as a foolish Venetian gentleman about town, but as a clown. The king in Hamlet and Ham Peggotty might have been twins except for the costume, because the heavy man had to play Ham, the juveniles being used up for Copperfield and Steerforth."[21]

However, the severest limitations of the stock-company solution, Shaw found, were not in the scheme of classification but in the conditions of repertory and rehearsal. Leman Rede sketched the problem in the *Road to the Stage* (p. ii):

"A country actor in a small company, and aspiring to a first-rate situation, will invariably have to study about *five hun-*

[19] "I am a Classic But Am I a Shakespear Thief?" *Hearst's Magazine* 38 (Sept. 1920), reprinted in West, *Shaw on Theatre*, p. 132.

[20] Rede, *Road to the Stage* (1827), pp. 27, 26. In the 1872 edition, costume requirements remain unchanged.

[21] *Ellen Terry and Bernard Shaw*, pp. xv, xvi.

dred lines [of text] *per diem*—it is astonishing how many persons are cured by this alone; this will occupy the possessor of a good memory for six hours—his duties at the theatre embrace four hours in the morning for rehearsal, and about five at night; here are sixteen [*sic*] hours devoted to labour alone, to say nothing of the time required to study the character, after the mere attainment of the words."

"Under such circumstances," wrote Shaw, "serious character study was impossible; and the intensive elaboration of an impersonation which an actor can achieve when he can repeat his performance without having anything else to do in the theatre was out of the question. The actress learnt, not how to interpret plays, but how to appear sweet and gentle, or jealous and wicked, or funny, or matronly, or deaf and palsied, and how to make up her face and wear wigs. The actor learnt how to appear sprightly, or romantic, or murderous, or bucolic, or doddering, and to make funny faces."[22]

On these grounds Shaw objected to having *Heartbreak House* presented by a repertory company in a Vienna première. The play, he felt, depended, as other of his plays did not, on nuances and subtleties rather than on the big bones beneath. He objects to a repertory interpretation not because his characters belong to no line—indeed, he precisely identifies them by line—but because he won't leave the nuances to chance. Shaw warns his translator that the director of the Burg Theater will insist that Hesione be played by "our Heavy Lead Frau Grimmigen," and that "Ellie is the Juvenile Lead, and as such belongs to Fraulein Shönaugen. . . . You will reply in despair 'But, good God! Ellie must be utterly virginal and Hesione utterly voluptuous. Fraulein Schönaugen is forty; and . . . Frau Grimmigen . . . will have to look sixty and make the whole play ridiculous.' " Shaw continues that he has a great deal of sympathy with the repertory system, having suffered so much from the shortcomings of the

[22] *Ibid.*, p. xvi.

London system, and that most of his plays can be cast anyhow, if the company is a good one and the direction reasonably artistic. "But H. H. is a peculiar play, as dependent on
atmosphere and on subtleties of personality in the performers
as any of Tchekov's. Therefore the Burg system *may* smash
it."[23]

The utter virginity of Ellie and the utter voluptuousness
of Hesione are patently nothing less than the essence of the
ingénue and of the female heavy lead. It is the failure of an
actual female heavy lead to live up to the ideal Hesione that
Shaw dreads for this play.

Within each "line" of acting in the nineteenth-century
stock-company theater were a number of strongly marked
types developed from the original peculiarities of notable
actors, from influential character-classics in the repertory, or
simply from variations in genre. Vincent Crummles says
to Nicholas, when recruiting him as Gentleman-Juvenile,
"There's genteel comedy in your walk and manner, juvenile
tragedy in your eye, and touch-and-go farce in your laugh,"
thus naming the chief departments of the line by genre. As
for Smike, "he'd make such an actor for the starved business
[e.g. Romeo's apothecary] as was never seen in this country."[24]
Such specialization, by line and within each line, resulted in
the nineteenth-century dramatic stereotypes: figures which,
however variously combined in various plots and circumstances, could be relied upon to behave in a particular manner and to possess certain defined moral and psychological
qualities. Like their masked predecessors in Roman comedy,
many of the nineteenth-century stereotypes were instantly
recognizable on appearance, and others through a combination of appearance and speech peculiarity. The nineteenth-

[23] MS letter to Siegfried Trebitsch, 16 Sept. 1920.
[24] *Vincent Crummles: His Theatre and His Times*, arranged by F. J.
Harvey Darton (London, 1926), pp. 49, 46.

—·[21]·—

century villain did not have to establish his wickedness for the audience; his exterior immediately gave him away.

Extreme specializations, like the "starved business," were dignified with a particular classification. In playbooks and promptbooks of the period, in addition to parts designated as belonging to one of the usual lines, there may be parts assigned to "Character Lead," "Character Comedy," "Eccentric." These descriptions were for types like the Stage Swell or the Stage Irishman, originally perhaps, like Sothern's Lord Dundreary, a foppish Walking Gentleman made into the main attraction of a play by elaborate and ingenious acting, or like Boucicault's Shaun the Post, Low Comedy in an Irish accent made into the Leading Business of a full-length thrilling melodrama. The Stage Jew, the Stage Irishman, the Stage Frenchman, the Stage Lunatic, the Stage Swell, most of them parts that required a comically affected manner of speech, were character parts. Once established they were recognizable on appearance. No one, for example, would fail to recognize Mr. John Chodd, Jr., in Robertson's *Society* (1865): "*a supercilious, bad swell; glass in eye; hooked stick . . .*"; or the more sympathetic and eccentric Talbot Champneys in H. J. Byron's *Our Boys* (1875): "Velvet coat and vest, light pants, eye-glasses, flashy necktie, blonde wig parted in centre, blonde side whiskers ['Dundreary whiskers'] and small blonde mustache."[25]

The existence of theatrical types affected as a matter of course the drama as written and adapted, so that conventions of interpretation became conventions of playwriting. In the nineteenth century, as opposed to the Restoration, for example, it was snobbishly and professionally important to a playwright to be recognized as "a practical man of the theater"; and one test of the dramatist's professionalism was whether he could create character according to line and spe-

[25] *The Principal Dramatic Works of Thomas William Robertson* (London, 1889), p. 687; and *Our Boys* (*French's Parlor Comedies*) , introductory costume list.

cialty. In a sense this was putting the cart before the horse; but in another sense it was clearly necessary to write plays with parts for as many of the regularly-paid leading members of the stock company as possible. W. S. Gilbert, in a sketch which purports to "trace the progress of a modern three-act comedy from the blank-paper state . . . to production," has his author presented with a specific commission to write a play with important parts for Jones, Brown, and Robinson, the light comedian, the "leading 'old man,'" and the "handsome lover or *jeune premier*" of a given company.[20] Add only Miss Smith, who plays "the interesting young ladies whose fortunes or misfortunes constitute the sentimental interest of every piece in which she plays," and the drama seems practically written before Horace Facile (Gilbert's "playwright") has dipped his pen. As in his own plays, Gilbert achieves considerable novelty with Facile's conventional personages, by making them into partial burlesques of themselves. Still, long after the passing of the particular kind of stock company for which Facile was supposed to be writing in 1873, the theatrical stereotypes persisted in the minds of actors and dramatists as the image of nature itself.

The basic stereotypes appeared at their purest in Melodrama, the most characteristic form of the nineteenth-century popular theater. A theatrical poster (Figure 1) of H. J. Byron's *The Lancashire Lass; or, Tempted, Tried, and True* (1867) illustrates a number of these stereotypes, and Byron's "Domestic Melodrama" presents them performing their typical functions. The plot runs as follows: Robert Redburn, an unprincipled gentleman, attempts to seduce the innocent country girl Ruth Kirby into running off with him and forsaking her mechanic lover, Ned Clayton. Redburn is assisted by Kate Garstone, who wants to revenge herself on Clayton for a fancied slight in love. The conspirators nearly succeed; but

[20] W. S. Gilbert, *A Stage Play*, introd. William Archer, *Papers on Playmaking*, 3rd Ser., III (New York, 1916), p. 15.

—·[23]·—

through the blunderings of Spotty, their impromptu messenger, Ruth's compromising and immediately regretted letter of consent goes astray. Ned Clayton saves Ruth from disgrace by pretending to her illiterate father that the letter rejects Redburn; but Clayton himself is heartbroken. Clayton then tries to forget his sorrow by drink and dissipation in Liverpool, where the seducer is meanwhile concentrating his charm on the girlish, rich and spoiled Fanny Danville. He is opposed by Fanny's father, Gregory Danville, and Fanny's much-chastened companion, Ruth Kirby. A disreputable and mysterious "party by the name of Johnson" proposes to assist Redburn by blackmail, and succeeds in intimidating Danville. However, under intense pressure, Danville stabs Johnson one night on the waterfront, and, on Redburn's evidence, Ned Clayton is held for the murder. Ultimately Clayton escapes to Australia with the help of Ruth Kirby (thus redeemed in his eyes) and Jellick, a foolish doddering old man who once paid Ruth court. Redburn, who comes to prevent the escape, is recognized as the notorious "Slippery Dick" and arrested by Sergeant Donovan. In Australia, just as the hero and heroine receive news of a death-bed vindication by Danville, they once more encounter the now sunken and degraded Redburn. Redburn is on the point of killing an unarmed Clayton when he himself is shot down by irate miners, led by a resurrected Johnson. Innocence triumphs and villainy is defeated.

It should be clear, even from this bald narration, that the legitimate creative aim of the author, as far as his personages were concerned, was not originality but vividness, achieved by giving as strong an accent as possible to the leading characteristics of established dramatic stereotypes. Nearly all the personages, including most of the minor ones, are exemplars of such boldly marked dramatic stereotypes. Spotty, for example, whose part though peripheral to the action looms large in the economy of the play, belongs to one of the most popular types in the low comedian's "line," the Comic

Countryman. Spotty is shown as shrewd and foolish and easily terrorized. He speaks a country dialect and laughs a country laugh (transcribed as "Hur! Hur!"). The playbook reports his appearance as "Countryman; drab felt hat; corduroy breeches; gray stockings, ankle-boots; jacket; loose neckcloth; chews a straw at opening of Scene I."[27] Similarly Jellick (in the line of the Comic Old Man) is the type of the Aged Suitor (for other examples, see below, Chapter 12). Danville is the *père noble*, the aristocratic Heavy Father. Sergeant Donovan, described in the cast of characters as "Irishman," is actually a combination of two invariably comic types: the Stage Irishman and the Stage Policeman.

Kate Garstone is an example of a dark, volcanic stereotype of melodrama which owed much to the tempestuous heavy heroines of tragedy. She is "black-haired, with black eye-brows and slightly browned complexion, supposedly of gipsey descent" (Costumes, p. 5). In the earlier scenes where Ruth Kirby wears light-colored, chaste, and girlish clothing, Kate wears "Cheap striped shawl; dark dress; bonnet with showy ribbons; ear-rings." Later, when she degenerates (by implication) into a street-walker on the point of doing away with herself through remorse and despair, she wears "Black shawl and dark dress, ragged; torn shoes; hair in disorder; no bonnet." She is moved by a violent passion for Ned Clayton which, frustrated, turns to "Revenge and hate. . . . Two powerful incentives to evil, in the female breast." Redburn tells her he would rather be despised than "the object of your hate. There is at times an ominous glitter of your dark eyes, and a grasping action of your hands that bodes no good. I have noticed it when the name of Mr. Clayton (KATE *starts and looks hateful*) is spoken" (p. 9). However, Kate herself is presented as the ultimately pitiful victim of her own law-

[27] *World Acting Drama* (Dramatic Publishing Co.), "Costumes," p. 5. Descendants of the Comic Countryman in Shaw's drama include Christy Dudgeon (*Devil's Disciple*), and, with an infusion of Stage Irish, Patsy Farrell (*John Bull's Other Island*).

less passions. When driven to the river by "my remorse and despair," she cries to Ned Clayton, "Oh, don't think of me as you see me now in these cruel streets of Liverpool, but think of me as I once was, the girl that you loved in our quiet village" (p. 29).

Ned Clayton, the hero, is defined by his contrast with the type of Robert Redburn. Clayton is clean-shaven, fair, curly-haired, generous and forthright, and given to knocking people down. What he lacks in Redburn's suavity and fierce passion he makes up for in honesty and "manly sentiment." He is identifiable on appearance, for though a mechanic he wears a costume reminiscent of the sailor-heroes of nautical melodrama (Figure 1).

Redburn is a classic example of the dark, passionate, Byronic, gentleman-villain stereotype of melodrama. His appearance is saturnine (he was originally played by the young Henry Irving); he wears "Moustache; light suit; walking-coat; black soft felt hat" in the first scene; "may smoke a cigar, watch and chain; ring; pin." The mustache, elegance, and jewelry are characteristic, as are the beetling brows, dark hair, and complexion of the illustration.[28] As he sinks into evil, his clothes get darker, his mustache more ragged, and his manner more satanic. His charm for women is presented as something almost mesmeric. Ruth describes him as "handsome, tall, dark, with a smile of conscious power," and Fanny, who is helpless before his fascination, contrasts him with all other young men of her acquaintance who have no hearts,

[28] Compare descriptions of the gentleman-villain, Chandos Bellingham, in Boucicault's *After Dark* (1868): "BELLINGHAM.—Black moustache; white overcoat, light; black hat; black suit; white vest; gloves; sporting-man type; watch and chain; finger-ring; breast-pin"; and of Compton Kerr in the same author's *Formosa; or, The Railroad to Ruin* (1869): "long black moustache, hair rather long and straggling down on forehead; eyebrows shaped to indicate determination." Gilbert burlesques the type in *Engaged* (1877) with Belvawney, dressed in "Black frock coat and trousers, black tie, ample black cloak, long black wig and moustache, pale face, green spectacles." The green spectacles are for his "dreadful" eyes with which he exercises a Svengali's power over the hero, Cheviot Hill.

"only eye-glasses! Why do all of my acquaintances seem to take pride in suppressing their natural emotions" (p. 22). Violent passion, not a taste for evil, is Redburn's leading quality, and he himself dreams of regeneration through the love of a good woman. "Who knows what this fresh, innocent girl may make of me when I bear her away from her home? I may be a changed man, why not? She may make me something like the thing she fancies I am. Kate, you think this the mere passing fancy of a lawless man—but it is not so! I really love Ruth Kirby. I will stick at nothing to have her for my own. I tell you, I love her—she is my fate and destiny" (p. 9). As with Kate Garstone, the frustration of his passion turns it into a passion for revenge.

Stage villainy in nineteenth-century drama had two aspects: a smooth and a rough, a high and a low. The "Party by the Name of Johnson" belongs to the stereotype of the low-comedy or "Character-comedy" villain. He is more immediately terror-inspiring than Redburn, but there is a constant, macabre jocularity in his speech and action. In contrast with the elegance of the gentleman-villain, he has an "Unshaven look about the cheeks; hair short crop, with a small lock on each temple. . . . Long drab coat, with buttons of different kinds, one sleeve torn and tied with string, ragged handkerchief; gray pants; shoes, all old and ragged; cigar, match-box and a revolver in his breast-pocket, old drab hat, with worn rim." Like Redburn, he is motivated by revenge, though unlike Redburn he has been deeply wronged in the past and may be allowed to survive into the future.[29]

[29] The macabre Johnson ("Character Lead") shows the influence of the great actor Lemaître's germinal character-creation, "Macaire" (see below, pp. 215-16), on the conventional rough, hoarse, and grimy Heavy Villain like Captain Grampus in J. B. Buckstone's *Wreck Ashore* (1830). (Grampus complements a Byronic Gentleman-Villain named Miles Bertram.) In the course of the century the low-comedy villain seems to have replaced the simpler stereotype. Note that Michael Feeny, the villain in Boucicault's *Arrah-na-Pogue* (1864; *De Witt's*), is assigned to "1st Low Comedy." The costume list directs the actor to "Make up the face very

A sweeping revolution in the English theater, whose beginnings in the late 1860s were contemporaneous with *The Lancashire Lass*, had as one of its chief objects the liquidation of the dramatic stereotypes (see below, Chapter 3). The stereotypes persisted, though with accents somewhat softened, even in the very camp of the revolution; but by the late eighties and nineties, when Shaw began writing, it was impossible for a playwright with either fashionable or intellectual pretensions to use the stereotypes without considerable disguise or self-consciousness. Shaw's incorporation of the popular dramatic stereotypes in his drama of ideas can scarcely be overlooked; but neither, considering the dates of his writing, can it be taken for granted.

The full significance of Shaw's incorporation of the conventional stereotypes will emerge in the course of examining his exploitation of popular dramatic genres (Part III below). However it is possible to suggest in advance the nature of his use of the stereotypes, and to cite some of the more striking examples of that use.

There are clear strains of "character" in Shaw's plays that seem to have little to do with nineteenth-century acting lines. There is a strain of imaginative realists, for example, which includes Bluntschli, Caesar, Don Juan, Undershaft, King Magnus, and Saint Joan (Bluntschli, Undershaft, and Joan would clearly have been assigned to three different lines in a nineteenth-century stock-company theater). Such recurrent strains generally owe their likeness to a common philosophical notion; but though some of these strains cut across stock-company categories, others seem to coincide exactly with a

---

repulsive, unwashed, two days' growth of black beard, lines of face marked prominently; black close-crop wig. Suit of rusty black, battered high-crown hat, soiled white vest. Very cringing in his bearing, nervous, glancing to the side and downwards when speaking to anyone." (Nervous starts, involuntary trembling, and uneasiness in the presence of virtue were characteristic of all types of villainy.)

particular acting line or stereotype, and are simply that line or stereotype raised to a greater power. For example, there is a strain of passionate "womanly women"—Shaw mocks the idolatrous proponents of the concept, but again and again projects the type—which includes such personages as Julia Craven, Blanche Sartorius, Ann Whitefield, Hesione Hushabye, and King Magnus's Orinthia. On the philosophical plane, they body forth Shaw's two Venuses, the urgent generative aspect of the Life Force and the spirit of sexual romance; but at the same time they are all generic variations on the dark, passionate, female Heavy of Melodrama. Julia Craven in *The Philanderer* is, like Kate Garstone in *The Lancashire Lass*, identifiable on appearance. The stage is prepared; the characters already present hear Julia's voice and stand transfixed: "*A beautiful, dark, tragic looking woman, in mantle and toque, appears at the door, raging*" (pp. 74-75). Since *The Philanderer* is explicitly concerned with theatrical conceptions and conventions, Shaw takes care to make Julia self-consciously theatrical; but it is Shaw who employs the theatrical convention in the dramatic situation. When, for example, "*Julia stops as she catches sight of Charteris, her face clouding, and her breast heaving*" (p. 102), she is suffering, like all the dark and tragic women of her line, from jealousy and the torments of unappreciated love.

Violent passion, sensual passion, uncontrollable passion, were the distinguishing marks of the frequently wicked, always tormented, and never triumphant Heavy of Melodrama. And Blanche Sartorius, Shaw's first passionate woman in the drama and Julia's immediate predecessor, pants and rages ungovernably, beats her snivelling maid, and ends "*provocative, taunting, half defying, half inviting* [the hero] *to advance, in a flush of undisguised animal excitement. It suddenly flashes on him that all this ferocity is erotic: that she is making love to him*" (*Widowers' Houses*, p. 63). Aside from the politics, it was not the spectacle of passion and eroticism which provoked the disproportionate fury of the critics upon the play's first unimportant production. The critics were quite, or nearly accustomed to such goings-on by the stereotyped heavy heroine. It was the sheer indecorum of Shaw's placing a woman of this type, of this line, in the plot position normally reserved for the fair, innocent, and sweet-tempered heroine. *The Streets of London* (in America, *The Poor* [or *Streets*] *of New York*) by Dion Boucicault (1864) handled the same motif in a theatrically conventional way and was not found objectionable. In Boucicault's drama the villain, Gideon Bloodgood (compare Sartorius, Blanche's heavy father), is a successful financier who cheats, steals, and burns to build a fortune for his daughter. His daughter, Alida Bloodgood, is selfish, tempestuous, and (it is hinted) morally suspect. She wants the *jeune premier* for her husband, and orders her father to buy him for her:

> A L I D A . I want to make a purchase.
>
> B L O O D G O O D . Of what?
>
> A L I D A . Of a husband—a husband who is a gentle-man—and through whom I can gain that position you cannot with all your wealth obtain—you see—the thing is cheap—there's the pen.[30]

But Alida fails in her project. And Alida is contrasted to the sweet, suffering Lucy, who succeeds. It is curious that Shaw's simple rearrangement of such a simple convention could have been mistaken for the depths of brutal realism.

Blanche's passion, in contrast to that of Alida, is not intended as the expression of her depravity but rather as the expression of her vitality. Shaw does not abandon the characteristics of the stereotype; he construes them differently. One effect of this procedure was to make viable his drama of ideas. Eventually Shaw's heavy heroine, in the person of

[30] *French S. D.*, pp. 20, 21. Compare Hypatia in *Misalliance* (p. 189) when Percival protests he is too poor to marry: "Papa: buy the brute for me."

Mrs. George (*Getting Married*), will speak for the *Ewig-Weibliche*. In *Back to Methuselah* she appears as Cleopatra-Semiramis, the flesh-and-blood doll who embodies the essence of sterile, passionate, and theatrical sexual romance, and as Lilith, the primal embodiment of the Life Force itself.

In the male heavy line, the most obvious of Shaw's various drafts upon the stereotypes was Captain Brassbound, dark, passionate, Byronic, and burning with a purpose of revenge. He is described on his first entrance:

> An olive complexioned man with dark southern eyes and hair comes from the house. Age about 36. Handsome features, but joyless; dark eyebrows drawn towards one another; mouth set grimly; nostrils large and strained: a face set to one tragic purpose. A man of few words, fewer gestures, and much significance. On the whole, interesting, and even attractive, but not friendly. He stands for a moment, saturnine in the ruddy light, to see who is present, looking in a singular and rather deadly way at Sir Howard; then with some surprise and uneasiness at Lady Cicely. (*Brassbound*, p. 224).

Shaw takes the convention of the Byronic Heavy with his glowering personal power and uses it to dramatize his own notions of the hapless victim of romance and of the natural leader and vital genius. Brassbound figures chiefly as the victim of romance. His theatrical and romantic notions of vengeance (which Shaw carefully equates with existing law) render him impotent, frustrated, and easily manipulated, like Hardress Cregan, for example, the Byronic Heavy in Boucicault's *Colleen Bawn* (1860), who hovers on the edge of passionate crime, but is paralyzed, in effect, by his conflicting base and noble passions. Cregan is ultimately redeemed and reduced, a little like Bertram in *All's Well That Ends Well*, by the persistent faith of a noble woman. In *Captain Brass-*

bound's Conversion, the hero's bonds are loosened and his vital power restored by the lesson on romance and reality administered by Lady Cicely.

Characteristic of Shaw's Heavies is the most blatant talent of the line: the peculiar mesmeric power, common to Svengali and to Gilbert's Belvawney, which regularly fascinated so many innocent heroines in the course of the century. Sartorius has this quality in the early acts of *Widowers' Houses*, before surrendering to the will of his daughter and the financial leadership of Lickcheese. Bohun, the Jaggers of *You Never Can Tell*, is endowed with sinister pallor, oiled black hair, *"and eyebrows like early Victorian horsehair upholstery."* He has a *"powerful menacing voice, impressively articulated speech, strong inexorable manner, and a terrifying power of intensely critical listening"* (p. 278). He is a *deus ex machina* who so dominates and paralyzes the various lively personages of the play that the audience accepts without a murmur his claim to have disposed of their various unsolved problems. Brassbound is similarly gifted with eyebrows and dark power. His leadership of a band of lawless scoundrels is based on a magnetic force; and at the end of the play, in discovering the secret of true command, he puts Lady Cicely into a virtual hypnotic trance.

Undershaft in *Major Barbara* is the most notable embodiment in Shaw's drama of ideas of the melodramatic Heavy as vital genius (see below, pp. 296-302). Both Undershaft and Mendoza, another Shavian leader of great natural energy and passion, have the Heavy's mesmeric force; but Mendoza, like Brassbound, is factored into impotence by his romanticism, while Undershaft is multiplied into irresistible force by his visionary sense of reality. To Louis Calvert (who played a number of his personages in the heavy line) Shaw wrote:

"I am getting on with the new play, scrap by scrap, and the part of the millionaire cannon founder is becoming more and more formidable. Broadbent and [K]eegan rolled into one, with Mephistopheles thrown in: that is what it is like. . . . Undershaft is diabolically subtle, gentle, self-possessed, powerful, stupendous, as well as amusing and interesting. . . . That penny-plain and twopence-colored pirate Brassbound will be beneath your notice then."

Shaw dictated to Calvert that Undershaft, like Bohun, should absolutely take charge of the end of the play. "Undershaft must go over everybody like Niagara from that moment. . . . His energy must be proof against everybody and everything."[31]

With the Heavy Male, as with the Heavy Female, Shaw seizes on essential characteristics of the type, in this case his energy and his power, and construes them for his own dramatic and philosophic purposes. Just as Shaw's Heavy Female took two forms in his drama of ideas, appearing ultimately as both Lilith and Cleopatra-Semiramis, so Shaw's Heavy Male took final form in both the awesome elders of *Methuselah*, with their vast spiritual energy and passion for reality, and in the murderous, sterile idealist, Cain.

The line associations of many of Shaw's personages, evident enough in his texts, were made explicit in his commerce with people of the theater. For example, Shaw wrote to Richard Mansfield, the American actor-manager, on the casting of *Candida*:

"There are six parts only. One of them is an old man, vulgar, like Eccles in Caste, only not a drunken waster, but a comfortably well off vestryman who has made money in trade. He must be a genuinely funny low comedian, able to talk vulgar English—drop his Hs and so forth. And he must be really a middleaged or elderly man and not a young man made up old, which is one of the most depressing things known to the stage. Then there is a young woman of the standing of a fe-

[31] "George Bernard Shaw as a Man of Letters," *NY Times*, 5 Dec. 1915, Sec. VI, p. 6.

—·[33]·—

male clerk, rather a little spitfire, a bit common, but with some comic force and a touch of feeling when needed. She must not be slowtongued: the part requires smart, pert utterance. If you know any pair who could play Eccles and Polly Eccles thoroughly well, you may engage them straight off for Candida. Then there is a curate. Any solemn young walking gentleman who can speak well will do for him."[32]

Similarly, Shaw sent to Golding Bright, then a theatrical paragraphist, a sketch of the cast and action of *You Never Can Tell* which included the following notes:

> Valentine—a dentist (Comedian—Wyndham style of part) Allan Aynesworth
>
> Crampton—old man—strong part—the father Brandon Thomas.
>
> .   .   .   .
>
> Bohun—an eminent Q. C. (only appears in last act, but very good character part) [Henry] Kemble.[33]

Valentine, it should be noted, sports a generic name. He belongs to one of Shaw's commonest types, a particularly verbal and volatile kind of Light Comedy hero. The Comedy Lover of the nineteenth century, unlike the generality of stereotypes, was notable for an absence of strong markings. George Henry Lewes wrote of the type: "It is a rare assemblage of qualities that enables an actor to be sufficiently good-looking without being insufferably conceited, to be quiet

[32] Letter of 9 March 1895, quoted in Henderson, *Man of the Century*, p. 433. Other Shaw personages in the line of Burgess and T. W. Robertson's Eccles are Lickcheese in *Widowers' Houses* and Doolittle in *Pygmalion*. Polly Eccles and Shaw's "female clerk" as here characterized belong to the line of the pert soubrette or Chambermaid. (Compare G. H. Lewes' description of Mrs. Keeley's sharp, "common," and pathetic qualities in the line in *On Actors and the Art of Acting* [London, 1875], pp. 81ff.)

[33] Letter card of 10 March 1897 in *Advice to a Young Critic*, ed. E. J. West (New York, 1955), p. 68.

without being absurdly insignificant, to be lively without being vulgar, to look like a gentleman, to speak and move like a gentleman, and yet to be as interesting as if this quietness were only the restraint of power, not the absence of individuality."[34] The rare assemblage was rarely encountered, and the *jeune premier* was notoriously bland. On Tavy's first appearance in *Man and Superman*, Shaw writes for the closet audience, "*He must, one thinks, be the jeune premier; for it is not in reason to suppose that a second such attractive male figure should appear in one story*" (*Man and Superman*, p. 4). But Tavy is typically bland; and Shaw uses his lineal insipidity for his own dramatic and philosophical ends: to set off the character and individuality of Jack Tanner. Tavy is Juvenile to Jack Tanner's Lead.

Shaw's view of the Stage Lover was vigorously expressed in his criticism. "The plague of the stage at present," he wrote, "is the intolerable stereotyping of the lover: he is always the same sort of young man, with the same cast of features, the same crease down his new trousers, the same careful manners, the same air of behaving and dressing like a gentleman for the first time in his life and being overcome with the novelty and importance of it" (*OTN*, III, 247). On another occasion Shaw notes, of the romantic hero, that even actor-managers must struggle "with the habits of the days when they were expected to supply this particular style of article, and to live under the unwritten law: 'Be a nonentity, or you will get cast for villains' " (*OTN*, I, 70).

Shaw's solution, as a writer of comedy, was to exploit a specialization in the line established by Charles James Mathews and in recent years continued and raised to great heights, in Shaw's view, by Charles Wyndham. Shaw had a particularly vivid recollection of Mathews in his most famous

---

[34] G. H. Lewes, *On Actors and the Art of Acting*, p. 61. Shaw calls Lewes "the most able and brilliant critic between Hazlitt and our own contemporaries" (*OTN*, III, 155). He sees Lewes, in some sort, as his precursor (*OTN*, II, 161).

part, and he writes in the preface to *Immaturity* (pp. xliii-xliv):

> In my boyhood I saw Charles Mathews act in a farce called Cool as a Cucumber. The hero was a young man just returned from a tour of the world, upon which he has been sent to cure him of an apparently hopeless bashfulness; and the fun lay in the cure having overshot the mark and transformed him into a monster of outrageous impudence. I am not sure that something of the kind did not happen to me; for when my imposture was at last accomplished, and I daily pulled the threads of the puppet who represented me in the public press, the applause that greeted it was not unlike that which Mathews drew in Cool as a Cucumber. Certainly the growls of resentful disgust with which my advances were resisted closely resembled those of the unfortunate old gentleman in the farce whose pictures and furniture the young man so coolly rearranged to his own taste.

In Shaw's plays, also, the outrageous impudence of his light comedians upsets the representatives of the older generation and of respectable opinion. Shaw uses the cool and shocking manners and opinions of the line to attack what he looks upon as antiquated notions and philistine complacency. The comedy values, however, remain the same. The most notable Shavian examples of the type are Charteris (*Philanderer*), Frank Gardner (*Mrs. Warren*), Bluntschli (*Arms*), Marchbanks (*Candida*), Valentine (*You Never Can Tell*), Apollodorus (*Caesar*), Dubedat (*Dr.'s Dilemma*) and Bentley Summerhays (*Misalliance*). Wyndham evidently recognized his characteristic line of work in Bluntschli, for Shaw wrote to Golding Bright, "Wyndham asked me to do something for him on seeing 'Arms and the Man'; and I tried to persuade him to play The Philanderer . . . But this involved so long a delay that I withdrew the play, and am now looking round to see whether the world contains another actor who can philander as well as Wyndham."[35] All Shaw's characters in the Mathews-Wyndham line are voluble, witty, more or less graceful, shockingly frank and seemingly shameless, light in style and manner. They are indispensable in what Shaw calls "my sort of play [which] would be impossible unless I endowed my characters with powers of self-consciousness and self-expression which they would not possess in real life" (*Sixteen Self Sketches*, p. 99).

Shaw was fond of pointing out that you don't taste water because it is constantly in your mouth. It is difficult to recognize many of the conventions of Shaw's theater, not simply because some of them are dead and forgotten, but also because some of them are taken for granted as the staple of our own entertainment. However, it is convention, not nature, which composes the cast of *Widowers' Houses*, for example, where the regular leading couple who will surmount all bars to marriage by the end of the play are supported by Sartorius, a Heavy Father; Cokane, a Walking Gentleman in the tradition of the Stage Swell; Lickcheese, a Low Comedy vulgarian; a Chambermaid of the comic-pathetic variety; and a Utility waiter and porter. There is nothing essential to drama in this particular familiar range of age, sex, and social position, this particular familiar range of comedy and pathos. Shaw was intensely aware and intensely concerned with theatrical convention, both as critic and playwright. A Fabian in the drama as in politics, he was concerned to do something with the available machinery, and not, like many revolutionaries and some reactionaries, simply to do without it. It was on the broad back of the nineteenth-century lines, casts, and stereotypes that Shaw built his drama of ideas.

[35] Letter of 2 Dec. 1894, *Advice to a Young Critic*, p. 15. For Wyndham's qualities as the ideal hero of farcical comedy, and his importance in Shaw's dramatic conceptions, see below, pp. 249-52.

2

OPERA AND DRAMA

"My method, my system, my tradition, is founded upon music. It is not founded upon literature at all. I was brought up on music. I did not read plays very much because I could not get hold of them, except, of course, Shakespear, who was mother's milk to me. What I was really interested in was musical development. If you study operas and symphonies, you will find a useful clue to my particular type of writing."—S H A W at Malvern, 1939.[1]

IN THE theater of Barry Sullivan, opera and drama were much closer to each other than they are today. The two forms supplied each other with conventions and materials, and the playhouse was the opera house. The attitude of the audience for both forms was very like that of a modern opera audience; for in a day of permanent companies, great touring stars, and a familiar grand repertory, the audience judged not the play but the performance. They expressed instant approval and disapproval, waited expectantly for the virtuoso bits, and, when particularly pleased, stopped the performance and demanded the same aria or the same bravura passage over again. The actors also moved more freely between opera and drama. Barry Sullivan, Shaw's favorite among all actors, sang in opera at the beginning of his career, and Shaw classed his kind of acting with Chaliapin's (see below, p. 102, n.15). On the London stage, the gap between opera and drama widened more rapidly than in the provinces. Consequently Shaw's experience in Dublin of a more intimately related opera and drama had great importance for his later critical thinking, and ultimately for his playwriting.

More than any other form of music or drama, opera in

[1] In Robert F. Rattray, *Bernard Shaw: A Chronicle* (London, 1951), p. 20.

Dublin was fashionable and distinguished. Dublin saw grand opera with the great singers of the age, usually at the Theatre Royal, three to six weeks each year. The stars of the visiting company included the legendary Mario, Zelia Trebelli, Thérèse Titiens, Ilma de Murska, and Charles Santley. From 1864 to 1876 these singers presented some three dozen different operas, mostly in Italian; but the schedules were heavily weighted with the dozen or so favorites in the repertory.[2] In addition to the regular season, there were visiting "English Opera" companies singing nearly the same repertory in English, Offenbach companies, comic opera companies, and occasional nights of amateur opera, at the Theatre Royal and later at the Gaiety, under the direction of George John Vandeleur Lee.

Lee was one of the leading musical personages in Dublin, and Shaw has described at length, in various autobiographical reminiscences, the remarkable intimacy between Lee and the Shaw family. Shaw's mother became Lee's leading mezzo-soprano, disciple, and factotum, and took leading roles in various productions which were rehearsed in the joint Shaw-Lee household. She sang Azucena in *Il Trovatore*, Donna Anna in *Don Giovanni*, Margaret in Gounod's *Faust*, and the title role in *Lucrezia Borgia*.[3] Meanwhile Shaw's sister Lucy

[2] See *Annals of the Theatre Royal, Dublin*, esp. pp. 224-58. Except for one year, during Shaw's residence in Dublin the company was brought by the notable London impresario, James Henry Mapleson. (See Shaw's critical comments on Mapleson and the opera of the seventies in *London Music in 1888-1889*, pp. 39-40.) For Shaw's recollection of the astonishment and delight of his first trip to the opera, see Pref. to *Heartbreak House*, pp. 29-30.

[3] Letter to Archibald Henderson, reprinted in *Shaw, Man of the Century*, pp. 36-37. A review of Lee's *Il Trovatore*, presented at the Theatre Royal on 31 Mar. 1868, is of particular interest for the notice it gives to Mrs. Shaw: "Mrs Shaw made much of the part of Azucena. She does not possess the rich contralto voice we are accustomed to associate with the character, but she sings with great care and accuracy, and her acting for a non-professional is exceptionally good" ("Amateur Italian Opera," *D.E.M.*, 1 April 1868).

became Lee's star pupil, and later went on to a modest career as a singer.

Shaw took no direct part in all this musical activity; he taught himself the piano, he declared, only after Lee and his mother and Lucy had gone to London and he found the dearth of music intolerable. But all through his childhood Shaw had been surrounded by music, especially great choral music and the music of Italian Opera. "At the end of my schooling I knew nothing of what the school professed to teach; but I was a highly educated boy all the same. I could sing and whistle from end to end leading works by Handel, Haydn, Mozart, Beethoven, Rossini, Bellini, Donizetti and Verdi" (*London Music*, p. 15). Shaw claimed that music, and particularly vocal and operatic music, was the only power in the parochial Ireland of his boyhood "religious enough to redeem me from this abomination of desolation" (*Sixteen Self Sketches*, p. 46). What he believed had saved his soul remained a power throughout his life. "From my earliest recorded sign of an interest in music when as a small child I encored my mother's singing of the page's song from the first act of Les Huguenots . . . music has been an indispensable part of my life. Harley Granville-Barker was not far out when, at a rehearsal of one of my plays, he cried out 'Ladies and gentlemen: will you please remember that this is Italian opera' " (*London Music*, p. 28).

As a critic of all the arts in turn, Shaw recognized no fixed invisible bar between opera and drama such as, in some quarters, made the opera house respectable and the theater immoral. Shaw persisted in considering opera as a specialization of drama, and drama as a broad spectrum which terminates at one end in opera. Many of his most acute comments on the drama depend upon his clear perception of this continuity.

Opera was, for Shaw, above all other forms of theatrical

expression, the drama of the passions. Music could carry the passions alive into the heart as mere words could never hope to do. In a significant article urging "The Religion of the Pianoforte" on an unmusical generation, Shaw asks, "how if you could find a sort of book that would give you not merely a description of these thrilling sensations, but the sensations themselves—the stirring of the blood, the bristling of the fibres, the transcendent, fearless fury which makes romance so delightful, and realizes that ideal which Mr. Gilbert has aptly summed up in the phrase, 'heroism without risk'?" Just take an operatic vocal score to the piano, Shaw urges, and pound away. "In the music you will find the body and reality of that feeling which the mere novelist could only describe to you."[4] And just as an opera score is superior to a romantic novel, an opera presenting a tale of passions will be far more real to a spectator than a play presenting the very same story, because of the greater intensity of musical expression.

"The fact is, there is a great deal of feeling, highly poetic and highly dramatic, which cannot be expressed by mere words—because words are the counters of thinking, not of feeling—but which can be supremely expressed by music. The poet tries to make words serve his purpose by arranging them musically, but is hampered by the certainty of becoming absurd if he does not make his musically arranged words mean something to the intellect as well as to the feeling.

"For example, the unfortunate Shakespear could not make Juliet say:

    O Romeo, Romeo, Romeo, Romeo, Romeo;

and so on for twenty lines. He had to make her, in an extremity of unnaturalness, begin to argue the case in a sort of amatory legal fashion . . .

[4] *Fortnightly Review*, 61 (1894), 257.

"Now these difficulties do not exist for the tone poet. He can make Isolde say nothing but 'Tristan, Tristan, Tristan, Tristan, Tristan,' and Tristan nothing but 'Isolde, Isolde, Isolde, Isolde, Isolde,' to their hearts' content without creating the smallest demand for more definite explanations; and as for the number of times a tenor and soprano can repeat 'Addio, addio, addio,' there is no limit to it. . . . Nay, you may not only reduce the words to pure ejaculation, you may substitute mere roulade vocalization, or even balderdash, for them, provided the music sustains the feeling which is the real subject of the drama. . . ." (*Music in London*, III, 228; 133-34).

With opera possessed of the overwhelming advantage of being the drama of passions *par excellence,* it was evident to Shaw that verbal drama had to develop its own specializations, according to its own qualities. Yet, the nineteenth-century drama was intensely operatic. It was above all a drama of passions. Even if we ignore the ordinary theatrical burlesque of opera, there was scarcely an opera libretto which lacked a serious version in the spoken drama. And if opera drew upon the drama for its libretti, the play was sometimes written to exploit the success of the opera.[5] The kinship was close; and in Melodrama, the most popular and characteristic form of the century, a drama of passions was acted out to music. The aspiring actor was advised that:

"In melo-drame, and serious pantomime, a slight knowledge of music is indispensable, where a certain number of things are to be done upon the stage during the execution of so many bars of music; the cues too for entrances and exits are frequently only the changes of the air, and unless the ear is

[5] For example, Tom Taylor's *The Fool's Revenge* (1859). "In the 'Fool's Revenge,' Mr. Tom Taylor has transformed the nightmare story, best known to Londoners in association with the opera of 'Rigoletto,' into a wholesome English-natured plot."—Henry Morley, *The Journal of a London Playgoer, From 1851 to 1866* (London, 1866), p. 236. The opera in turn was based on Victor Hugo's play *Le Roi s'amuse.*

cultivated (if naturally bad) the performer will be led into error. . . . when, as continually occurs, a certain act is to be done to a single note, nothing but learning the music, or counting the time, can insure correctness."[6]

At the end of the dramatic spectrum occupied by the pure drama of passions, Shaw saw opera and play losing all distinctions. When Verdi died, Shaw wrote of him: "Verdi's genius, like Victor Hugo's, was hyperbolical and grandiose: he expressed all the common passions with an impetuosity and intensity which produced an effect of sublimity. If you ask What is it all about? the answer must be that it is mostly about the police intelligence melodramatized" (*London Music*, p. 390). On the other hand, Shaw declares that, uniquely among Shakespeare's works, "Othello is a play written by Shakespear in the style of Italian opera." It has a "prima donna, with handkerchief, confidante, and vocal solo all complete." Iago, as Stage Villain, is scarcely more lifelike than the Count di Luna. And "Othello's transports are conveyed by a magnificent but senseless music which rages from the Propontick to the Hellespont in an orgy of thundering sound and bounding rhythm. . . ." (*London Music*, p. 394).

But Shaw would have it that what Shakespeare had leave to do, by virtue of his supreme musicianship and the undeveloped state of an operatic rival, the modern playwright mistakenly imitates. It is on these grounds that Shaw scolds the audiences for crowding to see Sarah Bernhardt in Sardou's *Gismonda*. "It seems a strange thing to me that we should still be so little awake to the fact that in these plays which depend wholly on poignant intensity of expression for the

[6] *Road to the Stage* (1827), p. 62. The same advice is still offered as useful in French's edition of 1872 (p. 5): "In melo-drama and serious pantomime a little knowledge of music is quite indispensable. A great many of the *cues* are given in some of our melo-dramas merely by a change of the tune, and exits, entrances, and deaths are often regulated simply by a change of the air." Compare "melodrame," or speech, against a musical background, in opera.

simple emotions the sceptre has passed to the operatic artist" (*OTN*, I, 138). On another occasion, he writes:

"The drama of pure feeling is no longer in the hands of the playwright: it has been conquered by the musician, after whose enchantments all the verbal arts seem cold and tame. . . . there is, flatly, no future now for any drama without music except the drama of thought. The attempt to produce a genus of opera without music (and this absurdity is what our fashionable theatres have been driving at for a long time past without knowing it) is far less hopeful than my own determination to accept problem as the normal material of the drama" (*Mrs. Warren*, pp. 161-62).

Yet, to banish from grace the drama of pure feeling was by no means to banish all feeling from the non-operatic play. And to condemn "a genus of opera without music" was to condemn neither a play with music, verbal or instrumental, nor a genus of opera with thought. There was room in Heaven for Wagner, from whom Shaw borrowed many of his categories, and for the allegorical music-drama of ideas, as Shaw understood *The Ring*. There was room for Shaw's own drama, with its musically conceived overtures, arias, and ensembles, thematic development, and tonal relations. There was room for a drama in which ideas are charged with emotion, "and for the drama in which emotion exists only to make thought live and move us" (*OTN*, I, 138).

Shaw's thinking as a critic, like his earlier experiences as a spectator, bore ultimate fruit in his playwriting. However, it is by no means easy to define the practical significance in his art of his musical heritage, "which is so important in my development that nobody can really understand my art without being soaked in symphonies and operas, in Mozart, Verdi and Meyerbeer, to say nothing of Handel, Beethoven and Wagner, far more completely than in the literary drama and

its poets and playwrights."[7] Numerous similar statements by
Shaw, general but positive, have led his critics into numerous
reiterations, general but uncertain, because what Shaw means
changes with the occasion and context.[8] When he says, "My
own practice varies, as far as the mechanical conditions allow
me, from the ultra-classic to the ultra-operatic,"[9] he is talking, in context, about *mise en scène*, and the classical ob-
servance or baroque neglect of the unities. When he asserts
that Herman de Lange, "though an excellent comedian and
intelligent enough to have a foible for omniscience, was in
complete reaction against the rhetorical, declamatory, Italian
operatic tradition of acting; and neither he nor anyone else
could imagine that Shaw, nursed on Italian Opera, was bent
on reviving it as the classical stage method," he is talking,
plainly, about acting.[10] When he writes, "the fact that I was
brought up on Italian and German opera must have influenced me a good deal: there is much more of 'Il Trovatore'
and 'Don Giovanni' in my style than of 'The Mourning
Bride' and 'The School for Scandal'; but it would take me
too far to pursue this,"[11] it is not at all certain what he is
talking about.

It appears eventually that the relevance of Shaw's operatic
background to his spoken drama is at least fourfold: He uses

[7] Letter to Nora Ervine, 12 May 1934, in St. John Ervine, *Bernard
Shaw; His Life, Work, and Friends* (London, 1956), p. 555.

[8] Two exceptions are Edmund Wilson in "Bernard Shaw at Eighty,"
Eight Essays (New York, 1950), where Mr. Wilson presents a symphonic
analysis of *The Apple Cart* with ideas treated as musical themes, and
Terrence J. Spencer in *The Dramatic Principles of George Bernard Shaw*,
unpub. diss. (Stanford, 1957), pp. 116-22, where Mr. Spencer makes a
similar analysis of *Caesar*.

[9] "Playhouses and Plays," *New York Tribune*, 14 Nov. 1926, reprinted
in *Shaw on Theatre*, p. 182.

[10] From the foreword to Michael Orme's *J. T. Grein: The Story of
a Pioneer 1862-1935* (London, 1936), p. 12. "Written by Conal O'Riordan
and Censored and Revised by George Bernard Shaw." O'Riordan makes
plain in an introductory note that most of the personal reminiscences
are his, and most of the objective criticism is Shaw's.

[11] "Mr. Shaw on Mr. Shaw," *New York Times*, 12 June 1927.

direct operatic allusion, because of the arch-romantic associations of opera, as part of his attack on romantic sentiment. He uses operatic conceptions in combining the *dramatis personae* of each play. He uses operatic conceptions in creating scene and dialogue, shaping them as overtures, arias, ensembles, and duets. He brings operatic ideas to acting, and seeks a rhetorical notation based on musical pitch and dynamics.

The first of these four reflections of Shaw's operatic background appears in *Arms and the Man* ("An Anti-Romantic Comedy"), where opera is put on a level with Byron and Pushkin as a source of romantic ideals. Bluntschli declares of Sergius in the charge, "He did it like an operatic tenor" (p. 15). Raina announces "We go to Bucharest every year for the opera season," and asks Bluntschli if he knows *Ernani*.

> RAINA. I thought you might have remembered the great scene where Ernani, flying from his foes just as you were tonight, takes refuge in the castle of his bitterest enemy, an old Castilian noble. The noble refuses to give him up. His guest is sacred to him.
>
> THE MAN (*quickly, waking up a little*) Have your people got that notion? (*Arms,* p. 19)

Needless to say, Shaw draws a double benefit from *Ernani*. First of all, it plays its part in the ridicule of romance; and secondly, since Raina acts on her operatic inspiration, the motif of the hunted quarry (Bluntschli) who takes shelter in the bosom of his enemies actually enters the plot.

Ernani appears again, in *Man and Superman*, in a less obvious invocation of operatic high romance for anti-romantic purposes. The opening scene of the opera presents Ernani, a brigand chief of noble blood, on a summit in the mountains of Aragon. He gazes sadly down the valley at a castle in the distance where Elvira, his true love, is about to be married unhappily. Nearby his followers, in conventional brigand style, make merry around the campfire with a drinking song.

The third-act opening of *Man and Superman* is a precise visual allusion to this scene. But the solitary man on the summit is only a lookout, and the men around the smouldering fire, with "an air of being conscious of themselves as picturesque scoundrels honoring the Sierra by using it as an effective pictorial background," are engaged in a political meeting with their chief in the chair, and in place of the chorus of "beviam, beviam," we hear that they have spent three evenings in discussing the question, "Have Anarchists or Social-Democrats the most personal courage?" Most of the brigands are dressed in bowler, coat, and muffler; and their leader, in boots, cloak, and sombrero, "with a striking cockatoo nose, glossy black hair, pointed beard, upturned moustache, and a Mephistophelean affectation," seems scarcely to belong among them (pp. 71-72).

Like Ernani, Mendoza, the brigand chief, is pining for a love that is denied him. (Elvira in the opera is about to be married, reluctantly, to her guardian. It is worth noting Shaw's reversal of this convention with Ann and Jack Tanner, where it is the designing ward who pursues the reluctant guardian.) But Shaw's point about the consciously picturesque and sentimental Mendoza is that his romantic love-affliction is driving him to waste, absurdly, his remarkable gifts of energy, intelligence, and imagination in the mountains of the Sierra Nevada. Here, as in *Arms and the Man*, the arch-romantic associations of opera are being used for anti-romantic purposes. The comedy is in the irreverence.

The second influence of Shaw's operatic background on his art was in the forming of his casts of characters. In opera, range of character and character balance were not, as in drama, chiefly a matter of age, station, and comic-pathetic quality; they were a matter of voice. When Shaw contrived his casts of characters, it was with an eye to vocal balance in addition to everything else. As advice to directors of any play, not just his own, Shaw wrote:

"In selecting the cast no regard should be given to whether the actors understand the play or not (players are not walking encyclopedias); but their ages and personalities should be suitable, and their voices should not be alike. The four principals should be soprano, alto, tenor, and bass. Vocal contrast is of the greatest importance, and is indispensable for broadcasting. . . .

"The director must accordingly take care that every speech contrasts as strongly as possible in speed, tone, manner, and pitch with the one which provokes it, as if coming unexpected as a shock, surprise, stimulant, offence, amusement, or what not. It is for the author to make this possible; for in it lies the difference between dramatic dialogue and epic narrative."[12]

In his author's task, Shaw was immensely assisted by the unmistakable coincidence of dramatic line and operatic voice which further underlines the operatic quality of so much of nineteenth-century drama. In the drama itself certain voice qualities were associated with certain types. Heavy Villains, for example, were expected to speak in deep, reverberating tones.[13] In opera, where vocal qualities were paramount and where vocal balance had to be attained, there was a much more thorough-going identification of particular plot functions with particular kinds of voice. Since the operatic and dramatic stages shared stories and materials, a list of cor-

[12] "Shaw's Rules for Directors," *Theatre Arts*, 33 (Aug. 1949), 7, 9.
[13] See Thomas W. Erle, *Letters from a Theatrical Scene Painter* (London, 1880), pp. 48-49. Of the "strong-minded and bold villain" (as distinguished from the "cowardly or white-livered villain"), Erle notes: "His voice is a basso profundo, or rather profundissimo. . . . It is as gruff as the sound of a Christmas wait's trombone . . ."

respondences may be drawn between dramatic and operatic lines of work. For example, corresponding to the male Heavy parts in the written drama were the bass or baritone parts in opera (as, drawing on opera available in Dublin, Pizarro in *Fidelio*, Kaspar in *Der Freischütz*, Rigoletto and Sparafucile in *Rigoletto*, the Count di Luna in *Trovatore*, Mephistopheles in *Faust*, Telramund in *Lohengrin*). Corresponding to the female Heavy parts were the contralto or mezzo-soprano parts (as Azucena in *Trovatore*, Amneris in *Aïda*, Ulrica in *Un Ballo in Maschera*, Ortrud in *Lohengrin*). Corresponding to the Juvenile Leads or leading lovers were the tenor and soprano parts (as Florestan and Leonore in *Fidelio*, Manrico and Leonora in *Trovatore*, Ernani and Elvira in *Ernani*, Faust and Marguerite in *Faust*, Edgardo and Lucia in *Lucia*, Radames and Aïda in *Aïda*, Alfredo and Violetta in *Traviata*). "The operatic artist of today," wrote Shaw in a scathing criticism of operatic acting, "is a 'stock company' artist. He calls himself a *primo tenore* or a *basso cantante* instead of a juvenile lead or a first old man; but the difference is only technical."[14]

In providing his casts of characters, Shaw did not obviously equip each play with a leading quartet of soprano, alto, tenor, and bass, though a number of his plays are precisely so equipped, and scarcely one strays further from this ideal than the ordinary opera. Among those plays with an obvious operatic quartet are *Major Barbara* (Barbara, Lady Britomart, Cusins, and Undershaft), *Heartbreak House* (Ellie, Hesione, Hector, and Shotover) and *The Dark Lady of the Sonnets* (the Dark Lady, Queen Elizabeth, Shakespeare, the Warder). However, in all his plays, in each cast, and in each scene, Shaw takes care to contrive the best possible vocal range and balance in the interests of liveliness and harmony. The operatic translation of dramatic line into voice quality usually

[14] "The Opera Season" (1889), reprinted in *How to Become a Musical Critic*, ed. Dan H. Laurence (New York, 1961), p. 152.

provides him with a proper variety, but occasionally these vocal associations are not sufficient. For example, in the "Don Juan in Hell" episode of *Man and Superman*, to achieve a proper balance and contrast Shaw must excuse himself and make the Statue a tenor—indeed, a counter-tenor—in spite of Mozart, decorum, and the convention of the *père noble* who in opera was always baritone or bass. By tuning Doña Ana, the Statue, Don Juan, and the Devil like a family of viols, Shaw provides a quartet better capable of sustaining a concert-length scene of difficult and highly developed intellectual substance. Similarly, in *The Apple Cart*, where Act I is largely a discursive meeting between King and Cabinet, Shaw takes care to make two of the ministers women: Amanda, a music-hall soprano who wins elections with comic songs, and Lysistrata, *"a grave lady in academic robes"* who speaks *"in a sepulchral contralto"* (pp. 210, 218).

The third aspect of musical and operatic conceptions in Shaw's dramatic art was in the composition, instrumentation, and succession of scenes. Scenic composition and instrumentation was the immediate practical consideration which required a vocally balanced and distributed cast. Sybil Thorndike said of Shaw's reading of *Saint Joan*, "It was like listening to a great executant who knows intuitively how every note should be played. The lines came like music; each character was a different instrument in the orchestra, and he could play them all. Listening to that symphony was the greatest experience of my life."[15] Shaw read like an orchestra because he had conceived each scene musically and operatically. "Opera taught me to shape my plays into recitatives, arias, duets, trios, ensemble finales, and bravura pieces to display the technical accomplishments of the executants. . . ."[16] The

[15] Quoted by Hesketh Pearson in *Bernard Shaw: His Life and Personality* (London, 1942), p. 377.

[16] Shaw, "The Play of Ideas," *New Statesman and Nation*, n.s., 39 (1950), 511.

"verbal music" of Shakespeare, the verbal texture which Shaw cried up vigorously and consistently while crying down Shakespeare's philosophical attitudes, he conceived as taking musical and operatic forms. "To Shaw," he wrote of himself, "the wonderful storm trio [in *Lear*] in which the king, the fool, and the sham madman have their parts 'concerted,' as musicians say, like the statue, the hero, and the comic valet in Shaw's favorite *Don Giovanni*, is the summit of Shakespeare's achievement as poet and playwright."[17]

Shaw's own equivalent in a "concerted" trio is perhaps what Sybil Thorndike calls "that marvellous three-handed scene between Cauchon, Warwick and de Stogumber" in *Saint Joan*, "the pith and essence of what the play means." In reading the play to her, Shaw said: "That's all flapdoodle up to there—just 'theatre' to get you interested—now the play begins."[18] Up to this point of the play we have had considerable stage action, some melodrama, and even some farce; but Scene IV, which follows, unmasks the drama of ideas. It is "concerted," as in *Don Giovanni*, between a comic buffo, a worldly baritone, and an other-worldly bass. In the storm scene and the supper scene in *Lear* and *Don Giovanni*, the total effect depends upon a counterpoint of three distinct melodic lines carried by three distinct voices playing against each other: for example, terror in the servant, bravado in the Don, awesome sternness in the statue. In Shaw's concerted trio, it is the ideas as well as the tones and emotions which play against each other: de Stogumber's simple chauvinism, Warwick's feudalism, the Bishop's catholicism. The final blending of the three voices comes not so much from connection in their discourse—the Bishop, the Earl, and the Chauvinist are rather impervious to each other's point of

[17] Part of a comparison, by Shaw, of Molière and himself in Henderson, *Man of the Century*, p. 741.
[18] Dame Sybil Thorndike, "Thanks to Bernard Shaw" in Raymond Mander and Joe Mitchenson, *Theatrical Companion to Shaw* (London, 1954), p. 14.

view and seem to talk past each other—as from parallelism in their situation with respect to Joan. The three vocal and intellectual lines finally join in the resolve to destroy Joan. This is not unity, but a temporary harmony emerging from the counterpoint. The counterpoint of ideas and points of view in "concerted" scenes was not restricted to *Saint Joan*; rather it was an intrinsic part of Shaw's dramatic art. As early as 1895 he wrote to the actor Charles Charrington, "when you see a man like me, trying to do in counterpoint in even so few as three real parts, as in *Candida*, or in seven, as in the finale of *The Philanderer*, never tell him he ought to go and write choruses instead."[19]

Though many of Shaw's characters are, like Warwick and Cauchon, intended as equals in ideological significance and personal force, a developed scene involving these characters rarely takes the form of a witty tennis match. Shaw's technique is not to shift the lead with each stroke, but rather to allow a character to retain the lead through a repeated pattern of speeches before losing the lead to someone else. Each part dominates the others in turn. The shifts are crucial, of course, and the character emerging with final dominance has usually won something substantial. An illustration is the beginning of the second act of *Mrs. Warren*. Mrs. Warren enters with Frank Gardner in attendance, Mrs. Warren very much in the lead, even flirting with Frank, until Frank unabashedly declares he has made love to her daughter Vivie. Mrs. Warren is taken aback and positions are briefly reversed, until the entrance of Crofts and the Reverend Samuel Gardner. Frank subsides, and Mrs. Warren leads all four voices, until the question of Frank and Vivie is once more raised. The voices of the quartet are the clergyman's hollow bass, Crofts' nasal baritone, *"reedier than might be expected from his strong frame,"* Frank's tenor, and Mrs. Warren's alto.

The Reverend Samuel Gardner, Frank's father and Mrs.

[19] Letter of 1 March 1895 in St. John Ervine, *Bernard Shaw*, p. 257.

Warren's former lover, is shocked and startled at the thought
of a match between the children. As he takes the lead (p. 197),
the conversation assumes a characteristic pattern (each line
below represents a speech):

> BASS *rising, startled . . . into real force and sincerity*
>   Baritone [*assenting*]
>   Tenor *with enchanting placidity*
>   Alto *reflectively*
> BASS *astounded*
>   Baritone [*assenting*]
>   Alto *nettled*
>   Bass [*plaintively—losing the lead*]
> ALTO *defiantly*
>   Bass *collapsing helplessly into his chair*
>   Tenor [*continuing unperturbed*]
>   Baritone *gets up . . . frowning determinedly*
> ALTO *turning on him sharply*
>   Tenor *with his prettiest lyrical cadence*
>   Baritone [*defending his challenge for the lead*]
>   Bass [*supporting Baritone*]—*Mrs Warren's face falls*

Up to this point there has been a four-part counterpoint
with a leading part defined, passing from Bass to Alto. Instead of supporting Gardner in declaring a marriage between
their children "out of the question," Mrs. Warren has taken
the stand "Why not?" and Frank's father dares not give the
reasons. Crofts, however, who has his own designs on Vivie,
raises the question of money. Gardner declares Frank will get
no money, and *"Mrs Warren's face falls."* Then Crofts utters
a triumphant "There! I told you" and sits down *"as if the
matter were finally disposed of,"* to crown his displacement
of the Alto theme and as transitional punctuation; for the
rhythm speeds up, the four voices become two, and Frank,
who has heretofore taken an unobtrusive part, starts his own
melody:

TENOR *plaintively*
Alto [*firmly*]
TENOR *much amused* [*to Bass*]
Bass [*weakly*]
TENOR [*patronizingly, to Baritone*]
Baritone *turning angrily on his elbow*
TENOR *pointedly*
Baritone *contemptuously . . . he turns away again*
TENOR *rising* [*to Alto*]
Alto *muttering*
TENOR *continuing* [*he is metaphorically still rising*] *They stare at him and he begins to declaim gracefully*

Frank announces he shall place his case before Vivie. While the others stand stupefied, he actually rises into verse, a short aria signalizing his temporary triumph. Then the cottage door opens and all relations change.

The quality of the scene, in its energy and vivacity, is typically Shaw's. It is operatic in a number of ways (character balance, vocal quality); but is musical chiefly in that much of the pleasure, conscious or unconscious, comes from the repetitions, variations, and transformations of a pattern. The clarity and handling of the pattern are what seem to justify Shaw's frequent remark that "I still call myself a pupil of Mozart in comedy much more than of any of the English literary dramatists."[20]

Shaw imagined, not only voice, cast, and scene in the conceptual framework of music and opera, but also the succession

[20] MS letter to Siegfried Trebitsch, 1 July 1902. See also *Music in London*, I, 296: "In my small-boyhood I by good luck had an opportunity of learning the Don thoroughly, and if it were only for the sense of the value of fine workmanship which I gained from it, I should still esteem that lesson the most important part of my education. Indeed, it educated me artistically in all sorts of ways, and disqualified me only in one—that of criticizing Mozart fairly. Everyone appears a sentimental, hysterical bungler in comparison when anything brings his finest work vividly back to me."

of scenes, and the play as a whole. Fretting over Max Reinhardt's German production of *The Apple Cart*, Shaw complains to his translator that Reinhardt has attempted to
transform Shaw's original Mozart into vulgarized Offenbach.
He objects to Maria Bard's making Orinthia a whore and
Magnus a libertine. "Naturally, when the play is transposed
into that amusing and popular but utterly vulgar key, everything that establishes my own higher key has to come out."
He gives as an example "my little overture for Sempronius
& Pamphilius," whose tone of quiet refinement gives relief
and effect to the violent entrance of Boanerges; "so Max
has to cut it out and begin with a vulgarized Boanerges waiting for a vieux marcheur king, a male Duchess of Gerolstein."[21] Both in its debased and "higher" version, everything in the play seems operatically conceived; Mozart or
Offenbach.

Shaw habitually referred to questions of tone and style as
a matter of "key." Writing about the drama of sex in the
preface to *Overruled*, he declares, "Now if all this can be
done in the key of tragedy and philosophic comedy, it can, I
have always contended, be done in the key of farcical comedy;
and Overruled is a trifling experiment in that manner" (pp.
164-65). In a note to Lillah McCarthy concerning *Man and
Superman*, Shaw makes certain corrective suggestions on a
transition from a scene of bustle: "Otherwise you will not
get the new key and the slow movement."[22] He writes to Siegfried Trebitsch of Trebitsch's own play, *Die Letzte Wille*,
"let the people in your next play have a little will and a
little victory [*Sieg*], and then you will begin to enjoy yourself
and write your plays in the Shavian Key—D flat major, viva-
cissimo."[23] The irrepressible tempo is strictly Shavian; but
the tonality, a good key for brass intruments, Shaw would
associate with *The Ring*.

[21] MS letter to Siegfried Trebitsch, 23 April 1930.
[22] Lillah McCarthy, *Myself and My Friends* (London, 1934), p. 70.
[23] MS letter to Trebitsch, 28 March 1906.

The fourth influence of Shaw's musical and operatic experience on his dramatic art was the effect on his notions of acting, or "performance." Up to 1920, Shaw was his own director. The extensive descriptions of character and the parenthetical characterizations of almost every speech in his printed texts were attempts to reproduce for the reader all that Shaw as director would bring out of the play. Shaw genuinely lamented the lack of a musical-rhetorical notation which could send his plays to posterity as he conceived them:

"But I must repeat that the notation at my disposal cannot convey the play as it should really exist: that is, in its oral delivery. I have to write melodies without bars, without indications of pitch, pace, or timbre, and without modulation, leaving the actor or producer to divine the proper treatment of what is essentially word-music. I turn over a score by Richard Strauss, and envy him his bar divisions, his assurance that his trombone passages will not be played on the triangle, his power of giving directions without making his music unreadable. What would we not give for a copy of *Lear* marked by Shakespear 'somewhat broader,' 'always quieter and quieter,' 'amiably,' or, less translatably, 'mit grossem Schwung und Begeisterung,' 'mit Steigerung,' much less Meyerbeer's 'con esplosione,' or Verdi's *fffff* or *pppppp*, or *cantando* or *parlando,* or any of the things that I say at rehearsal, and that in my absence must be left to the intuitions of some kindred spirit?"[24]

Though Shaw had no hope of developing an adequate rhetorical notation, he made shift with the language of music in directing his actors. Winifred Loraine, in the biography of her actor-husband, writes, "Shaw annotated *Don Juan,* the

[24] "Shakespeare: A Standard Text," *Times Literary Supplement,* 17 March 1921, p. 178; in *Shaw on Theatre,* p. 144.

dream in the third act of *Superman*, like a symphony for Robert. The margin in the book twinkled with crotchets, crescendoes and minims; with G clefs, F clefs, and pianissimos; and Robert, who did not know how to read music, learned how to do so by this."[25] G. W. Bishop, writing on Shaw as a rehearsalist, declares:

"It would not be a misstatement to say that he orchestrates the parts for the actors, and in one instance he actually annotated a copy of the play in musical terms. This was for Scott Sunderland who appeared as Cain in Act 2 of the first part of *Back to Methuselah*, and as the Elderly Gentleman in Part 4.

.   .   .   .   .   .

"The actor is told to pitch his first long speech—'Whose fault was it that I killed Abel . . .'—'say, in, C Major.' 'He is to be happy and condescending.' When he gets down to the line, 'I envied his happiness, his freedom . . .' he is told to 'drop without modulation to A flat, and abandon all affectation. He is now *talking about himself*, and much more serious than when he was talking about Abel.'

"[In the speech following Cain's protest 'I do not want to kill women,'] 'begin at a low pitch and drag the time a little; then take the whole speech as a *crescendo—p.* to *ff*.' Against the words 'fighting, fighting, killing, killing!' there is a note: '*martellato*,' and after 'burning, overwhelming life,' Mr. Shaw has written '*meno mosso*.'

.   .   .   .   .   .

"With the line, 'I revolt against the clay,' he is to reach 'his top note; it is the climax—and indeed the end—of this part. His style in this speech is large and grand and harmonious, in longer bars, a little restrained in speed, but otherwise all out.' "

Most significant is Bishop's final statement: "I have quoted

[25] Winifred Loraine, *Head Wind* (New York, 1939), p. 90.

—·[57]·—

a few of the more important notes—leaving out most of the technical musical terms that are scattered through the part. . . ."[26]

Further traces of Shaw's musical-rhetorical notation may be found among the scrawled rehearsal notes in his hand which survive in the Enthoven Collection of the Victoria & Albert Museum. For *Arms and the Man* (produced April, 1894) Shaw noted:

> Raina   Chocolate cream soldier—much longer ⌒;

for *Getting Married* (produced May, 1908):

> [Collins] No maam: it didnt come natural ⎱
>   Oh yes, maam, yes: very often   ⎰ same song;

for *Fanny's First Play* (produced April, 1911):

> Gilby   The solo on a lower note
> Mrs K   Revenlations [sic]—But I do say—*sf*
> Mrs K   But dont *you* think—a third lower.

Though sharps and flats, clefs and key signatures, are almost entirely barred from Shaw's printed texts, occasionally the musical conception of an actor's part in a scene shows through, as for example in the brief "Recruiting Pamphlet" *O'Flaherty V. C.*

> MRS O'FLAHERTY (*solo*): You impudent young heifer, how dar [sic] you say such a thing to me? (*Teresa retorts furiously; the men interfere; and the solo becomes a quartet, fortissimo*). (p. 216)

Other examples occur in the bravura sections of the waiter's part in *You Never Can Tell*. As the waiter greets Valentine and Crampton, he begins a line of chatter designed to soothe and at the same time to reveal to Crampton, as delicately as possible, that Crampton is the father of the family that has

[26] G. W. Bishop, *Barry Jackson and the London Theatre* (London, 1933), pp. 28, 29.

asked him to lunch (pp. 230-31). In the course of the revelation, the waiter bustles professionally, helps Crampton with his coat, takes a stick from Valentine. The directions for all this are musical directions. The waiter begins *"smoothly melodious"* [*legato cantabile*]; then speaks *"Quickly, to Crampton, who has risen to get the overcoat off."* Rid of his overcoat, Crampton sits down, *"and the waiter resumes the broken melody."* He drops a hint which startles Crampton, and continues *"With gentle archness;"* then turns to Valentine, *"(Again changing his tempo to say to Valentine, who is putting his stick down against the corner of the garden seat) If youll allow me, sir?"* Capturing the stick, *"The waiter turns to Crampton and continues his lay,"* to the point of the catastrophic revelation.

It was such bravura acting that Shaw had in mind when he wrote to one of his critics, "You are right in saying that my plays require a special technique of acting, and, in particular, great virtuosity in sudden transitions of mood that seem to the ordinary actor to be transitions from one 'line' of character to another. But, after all, this is only fully accomplished acting; for there is no other sort of acting except bad acting, acting that is the indulgence of imagination instead of the exercise of skill."[27] And it was to secure such acting for a drama which came to depend more and more for its interest on the rapid fire of its words and ideas that Shaw wished for something like a musical-rhetorical dramatic notation.

In revolting against "a genus of opera without music," the drama of pure emotion, Shaw committed himself to a species of drama much more musical in its fundamental nature: the drama of ideas. For "If you want to produce anything in the way of great poetic drama," he declared, "you have to take a theme, as Beethoven did in his symphonies, and keep ham-

[27] "Mr. Shaw on Mr. Shaw," *NY Times*, 12 June 1927.

mering at the one theme."[28] As Shaw developed from his first exploitations of popular genres to the full-fledged Discussion Play, he became more and more adept at the development and counterpointing of ideas as if they were musical themes. At the same time, he became less and less patient with the requirement of first-night comprehensibility. He wrote, at about the time of *Misalliance* and *Getting Married,*

"Even when the author raises no hostility or misunderstanding by breaking new ground, as Beethoven did, yet it is not in the nature of things possible for a person to take in a play fully until he is in complete possession of its themes; or, to put it in another way, nobody can understand the beginning of a play until he knows the end of it: a condition which cannot be fulfilled at a first hearing . . . In music this goes without saying: no one pretends to be able to follow the Ninth Symphony until he knows all the themes as well as he knows God Save the King. Now probably there are many more people who can pick up and remember a new tune at one hearing than can master a new idea at its first utterance."[29]

The play, in this passage, is conceived as a musical composition, built from the progression, development, and counterpointing of themes. Theme as melody and theme as idea are equated. The playwright is regarded as a composer, and the spectator is required to adopt the concert-goer's frame of mind.

Shaw's conception of *Back to Methuselah* was similar. He conceived of it, on the analogy of Wagner's *Ring* cycle, as an allegorical music-drama in which ideas were made flesh.[30] After an unsatisfactory reading of the work in progress, he wrote to Granville-Barker, "To the end I may have to dis-

[28] Rattray, *Bernard Shaw: A Chronicle*, p. 20, quoting a statement by Shaw at Malvern in 1939.

[29] "Mr. Trench's Dramatic Values," a letter to *The Saturday Review,* 110 (2 July 1910), reprinted in West, *Shaw on Theatre*, p. 114.

[30] See MS letters to Siegfried Trebitsch, 20 July 1919 and 15 Sept. 1920.

regard the boredom of the spectator who has not mastered all the motifs, as Wagner had to do; but I daresay I shall manage to make the people more amusing, some of them more poetic, and all of them more intelligible than they now are in this first draft."[31]

When Shaw defined opera as the extreme and supreme drama of the passions, he was careful to distinguish opera from Wagnerian music-drama. Thereafter, he campaigned against those dramatists who still attempted to beat opera at its own game, but he nevertheless exploited aspects of opera in writing his own plays. He used its arch-romantic associations in attacking the romantic view of the world; he imported its vocal and structural concepts for forming his casts, and for constructing scenes and creating dialogue; he borrowed its fundamentally musical idea of performance and infused it into the acting his scenes and dialogue require. All this he took largely from a form whose purest expression, Shaw declared, was a tenor and soprano infinitely repeating "Addio, addio, addio."

But in Wagner's music-drama Shaw believed he had found the possibility of conveying impassioned thought to an audience, thought interpenetrated with intense feeling. "It is only when a thought interpenetrated with intense feeling has to be expressed," he wrote, "as in the Ode to Joy in the Ninth Symphony, that coherent words must come with the music."[32] The converse seemed to follow: if thought was to be conveyed with all possible passion, music would have to come with the coherent words; to infuse thought with the life and passion he had found in opera as a boy, Shaw would have to bring the world of music to his playwriting. The consistent aesthetic direction of Shaw's entire playwriting career was toward the creation of a drama of impassioned thought, a heroic drama of ideas.

[31] 18 Dec. 1918, *Bernard Shaw's Letters to Granville Barker*, ed. C. B. Purdom (New York, 1957), p. 198.
[32] *Music in London*, III, 134. (Compare Wagner on the Ninth Symphony in *Opera and Drama*.)

II

LONDON: CURRENTS AND
CROSSCURRENTS

3

DRAMA

T H E London theater of the late eighties and nineties, when Shaw sat in judgment as a critic, was an active, uncertain theater of complex character and multiple traditions whose strengths bore no relation to their venerability, where reactionary bursts of primitive melodrama jostled polite comedies, "problem plays," matinee experiments, and full-scale productions of Ibsen, Sudermann, Henry James, Barrie, and Oscar Wilde. Since the middle of the century it had been changing rapidly from a theater of flamboyant make-believe to a theater of sophisticated verisimilitude. Its dramatic traditions were not only multiple, they were conflicting. There was an ascendant strain of fashionable or drawing-room drama devoted to an ideal of cultivated truth-to-life, and a surviving strain of romantic-rhetorical drama devoted to an ideal of impassioned flamboyance. There was the purely formal ideal of the well-made play attached to the names of Scribe and Sardou, and the challenging ideal of the social-didactic play attached to the name of Ibsen. These were the conflicting strains in the London theater whose relevance to Shaw's beginnings as a playwright appears in his writings as a critic. These were the dramatic traditions which provided the immediate context of Shaw's own dramatic work.

As a critic of end-of-the-nineteenth-century drama, no less than as a critic of music and painting, Shaw disclaimed objectivity and impartiality. For example, he warned the readers of his music criticism that:

"in dealing with the drama, I find that the forces which tend to make the theatre a more satisfactory resort for me are rallied for the moment, not round the so-called French realists, whom I should call simply anti-obscurantists, but around the Scandinavian realists; and accordingly I mount their platform, exhort England to carry their cause on to a glorious victory, and endeavor to surround their opponents with a subtle atmosphere of absurdity. . . . Never in my life have I penned an impartial criticism; and I hope I never may. As long as I have a want, I am necessarily partial to the fulfilment of that want, with a view to which I must strive with all my wit to infect everyone else with it." (*Music in London*, II, 129)

In 1906, when his dramatic criticism was first collected and republished, Shaw wrote in "The Author's Apology":

". . . I must honestly warn the reader that what he is about to study is not a series of judgments aiming at impartiality, but a siege laid to the theatre of the XIXth Century by an author who had to cut his own way into it at the point of the pen, and throw some of its defenders into the moat.

"Pray do not conclude from this that the things hereinafter written were not true, or not the deepest and best things I knew how to say. Only, they must be construed in the light of the fact that all through I was accusing my opponents of failure because they were not doing what I wanted, whereas they were often succeeding very brilliantly in doing what they themselves wanted." (*OTN*, I, v)

Shaw's partisan advocacy of the "Scandinavian realists" shaped his attitude toward drawing-room drama, romantic-rhetorical drama, and the ideal of the well-made play. However, it was not simply Ibsen and Ibsenism for which he campaigned; it was for the underlying notion of a critical-realistic drama in which ideals and conventions were criticized, tested, examined, ridiculed, and proposed, and in which dramatic situations had no value except as instruments to test ideals and conventions, and to reveal character. In contrast, the rival traditions supported a "conventional" drama. In the well-made play, for example, in which an intriguing dramatic situation was the center of interest and the structural core, ordinary social ideals and conventions formed a background which had to be taken for granted or the situation would disappear. Drawing-room drama was similarly conventional. As its name suggests, it aimed at creating a photographic image of life and manners in a fashionable, or West End drawing room. It was concerned with a realism of surface and confined itself to that genteel area of life which could be reproduced most attractively, with the greatest apparent verisimilitude and with the least offense, on a fashionable stage. Actually, drawing-room drama simply toned down ordinary dramatic conventions to the pitch of polite discourse while reproducing on the stage the very stronghold of accepted social ideals. As in the well-made play, ordinary social ideals and conventions formed a background which had to be taken for granted.

In England, "well-made" construction and "drawing-room" surface were linked by history, though by no apparent internal necessity. The line of the drawing-room play descended visibly from T. W. Robertson to Arthur Wing Pinero among Shaw's contemporaries, though as William Archer pointed out it had its effective beginnings in "the humble bourgeois movement headed by Eugène Scribe and his innumerable collaborators."[1] The line of the well-made play was also identified with Scribe; and similarly, its most skilled and fashionable continuator among Shaw's contemporaries was Arthur Wing Pinero. Shaw lumped together "well-made" construction and "drawing-room" verisimilitude in his attack on conventional drama and bombarded them indiscriminately.

The existing romantic-rhetorical drama was also conven-

[1] *The Old Drama and the New; an Essay in Re-Valuation* (Boston, 1923), pp. 250-51.

tional in its presuppositions and was, as the name implies, violently and openly romantic. However, except for the branch at the august Lyceum, it was much less fashionable, and in Shaw's view much less dangerous to his strategic objectives, than the superficially realistic modes. Consequently Shaw used its most "popular" and unpretentious form—Melodrama—as a stick to beat the other modes.

Shaw's major strategy, however, in his war to convert the theater of the nineteenth century, was to blow up the enemy with its own critical assumptions. Invoking the criterion of stage realism, he demonstrated "conventionality" everywhere. All through his criticism in the nineties, he delights in naming, dissecting, and ridiculing particular stage conventions, especially when they appear in plays pretending to superficial truth-to-life. The "subtle atmosphere of absurdity" with which Shaw hoped to surround the "French realists" was the absurdity inherent in any lapse from advertised virtue and was achieved by exposing their theatrical artifice. Shaw's sleight of hand here, in criticism as in playwriting, was to substitute particulars of stage convention for moral conventionalism, which was the true antagonist of his philosophical realism and his drama of unsettled ideals.

Apart from this strategy, Shaw recognized the existence, indeed the necessity, of the artifices of the world of the stage which make performance, communication, and illusion possible. He knew perfectly well, for example, that actors must not whisper inaudibly and that "you do not write parts for six-legged actors or two-headed heroines, though there is great scope for drama in such conceptions."[2] He even went so far as to declare that, to him, the object of drama was "the expression of feeling by the arts of the actor, the poet, the musician. Anything that makes this expression more vivid,

[2] Shaw, "The Heroic Actors," in Raymond Mander and Joe Mitchenson, *Theatrical Companion to Shaw: A Pictorial Record of the First Performances of the Plays of George Bernard Shaw* (London, 1954), p. 63.

whether it be versification, or an orchestra, or a deliberately artificial delivery of the lines, is so much to the good for me, even though it may destroy all the verisimilitude of the scene" (*OTN*, I, 91-92). Shaw frequently discussed the artifice in his own dramatic practice; thus, he writes of Major Barbara's loss of Bill Walker's soul when the Army accepts Bodger's conscience money: "In real life Bill would perhaps never know this. But I, the dramatist whose business it is to shew the connexion between things that seem apart and unrelated in the haphazard order of events in real life, have contrived to make it known to Bill . . ." (*Major Barbara*, p. 230). To Siegfried Trebitsch, who was a playwright on his own account as well as Shaw's translator, Shaw declares that in writing a play there are "two points on which all ordinary probability and naturalness must be thrown to the winds." The playwright must make "a reckless use of coincidences"; and his characters must be able to "understand themselves and describe themselves much better than any real human being ever does or can." Shaw offers Doolittle as an example of such a character and contrasts him with Higgins, a character so unaware of his own nature that he complains continually about the unreasonable views others take of him. The latter method is perhaps more natural, Shaw notes; but "natural or not . . . either by self-portraiture or self-betrayal every character has to be defined to the audience."[3]

In their elementary nature, stage convention and moral conventionalism are totally different things. Shaw recognized that stage convention inhered in the very idea of theater; but moral conventionalism was something opposed to moral realism. Moral conventionalism was self-blinding and self-illuding and, to Shaw, the offspring of romantic idealism. It was the unquestioning acceptance of laws, customs, attitudes, and ideals as standards of judgment long after the social necessity which created them had passed. It was plain to

[3] ms letter, 8 May 1914.

Shaw that many theatrical conventions reflected moral conventions, or had moral implications. "The whole point of an Ibsen play," he wrote in 1891, "lies in the exposure of the very conventions upon which are based those by which the actor is ridden."[4] It was also plain to Shaw that, for the intelligent playgoer of the nineties to whom "the moral conventions" were sacred, the theatrically "conventional" was an obsolete and inferior species, and the term was a term of derogation. Consequently, Shaw in his criticism sets up an ambivalent polarity between "convention" and "realism"; but what he thereby stigmatizes as an outdated dramatic convention is usually a habit of the theater embodying an outdated or untenable moral convention in a presumably modern play.

Shaw's theatrical criticism reveals him during the period when he was cutting his way into the theater as a coterie playwright still largely unacted in London. It is clear that he was not then a naïve genius whose originality was bound up with provincial or academic innocence, but an experienced man of the theater, professionally aware of a general condition of ferment and of a number of vigorous and conflicting currents in the drama which would be useful or inimical to his own work and to the world at large.

DRAWING-ROOM DRAMA

A revolution took place on the London stage of the late sixties and seventies while Shaw was enjoying the theater of flamboyant make-believe in Dublin. Shaw wrote of this revolution in 1896:

"I need not tell over again the story of the late eclipse of the stagey drama during the quarter-century beginning with the success of Robertson, who, by changing the costume and the form of dialogue, and taking the Du Maurieresque, or garden

---

[4] *Quintessence of Ibsenism* (London, 1891), p. 137.

party, plane, introduced a style of execution which effectually broke the tradition of stagey acting, and has left us at the present moment with a rising generation of actors who do not know their business." (*OTN*, II, 237)

As Shaw's comment suggests, the most obvious effect of the Robertsonian revolution was on acting (see Chapter 4, below), though the style and matter of performance were inextricably mixed. Shaw's critical contemporaries looked upon T. W. Robertson as the fountainhead in English drama of the movement that William Archer was pleased to characterize as "that elimination of exaggerative and rhetorical conventions which was the predestinate line of progress."[5] The Robertsonian movement, Archer felt, had its full accomplishment in the drama of Jones and Pinero. "As we listen to the dialogue," he writes of a play by Jones, "we cannot but be conscious that we have got utterly away both from the convention of wit and the convention of rhetoric—from the whole exaggerative and falsifying apparatus, in short, that had come down to our own time from the days when drama was a rite of hero-worship or a propitiation of the deities, the daimons, of corn and wine" (p. 302).

For Shaw, the Robertsonian tradition in the theater of the nineties was not Archer's projected ideal of 1886: "the ultimate evolution of a form of drama which shall soberly and simply reproduce the everyday aspects of modern life."[6] Rather, looking at the vast bulk of undistinguished fashionable drama, Shaw declared it nothing but "a tailor's advertisement making sentimental remarks to a milliner's advertisement in the middle of an upholsterer's and decorator's advertisement" (*OTN*, III, 58). Shaw found nothing to delight him in the absence of wit and rhetoric, and little to celebrate in the whole tradition which had led to the reduc-

[5] *Old Drama and the New*, p. 228.
[6] Archer, "Are We Advancing?" *About the Theatre* (London, 1886), p. 19.

tion of drama to sentimental conversation in a drawing-room. And, of course, he found the approximation of a naturalistic surface a deceptive substitute for a genuine critical realism.

The line of Robertson was traceable, Shaw felt, not only in a progressive freedom from exaggeration and from the conventions of wit and rhetoric but also in a method of disguising pure conventionality by an increase in superficial naturalness. The freshness, nature, and humanity which delighted ordinary audiences in Robertson's *Caste* (1867) Shaw ascribed merely to the relief provided from "years of sham heroics and superhuman balderdash." He declares:

"The characters are very old stagers, very thinly 'humanized.' Captain Hawtrey . . . began by being a very near relation of the old stage 'swell,' who pulled his moustache, held a single eyeglass between his brow and cheekbone, said 'Haw, haw' and 'By Jove,' and appeared in every harlequinade in a pair of white trousers which were blacked by the clown instead of his boots. . . . Polly is comic relief pure and simple; George and Esther have nothing but a milkcan to differentiate them from the heroes and heroines of a thousand sentimental dramas . . . the 'Marquizzy' . . . is not an original study from life, but simply a ladyfication of the conventional haughty mother whom we lately saw revived in all her original vulgarity and absurdity at the Adelphi in Maddison Morton's All that Glitters is not Gold, and who was generally associated on the stage with the swell from whom Captain Hawtrey is evolved. Only, let it not be forgotten that in both there really is a humanization, as humanization was understood in the 'sixties: that is, a discovery of saving sympathetic qualities in personages thitherto deemed beyond redemption." (*OTN*, III, 166-67)

The humanization of stage types made scarcely any difference in the conventionality of situation, relationships, or the background of values and assumptions. Robertson provided a conventional action for conventional types, methodically toned down to harmonize with the genuine furnishings of his elegant interiors, and he reveals as much in his nervous notes to the actor. For example, in *M.P.* (1870), Dunscombe, an aristocratic man of the world who has gone bankrupt, hears an auctioneer in the next room selling a portrait of his mother as a little girl. The annotated stage direction reads:

> CECILIA goes to DUNSCOMBE and lays her hand upon his shoulder. CHUDLEIGH takes his hand. DUNSCOMBE masters his emotion.*
>
> *NOTE.—The actor playing Dunscombe is requested not to make too much of this situation. All that is required is a momentary memory of childhood—succeeded by the external phlegm of the man of the world. No tragedy, no tears, or pocket-handkerchief.[7]

The sole departure from conventions is the underplaying. In *War* (1871), the highly conventional tale of Lotte (a German girl) and Oscar (a French officer) whose love is crossed by the outbreak of the Franco-Prussian war, Robertson requests that Oscar's father "be played with a *slight* French accent. He is not to pronounce his words absurdly, or shrug his shoulders, or duck his head towards his stomach, like the conventional stage Frenchman. COLONEL DE ROCHE-VANNES is to be played with the old pre-Revolutionary polite-ness—knightly courtesy, with a mixture of ceremony and *bonhommie.*" Similarly, on the first appearance of Lotte's father, the actor is instructed: "*This part to be played with a slight German accent, and not to be made wilfully comic. Herr Karl Hartmann is to be a perfect gentleman, with a touch of the scholar and pedant in his manner—but always

[7] *The Principal Dramatic Works of T. W. Robertson* (London, 1889), I, 365.

a gentleman."[8] Here is a humanization of "personages," though the personages are still the old stage types, while the action, clichés of sentiment, and conceptual frame of reference remain the same.

For England the theater with which Robertson became identified was revolutionary in nothing so much as its idea of dramatic ensemble, and Robertson wrote ensemble acting into his plays in such a way as to make grandly rhetorical drama impossible. Characteristic of his dialogue is the conversation composed of short, linked speeches, each speaker picking up the thread from the one before. Also characteristic is the scene with two independent (though perhaps amusingly related) dialogues in progress on stage at once. In *Caste*, Robertson's most notable play, Sam and Polly (the comic couple) quarrel, while George persuades Esther (the sentimental heroine) to marry him. The superb sustained counterpointing of the two conversations gives the scene the warmth of sentimental comedy without compromising the serious sentimental characters. Here and elsewhere, it also gives an effect of business, movement, and keeps audience, actors, and stage from settling into the earnest, static, more profound concentration of rhetorical drama.

Robertson had an immediate successor in James Albery, who was even more skilled at the gentle grey-dusting of conventions, the muting of loud colors. In *Two Roses* (1870), the dialogue is swifter, subtler, and more fragile than Robertson's, requiring greater attention and containing many delicate poetically-phrased lines that fit perfectly into the flow of the discourse. A scene is made out of a bit of sewing, writing a letter, counting roses: details seemingly slight and peripheral to the dramatic action, but in fact the real substance of the drama. The utterly conventional plot needs very little attention, and it is constantly underplayed by Robertsonian counterpointing. Albery's talent waned, and H. J. Byron, who

[8] *Ibid.*, II, 755, 756.

also felt Robertson's influence, and whom Archer declares was "from the death of Robertson . . . to the coming of Pinero . . . the most prominent and popular dramatist of the day,"[9] was gifted in other directions. Of his longest running hit, one critic in the nineties observed: *"Our Boys* resembles Robertson's comedies just as a cook resembles her mistress when she is decked out in her mistress's hat and gown. . . ."[10] Robertson's true succession flourished in the nineties, particularly in Arthur Wing Pinero, the most esteemed and approved writer of the period, and the particular object of Shaw's castigation.

Pinero, who served his dramatic apprenticeship as an actor in the seventies, revealed his indebtedness in a number of ways. For example, Robertson's *School* (1869), and a number of Robertson's and Albery's other plays, presented a group of young school-age girls who dominated the stage and set the tone. Pinero's *The Schoolmistress* (1886) imitates these plays forthrightly. Pinero's *Trelawny of the "Wells"* (1898) is actually a play about Robertson himself in the person of Tom Wrench, a minor actor who has written a play that calls for a new style of acting. Tom Wrench's story is part of a typically Robertsonian plot of a love affair between Miss Rose Trelawny, juvenile lady of the Wells, and the grandson of a vice-chancellor. The lovers are finally brought together by Tom Wrench (who quietly loves Trelawny himself) in his new play called *Life* when it unexpectedly finds a theater and a backer. In a review entitled "Mr Pinero's Past" Shaw dryly remarks, "I cannot pretend to think that Mr Pinero, in reverting to that period, has really had to turn back the clock as far as his own sympathies and ideals are concerned" (*OTN*, III, 309).

Pinero reveals how earnestly his aesthetic completes the revolution announced by Robertson in an illuminating lec-

[9] *The Old Drama and the New*, p. 273.
[10] Augustin Filon, *The English Stage* (London, 1897), p. 134.

ture on Stevenson as a dramatist. Even in *Beau Austin*, which he considers almost successful, Pinero objects that "still the author evidently conceived that the essence of the drama resides in rhetoric, in fine speeches."[11] In his peroration, on the hard work and earnest concentration the art of playwriting demands, Pinero declares: "When you sit in your stall at the theater and see a play moving across the stage, it all seems so easy and so natural, you feel as though the author had improvised it. The characters being, let us hope, ordinary human beings, say nothing very remarkable, nothing you think— (thereby paying the author the highest possible compliment)—that might not quite well have occurred to you" (pp. 70-71).

Eventually Pinero brought this ideal of the easy and natural to complete fruition. In such a fine play as *Mid-Channel*, the dialogue is laconic, idiomatic, expressive in understatement and implication. There is no trace of Archer's "convention of wit" or "convention of rhetoric." The story is free of the artificialities of "well-made" plotting and even of stock and line. For example, Lena, the maid, is neither a soubrette nor a nonentity, but an ordinary intelligent and sympathetic person, on the same plane of humanity as all the other characters—very different in this respect from Enry Straker in *Man and Superman*, or Nurse Guinness in *Heartbreak House*.

Shaw consistently attacked Pinero's conventionality, not his efforts at naturalistic surface. But he complained particularly of Pinero's ability to create naturalistic surface and smuggle in, under its cover, clichés of character, plot, and sentiment. As a social thinker Shaw had to consider this dangerous, particularly when Pinero broached a theme of social concern. The staginess of romantic drama at least alerted the audience that what they were seeing took place in a world apart. But there was no such clue in Pinero, or in the dramatists

[11] *Robert Louis Stevenson as a Dramatist*, reprinted in *Papers on Play-Making* (New York, 1914), p. 59.

of his school, unless someone took the trouble to advertise the unrealities. Therefore, at his first opportunity as a Saturday Reviewer, Shaw declared that though Pinero cultivates "that peculiar stage effect of intellectual drama, of social problem, of subtle psychological study of character," it was all merely stage effect. In *The Profligate* and *The Second Mrs. Tanqueray* "he was careful to support this stage effect with a substantial basis of ordinary dramatic material, consisting of a well worked-up and well worn situation which would have secured the success of a conventional Adelphi piece." At *Mrs. Tanqueray*, the "commonplace playgoer, as he admired Mrs Patrick Campbell, and was moved for the twentieth time by the conventional wicked woman with a past, consumed with remorse at the recollection of her innocent girlhood, and unable to look her pure step-daughter (from a convent) in the face, believed that he was one of the select few for whom 'the literary drama' exists . . ." (*OTN*, I, 59-60).

While marking Pinero's conventionalities of character, Shaw did not neglect his artificialities of plot under the realistic surface: the confidant, the intercepted letters, or "sendings of one set of people to France and another to India in order to enable a lady to arrive unexpectedly or a gentleman to walk in by night at the drawing room window"—all the expedients of well-made drama. When Shaw gave his approval to *The Benefit of the Doubt*, it was, he declared, because Pinero had stayed within the limits of what he knew, and hadn't been driven back on "the conventional figures which inevitably appear in his plays whenever he conceives himself to be dealing as a sociologist with public questions of which he has no solid knowledge, but only a purely conventional and theatrical conceit" (*OTN*, I, 217-18).

Shaw's disparaging criticism was not provoked simply by Pinero's use of convention, any more than it was by Pinero's attempt to achieve a true-to-life surface. Shaw's own plays written in the nineties abounded in convention, social and theatrical. But in Shaw's eyes, Pinero's method was an amalgam-with-convention, whereas Shaw introduces the conventions in order to slight them, expose them, laugh at them, or transmute them. Shaw's method in playwriting, from first to last, was exactly opposite to the method of the playwrights in the line of Robertson, for Shaw put all the conventions on the surface, and the truth-to-life underneath.

THE WELL-MADE PLAY

Paralleling his campaign against drawing-room drama, Shaw waged his war against the well-made play by systematically exposing its essential unreality. Like drawing-room drama, the well-made play was committed to producing an illusion of reality, though on a different level of dramatic activity.

In the late nineteenth century, the prolonged influence of the Parisian theater upon English drama had been finally reduced, through assimilation and international copyright laws, to the point where an ideal, the ideal of the "well-made" play, was much more significant than actual imports and adaptations. In England, through the work of dramatists like Pinero and through the Anglo-French repertories of actors like the Bancrofts and the Kendals, there had been a native fusion of "drawing-room" and "well-made" traditions, one concerned with surface, and the other with "construction."

The ideal well-made play was built around a single situation with a high charge of intriguing emotion or amusing piquancy. "Once this scene was invented," Shaw declared, "nothing remained for the author to do except to prepare for it in a first act, and to use up its backwash in a third" (*OTN*, I, 2). He lectures Sydney Grundy for "writing a play round a 'situation,' instead of developing a situation into a play" (*OTN*, I, 72). He refers to well-made plays as mechanical rabbits, clockwork mice, and, in contrast to a play like

James's *Guy Domville*, "a mere situation hung out on a gallows of plot" (*OTN*, I, 8).

Truth-to-life in the well-made play was sought in the neat and plausible explanation of its ingenious and unlikely principal situations. The illusion of reality was identified with an entirely visible and unbroken chain of circumstantial causality. In practice, however, to achieve a logic of events the well-made play developed a set of plot conventions suited to the conditions of the stage. These conventions Shaw advertised and ridiculed. Labelling them "Sardoodledom," he attacked "The postal arrangements, the telegraphic arrangements, the police arrangements, the names and addresses, the hours and seasons, the tables of consanguinity, the railway and shipping time-tables, the arrivals and departures, the whole welter of Bradshaw and Baedeker, Court Guide and Post Office Directory, whirling round one incredible little stage murder and finally vanishing in a gulp of impossible stage poison" (*OTN*, I, 133). He attacks the "naïve machinery of the exposition" in *Mrs. Tanqueray*, "in which two whole actors are wasted on sham parts, and the hero, at his own dinner party, is compelled to get up and go ignominiously into the next room 'to write some letters' when something has to be said behind his back." Shaw points out the artifice of the confidant "to whom both Paula and her husband explain themselves for the benefit of the audience," counts the number of doors, notes the activity of the postman, and declares: "it is impossible to avoid the conclusion that what most of our critics mean by mastery of stage craft is recklessness in the substitution of dead machinery and lay figures for vital action and real characters" (*OTN*, I, 45-46). The final effect of Shaw's comments was not only to expose the artificialities of the "well-made" method, but to reject the "realistic" criterion of circumstantial plausibility altogether as "elaborating a tissue of artificialities to lead us to accept a situation which we would willingly have taken for granted without any explanations at all" (*OTN*, I, 3).

Shaw's root objection to the "well-made" formula was that any serious play whose ultimate dramatic values lay in an intriguing situation and its circumstantial plausibility was likely to depend upon conventional moral and social values in its characters and in its audience. For example, Shaw writes of *The Second Mrs. Tanqueray*, "I find little except a scaffold for the situation of a step-daughter and step-mother finding themselves in the positions respectively of affianced wife and discarded mistress to the same man. Obviously, the only necessary conditions of this situation are that the persons concerned shall be respectable enough to be shocked by it, and that the step-mother shall be an improper person" (*OTN*, I, 46). Such a formula, Shaw felt, depended upon static attitudes and moral commonplaces. It was conventional in the deepest sense, "essentially mechanistic and therefore incapable of producing vital drama."[12]

ROMANTIC-RHETORICAL DRAMA

In a *Saturday Review* article defining London theater management as a precarious "speculation in fashionable drama," Shaw makes an exception of the Lyceum, the Criterion, the Haymarket, and the Adelphi, where, "given a tolerable play, new or old, their reputation and the acting of their companies will pull it through, even triumphantly. Thus," he concludes, "roughly speaking, the West End of London seems capable of maintaining about four theatres, one classical, one popular, and two intermediate, in tolerable security" (*OTN*, III, 185). The classical theater and the popular theater were Irving's Lyceum and the Adelphi, a theater devoted to melo-

[12] "How William Archer Impressed Bernard Shaw," *Pen Portraits*, p. 22. See Shaw's discussion of "well-made" construction in his preface to *Three Plays by Brieux* (New York, 1911), pp. xx-xxiii.

drama; and it was at these extremes that the romantic-rhetorical tradition persisted.

With the rise of drawing-room drama and the well-made play, the romantic-rhetorical tradition had lost its primacy. Fifty years before, what Shaw called the "pure-bred drama engendered solely by the passion of the stage-struck" fairly dominated the stage. "Stage kings and queens, stage lovers, stage tyrants, stage parents, stage villains, and stage heroes were alone to be found in it; and, naturally, they alone were fit for the stage or in their proper place there." Even in Shakespeare, "It was the stagey element that held the stage, not the natural element," and a style of acting proper to these plays, "an excessively stagey style, was evolved and perfected." But there came a change, and Shaw, virtually alone among his respectable contemporary critics, questions that the change was for the better (*OTN*, II, 236-37).

Of the two areas in which a stagey, rhetorical, and overtly romantic tradition survived, the Lyceum commanded an extraordinary reverence and melodrama commanded an unshakable popularity, even in the West End. In suburban theaters and "penny gaffs" Melodrama flourished without serious abatement. When Shaw wrote on the romantic-rhetorical survivals in the nineties, he made a point of treating the august Lyceum as if it had no claim to an extra measure of reverence; but if Shaw was disrespectful to the lady, he seems by contrast cordial to the flower-girl. Shaw spends as much time pointing out virtues in melodrama as in acknowledging its shortcomings. Moreover, in all comparisons with drawing-room drama, melodrama was certain to come off with honor. For example, Shaw writes of the invasion of the St. James's Theatre, heretofore devoted to fashionable drama, by Paul M. Potter's melodrama *The Conquerors* (1898): "When civilization becomes effete, the only cure is an irruption of barbarians. When the London dramatist has driven everybody out of the theatre with his tailor-made romances and suburban love affairs, the bushranger and the backwoodsman become masters of the situation." After cataloguing the crudities of such "barbarian melodramas," Shaw adds, "All the same, these bushwhacking melodramatists have imagination, appetite, and heat of blood; and these qualities, suddenly asserting themselves in our exhausted theatre, produce the effect of a stiff tumbler of punch after the fiftieth watering of a pot of tea" (*OTN*, III, 365). On another occasion, he writes of an adaptation from Sardou, "Delia Harding is the worst play I ever saw. Taking it as a work bearing the same relation to the tastes of the upper middle class as the Adelphi drama to those of the lower middle class, I declare enthusiastically in favor of the Adelphi" (*OTN*, I, 97).

But if Shaw's appreciation of melodrama sometimes rose to enthusiasm over a revival of an ancient piece like *Black-Ey'd Susan* (*OTN*, III, 6), it also sank to hopelessness over Adelphi plays in general, all "like Messrs Chubb's locks: each of them presents a fresh combination and permutation of the standard component parts, and so can be described as 'new and original'; but the parts are the same, and the manufacture would probably be carried on by machinery if hand labor were not cheaper" (*OTN*, III, 186). If he declared that "A really good Adelphi melodrama is of first-rate literary importance, because it only needs elaboration to become a masterpiece," he added that "Unfortunately, a really good Adelphi melodrama is very hard to get" (*OTN*, I, 93). Shaw objected strenuously, of course, to a tendency William Archer had noted in 1886 as "the unexampled vogue of modern and so-called realistic melodrama,"[18] in which a renaissance of Melodrama was marked by an increase in superficial verisimilitude, in the direction of the fashionable play (*OTN*, I, 204-05). Shaw objected, not to the continuing renaissance of melodramatists in the West End, but to the well-made "explanations and contrivances with which they burden their

[18] "Are We Advancing?" p. 18.

pieces," since "melodramatic stage illusion is not an illusion of real life, but an illusion of the embodiment of our romantic imaginings" (*OTN*, II, 83). He also objects profoundly to some of the secondary characteristics of Melodrama, particularly the Drury Lane Melodrama of Sir Augustus Harris: "their open exploitation of the popular worship of sport, fashion, and jingoism, in scenes which it did nobody any good to gloat over" (*OTN*, II, 204).

It should not be imagined that, because of some approximation to fashionable forms, the language and substance of the Melodrama of the nineties ceased to be strongly romantic and rhetorical. As in drawing-room drama, the style and matter of the play were inseparable from a style and manner of performance, and in 1895 Shaw could report of Charles Cartwright in a modern Adelphi melodrama, "Mr Cartwright . . . gives us the Adelphi voice, the Adelphi suffusion of suppressed emotion, and the Adelphi unction in remarking, in the character of a leading counsel in the thick of a heavy murder case, that 'the happy day is enamelled blue and gold like some old missal.' He leans much on the orchestra, also in the Adelphi manner, turning on the band and the deeper springs of emotion simultaneously" (*OTN*, I, 209). It is evident from the generic adjective that such language and such acting were not merely present in the particular Melodrama under review, but were the hallmarks of the Adelphi play.

Shaw's attitude toward Melodrama was determined in part by its utter lack of pretension and indeed of respectability as compared to what he called upper-middle-class drama. His attitude toward that other survival of the rhetorical-romantic mode at the "classical" Lyceum was radically different. Shaw was particularly annoyed that the romantic drama at its most conservative should monopolize the energies and prestige of the leading theater of the empire. Of Irving as actor-manager,

Shaw later wrote that the engagement of Ellen Terry "was his first and last enlightened stroke of policy. For he immediately turned back to the old Barry Sullivan repertory of mutilated Shakespear and Bulwer Lytton, to which he actually added The Iron Chest of the obsolete Colman. . . . As far as the drama was concerned he was more old-fashioned than the oldest of his predecessors."[14] Irving's repertory was rooted in "the classically romantic phase which held the English stage from the time of Otway to that of Sheridan Knowles and Westland Marston" (OTN, II, 235). Looking back with considerable historical acumen, Shaw felt that a century of actors like Kean, Macready, Barry Sullivan, and Irving ought to have inspired a group of monumental heroic plays, "comparable in intensity to those of Aeschylus, Sophocles, and Euripides"; but instead:

"Sheridan Knowles, Bulwer Lytton, Wills, and Tennyson produced a few glaringly artificial high horses for the great actors of their time; but the playwrights proper, who really kept the theatre going, and were kept going by the theatre, did not cater for the great actors: they could not afford to compete with a bard who was not of an age but for all time, and who had, moreover, the overwhelming attraction for the actor-managers of not charging author's fees. The result was that the playwrights and the great actors ceased to think of themselves as having any concern with one another: Tom Robertson, Ibsen, Pinero, and Barrie might as well have belonged to a different solar system as far as Irving was concerned; and the same was true of their respective predecessors." (Great Catherine, Pref., p. 149)

In the nineties, with a new kind of heroic drama of his own taking shape, and rhetorical-realistic comedies of his own in existence, Shaw understandably deplored the gap between the heroic stage and the drama of the day.

[14] *Ellen Terry and Bernard Shaw,* p. xxi.

SOCIAL-DIDACTIC DRAMA

Shaw recognized and enjoyed the association between Ibsen and the aesthetic ideals of the well-made play and of the true-to-life surface, for he saw Ibsen converting them to the purposes of a drama that was critical of social and moral convention.[15] In *A Doll's House*, the conventional attitudes in audience and characters upon which the tensions of the master situation depend are the very things brought into question. Ibsen uses the machinery of the well-made play to implicate the audience and then exploits its conventional expectations in the shock of the last scene. The audience discovers there can be no satisfying sentimental reconciliation, though nothing in the plot stands in the way. The machinery breaks down and the artificiality of its conventions is exposed. It should not be overlooked that the offense given to such reigning critics as Clement Scott (caricatured as "Cuthbertson" in Shaw's *Philanderer*) was not simply moral; there was a much deeper aesthetic offense. In his earlier plays, Shaw gave similar offense, though the effectiveness of the shock achieved in *A Doll's House* precluded its direct imitation. *Arms and the Man*, for example, is a continuous, simultaneous exploitation and exposure of the conventions of military romance. William Archer, who devoted much of his life's energies to Ibsen, wrote retrospectively, "If I were asked to lay my hand on a single English play which was obviously imitated from, or directly influenced by Ibsen, I should not know where to turn. Mr. Bernard Shaw was, of course, his doughtiest champion and in some sense his disciple; but as for imitating him— well, I can only say I wish he had. But of indirect and what may be called pervasive influence, Ibsen had more, perhaps, than any other European writer since the time of Byron."[16]

In the columns of *The Saturday Review*, Shaw asked his

[15] See *The Quintessence of Ibsenism* (rev. ed.) in *Major Critical Essays*, p. 138.
[16] *The Old Drama and the New*, p. 307.

readers to compare the box office successes of the eighties with those of the nineties (Wilde, Pinero, and Jones): "The change is evident at once. In short, a modern manager need not produce The Wild Duck; but he must be very careful not to produce a play which will seem insipid and old-fashioned to playgoers who have seen The Wild Duck, even though they may have hissed it" (OTN, I, 165). But from the standpoint of 1900, Shaw could look back on the advent of the problem play and declare that "the manager, and sometimes, I suspect, the very author, firmly believed the word problem to be the latest euphemism for what Justice Shallow called a bona roba, and certainly would not either of them have staked a farthing on the interest of a genuine problem. In fact these so-called problem plays invariably depended for their dramatic interest on foregone conclusions of the most heartwearying conventionality concerning sexual morality. The authors had no problematic views: all they wanted was to capture some of the fascination of Ibsen" (Three Plays for Puritans, p. xii). In short, though the naïveties of the pre-Ibsen eighties might no longer go down in the nineties, the more sophisticated "problem plays" of the nineties were neither critical, nor in Shaw's definition, realistic, but as conventional as the plays they succeeded.

As Archer was well aware, the relation between Ibsen and Shaw as dramatists is certainly not readily apparent. The two dramatists seem utterly distinct in general methods and particular qualities. Yet the kinship Shaw felt with Ibsen was fundamental—more fundamental than questions of simple dramaturgy. Current drama in the rhetorical tradition, in the naturalistic tradition, and in the line of the well-made play, was in Shaw's definition conventional drama. It occurred against a background of widely accepted conventional attitudes. However, in some of the new plays, in the plays genuinely inspired by Ibsen, "the drama arises through a conflict of unsettled ideals rather than through vulgar attachments,

rapacities, generosities, resentments, ambitions, misunderstandings, oddities and so forth as to which no moral question is raised. The conflict is not between clear right and
wrong: the villain is as conscientious as the hero, if not more
so: in fact, the question which makes the play interesting
(when it *is* interesting) is which is the villain and which
the hero. Or, to put it another way, there are no villains and
no heroes" (*Quintessence*, p. 139). This was Shaw's characterization (in 1912) of the essential quality of Ibsen's drama
in his treatise on Ibsen; and it suits his own plays better than
Ibsen's.

The highly unpopular, almost unproduced, but widely
publicized plays of Ibsen were not the only factor in the
English theater which could be drawn upon in the interests
of a drama critical of convention and society. Much of the
conventionality of the drawing-room drama, rhetorical-romantic drama, and well-made drama of the nineties stemmed
from the simplicity of its desire to amuse and entertain. And
yet, Shaw observed in his preface to *Three Plays for Puritans,*
"the rich purchasing-powerful Englishman prefers politics
and church-going." This spectator will never support a simply
"voluptuous" drama because the pleasures are too feeble for
him. "From the play of ideas—and the drama can never be
anything more—he demands edification, and will not pay for
anything else in that arena" (p. ix).

There was a latent strain of edification and didacticism in
English drama long before the impact of Ibsen. Even apart
from such "improving" genres as temperance drama, both
comedy and melodrama in the nineteenth century were likely
to burst into open didacticism. For example, J. B. Buckstone's *Married Life; a Comedy in Three Acts* (1834) has
the form of a stage sermon with exempla. The final speech
of the play sums up the lesson and is delivered directly at the
audience:

There, this is the way that all matrimonial quar-
rels should end; and if *you* are of the same opinion
. . . then, indeed will our conjugal joy be complete,
and our light lesson not have been read in vain. You
have seen the result of perpetual jealousy, in the
case of Mr. and Mrs. Lynx; of continual disputes
and contradiction in that of Mr. and Mrs. Young-
husband; of a want of cheerfulness in Mr. and Mrs.
Dismal; of the impolicy of public correction, in the
instance of Mrs. Dove; and of the necessity of as-
similating habits and tempers in the singular case
of Mr. and Mrs. Coddle. . . . So think of us, all ye
anticipating and smiling single people; for you *must*
or *ought*, all to be married, and the sooner the better
—and remember us, ye already paired; and let our
example prove to you, that, to mutual forbearance,
mutual confidence, mutual habits, mutual everything,
must we owe mutual happiness. (*French S. D.*)

The simple formulae of traduced innocence and its ultimate triumphant vindication, assaulted virtue and the final
discomfiting of wickedness, brought melodrama close to the
morality play. Of three recent melodramas, Shaw wrote in the
nineties, "Dick Hallward, Her Advocate, and The Manxman
were nothing but lame attempts to compete with the con-
venticle by exploiting the rooted love of the public for mor-
alizing and homiletics." Of the hero in *Her Advocate*, he declares that the revivalist preacher "cannot elude my recognition by merely taking refuge in a theatre. In vain does he
mount the stage in a barrister's wig and gown and call his
familiar emotional display acting. I am not to be deceived:
in his struggles with his mock passion for the leading lady I
recognize the old wrestle with the devil: in his muddy joy and
relief at having won a verdict of acquittal for her I detect
the rapture of the sinner saved" (*OTN*, I, 263, 265). In out-

lining the qualities of a really good melodrama, Shaw writes that the characters must be ideal types, and that "The whole character of the piece must be allegorical, idealistic, full of generalizations and moral lessons; and it must represent conduct as producing swiftly and certainly on the individual the results which in actual life it only produces on the race in the course of many centuries" (*OTN*, I, 93).

A play which simply dramatized the eternal war of good and evil, or exhorted to domestic mutuality and forbearance, or urged each man to reform himself, could bark no shins. However edifying the homily, the acceptability of the play was guaranteed by the conventionality of the morality, under whose protection much thrilling wickedness could flourish and delight. But there was also in the drama an edifying strain with a genuine critical intent: a play which touched on social conditions, and even social convictions, which Shaw called the "bluebook play" after the official blue-bound reports of Parliament and the Privy Council, and which he claimed for his own immediate ancestry in an appendix to his first-published drama. What he *did* expect the critic to know, Shaw wrote, "is that 'bluebook plays' hold the stage far better than conventionally idealist dramas. I need only mention the irrepressible *Never too Late to Mend* to prove that *Widowers' Houses,* far from being a play of so new a sort that its very title to the name of drama is questionable, is, on its bluebook side, a sample (whether good or bad is not here in question) of one of the most familiar, popular, and firmly established *genres* in English dramatic literature."[17]

Charles Reade wrote the drama (1864) as well as the novel of *It's Never Too Late to Mend.* The second act, which has almost nothing to do with the rest of the melodrama of innocence and villainy, is a frightening presentation of prison life, exposing the sadism, illegality, pernicious cruelty, harsh

---

[17] "The Author to the Dramatic Critics," in *Widowers' Houses,* Independent Theatre Edition (1893), p. 113.

punishments, and brutal administrators of "The System." It ends with the near suicide and pathetic death through harsh treatment of a fifteen-year-old victim of The System. Except for the second act and a few stray glances at the exploitation of the English poor, the drama is quite conventional.

Several of the dramas of Tom Taylor, who often collaborated with Reade, make a critical social point. The *Ticket-of-Leave Man* (1863) makes the point (sandwiched between the sentimental romance of Bob Brierly and May Edwards and the melodramatic contest of Hawkshaw the Detective and James Dalton alias The Tiger) that the ticket-of-leave man doesn't have a chance between the Criminal and the Respectable classes. This point is somewhat beclouded by Bob Brierly's innocence of the crime which sent him to prison.

Another Taylor play with a critical social point is *Still Waters Run Deep* (1855), a comparatively complex domestic drama with an oddly injected critique of *laissez-faire* economics running throughout. The economic doctrine is analogized with John Mildmay's domestic doctrine of *laissez-aller*, a policy which almost leads to catastrophe. Furthermore, in a stock-selling scene at the climax of the play, Mildmay firmly rejects the Manchester notion that general good can come, as he puts it, from the sum of particular harms, and financiers are compared very unfavorably with gamblers, even by the villain.

It is evident that in all these plays the "bluebook" or critical portions are extraneous to the rest, whose dramatic values are altogether conventional. Shaw occasionally proclaimed his awareness that, though there was an audience which might come to the theater to be edified and educated, nevertheless:

"the ordinary man's life-struggle is to escape from reality, to avoid all avoidable facts and deceive himself as to the real nature of those which he cannot avoid. . . . Hence the more unnatural, impossible, unreasonable, and morally fraudulent a theatrical entertainment is, the better he likes it. He abhors the play with a purpose, because it says to him, 'Here, sir, is a fact which you ought to attend to.' This, however, produces the happy result that the great dramatic poets, who are all incorrigible moralists and preachers, are forced to produce plays of extraordinary interest in order to induce our audiences of shirkers and dreamers to swallow the pill." (*Music in London*, III, 139)

In his own practice, however, Shaw does not cover his pill with an unrelated sugar-coating of conventional drama. Rather he combines edification with a comedy in which the conventions are themselves the butt of the joke, and in which the fun relieves the spectator of an immediate obligation to damn or say "Amen."

The sharpest distinction Shaw ever made between writers was not between good and bad, though he deliberately chooses the terms "writers of the first order" and "writers of the second order." A work of a writer of the first order is one "in which the morality is original and not ready-made." Ibsen is offered as the prime example of such a writer. "By writers of the second order the readymade morality is accepted as the basis of all moral judgment and criticism of the characters they portray, even when their genius forces them to represent their most attractive heroes and heroines as violating the readymade code in all directions" (*The Irrational Knot*, preface [added 1905], pp. xvii, xviii). Shaw found that even the "novels of his nonage" were, in this sense, works of the first order (though not without an amused sense of their undistinguished quality). And the whole strategy of his dramatic criticism was to create an attitude favorable to writers of the first order.

Of the currents active in the theater for which he began writing, Shaw committed himself immediately to the drama critical of moral and social ideals. He attacked or held himself aloof from the well-made play and the elevated rhetorical-romantic play, but he borrowed conventions from them, to slight, to expose, to laugh at, to convert to his own uses. Thus, he creates convention-bound characters, frequently stage-struck romantics, who are contrasted with clear-eyed "realists"; and he exploits conventional dramatic situations, which are brought to unconventional, "realistic" conclusions.

Shaw could not find even a negative use, however, for drawing-room naturalism. Later, he reasoned that Ibsen's introduction of the discussion had brought about "the substitution of a forensic technique of recrimination, disillusion, and penetration through ideals to the truth, with a free use of all the rhetorical and lyrical arts of the orator, the preacher, the pleader, and the rhapsodist" (*Quintessence* [rev. ed.], p. 146). Shaw turned to popular rhetorical drama for his method rather than to drawing-room naturalism, despite the stagey unreality and arch-romantic associations of the former, and imbedded his sermons and his "drama of unsettled ideals" in a fabric of rhetorical, operatic, and ironic techniques.

The question which lay at the bottom of all Shaw's dealings with convention and conventionalism, reality and realism, was simply that fundamental consideration of humanistic aesthetics, the relation of art to life. Late in his life, Shaw gave final expression to his position and his practice. His position was directly opposite to the aesthetics of realism in all senses of that word but the Platonic:

"Holding a mirror up to nature is not a correct definition of a playwright's art. A mirror reflects what is before it. Hold it up to any street at noonday and it shews a crowd of people and vehicles and tells you nothing about them. A photograph of them has no meaning. They may be in love with one another, they may intend to murder one another. They may be husbands and wives, parents and children, or doctors and patients, in the most comic or tragic relations to one another; but the mirror or photograph tells you nothing of all this, and cannot give the playwright any material whatever. Shakespear's mirror was for the actor, to teach not to saw the air and look like nothing on earth. The playwright has more to do than to watch and wave: the policeman does that much; but the playwright must interpret the passing show by parables."[18]

[18] MS letter to Alan S. Downer, 21 Jan. 1948. Compare "The Author's Apology" to *Mrs Warren's Profession*, p. 162: ". . . drama is no mere setting up of the camera to nature: it is the presentation in parable of the conflict between Man's will and his environment: in a word, of problem."

ACTING

"When will you understand that what has ruined you as a manager is your love for people who are 'a little weak, perhaps, but just the right tone.' The right tone is never a little weak perhaps; it is always devastatingly strong. Keep your worms for your own plays; and leave me the drunken, stagey, brassbowelled barnstormers my plays are written for."—BERNARD SHAW to HARLEY GRANVILLE-BARKER, 19 January 1908[1]

SHAW'S criticism of acting in the nineties was as strategic as his criticism of playwriting, which it paralleled in several respects. With an eye to his own acting needs and to a climate of taste favorable to his own kind of drama, Shaw attacks the most fashionable of the current modes (the so-called cup-and-saucer school) and uses an older, more flamboyant mode as a stick with which to beat it. His attitude toward the flamboyant mode is complicated by his perception of its shortcomings in the past, by his experience of its conservatism in the present, and by his vision of a new school of acting, to suit his new drama, in the future. Nevertheless, it was with this older tradition that Shaw identified the acting to come. The history of Shaw's dealings with nineteenth-century acting has a dramatic development of its own: it begins in his reaction to the "modern" mode, it continues in his identification with the older tradition, and it resolves in his modification of that older tradition to suit his newer dramatic needs.

The revolution in acting which began with T. W. Robertson and the Bancrofts at the Prince of Wales was in victorious possession of the fashionable theater of the nineties, except

[1] *Bernard Shaw's Letters to Granville Barker*, p. 115.

for Irving's Lyceum. Like many revolutions, its sweeping success was rather appalling to those, like Shaw, who had squirmed under the abuses of the *ancien régime*. Prince-of-Wales acting meant refinement, delicacy, a skillful ensemble, and the quiet good manners appropriate to the drawing-room settings of the plays. The concept of "the natural" in acting is a perilous one; but the new school was more "natural" than those it succeeded in the sense in which Garrick's Hamlet was more "natural" than the King Claudius whom Partridge preferred. The King, Partridge notes, "speaks all his words distinctly half as loud again as the other.—Anybody may see he is an actor." The Bancrofts retired in 1885, leaving the fashionable stage to actors associated with their playhouse, such as John Hare and the Kendals, who provided the models for a rising generation. Hare and the Kendals, Shaw wrote, ". . . represented a generation of actors who had toned their acting down and their dress and manners up to stockbroker-civil-servant pitch. This was all very well whilst it lasted; but unfortunately the drawing room drama, being artistically a sterile hybrid, could not renew the generation of actors; and now the Kendals are replaced by couples equal to them in dress, manners, good looks, and domestic morality, but subject to the disadvantage of not possessing in their two united persons as much power of acting as there was in the tip of Mrs Kendal's little finger-nail." (*OTN*, I, 279)

Shaw was not consoled by knowing from his Dublin days that the pre-revolutionary journeyman actor was often stagey and impossible; that (of their rhetorical and hyperbolical style) "Actors of gigantic or intense personalities could carry it off; but it made commonplace actors ridiculous."[2] The rhetorical approach of the pre-Robertsonian actor was precisely the capability Shaw yearned for in contemporary actors; and drawing-room acting was sufficiently general to spoil Shaw's chances of production, even by such pioneers

[2] *Ellen Terry and Bernard Shaw*, p. xvii.

as the Independent Theatre. One reason for the rejection of *The Philanderer* in 1893, wrote J. T. Grein, was the conviction "that the English actors of that day could not possibly cope with the flood of dialogue—that their tongues were not glib enough to rattle it off at the lightning speed required."[3]

The revolution had produced a journeyman actor without the equipment to sustain a part in a drama of unsettled ideals and forensic techniques, using "all the rhetorical and lyrical arts of the orator, the preacher, the pleader, and the rhapsodist." Long speeches, rapid transitions, violent verbal exchanges, and flamboyant presentations were all beyond "the smart nullity of the London person" (*OTN*, I, 274). Pinero knew what he was at in *Trelawny of the "Wells"* when, sketching the beginnings of the new school, he shows Rose Trelawny as "spoiled"—that is, subdued and ladylike in her acting—after she returns from living with the family of her aristocratic fiancé. Pinero draws an elaborate contrast between the flamboyantly individual "line" actors at the Wells, and the young, polished, "outwardly greatly superior," but totally indistinguishable ladies and gentlemen who play the parts in Tom Wrench's play. Rose, who has been "spoiled," and the smart young indistinguishables are perfectly suited to the play. But the expansive tragedy lead of the first act, now out of work, can only be given the part of "an old, stagey, out-of-date actor." When Rose asks him, "Do you like the play?" he answers, "Like it! there's not a speech in it, my dear—not a real *speech*; nothing to dig your teeth into—."[4]

[3] J. T. Grein, *The New World of the Theatre* (London, 1924), p. 23. In his article, "Barker's Wild Oats," *Harper's*, 194 (1947), p. 49, Shaw begins by listing the reasons why his plays were not acted in London before the Vedrenne-Barker management at the Royal Court: "Although the rule of the stage was that any speech longer than twenty words was too long, and that politics and religion must never be mentioned and their places taken by romance and fictitious police and divorce cases, my characters had to declaim long speeches on religion and politics in the Shakespearean or 'ham' technique."

[4] Pinero, *Trelawny of the "Wells"* (London, 1925), p. 176.

Disuse precedes atrophy; and when Shaw provided speeches, he found actors without teeth. He declared himself in terror of the current generation of leading men and ladies, who had been spared the old-fashioned training which taught "an old-fashioned stage-walk, an old-fashioned stage-voice, an old-fashioned stage way of kneeling, of sitting down, of shaking hands" (*OTN*, I, 212), and who instead had become the smart nullities who couldn't walk, speak, or sit down at all. "Let us by all means congratulate ourselves to the full on the fact that our young actresses are at least not stagey," Shaw wrote; "but let us also be careful not to confuse the actress who knows too much to be stagey with the actress who does not know enough" (*OTN*, II, 239).

Cramped by the limitations of the present-day crop of journeyman actors, Shaw as a critic of the theater campaigned vigorously against the current school. As a playwright and as a director he looked for actors capable of producing his effects, which he demonstrated at rehearsals and urged upon backsliders in furious correspondence. He asked for a new mode of heroic acting suited to the heroes of the modern stage; and from his journeyman actors he sought "a combination of the proficiency and positive power (as distinguished from negative discretion) of the old stock actor, with the spontaneity, sensitiveness, and touch with the cultivated non-professional world which the latest developments of the drama demand" (*OTN*, I, 70).

The pre-Robertson traditions of acting had by no means utterly vanished from the London stage. Melodrama kept alive a form of the grand style, as, conversely, Irving's acting at the Lyceum kept alive what Shaw called the "artificial high horses" of rhetorical drama. And just as Shaw had used Adelphi drama to set off the tiresomeness of the drawing-room play, so he used Adelphi acting to contrast with the insipidities of drawing-room acting. He asks his readers, on the occasion of the revival of *Black-Ey'd Susan*,

"Is it not odd that the Adelphi is the only theatre in London devoted to sentimental modern drama where the acting is not vulgar? In other houses the actors' subordination of drama to 'good taste,' their consciousness of the stalls, their restrained drawing room voices, made resonant enough for the theatre by clarionet effects from the nose, their perpetual thinking of their manners and appearance when they ought to be thinking of their work, all produce a destestable atmosphere of candidature for social promotion. . . . At the Adelphi the actors provide for their appearance in their dressing rooms, and when they come on the stage go straight for the play with all their force, as if their point of honor lay in their skill, and not in persuading smart parties in the boxes that it would be quite safe to send them cards for an 'At Home' in spite of their profession. The result is that they look better, dress better, and behave better than their competitors at the intentionally fashionable theatres. . . . In short, the secret of the Adelphi is not, as is generally assumed, bad drama, but simply good acting and plenty of it. And, unlike most critics, I am fond of acting." (*OTN*, III, 6, 7)

Melodrama provided one home for the remains, good and bad, impressive or merely "stagey," of the grand style, and the Lyceum provided another, though Irving's acting was no more a simple continuation of the grand-and-lofty tradition than was Adelphi acting. Shaw described his own views of acting as "pre-Irving,"[5] and excluded him from the line of great actors in the heroic tradition: "the hierarchy of great actors should be from Burbage and Betterton to Edwin

[5] *Ellen Terry and Bernard Shaw*, p. 13.

Booth and Barry Sullivan. Neither Barrymore nor Irving have a place in it."[6]

Nevertheless, even with Sullivan still fresh in his mind, Shaw had been permanently impressed by his first sight of Irving with the *Two Roses* company in Dublin. "I instinctively felt that a new drama inhered in this man, though I had then no conscious notion that I was destined to write it; and I perceive now that I never forgave him for baffling the plans I made for him (always, be it remembered, unconsciously)."[7] In the *Saturday Review*, Shaw consistently urged Irving to try his hand at Ibsen; and Irving had the refusal of at least two of Shaw's own plays. But nothing came of it, though in later years Shaw wrote regretfully of Irving and his leading lady, "If ever there were two artists apparently marked out by Nature to make a clean break with an outworn past and create a new stage world they were Ellen Terry and Henry Irving."[8]

When Shaw first saw him, Irving had not yet developed his cultivated Lyceum style (see *OTN*, III, 145), but Shaw was fascinated by his singularity and by his peculiar force despite physical and technical inadequacies. "He was utterly unlike anyone else: he could give importance and a noble melancholy to any sort of drivel that was put into his mouth; and it was this melancholy, bound up with an impish humour, which forced the spectator to single him out as a leading figure with an inevitability that I never saw again in any other actor until it rose from Irving's grave in the person of . . . Charlie Chaplin."[9] At this stage, Shaw felt, Irving's idiosyncratic combination of melancholy and humor held at least the promise of a style for the modern unheroic or partly-

[6] Typescript letter to Alan S. Downer, 12 Nov. 1947. On 21 Jan. 1948, Shaw writes again: "The tradition of heroic acting in Shakespearean tragedy did not end with Macready nor include Irving: it ended with Barry Sullivan (1821-91), perhaps the greatest of them all, and certainly the most successful."

[7] *Ellen Terry and Bernard Shaw*, p. xx.   [8] *Ibid.*, p. xxi.
[9] *Ibid.*, p. xx.

heroic hero, too self-conscious of his failings and too complex in his knowledge of himself not to be either ridiculous, like Sergius, or, like Caesar, something of a rueful clown.

But by the time of Shaw's criticisms in the nineties, Irving's melancholy and humor had been rather successfully separated from each other in the Lyceum repertory. Moreover, in spite of apparent vocal handicaps, he had developed an acceptable declamatory technique for presenting the grand repertory of the English theater (see *OTN*, I, 271-73). Yet his great gift remained an ability to "give importance and a noble melancholy to any sort of drivel that was put into his mouth," as in the success which established his reputation, Leopold Lewis's *The Bells*. Irving was able to transcend the words; to create a part, even where there was no part, between the lines.

Archer declared that self-accentuation rather than self-suppression was the necessary basis of Irving's acting and that "a more marked and less pliant personality than his it would be difficult to discover, on or off the stage."[10] Shaw gave a subtler form to this analysis in a review of the Lyceum *Cymbeline*. According to Shaw, Irving was a "creative" as opposed to an "interpretive" actor. "The truth is that he has never in his life conceived or interpreted the characters of any author except himself. . . . he was compelled to use other men's plays as the framework for his own creations." In the *Merchant of Venice*, "he was simply not Shylock at all; and when his own creation came into conflict with Shakespear's, as it did quite openly in the Trial scene, he simply played in flat contradiction of the lines, and positively acted Shakespear off the stage" (*OTN*, II, 198). Shaw found this phenomenon intensely interesting; he even considered Irving's Iachimo greatly superior to Shakespeare's. But his King Lear, according to Shaw, was a dreadful failure. His

[10] William Archer, *The Theatrical 'World' of 1896* (London, 1897), pp. 343-44.

idiosyncratic talent prevented a genuine impersonation, and Shakespeare's King Lear refused to be effaced from the play by Irving's rival creation.

As Shaw's conception of his own work matured and he became more aware of the values upon which his plays depended, he seems to have realized that "creative" acting, however splendid, was useless to him. Barrymore's Hamlet, which was charged with "creative" byplay, provoked Shaw to declare: "I write plays that play for three hours and a half even with instantaneous changes and only one short interval. There is no time for silences or pauses: the actor must play on the line and not between the lines, and must do nine-tenths of his acting with his voice. Hamlet—Shakespear's Hamlet—can be done from end to end in four hours in that way; and it never flags nor bores."[11]

Like Irving, Barrymore impressed Shaw as a creative actor, and, like Irving, Barrymore was excluded from the dynasty of heroic actors. As an author Shaw demanded "interpretive" rather than "creative" acting, and verbal rather than picturesque heroics, to exploit the values upon which his plays had to stand or fall: "My plays do not consist of occasional remarks to illustrate pictures, but of verbal fencing matches between protagonists and antagonists, whose thrusts and ripostes, parries and passados, follow one another much more closely than thunder follows lightning. The first rule for their producers is that there must never be a moment of silence from the rise of the curtain to its fall."[12]

As a critic and as a propagandist for the new forces in the drama, it was worth Shaw's while to try to tempt or provoke an Irving into forsaking his conservative repertory. As a playwright, however, Shaw found as little satisfaction among the surviving elements of the grand school as among the actors

[11] Letter of 22 Feb. 1925 in John Barrymore, *Confessions of an Actor* (Indianapolis, 1926), unpaged, reprinted in *Shaw on Theatre*, p. 168.
[12] "My First Talkie," *Malvern Festival 1931* (a souvenir booklet), reprinted in *Shaw on Theatre*, p. 205.

of the modern or "cup-and-saucer" school. Therefore Shaw declared himself pre-Robertson and pre-Irving and claimed as his masters the interpretive and rhetorical giants of the past.

The three masters of the grand school whom Shaw almost invariably named in the same breath were Sullivan, Salvini, and Adelaide Ristori. From these, Shaw declared, "I learned my stage technique and what great acting can do."[13]

"In a generation which knew nothing of any sort of acting but drawing-room acting, and which considered a speech of more than twenty words impossibly long, I went back to the classical style and wrote long rhetorical speeches like operatic solos, regarding my plays as musical performances precisely as Shakespear did. As a producer I went back to the forgotten heroic stage business and the exciting or impressive declamation I had learnt from oldtimers like Ristori, Salvini, and Barry Sullivan. . . . [My methods] would have seemed the merest routine to Kemble or Mrs. Siddons; but to the Victorian leading ladies they seemed to be unleadingladylike barnstorming."[14]

To Ristori, Salvini, and Sullivan, Shaw frequently added Chaliapin and Coquelin and occasionally Ada Rehan, "the only British-speaking successor to Barry Sullivan within my experience."[15] Sullivan and Ristori came to Dublin before

[13] "Sullivan, Shakespear, and Shaw," *Atlantic Monthly*, 181 (March 1948), p. 57.
[14] Shaw's introductory "Aside" to Lillah McCarthy, *Myself and My Friends* (London, 1934), p. 4.
[15] "Sullivan, Shakespear, and Shaw," p. 58. Elsewhere, Shaw writes of Granville-Barker and the heroic line from Burbage to Sullivan: "Note also that Barker, 20 years my junior, had never seen their sort of acting except too late from Chaliapine (a Russian opera singer) and Coquelin (a Frenchman), whereas Sullivan was the stage hero of my boyhood and may be said to have formed my theatrical mind. I had also studied Ristori

Shaw's departure while Salvini came a month after, so that Shaw had to see him in London. Coquelin first came to England in 1879, and Chaliapin didn't appear until 1913. Of the entire group only Ada Rehan acted with some regularity in London during Shaw's career as a critic. In the nineties, however, Shaw was also stirred by Eleonora Duse as "the first actress whom we have seen applying the method of the great school to characteristically modern parts or to characteristically modern conceptions of old parts" (*OTN*, I, 145); but in later years, it was to the more strictly heroic and operatic group that he always alluded.

In his worshipful memoir of Henry Irving, Gordon Craig makes an illuminating comparison of Gladstone and Salvini with Irving and Disraeli:

"Gladstone and Salvini roll their words out, they stride, they glare very grandly and are spacious: you want to look and listen to them. Disraeli and Irving do something quite different. They glide, they are terribly self-possessed, their eyes dart flame: you *have* to look and listen to them, whether you want to or no. Rhetoric is for whoever likes to use it—not for Disraeli or Irving. 'He will say something fine' is what listeners would murmur to themselves in the presence of Gladstone or of Salvini—and fine it was. But the same listeners, when watching Disraeli or Irving, would not know where they were, who exactly this being in front of them could be, and would think to themselves, 'What will he say—what will he do now?' "[16]

Compared to Irving, Salvini was grandly rhetorical. According to Shaw he was also able "to make his audiences

---

and Salvini at first hand. I had 20 years experience as a playgoer before Barker began as a boy actor" (Typescript letter to Alan S. Downer, 12 Nov. 1947).

[16] *Henry Irving* (New York, 1930), pp. 80-81.

imagine him a volcano in eruption when he was in sober fact hardly moving. . . ."[17]

Shaw was acutely aware of the differences between actors such as Salvini and Sullivan, but his concern lay in their common qualities, and he classed them together as the grand school. Of Sullivan, whose violence was more real than illusory, Shaw wrote in the nineties, "there was hardly any part sufficiently heroic for him to be natural in it" (*OTN*, I, 271). Shaw admired his stage walk as "the perfection of grace and dignity," his "cultivated resonant voice," his attitudes, his gestures, "his lightning swiftness of action, as when in the last scene of Hamlet he shot up the stage and stabbed the king four times before you could wink."[18] Sullivan carried with becoming ease all the paraphernalia of the grand manner. In Hamlet, his greatest part, "His secret, which was no secret, was simply that he presented himself as what Hamlet was: a being of a different and higher order from Laertes and the rest."[19]

From Ristori's visit to Dublin Shaw claimed to have learned "how far the grand style in acting can be carried by women."[20] He recalled to the audiences of the nineties "that scene in which Queen Elizabeth and her court seemed to vanish miraculously from the stage, apparently swept into nothingness when Ristori let loose her wrath as Marie Stuart," and he compared it with the effect produced by Salvini in the play scene in *Hamlet* (*OTN*, I, 160). Shaw as a critic in the nineties never had occasion to write on Ristori as he wrote on the visits of Duse. However, a contemporary description of the impact of Ristori under similar conditions to those of her Dublin appearance can be found in the theater criticism of Henry James. Young American spectators should be assured, James writes, "that in witnessing the last act of *Mary*

[17] *Ellen Terry and Bernard Shaw*, p. xviii.   [18] *Ibid.*, p. xvii.
[19] "Sullivan, Shakespear, and Shaw," p. 56.
[20] *Ellen Terry and Bernard Shaw*, p. xix.

Stuart, or certain of the great points in *Medea,* they are looking at a supreme exhibition of the grand style of acting. No
one whom we have seen, or are likely to see in this country,
can interpret tragedy in the superbly large way of Madame
Ristori—can distribute effects into such powerful masses."[21]

Shaw's criticisms of Ada Rehan were affected by his desire
to lure the contemporary actress into the modern repertory.
He compares her to Barry Sullivan at his prime, "an actor who
possessed in an extraordinary degree just the imposing grace,
the sensitive personal dignity of style, the force and self-re-
liance into which Miss Rehan's style is settling." He professes
discomfort, however, at recognizing characteristics brought
out by acting, in the grand style, exclusively in the rhetorical
drama of the past. Shaw urges Ada Rehan forward with Duse,
not "back with Barry Sullivan, who would in just the same
way, when led into it by a touch of stateliness and sonority
in the lines, abandon his part, and become for the moment a
sort of majestic incarnation of abstract solemnity and magnificence" (*OTN,* I, 182-83). Nevertheless, of Ada Rehan de-
claiming Shakespearean blank verse, Shaw declares: "She
gives us beauty of tone, grace of measure, delicacy of articu-
lation: in short, all the technical qualities of verse music,
along with the rich feeling and fine intelligence without which
those technical qualities would soon become monotonous.
When she is at her best, the music melts in the caress of the
emotion it expresses, and thus completes the conditions necessary for obtaining Shakespear's effects in Shakespear's way"
(*OTN,* I, 181-82).

Several qualities are involved in Shaw's claim that he
turned to these great actors and the tradition of the "grand
style" for his playwright's conception of play and performance. Extremely important was primacy of language: the

[21] "Madame Ristori" (1875), in *The Scenic Art,* ed. Allan Wade (New
York, 1957), p. 29.

ability of the actor to deal masterfully and beautifully with complicated structures of poetry and argument. Equally important was largeness of effect: a spaciousness in gesture, presence, creation of character, and delivery of speech. These are the demands Shaw made of his actors: to let the language take precedence, to deliver it with breadth and accomplished virtuosity, and to act with verve and spaciousness. While his plays would seem to state their own requirements, Shaw was even more explicit in dealing with the actors as author and director. While directing a play he rained notes and postcards upon the actors; and upon visiting a production during its run he was sure to obtrude his advice and correction. Accordingly, he writes to Irene Vanbrugh in a warm letter on her performance as Lina in *Misalliance* (26 March 1930): "The great final speech is effective but not yet quite impetuous enough. There should be an agony of indignant shame carrying it along like a torrent. I think that with practice you will have no difficulty in hurling it out as Coquelin could hurl out a tirade."[22] On another occasion, Shaw tells Mrs. Patrick Campbell about the shortcomings in a revived *Pygmalion*:

"It is now really good Victorian drawing-room drama, pleasant and sweet, and in what you (bless you!) call good taste. You are not a great actress in a big play or anything disturbing or vulgar of that sort; but you have your hearts desire, and are very charming. Kate Rorke at her best could not have improved on it. I enjoyed it and appreciated it in its

[22] Irene Vanbrugh, *To Tell My Story* (London, 1948), p. 205. Of Coquelin, whom Shaw in the nineties called "the greatest comedian known to us" (*OTN*, I, 280-81), James wrote, "It is true as a rule that whenever M. Coquelin has a very long and composite speech to utter, be it in verse or prose, there one gets the cream of his talent, or at least of his virtuosity. . . . In the great cumulative *tirades* of the old comedy, which grow and grow as they proceed, but the difficulties of which are pure sport for our artist's virtuosity, [his voice] flings down the words and the verses as a gamester precipitated by a run of luck flings *louis d'or* upon the table" (*The Scenic Art*, p. 207).

little way. And that was magnanimous of me, considering how I missed the big bones of my play, its fortissimos, its allegros, its precipitous moments, its contrasts, and all its big bits. My orchestration was feeble on the cottage piano; and my cymbals were rather disappointing on the cups and saucers."[23]

In the three seasons of the Vedrenne-Barker management of the Royal Court Theatre (1904-1907), eleven of Shaw's plays were produced for a total of 701 performances.[24] Up to that time only two of Shaw's dozen published plays had received more than two performances in London. Shaw had directed matinee casts and advised foreign productions of his plays, but it is only with the Court enterprise that the solid history of Shaw's relations with the actors begins. Through the nineties Shaw had written and thought furiously about actors and acting. Here now were the fruits.

Granville-Barker was the central energy of the Court Theatre, the director of all but Shaw's plays, and one of the chief actors in Shaw's productions. On his qualities as an actor and director, Sir Lewis Casson wrote: "In speech especially he had an inspired knowledge of the exact melody and stress that would convey the precise meaning and emotion he wanted, and a power of so analysing it in technical form that he could pass it on to others. And with this he had at his command all the devices of rhetoric with which the actor or speaker can rouse the curiosity, the attention, the tears or the laughter of an audience."[25] Shaw himself declared: "My plays were the decisive and at first the sole V. B. stock-in-trade. I produced them all with Barker as my leading juvenile actor; and my throw-back to the art of Barry Sullivan and

[23] Letter of 15 May 1920, *Bernard Shaw and Mrs. Patrick Campbell: Their Correspondence*, ed. Alan Dent (London, 1952), p. 211.

[24] Desmond MacCarthy, *The Court Theatre, 1904-1907* (London, 1907), p. 123.

[25] "Granville Barker, Shaw and the Court Theatre," in Mander and Mitchenson, pp. 290-91.

Italian Opera, and my method of rehearsal, must have in-fluenced him considerably."[26]

But Barker never so completely suited Shaw as such com-ment suggests. Nearly all Shaw's contemporary communica-tions on the action or direction of his plays urge Barker in the direction of broader effects and more flamboyant acting. Retrospectively, Shaw points out that Barker was not really familiar with the grand school; that "His taste for low tones, which made his productions of Galsworthy's plays and of his own exquisite, did not suit mine: that was how . . . I had to upset his arrangement of Androcles. His Shakespear produc-tions were visibly beautiful; but he disliked Shakesperean [*sic*] acting (my specialty) and damaged A Midsummer Night's Dream by undercasting three of the chief quartet of char-acters."[27] Shaw wrote to Mrs. Patrick Campbell, annoyed with the difficulties of finding a Higgins for her Liza Doolittle, "You are happy playing with worms. Barker loves worms. Worms never give any trouble; and in plays which can be *produced*, they make the best casts. . . . But my plays must be acted, and acted hard. They need a sort of bustle and crepita-tion of life which requires extraordinary energy and vitality, and gives only glimpses and movements of the poetry be-neath. The lascivious monotony of beauty which satisfies

[26] Typescript letter to Alan S. Downer, 12 Nov. 1947.

[27] *Ibid.* Hesketh Pearson reports Shaw's invasion of the production of *Androcles* as follows: "Barker drilled us through August and Shaw entered like an avalanche when we were all standing about in our costumes and make-up before the curtain went up on the final dress-rehearsal. . . . In the course of four hours Shaw transformed the play from a comedy into an extravaganza. He danced about the stage, spouting bits from all parts with folded arms, turned our serious remarks into amusing quips and our funniments into tragedies, always exaggerating so as to prevent our imitating him, and making us all feel we were acting in a charade. Mean-while, Barker had retired from the contest and was looking on at the destruction of his month's work with a face that registered amusement and annoyance in about equal degree. Yet, though Shaw got every ounce of fun out of the acting, he did it with the sound Shakespearean object of putting every ounce of emotion into the play: by contrast with the com-edy, the tragedy was all the more grim" (*Bernard Shaw*, pp. 289-90).

those who are slaves of art instead of masters of it is hideous in my plays."[28]

To Barker himself, Shaw writes of Nigel Playfair as Broadbent in *John Bull's Other Island*: "Playfair is a born actor, just as Gurney is. You hate the thing because it is so blatant and unreal—because it is a garish projection of an overemphasized personality; but it draws and pays. And my plays are built to stand that sort of thing. The provinces stand it and like it." But elsewhere in the letter, Shaw notes, "Of course it will not be Calvert [the original Broadbent]; but then in the nature of things the future history of J. B.'s O. I. must be a history of broadly comic Broadbents, and not happy accidents like Calvert's personality."[29]

It is evident that Shaw's declarations to Barker, such as the one above and the roar which begins the chapter, were strategic, like so much of Shaw's professional criticism. Shaw regretted the loss of the sensitive side of Calvert's performance almost as much as Barker; but he preferred a Broadbent who was coarse but strong to one who was sensitive but weak.

As an actor in Shavian roles, Barker was evidently an admirable juvenile lead. Shaw picked him out immediately for the poet in *Candida*, and "His performance of this part—a very difficult one to cast—was, humanly speaking, perfect."[30] Barker also shone as Father Keegan (*JBOI*), but "His youth and charm made him an ideal Louis Dubedat" (*Dr.'s Dil.*).[31] He excelled in the line of the Charles Mathews *jeune premier* —as the impudent, voluble, and witty descendant of the hero of *Cool As a Cucumber* (see above, p. 36)—when his part permitted quiet shading or a note of delicate feeling. A. B. Walkley, the critic for the *Times*, declared that "Never was playwright more lucky in finding a born interpreter of his talent than Mr. Shaw in the case of Mr. Granville Barker. He is

[28] *Bernard Shaw and Mrs. Patrick Campbell*, pp. 23-24.
[29] *Bernard Shaw's Letters to Granville Barker*, p. 96 (20 July 1907).
[30] "Barker's Wild Oats," *Harper's*, 194 (1947), p. 50.
[31] MS response to Alan S. Downer's questionnaire on Granville-Barker.

so alert, so exuberant, so 'brainy,' so engagingly impudent, so voluble in his patter!"[32] But as John Tanner, a part according to Shaw with "a broad division . . . into two halves," Barker excelled as "the hunted man," and was apparently outdone by a more old-fashioned actor, Robert Loraine, as "the victorious comedian, full of resource, amusing, whimsical, and carrying everything before him."[33] Even before the Court management began, Shaw wrote of Barker to his fellow dramatist, Henry Arthur Jones, "he is always useful when a touch of poetry and refinement is needed: he lifts a whole cast when his part gives him a chance, even when he lets the part down and makes the author swear." Shaw adds, "He rebukes me feelingly for wanting my parts to be 'caricatured.' "[34] Like Charles Mathews, whom G. H. Lewes characterized as "eminently vivacious," with "a certain grace . . . an innate sense of elegance," Barker " '. . . wanted weight,' " but "had the qualities of his defects. . . ."[35]

Shaw had a great deal to do with the company of actors built up at the Court. Sir Lewis Casson reports that "the actors and actresses who made up the backbone of the old Court Theatre Company—like Louis Calvert, Lillah McCarthy, Robert Loraine, Henry Ainley and Harcourt Williams—were all brought up in the old tradition and could give clarity and significance to the quietest and most intricate dialogue with apparent 'naturalness.' "

"But for all the genius of Barker and Shaw, they would not have been able to achieve what they did had they not at their

[32] A. B. Walkley, *Drama and Life* (London, 1907), p. 232. Review of Court performance of *Man and Superman*, May 1905.
[33] Letter to Iden Payne, 3 Feb. 1911, in Julian Park, ed., "Some Unpublished Letters of George Bernard Shaw," *University of Buffalo Studies*, XVI (1939), 127.
[34] Letter of 20 Feb. 1902, in Doris Arthur Jones, *Taking the Curtain Call* (New York, 1930), p. 178.
[35] *On Actors and the Art of Acting*, pp. 61-62.

disposal actors of what are now almost an extinct type, trained speakers who had grown up in a tradition that there is an art of stage speech as definite and distinct from the speech of the street and drawing-room as the part of opera-singing or ballet is from everyday life, though the actual differences may not be so marked; a tradition of style, no longer consciously assumed because it had become instinctive, because in the theatre nothing else was heard. It included a much wider range of pitch, much more use of melody in conveying significance and meaning, and definite unwritten rules on phrasing (rhetorical punctuation, one might call it), on elision and on the carrying on of the final consonant, and so on."[36]

Lillah McCarthy was an excellent case in point. She was trained largely by reciting Milton, by playing in Ben Greet's provincial Shakespeare Company, and by touring and eventually starring with Wilson Barrett in plays like the *Sign of the Cross* (1896-1904). Shaw first saw her in 1895 as an amateur Lady Macbeth, and in his review assured her she was bad, though "she can hold an audience whilst she is doing everything wrongly. . . . and if the earlier scenes were immature, unskilful, and entirely artificial and rhetorical in their conception, still, they were very nearly thrilling" (*OTN*, I, 132-33).

Her eight years with Wilson Barrett were the keystone of her training. She writes of him in her recollections, "I was enthralled by his gestures, his voice, his 'presence.' Barrett had the traditional grand manner; now 'resting,' but presently to reappear."[37] Her prolonged absence from the influences of London, and her unrelieved experience of Barrett's kind of acting, placed her in an extremely awkward position on his

[36] "Granville Barker, Shaw and the Court Theatre," in Mander and Mitchenson, p. 291.
[37] *Myself and My Friends*, p. 42.

death; for "whilst we had been touring in the Southern Hemisphere a change had come over the English theatre. The romantic dramas of the Wilson Barrett school were passing out of fashion, and with them was passing also the broad, romantic style of acting in which for the last eight years I had been trained" (p. 49).

While Lillah McCarthy was having difficulty in finding plays to suit her acting, Shaw was having difficulty in finding actors to suit his plays.

"This difficulty was acute when I had to find a heroine for 'Man and Superman.' Everybody said that she must be ultra-modern. I said that I wanted a young Mrs. Siddons or Ristori, and that an ultra-modern actress would be no use to me whatever in the part. I was in despair of finding what I wanted when one day there walked into my rooms in the Adelphi a gorgeously goodlooking young lady in a green dress and huge picture hat in which any ordinary woman would have looked ridiculous, and in which she looked splendid, with the figure and gait of a Diana. . . . And with that young lady I achieved performances of my plays which will probably never be surpassed. For Lillah McCarthy was saturated with declamatory poetry and rhetoric from her cradle, and had learnt her business out of London by doing work in which you were either heroic or nothing. She was beautiful, plastic, statuesque, most handsomely made, and seemed to have come straight from the Italian or eighteenth century stage without a trace of the stuffiness of the London cup-and-saucer theatres. . . .

"On the stage she gave superb performances with a force and sureness of stroke and a regal authority that made her front rank position unassailable . . .

". . . her technique fell in with mine as if they had been made for one another, as indeed they had. She created the first generation of Shavian heroines with dazzling success.

. . . And she did this by playing my heroines exactly as she would have played Belvidera in 'Venice Preserved' if anyone had thought of reviving that or any other of Mrs. Siddons's great parts for her."[38]

Lillah McCarthy created the parts of Ann Whitefield and Doña Ana in *Man and Superman*, Jennifer Dubedat in *The Doctor's Dilemma*, Margaret Knox in *Fanny's First Play*, Lavinia in *Androcles*, and Annajanska the Bolshevik Empress in the frankly "bravura piece" of the same name written specifically for her. She also played Julia Craven in *The Philanderer*, Nora in *John Bull's Other Island*, and Gloria Clandon in *You Never Can Tell*. Almost all her parts belonged to the class of Shaw's passionate, dominating women (see pp. 29-31 above); and Shaw confirms the association between this strain and its "line" ancestor by referring to their actress as "a Siddonian 'heavy.' "[39] He consistently associates her with Mrs. Siddons, partly no doubt because he first saw her as Lady Macbeth. Shaw had never seen Mrs. Siddons, of course, but he knew the classics of dramatic criticism well enough to have formed an idea of her acting and presence. Particularly in Hazlitt's ecstatic characterizations, one can find recorded the kind of grandeur, range, controlled virtuosity, and heroic potential Shaw was seeking, and evidently heard echoed in Lillah McCarthy:

". . . Mrs. Siddons seemed to command every source of terror and pity, and to rule over their wildest elements with inborn ease and dignity. Her person was made to contain her spirit; her soul to fill and animate her person. Her eye answered to her voice. She wore a crown. She looked as if descended from a higher sphere, and walked the earth in majesty and pride. She sounded the full diapason, touched all chords of passion, they thrilled through her, and yet she preserved an

[38] Shaw's preface to *Myself and My Friends*, pp. 5-7. Compare his account in "Barker's Wild Oats."
[39] *Ibid.*, p. 205.

elevation of thought and character above them, like the tall cliff round which the tempest roars, but its head reposes in the blue serene! Mrs. Siddons combined the utmost grandeur and force with every variety of expression and excellence: her transitions were rapid and extreme, but were massed into unity and breadth—there was nothing warped or starting from its place—she produced the most overpowering effects without the slightest effort, by a look, a word, a gesture."[40]

Despite Shaw's remarkable opportunities to shape the style of the Court company, it was Johnston Forbes-Robertson, who had acted with the Bancrofts at the Prince of Wales and the Haymarket and with Irving at the Lyceum, whom Shaw held up as the supreme example of modern heroic acting in a modern heroic Shavian role. But Forbes-Robertson, Shaw declared, had "inherited the tradition handed down at rehearsal by Phelps" (*Pen Portraits*, p. 274) and was "the classic actor of our day."

"I wrote *Caesar and Cleopatra* for Forbes Robertson, because he is the classic actor of our day, and had a right to require such a service from me. He stands completely aloof in simplicity, dignity, grace and musical speech from the world of the motor car and the Carlton Hotel . . . Forbes Robertson is the only actor I know who can find out the feeling of a speech from its cadence. His art meets the dramatist's art directly, picking it up for completion and expression without explanations or imitations, even when he follows up the feat by turning to ask what the prosaic meaning of the sentence is, only to find the author as much in doubt as himself on that point. Without him *Caesar and Cleopatra* would not have been written; for no man writes a play without any reference to the possibility of a performance. . . ."[41]

[40] Hazlitt, from *The Examiner* (25 May 1828); in *Works*, ed. P. P. Howe (London, [1930-34]), XVIII, 408. For Shaw's familiarity with the criticism of Hazlitt, Forster, and Lewes, see *OTN*, II, 159-62, 291.
[41] "The Heroic Actors," in Mander and Mitchenson, p. 63 (reprinted

Forbes-Robertson's acting was "classic" and "interpretive" as distinguished from the "idiosyncratic" and "creative" acting of Irving and Herbert Beerbohm Tree. "For no uncommissioned author," Shaw declared in a memorial article on Tree, "can write for an idiosyncratic style and technique: he knows only the classical one. He must, like Shakespear, assume an executant who can perform and sustain certain physical feats of deportment, and build up vocal climaxes with his voice through a long crescendo of rhetoric. Further, he assumes the possession of an English voice and an English feeling for splendor of language and rhythm of verse" (*Pen Portraits*, p. 274). There was, however, a further significance which Shaw attached to the term "classical actor," highly relevant to the creation of a modern heroic drama of ideas. When Shaw reviewed Forbes-Robertson's *Hamlet* (2 October 1897), he explained: "What I mean by classical is that he can present a dramatic hero as a man whose passions are those which have produced the philosophy, the poetry, the art, and the statecraft of the world, and not merely those which have produced its weddings, coroners' inquests, and executions" (*OTN*, III, 201).

While Forbes-Robertson was looking for backers for a London production of *Caesar*, Shaw was trying to interest Richard Mansfield, who had had a substantial success with the *Devil's Disciple*, in an American production of the play.

---

from *Play Pictorial*, 10, Oct. 1907, pp. 110-11). Forbes-Robertson's association with Phelps began in 1874 at the Prince's Theatre, Manchester, when, as one of the stock company, he played Prince Hal to Phelps's Henry IV and Shallow. Robertson notes in his autobiography, "He bade me to his lodging the next day for further study, and this was the beginning of an interest he took in all my doings almost to the day of his death [d. 1878], and from that time on he seldom played an engagement without me. To be taken up so early in my career by one of the best of the old school was my supreme good fortune. He had been Macready's favourite actor. Macready had played with Mrs. Siddons, and she had played with Garrick, so that I may boast of a good histrionic pedigree, and I confess to pride at being a link with the great past in my calling" (*A Player Under Three Reigns* [Boston, 1925], p. 67).

He wrote to Mrs. Mansfield (after Mansfield had refused), describing Caesar as a heroic part in a modern heroic play:

". . . 'C and C' is the first and only adequate dramatization of the greatest man that ever lived. I want to revive, in a modern way and with modern refinement, the sort of thing that Booth did the last of in America: the projection on the stage of the hero in the big sense of the word. Whoever plays Caesar successfully will pass *hors concours* at once—get the sort of position Garrick, Kemble and Macready held, and that Irving holds here now without having ever quite achieved a heroic impersonation."[42]

The "modern way" and the "modern refinement" of Shaw's heroic play created the difficulty of the part. Caesar must seem, like Barry Sullivan's Hamlet, "a being of a different and higher order from Laertes and the rest," like Mrs. Siddons, "descended from a higher sphere"—but in the modern manner. Though Caesar is put on a plane with Christ at various points in the play, he is none the less regretfully balding and middle aged. "Our conception of heroism," Shaw wrote, "has changed of late years."

"The stage hero of the palmy days is a pricked bubble. The gentlemanly hero, of whom Tennyson's King Arthur was the type, suddenly found himself out, as Torvald Helmer in Ibsen's *Doll's House*, and died of the shock. It is no use now going on with heroes who are no longer really heroic to us. Besides, we want credible heroes. The old demand for the incredible, the impossible, the superhuman, which was supplied by bombast, inflation and the piling of crimes on catastrophes and factitious raptures on artificial agonies, has fallen off; and the demand now is for heroes in whom we can recognise our own humanity, and who, instead of walking, talking,

[42] Letter to Mrs. Mansfield, 3 May 1899, in Henderson, *Man of the Century*, p. 473.

eating, drinking, sleeping, making love and fighting single combats in a monotonous ecstasy of continuous heroism, are heroic in the true human fashion: that is, touching the summits only at rare moments, and finding the proper level of all occasions, condescending with humour and good sense to the prosaic ones, as well as rising to the noble ones, instead of ridiculously persisting in rising to them all on the principle that a hero must always soar, in season and out of season."[43]

Caesar is made perfectly free of heroic illusion, and some of his strength lies in his willingness to be prosaic, anticlimactic, and undignified. His humanity must not contradict his super-humanity. His finding the proper level for all occasions must not compromise his power to act up to the sublime moments. The actor must create the illusion of a relaxed and latent power. G. W. Bishop reports Shaw's opinion of the first Caesar: "Sir Johnston Forbes-Robertson . . . was, according to Mr. Shaw, the only actor on the English stage then capable of playing a classical part in the grand manner without losing the charm and lightness of an accomplished comedian."[44]

Shaw required actors adept at sustaining complex structures of language and thought and adept at creating and resolving the tensions of drama in sustained verbal heroics. In drama as in architecture, the taller the structure and the heavier with material, the larger the foundation and the more powerful the supports required. To secure the foundation he needed, Shaw declared he had had to revert to certain techniques of the heroic stage. But there was an essential difference between its acting and the heroic acting he required. The heroic stage was conceived of as presenting a drama of the passions, or in Shaw's terms, an opera. The actor was instructed to present himself in a series of passions

[43] "The Heroic Actors," Mander and Mitchenson, p. 63.
[44] *Barry Jackson and the London Theatre*, p. 44.

whose succession provided the continuity of his part (see Chapter 16). But Shaw was attempting to write plays of ideas; and however impassioned, the debaters in a Socratic dialogue cannot be represented by series of succeeding passions. In the old heroic mode a Barry Sullivan might be capable of only the top of the scale in drama of the passions and yet be great. But wit, irony, and the comedy of illusion and disillusion, of false logic and illogic and logic discomfited, also enter into the drama of impassioned ideas, and the actors must be skilled accordingly.

III

DRAMATIC GENRE AND THE DRAMA OF IDEAS

5

PREAMBLE TO GENRE

THE NINETEENTH CENTURY

A CHARACTERISTIC association of convention, tone, and subject matter defines a nineteenth-century "genre" as it proved useful to Shaw. In this sense, nineteenth-century genres are, first, the most prominent element in Shaw's exploitation of his immediate theatrical past and, second, the formal foundation of his creation of a drama of ideas. Evidence that Shaw conceived his plays with a strong sense of genre is abundant and convincing. Most of his fifty-odd plays and playlets were given subtitles, and most of the subtitles contain a genre identification: "A Melodrama," "A Romance," "A Political Extravaganza." Some of the nineteenth-century genres invoked, however, have since disappeared, and others have changed, so that an effort at historical recovery is necessary to confirm their genetic relevance and to grasp some of Shaw's meanings and some of his goals.

At some point in the modern history of English drama, the simple classical categories, Comedy, Tragedy, and Farce, and the useful Shakespearean categories, Comedy, Tragedy, and History lost their convenience and inclusiveness. Lists of nineteenth-century plays, such as those in Allardyce Nicoll's *History of English Drama*, seem to reflect either a bizarre proliferation of dramatic types or an utter chaos in contemporary nomenclature. Nicoll, who follows where possible the designations employed in the original bills, uses eighty-seven different terms to characterize his plays.[1] From these terms it is at least plain that the purpose of contemporary nomenclature was descriptive rather than classificatory, and that the

[1] *A History of English Drama, 1660-1900* (Cambridge U. P., 1952-59), IV, 246-47, and V, 230.

simple classical categories were inadequate as description. But they were also, very much of the time, irrelevant.

In the nineteenth-century popular theater there was no modern Tragedy, and the category dwindled into a vestigial descriptive term for surviving serious plays from the classical repertory and their archaizing imitations. Similarly, critics have argued that there was no modern Comedy. True comedy, which Shaw parenthetically defines as "the fine art of disillusion," is not popular, he writes, "except among men with a natural appetite for comedy which must be satisfied at all costs and hazards: that is to say, *not* among the English playgoing public, which positively dislikes comedy" (*OTN*, III, 85, 87). And a historian of this theater writes:

"A theatre which must offer *Money* and *Masks and Faces* as evidence of its comic spirit, and *London Assurance* and *Our American Cousin* as its popular choices, is clearly starved of comic inspiration.

"In fact the conditions of the Victorian theatre were almost uniformly unfavourable to comedy. The theatres themselves were too big, the audiences' understanding too small. The repertory of comedies from Dryden to Sheridan, many of which had retained their popularity for a hundred years, therefore disappeared from the bills."[2]

As a term, however, Comedy by no means disappeared from the bills. It continued as a vague and convenient designation for amusing plays with enough sentiment or enough pretension not to be called Farce. Plays with more distinctive qualities were ranged in other categories: Comic Drama, Comic Entertainment, Comic Interlude, Comic Opera, Comic Pantomime, Comic Romance, Comic Sketch, Comic Spectacle.

Farce was similarly an element in a number of individual alloys: Dramatic Farce, Operatic Farce, Pantomimic Farce. But Farce was one of the most vigorous and characteristic

[2] George Rowell, *The Victorian Theatre* (London, 1956), p. 63.

modes of the nineteenth century, and as such had a continuing claim to serve as a broad dramatic category. However, through the enervation of the other classical categories and the teeming of new or ambiguous types, Farce as a descriptive term shared the bills on an equal footing with Equestrian Drama, Burlesque, Domestic Drama, Burletta, Historical Drama, Pantomime.

The impulse behind the proliferation of descriptive categories and dramatic types is very much a matter of conjecture. It is clear, however, that if nineteenth-century dramatic terminology is on the whole less absurd than that put in the mouth of Polonius, it is because the nineteenth century had a greater terminological need. It is likely that the long monopoly of "legitimate" Tragedy and Comedy by the patent houses had much to do with the sapping of old terms and the forcing of new forms, so many of a semi-musical or otherwise "impure" nature. A further accounting is necessary, however, to explain the tastes embodied in the new, and by classical standards, ambiguous types; to explain the taste for the "serio-comic," for "harmless" laughter, for pity without terror and terror without pity. The root of the matter is perhaps in that perilous marsh, the sensibility of the age.

In view of the uselessness of traditional classifications and the complexity of nineteenth-century descriptive designations, the procedure in the succeeding chapters has been to isolate groups of plays which Shaw seems to be drawing upon with a sense of their common characteristics, and to treat these groups as genres or sub-genres. Occasionally, however, Shaw exploits simultaneously two play-groups not at all associated in their previous life on the stage (Christian Melodrama and Christmas Pantomime, in *Androcles and the Lion*), and in such case the dissimilar play-groups are considered together.

Shaw did not treat uniformly the genres he adapted. Some of them, like the Courtesan Play (*Mrs. Warren's Profession*) and Military Romance (*Arms and the Man*) he made into the opponents in a debate. Some of them, like Romantic Comedy (*Widowers' Houses*) and Domestic Comedy (*Candida*), he treated as useful springboards, or as sources of thematic material. During his Discussion Play period he used a number of familiar genres, treated allusively and with impressionistic exuberance, simply to set the discussion of a given subject in its familiar theatrical surroundings. Finally, he used three of the chief popular genres of the nineteenth-century theater, Melodrama, Farce, and Extravaganza, to create the three chief modes of his drama of ideas.

At three points in Shaw's playwriting career there is an artistic "breakthrough," where a genre provides not just material or suggestion coextensive with a single play, but a method for the writing of many plays. The three modes resulting from these "breakthroughs," which more or less succeeded each other, were Melodrama, Discussion, and Extravaganza. They by no means engross the whole of Shaw's significant drama of ideas. *Man and Superman*, for example, a high point of his philosophical drama, is a development out of Romantic Comedy (not counting the detachable "Discussion" in Hell). It is both "A Comedy and a Philosophy," as its subtitle proclaims, because conventional thematic materials of Romantic Comedy, such as the love-chase, are given philosophic and symbolic significance. But to turn the trick successfully was to exhaust the exploited aspects of the genre. Romantic Comedy could provide materials for the drama of ideas, but not a mode, not a method for many plays.[3]

Of the three modes, Melodrama and Extravaganza are straightforward continuations of extremely well-established

[3] Similarly, *Caesar and Cleopatra* and *Saint Joan* are both History Plays as well as plays of ideas and both are also attempts at a new heroic drama. But regarded as a drama of ideas, *Caesar* is primarily in the mode of spectacular Melodrama, while *Saint Joan* begins as Melodrama, resolves into a Discussion, and ends with an epilogue in the key of Extravaganza. Though Shaw exploited a dozen different popular genres for suggestion, framework, and familiarity, there were ultimately only those three versatile and recurring modes of the drama of ideas.

nineteenth-century genres. The Discussion Play is apparently an original genre, unless considered from a viewpoint Shaw frequently adopted, whereby genre is analogized with musical mode or "key." From such a viewpoint, the Discussion Play appears as an adaptation of the "key" qualities of nineteenth-century Farce (see below, pp. 263-64). It is significant that these three kinds, Melodrama, Extravaganza and Farce, should be at the root of Shaw's dramatic production; for two of them emerged only in the nineteenth century, in which they flourished mightily and with which they began to fade, while the three together formed, as far as the nineteenth-century popular theater was concerned, the triple pillar of the world.

PLEASANT AND UNPLEASANT

Though Shaw invoked recognizable popular genres in nearly all his plays and gave many of his plays an obvious genre label, he occasionally used other modes of classification significant in their total disregard of "professional" dramatic nomenclature. For example, when he decided in 1898 to publish his plays, as a rather daring move in his campaign for an audience, he collected them into two volumes called *Plays: Pleasant and Unpleasant*. The volume of *Unpleasant Plays* contained the three earliest plays of Shaw's professional career. Their classification is peculiarly significant, since the retrospective distinction into Pleasant and Unpleasant marks a change in Shaw's conception of himself as a playwright.

Pleasant and Unpleasant are categories that ignore formal distinctions and generic characteristics, though in the dawn of Shaw's playwriting career Unpleasant holds a place corresponding to the later genre-based modes, Melodrama, Discussion, and Extravaganza. The latter three categories, like all genre designations, called attention to the relation of a work to its artistic predecessors and contemporaries, to other plays. On the other hand, Pleasant and Unpleasant (like the title *Three Plays for Puritans*) called attention to the relation of a work to its audience.

Actually, of course, Shaw was preoccupied with both relationships in all his writing for the stage, and the Unpleasant Play could not have held the place of an initial mode in Shaw's career if it were not also, in some sense, a genre like its successors. But it is, as it were, a genre in spite of itself. It seems to reject explicitly, in its very name, all aesthetic considerations; yet there is a contemporary aesthetic consideration in this very rejection. The Unpleasant Play asserts, I ignore Art because I am concerned with Reality, Persuasion, and Society. And in this assertion it reflects and affronts the critical confusion of art with ennobling ideality and theater with comfortable entertainment, and the popular disqualification of certain kinds of subject matter. It declares itself, in the end, a genre with specific sociological concerns. The peculiar status of the Unpleasant Play, as a genre beyond genre, as well as its formidable position as a starting point, makes it a curious but revelatory prelude to the uses of genre in Shaw's subsequent dramatic career.

The word "unpleasant" had long been popular with reviewers to suggest qualities they might not care to name. Even Mr. Podsnap, in declining to pursue a discussion of starvation in the streets, declares the subject is "not pleasant," not fit to be introduced among our wives and young persons. And William Archer wrote in 1882, "A drama which opens the slightest intellectual, moral, or political question is certain to fail. The public will accept open vice, but it will have nothing to do with a moral problem. . . . Especially it will have nothing to do with a piece to whose theme the word 'unpleasant' can be applied. This epithet is of undefined and elastic signification, but once attach it to a play and all chance for it is past."[4]

[4] *English Dramatists of To-Day* (London, 1882), p. 9. Shaw ambiguously

Shaw's three Unpleasant Plays were *Widowers' Houses*, *The Philanderer*, and *Mrs. Warren's Profession*. The Pleasant Plays were *Arms and the Man*, *Candida*, *The Man of Destiny*, and *You Never Can Tell*. The seven plays (written in the above order) cut across half a dozen different genres, from Farce to Melodrama, and they will be treated accordingly in succeeding chapters. An Unpleasant Play, as Shaw himself suggested, was a "bluebook" play like *It's Never Too Late to Mend* (see above, p. 89); that is, it dealt with an immediate social problem. *Widowers' Houses* and *Mrs. Warren's Profession* were the first and last of the kind that Shaw ever wrote.

In elaborating the distinction between Pleasant and Unpleasant Shaw turned to Jonsonian categories. Jonson took it upon himself to prepare the audience of *Every Man In His Humour* for:

> . . . deeds and language such as men do use,
> And persons such as Comedy would choose,
> When she would show an image of the times,
> And sport with human follies, not with crimes.
>
> (Prologue, ll. 21-24)

Shaw prepares the readers of his *Unpleasant Plays* for a second volume containing "plays which, dealing less with the crimes of society, and more with its romantic follies and with the struggles of individuals against those follies, may be called, by contrast, Pleasant . . ." (p. xxiii). Jonson's distinction suggests the indecorum of Comedy sporting with crimes, these presumably falling in the province of Tragedy along with extraordinary deeds, noble persons, and elevated language. Still, Jonson's good sense left a loophole for Shaw's Unpleasant Plays, for his Comedy of Social Crime:

---

remarked to Archibald Henderson (*Man of the Century*, p. 531), "I called one of the volumes 'unpleasant' for fear that people, without reading them, might give them to children for Christmas presents."

And sport with human follies, not with crimes;
Except we make 'em such, by loving still
Our popular errors, when we know they're ill.

(ll. 24-26)

It is noteworthy that in all cases the social "crimes" of the Unpleasant Plays are paralleled among the human "follies" of the Pleasant Plays, so that, for example, the controlling action of both *Widowers' Houses* and *Arms and the Man* is the disillusioning of a central figure with current ideals. Similarly, both *Mrs. Warren* and *Candida* are about strong-minded women, one inside marriage and nominally respectable, the other outside marriage and nominally immoral, who make their decisions unconstrained by conventional niceties. The two heroines and their two predicaments present mentionable and unmentionable sides of the "woman question." Similarly, both *The Philanderer* and *You Never Can Tell* present the New Woman and the Old Adam in a "duel of sex." The parallels in subject and action in these three pairs of plays are obscured by the shift of accent in each pair: from the social institution, overwhelming individual compunction, to the private imagination, accessible to grace.

The Unpleasant Plays differ from those that succeeded them not only in their explicit concern with social crime, such as prostitution and slum-landlordism, but also in their relation to the audience. In these plays, Shaw wrote, "dramatic power is used to force the spectator to face unpleasant facts" (*Plays Unpleasant*, p. xxii). "Nobody's conscience is smitten except, I hope, the conscience of the audience. My intention is that they shall go home thoroughly uncomfortable."[5] Of *Widowers' Houses* Shaw wrote, "Sartorius is absolutely typical in his unconscious villainy. Like my critics, he lacks conviction of sin. Now, the didactic object of my play is to bring conviction of sin—to make the Pharisee who re-

[5] Letter to Golding Bright, 4 Nov. 1895, *Advice to a Young Critic*, p. 41, concerning *Mrs. Warren*.

pudiates Sartorius as either a Harpagon or a diseased dream of mine, and thanks God that such persons do not represent his class, recognize that Sartorius is his own photograph."[6]

It would have defeated Shaw's object, that of troubling the conscience of the honest citizen with guilt for the crimes of society, if as playwright he had provided an antisocial villain. His strategy in the Unpleasant Plays is rather to make audience-surrogates of the most self-righteous and honorable of his characters, those who stand closest to the audience in that their blamelessness seems to give them the right to judge and condemn according to conventional standards. These are the stage personages whom Shaw overwhelms with the knowledge of taint and sin. In *Mrs. Warren's Profession*, Vivie passes through such a spiritual crisis, and it makes her into the woman of the fourth act who shudders at Praed's "romance and beauty of life" and at Frank's "love's young dream." Challenged by Vivie as an avaricious scoundrel, Mrs. Warren's silent partner declares that he is no worse than the Archbishop who takes the ground rents, or anyone else in society, including Vivie herself:

> Do you remember your Crofts scholarship at Newnham? Well, that was founded by my brother the M. P. He gets his 22 per cent out of a factory with 600 girls in it, and not one of them getting wages enough to live on. How d'ye suppose they manage when they have no family to fall back on? Ask your mother. . . . If youre going to pick and choose your acquaintances on moral principles, youd better clear out of this country, unless you want to cut yourself out of all decent society.
>
> VIVIE (*conscience stricken*) You might go on to point out that I myself never asked where the money I spent came from. I believe I am just as bad as you. (p. 226)

[6] *Widowers' Houses* (Independent Theatre Edit., 1893), pp. 117-18.

Shaw's point is the inescapable complicity of all members in the social crime. When Crofts later damns Vivie, she answers, "You need not. I feel among the damned already" (p. 227).

Harry Trench in *Widowers' Houses* undergoes a similar crisis and revelation. When he discovers that Sartorius is the worst kind of slum landlord, he earnestly refuses to touch the money Sartorius was to have given with his daughter and thereby upsets the match. But Sartorius dispels Trench's illusions and proves his complicity in the social crime. He shows that Trench's own £700-a-year depends upon the exorbitant interest-rate of a slum-property mortgage, and that Trench's connections in the peerage live on the ground rents of that same property.

> TRENCH (*dazed*) Do you mean to say that I am just as bad as you are? . . .
>
> SARTORIUS . . . If, when you say you are just as bad as I am, you mean that you are just as powerless to alter the state of society, then you are unfortunately quite right.
>
> *Trench does not at once reply. He stares at Sartorius, and then hangs his head and gazes stupidly at the floor, morally beggared, with his clasped knuckles between his knees, a living picture of disillusion.* (p. 42)

The reforming play or novel which made its Sartorius an out-and-out melodramatic villain like Boucicault's Gideon Bloodgood, antisocial and malevolent by temperament and philosophy, presented precisely the view Shaw was out to combat; for a villainous scapegoat excused the audience from complicity and responsibility. Shaw wrote that the socialism of *Widowers' Houses* confused the critics, "who are in the habit of accepting as Socialism that spirit of sympathy with the poor and indignant protest against suffering and injustice which, in modern literature, culminated in Victor Hugo's *Les Miserables*. . . . This 'stage Socialism' is represented in my play by the good-natured compunction of my hero, who conceives the horrors of the slums as merely the result of atrocious individual delinquency on the part of the slum landlord."[7] In his preface to the Pleasant Plays, Shaw further declares, "the obvious conflicts of unmistakeable good with unmistakeable evil can only supply the crude drama of villain and hero, in which some absolute point of view is taken, and the dissentients are treated by the dramatist as enemies to be piously glorified or indignantly vilified. In such cheap wares I do not deal. Even in my unpleasant propagandist plays I have allowed every person his or her own point of view . . ." (pp. vi-vii).

With every person allowed the power to explain and justify himself in his own terms, each character becomes socially representative; becomes a generic figure rather than a particular instance of virtue or vice. For example, when Mrs. Warren uses the first person in her last great appeal to her daughter, her speech is overtly "representative." Shaw makes her speak as the Prostitute under Capitalism, for all her kind: ". . . the big people, the clever people, the managing people . . . do as I do, and think what I think. . . . I dont mean anything wrong: thats what you dont understand: your head is full of ignorant ideas about me. What do the people that taught you know about life or about people like me? When did they ever meet me, or speak to me, or let anyone tell them about me? the fools!" (p. 243). Shaw makes representative figures out of Mrs. Warren and Crofts (the "capitalist bully"), and Sartorius and Lickcheese (the rent-collecting tool), so that by justifying and explaining themselves they will send their audience home radically discontented with a society in which such justification is not only possible but logically impeccable.

[7] *Ibid.*, p. xv.

Precisely because each figure had to be so plausible, so convincing, and so free from special guilt, none could know more than his own partial truth. Moreover, to make an audience uncomfortable, each has to justify himself in terms of existing society, not in terms of the author's heterodox opinions. Therefore, though some figures in these plays represent segments of society and some represent the audience, there are no representatives of the author of all. There is no *raisonneur*.

In intellectual strategy the three Unpleasant Plays are essentially alike, despite *The Philanderer's* distinctly different tone. In each play, the truth to which no character penetrates is that the entire social framework is unwholesome, but remediable. In each play the characters view the social structure as if it were permanent and to be dealt with according to its permanence. Nevertheless, the implicit frame of reference for the paradoxical justifications and insoluble dilemmas of the characters is the necessity of social transformation. It is worth noting that, in Shaw's rapid change from the pamphleteer to the dramatist, his conscious effort was to eliminate all explicit solution and resolution from these plays. In the early drafts of *Widowers' Houses*, much more is made of the threat of the vestries and the London County Council, now "full of red radical republican revolutionizers that wants to cut us out by building what they calls municipal dwellings."[8] In the 1893 edition, Shaw declared that *Widowers' Houses* "deals with a burning social question, and is deliberately intended to induce people to vote on the Progressive side at the next County Council election in London."[9] But by the time of publication in 1898, the traces of propaganda for an explicit and easily achieved stopgap solution were removed, thus giving a finer dramatic conception to the play, and perhaps a greater power of conversion. Socialism is the almost

[8] Holograph ms of *Widowers' Houses* (in the Berg Collection, N.Y.P.L.), Act III, p. 30.
[9] *Widowers' Houses* (Independent Theatre Edit.), p. xix.

unnamed alternative to the seemingly insoluble state of affairs.[10]

There is no evidence that *Mrs. Warren* ever offered any explicit reform suggestion. The play demonstrates that prostitution as a profitable business is inextricably knit into the fabric of society as it exists and even suggests that this is not the worst alternative offered by the society. No one in the play makes the step to Shaw's overarching conclusion: if our social organization is so impossibly vicious that it taints us all, then let us make a new society. "In The Philanderer," Shaw writes in his introduction, "I have shewn the grotesque sexual compacts made between men and women under marriage laws which represent to some of us . . . an institution which society has outgrown but not modified, and which 'advanced' individuals are therefore forced to evade" (*Plays Unpleasant*, p. xxii). It is the "advanced" people, no doubt, who get the worst of the satire, but Shaw wishes to show that as long as the outgrown institution is unmodified there is no decent or dignified alternative to celibacy for "the intellectual and artistically conscious classes in modern society." Celibacy is practical only for some. Others in the play resort to clandestine expedients with all their embarrassments or to unwelcome marriage with all its shortcomings. Again, no personage

[10] Francis Fergusson suggests that Shaw's perspective through most of his work is "romantic irony," and that the basis of his theses, his rationalized characters, and the movement of his dialogue is the *"unresolved* paradox." Shaw maintains "logical consistency on the irrational premise"; but there is not, as in Molière, a final "appeal from logic to reality" (*Idea of a Theater* [New York, 1956], pp. 196, 203). There is in fact generally an unstated resolution to the paradox, available to few or none of the characters themselves, but available to the spectator. In the earlier plays, the implied resolution is in social revolution (however Fabian) and in ethical revisionism. In later plays the resolution is usually to be found in that well-defined assembly of ideas Shaw came to call his religion, which, however, like most religions, has its final inexplicable assumption. Shaw found such scaffolding as necessary to abundant and fruitful creation as did some of his contemporaries who invoked much more private religions.

in the play states the implicit conclusion of social transformation.

Shaw suggests the external viewpoint and the external resolution, which is the common method of his Unpleasant Plays,
in a letter to Golding Bright. He also reflects on the differences
between his Unpleasant and Pleasant Plays, guardedly using
the word "realist" in its school-of-literature sense:

"My first three plays, 'Widowers' Houses,' 'The Philanderer,' and 'Mrs. Warren's Profession' were what people would
call realistic. They were dramatic pictures of middle class
society from the point of view of a Socialist who regards the
basis of that society as thoroughly rotten economically and
morally. In 'Widowers' Houses' you had the rich suburban
villa standing on the rents of the foul rookery. In 'The Philanderer' you had the fashionable cult of Ibsenism and 'New
Womanism' on a real basis of clandestine sensuality. In 'Mrs.
Warren's Profession' you had the procuress, the organiser of
prostitution, convicting society of her occupation. All three
plays were criticisms of a special phase, the capitalist phase,
of modern organization, and their purpose was to make people
thoroughly uncomfortable whilst entertaining them artistically.

"But my four subsequent plays, 'Arms & The Man,' 'Candida,' 'The Man of Destiny' (the one-act Napoleon piece) and
the unnamed four act comedy just finished [*You Never Can
Tell*], are not 'realistic' plays. They deal with life at large,
with human nature as it presents itself through all economic
and social phases. 'Arms and The Man' is the comedy of youthful romance & disillusion, 'Candida' is the poetry of the Wife
& Mother—the Virgin Mother in the true sense, & so on & so
forth. . . . I am rather flattered than otherwise at the preference of my friends for those plays of mine which have no purpose except the purpose of all poets & dramatists as against

those which are exposures of the bad side of our social system."[11]

The Pleasant Plays, Shaw had said, would deal more with the romantic follies of society, and with the struggles of individuals against those follies, than with the crimes of society. It was no accident that Shaw echoed Ben Jonson's classical distinction, for it was essential tragedy to Shaw that a strong and capable woman whose instincts were all for respectability should be forced by society to choose between deprivation and a successful career in Mrs. Warren's profession.[12] On the other hand, the encounter of romantic infatuation and prosaic realism in *Arms and the Man* was to Shaw the primary stuff of comedy. However, both the Pleasant Play and the Unpleasant Play are joined at the root. Shaw writes in the preface to the Pleasant Plays, "To me the tragedy and comedy of life lie in the consequences, sometimes terrible, sometimes ludicrous, of our persistent attempts to found our institutions on the ideals suggested to our imaginations by our half-satisfied passions, instead of on a genuinely scientific natural history" (pp. xvi, xvii). The shift in attention from social crime to romantic folly, from the public institution to the private imagination, was for Shaw an easy shift from effect to cause.

The distinction between the Pleasant and Unpleasant Plays lay not only in their focus but in their relation to the audience. In the Pleasant Plays there is no strategy designed to make the audience uneasy while it is being entertained. On the contrary, if any strategy exists it is to charm the audience with the heterodox individuals and to amuse it with the orthodox, so that it will feel sympathetic to the one and superior to the other. The possible serious consequences of the subject matter are avoided. In *Widowers' Houses*, the disillusion of Trench leaves him "morally beggared" to such an extent that in the end he stands in with the thieves

[11] Letter of 10 June 1896, *Advice to a Young Critic*, pp. 49-50.
[12] See the Author's Apology, *Mrs. Warren*, pp. 166, 168-69.

in their plan to defraud the County Council. In contrast, in *Arms and the Man* the disillusion of Raina, the audience-surrogate, is an education to something better, a truer and healthier perception of reality. In *The Philanderer*, the "duel of sex" results in the general discontent of the duellists. Julia, the old-style woman, is trapped into a marriage she doesn't want, and Grace, the new-style woman, resolves not to have the philanderer after all; so that Grace says with some bitterness, "They think this a happy ending, Julia, these men: our lords and masters!" (p. 141). In contrast, in *You Never Can Tell*, the skirmish between Valentine, the "duellist of sex," and the New Woman results in the shattering of their foolish preconceptions, in the happy defeat of the duellist, and the final breathless love-match. In *Mrs. Warren's Profession*, the heroine has to choose between going on the streets and dying in the spirit and perhaps in the body as well. Her decision results in the Mrs. Warren we meet. In contrast, in *Candida*, the heroine must choose between the much more agreeable alternatives of comfortable domesticity and romantic idolatry. Candida is as unconstrained by conventional considerations in choosing between her husband and her lover as Mrs. Warren was in her harsher circumstances, and she chooses as common-sensibly, but, as it happens, respectably. Mrs. Warren becomes the proprietor of a chain of brothels, while Candida remains, for violently heterodox, anti-romantic reasons, the domestic angel of the Reverend James Morell.

When he abandoned the Unpleasant Play, Shaw began to change his orientation as a writer.[18] The change manifests

[18] In "A Dramatic Realist to His Critics" (*The New Review*, 11, 1894), his defense of *Arms and the Man*, Shaw presented himself as a realist in the most absolute literary sense. He claimed to have taken all his dramatic material "either from real life at first hand, or from authentic documents," and proceeded to document all the heterodoxies of the play with citations from memoirs of real soldiers and from articles by notable generals, thereby invoking the sociological-journalistic foundation of literary "realism." But after this *tour de force*, he rarely presents himself as a

itself as a shift in emphasis in Shaw's own comments on the problem play and particularly on his own examples of it. In 1893, Shaw described *Widowers' Houses* as a "bluebook play." In 1895, in a symposium on the question, "Should social problems be freely dealt with in the Drama?" he declares:

"Now the material of the dramatist is always some conflict of human feeling with circumstances; so that, since institutions are circumstances, every social question furnishes material for drama. But every drama does not involve a social question, because human feeling may be in conflict with circumstances which are not institutions, which raise no question at all, which are part of human destiny. . . . Abnormal greatness of character, abnormal baseness of character, love, and death: with these alone you can, if you are a sufficiently great dramatic poet, make a drama that will keep your language alive long after it has passed out of common use. Whereas a drama with a social question for the motive cannot outlive the solution of that question."[14]

But still he finds enormously praiseworthy Ibsen's deliberate turn to "prosaic topical plays." "A Doll's House will be as flat as ditchwater when A Midsummer Night's Dream will still be as fresh as paint; but it will have done more work in the world; and that is enough for the highest genius, which is always intensely utilitarian."[15] In 1902, Shaw wrote of his own social play, "Mrs Warren's Profession is no mere theorem, but a play of instincts and temperaments in conflict with each other and with a flinty social problem that never yields an inch to mere sentiment" ("The Author's Apology," p. 163). In 1919, Shaw had so altered his emphasis that he wrote, in an exasperated letter to one of his would-be biographers:

---

documentary realist, and he no longer writes plays with a purpose "except the purpose of all poets and dramatists."

[14] Reprinted in *Shaw on Theatre*, pp. 59-60, from *The Humanitarian*, VI (May 1895).

[15] *Ibid.*, p. 63.

"It is true that neither Widowers' Houses nor Major Barbara could have been written by an economic ignoramus, and that Mrs Warren's Profession is an economic exposure of the White Slave traffic as well as a melodrama. There is an economic link between Cashel Byron, Sartorius, Mrs Warren, and Undershaft: all of them prospering in questionable activities. But would anyone but a buffleheaded idiot of a university professor, half crazy with correcting examination papers, infer that all my plays were written as economic essays, and not as plays of life, character, and human destiny like those of Shakespear or Euripides?" (*Sixteen Self Sketches*, p. 89)

The change in emphasis was from social concern to human, and ultimately to divine concern. For Shaw's shift from social crimes to the individual follies of the romantic imagination, from Unpleasant to Pleasant, from effect to cause, was founded on his faith in the power of mind to shape reality, a faith which led him eventually into the imaginative projection of ultimate ideas.

BEYOND PLEASANT AND UNPLEASANT

Shaw distinguishes between two kinds of imagination: the romantic and the realistic. "One is the power to imagine things as they are not. . . . The other is the power to imagine things as they are without actually sensing them." The romantic imagination, with its visions of a domestic angel and of glorious ennobling cavalry charges does great mischief; "begins in silly and selfish expectations of the impossible, and ends in spiteful disappointment, sour grievance, cynicism, and misanthropic resistance to any attempt to better a hopeless world." On the other hand, the realistic imagination is "a means of foreseeing and being prepared for realities as yet unexperienced, and of testing the feasibility and desirability of serious Utopias" (*Misalliance*, Pref., p. 103). Appropriately, in Shaw's cosmology hell is the paradise of the romantic imagination and heaven is the home of the "masters of reality."

The theater as it existed at the beginning of his career Shaw represented as hell on earth, the stronghold of the romantic imagination, and it was his early strategy to discredit and replace that drama which accepted, supported, and indeed realized romantic conventions and idealized projections on stage. He desired to convert the power of the theater to the service of the realistic imagination, first for presenting "things as they are"; later for projecting "realities as yet unexperienced." Both Pleasant and Unpleasant Plays were part of Shaw's onslaught on the theater to win it from the propagation of unreality and to destroy it as a refuge from the comic and tragic consequences of importing its unreality into life. "I can no longer be satisfied," he wrote in the preface to *Plays Pleasant*, "with fictitious morals and fictitious good conduct, shedding fictitious glory on robbery, starvation, disease, crime, drink, war, cruelty, cupidity, and all the other commonplaces of civilization which drive men to the theatre to make foolish pretences that such things are progress, science, morals, religion, patriotism, imperial supremacy, national greatness and all the other names the newspapers call them" (p. xvi).

After the First World War, however, Shaw felt that mass literacy, cheap literature, and mass entertainment meant only that "the people . . . are so ignorant and incapable politically" that a statesman must deal with them "according to their blindness instead of to his own wisdom."

"But though there is no difference in this respect between the best demagogue and the worst, both of them having to present their cases equally in terms of melodrama, there is all the difference in the world between the statesman who is humbugging the people into allowing him to do the will of God . . . and one who is humbugging them into furthering his personal ambition and the commercial interests of the pluto-crats who own the newspapers and support him on reciprocal terms." (*Methuselah*, p. lxv)

This conviction ultimately resulted in a modification of Shaw's strategy of replacing the theater of romantic conven-tion with a drama that systematically questioned contempo-rary institutions and contemporary accepted ideals. He put forward *Back to Methuselah*, "A Metabiological Pentateuch," as "my beginning of a Bible for Creative Evolution" (p. lxxxvi). For despite the fact that the men engaged in "the starkly realistic practice of government" become arch-heretics themselves as to "gods, saviors, prophets, saints, heroes, and the like," yet "It is through such conceits that we are governed and governable"; though of course "only by debunking them can we evolve towards the goal" (*Methuselah*, "Postscript" [1944] pp. 264-65). From a strategy of heretical debunking, Shaw moved to a strategy of providing the provisional conceits for a future ruling orthodoxy.

The successive changes in emphasis, from the arrangements and institutions of contemporary society, to the ideals and attitudes of the private imagination, to the evolutionary scripture and utopian vision of unrealized future societies, paralleled the over-all movement in dramatic modes: from the Unpleasant Play, the "bluebook" play, with its associa-tions of documentary realism and clinical truth-to-life at the beginning of Shaw's career as a playwright; to Melodrama, with its ideal types and romantic content, and Discussion, with its dialectical dissections, in the middle of his career; to Extravaganza, with its associations of fairy tale, fable, and fantasy at the end.

COURTESANS AND MAGDALENS

EVEN in his primary phase of "bluebook" drama, Shaw turned to the popular genres of the nineteenth-century theater to provide the vehicle for his social and intellectual concerns. The simplest way of exploiting a popular genre for revolutionary purposes was by the method of systematic counter-convention, by the creation of a genre anti-type. *Mrs. Warren's Profession*, the first of Shaw's genre anti-types, is based upon the materials of the Courtesan Play. Like *Arms and the Man* with respect to Military Romance and *John Bull's Other Island* with respect to Irish Romance, it was designed to make the conventional uses of the materials artistically unacceptable to men of intellectual conscience.

In "The Author's Apology" to *Mrs. Warren's Profession*, Shaw sketches the officially allowable (and clichéd) Courtesan Play. He proclaims its dependence upon "an unwritten but perfectly well understood regulation that members of Mrs Warren's profession shall be tolerated on the stage only when they are beautiful, exquisitely dressed, and sumptuously lodged and fed; also that they shall, at the end of the play, die of consumption to the sympathetic tears of the whole audience [*La Dame aux Camélias*], or step into the next room to commit suicide [*The Second Mrs. Tanqueray*], or at least be turned out by their protectors and passed on to be 'redeemed' by old and faithful lovers who have adored them in spite of all their levities [*Formosa; Uncle Dick's Darling*]" (pp. 151-52). These were the glamorous and (to Shaw) dishonest conventions of the genre which made it the object of his particular antagonism. "I am not a pandar posing as a moralist," he wrote to Golding Bright (the pose of the officially allowable Courtesan Play was exceedingly moral). "I want to make an end, if I can, of the furtively lascivious Pharisaism of stage immorality, by a salutary demonstration of the reality."[1]

Magdalens of the nineteenth-century drama came in two varieties: domestic and vocational. The domestic Magdalen Play was a sentimental drama devoted to a weak but sympathetic woman whose fall was disinterested, usually adulterous, and always tearfully regretted. Epitomes of the type were *The Stranger* (1798), Benjamin Thompson's adaptation of Kotzebue's *Menschenhass und Reue*; the many dramatizations of Mrs. Henry Wood's novel *East Lynne* (1861); H. J. Byron's *Uncle Dick's Darling* (1869); and Augustin Daly's adaptation *Frou Frou; A Comedy of Powerful Human Interest* (1870). The Courtesan Play proper, a genre lastingly defined by *La Dame aux Camélias* of Dumas *fils* (1852), was a drama of contemporary setting featuring the magdalen by vocation. Through most of the century the domestic magdalen was considerably more feasible as a dramatic heroine in England than the "unmentionable woman." But a few plays in the courtesan genre made their mark in England: *La Dame aux Camélias* (despite the delay in performance),[2] Boucicault's *Formosa; or, The Railroad to Ruin* (1869), Wilkie Collins' *New Magdalen* (1873), and Pinero's *Second Mrs. Tanqueray* (1893). Both varieties contributed to the substance of Shaw's genre anti-type.

[1] Letter of 4 Nov. 1895, *Advice to a Young Critic*, pp. 41-42. At the time Bright was a free-lance journalist whom Shaw often used as an outlet for his own press-agentry.

[2] *Camille*, a translation, was refused by the censorship after having been announced at Drury Lane (1853). The action was approved by such liberal critics as G. H. Lewes, who nevertheless reported the play as "*the* success of the last ten years!" (*Dramatic Essays: John Forster; George Henry Lewes*, ed. William Archer and Robert W. Lowe, London, 1896, p. 241). However *La Traviata* (1853), Verdi's opera based on the play, was licensed and almost incessantly performed, in Italian and English. A version of *La Dame aux Camélias* by James Mortimer (*Heartsease*) took the stage in 1875, 1880, and 1892. A chastened American version (*Camille; or, The Fate of a Coquette*) was performed in England in 1888.

Shaw wrote *Mrs. Warren* in the latter half of 1893. The time is important because on May 24 of that year Eleonora Duse appeared in *La Dame aux Camélias* and on May 27, three days later, Mrs. Patrick Campbell opened in *The Second Mrs. Tanqueray*. Both the old play and the new had a remarkable reception.[3] But the connection between *Mrs. Warren's Profession* and *The Second Mrs. Tanqueray* is more explicit than the simple fact that in 1893 the theater was prolific of women with a past. All through Pinero's play references occur to the name that Paula Tanqueray used in the *demi-monde*, a name borrowed from one of her former patrons. Tanqueray identifies her by that name for his friend, Cayley Drummle. He declares he is going to marry "the lady—who is known as—Mrs. Jarman."[4] In his earliest biography of Shaw, Archibald Henderson reports (without comment) of *Mrs. Warren's Profession*, "In the first draft, the play was entitled *Mrs. Jarman's Profession*."[5]

[3] See the summing up of the critical reception of Duse and Pinero in *The Theatre*, 22 (n.s.), July 1893, pp. 1-8, 45. Over Duse's Marguerite Gautier (the reviewer declares) "*blasé* London was thrown into a fever." *The Second Mrs. Tanqueray* provoked essays in competitive appreciation for the next several years.

[4] *The Social Plays of Arthur Wing Pinero*, ed. Clayton Hamilton (New York, 1917), I, 74.

[5] *Life and Works*, p. 301n. Shaw denies such an earlier title in a letter to Golding Bright (19 Nov. 1894) : "The title 'Mrs. Jarman's Profession' is a curious illustration of the influence of Paula Tanqueray. The real title is 'Mrs. Warren's Profession.' The name Jarman never came into my head, nor is there any authority for it except some association of ideas in Grein's head which led him to give the wrong name to his interviewer" (*Advice to a Young Critic*, p. 9). Since Bright was engaged in dramatic paragraphing at this time, it is conceivable that Shaw was anxious to retrieve a slip by denying it had any basis at all. That J. T. Grein, the prospective producer, did have some authority for associating the plays is demonstrated in a letter Shaw wrote to Grein, in response to a request for particulars, as early as 12 December 1893. Shaw gives the title as "Mrs. Warren's Profession"; but in an account of the characters he lists "an amiable old bachelor, Praed, who could be played by anybody who can play Cayley in 'The Second Mrs. Tanqueray.' . . . The great difficulty is Mrs. Warren. . . . I should be content, myself, with Mrs. Patrick Campbell" (Orme, *J. T. Grein*, pp. 117-18).

Henderson also quotes from a letter by Shaw to the editor of the *Daily Chronicle* giving some of the origins of the play:

"Miss Janet Achurch mentioned to me a novel by some French writer as having a dramatisable story in it. It being hopeless to get me to read anything, she told me the story, which was ultra-romantic. I said, 'Oh, I will work out the real truth about that mother some day.' In the following autumn I was the guest of a lady of very distinguished ability [Beatrice Webb] . . . She suggested that I should put on the stage a real modern lady of the governing class—not the sort of thing that theatrical and critical authorities imagine such a lady to be. I did so; and the result was Miss Vivie Warren . . . I finally persuaded Miss Achurch, who is clever with her pen, to dramatise her story herself on its original romantic lines. Her version is called 'Mrs. Daintry's [*sic*] Daughter.' That is the history of 'Mrs. Warren's Profession.' "[6]

These materials were evidently precipitated in 1893, the season of the triumph of the Courtesan Play, into a counter-portrait of Mrs. Jarman. Shaw had precedent for his counter-

[6] "Mr. Shaw's Method and Secret," *Daily Chronicle*, 30 April 1898, p. 3. The play by Janet Achurch was performed for licensing 10 Feb. (July?) 1894, and is listed by Allardyce Nicoll as *Mrs. Daintree's Daughter* (under "Unknown Authors") in his *History of English Drama*.

In an article discussing in particular the relation of Shaw's play to Maupassant's *Yvette* (the "novel by some French writer") and to *Mrs. Daintree's Daughter*, Geoffrey Bullough reports that the Lord Chamberlain's typescript of *Mrs. Daintree's Daughter* shows that it was originally called *Mrs. Dartrey's Daughter*, and adds, "There are several alterations in names in the deposited copy, especially in Acts I and II" ("Literary Relations of Shaw's Mrs Warren," *Philological Quarterly*, 41, January 1962, p. 350). The original "Mrs. Dartrey" invokes another name once borne by Paula Tanqueray:

> DRUMMLE. I met her at Homburg, two—three seasons ago.
> AUBREY. Not as Mrs. Jarman?
> DRUMMLE. No.
> AUBREY. She was then—?
> DRUMMLE. Mrs. Dartry. (Pinero, *Social Plays*, I, 74-75)

The name change in what Shaw called Miss Achurch's "version" of the story supports the disputed metamorphosis of Mrs. Jarman.

portrait in Augier's *Marriage d'Olympe* (written 1855), a play intended as a deliberate corrective to *La Dame aux Camélias*, from which Augier draws names and a parallel situation. (In both of the French plays, a young man wishes to marry a seemingly redeemed courtesan. In *Olympe*, he succeeds.) Similarly, there are parallels in situation between *Mrs. Tanqueray* and *Mrs. Warren*. For example, both protagonists are suddenly confronted with their past. In the crucial incident of Pinero's play, a suitor for Paula's stepdaughter turns out to be one of Paula's former lovers. The discovery makes the match impossibly indelicate, and it is honorable in an anguished Paula to tell all and prevent it. The catastrophic consequences are the suitor's flight and Paula's suicide. In Shaw's play, Mrs. Warren's past catches up with her when her daughter's suitor turns out to be the son of a former lover. The apparent consequences for Mrs. Warren and the young couple seem grave; Vivie Warren and Frank Gardner may even be brother and sister. But the situation, emphasized by a melodramatic curtain, leads nowhere. Mrs. Warren is past feeling the embarrassments of promiscuity, and the shadow of incest is dismissed as having very little influence on the feelings of two young people who have only recently met.

The latter half of *The Second Mrs. Tanqueray* depends upon the confrontation of innocence and experience, and the judgment of daughter upon "mother." Ellean says, after the catastrophe, "But I know—I helped to kill her. If I'd only been merciful!" (p. 195). Similarly the whole of *Mrs. Warren* depends upon the confrontation of daughter and mother, of innocence or at least ignorance, and experience. Shaw describes Vivie Warren as "highly educated and respectably brought up in complete ignorance of the source of her mother's income. The drama of course, lies in the discovery and its consequences. These consequences, though cruel enough, are all quite sensible and sober, no suicide nor sensational tragedy of any sort."[7]

The specific connections between *Mrs. Warren* and *Mrs. Tanqueray* are unmistakable. But more important than any particular parallel, or any direct connection with any particular play, is Shaw's intention of creating a counter-portrait to the general image of the romantic, sentimentally attractive courtesan of the stage. It was by this counter-portrait that Shaw intended to make the conventional image artistically unacceptable to men of intellectual conscience. Insofar as Shaw's comment extends to sexual morality and sexual crime in general, he invokes the conventions of the domestic magdalen as well. To make plain the nature and context of Shaw's counter-portrait, it is only necessary to present the conventional characteristics of the ordinary stage types and juxtapose the contrasting qualities of Shaw's Mrs. Warren.

The conventional stage courtesan was a careless improvident who wasted her money and her life with sad recklessness, and died without the riches or the lover for which she had originally bartered everything else. To cap her unselfish improvidence with pathos, Marguerite Gautier on her deathbed lends her last few hundred francs to a parasite. A critic asked of Mme. Modjeska's performance in *Heartsease*, an adaptation of *La Dame aux Camélias*, "were ever satin robes and laces, diamonds and gems, worn with such evident carelessness— almost contempt . . . ?"[8] Boucicault's Formosa, troubled by love, is similarly altogether regardless of the presents of admirers and the lavishness that sorts with her condition. Paula

---

[7] Letter of 4 Nov. 1895, *Advice to a Young Critic*, p. 41. A similar situation occurs in Oscar Wilde's *Lady Windermere's Fan* (1892), where a high-principled daughter judges a woman of uncertain status whom she doesn't know to be her mother, and in *A Woman of No Importance* (1893), where a son who has been brought up "to be a good man," is confronted with the truth about his mother and his birth. "You have educated him to be your judge if he ever finds you out."

[8] R. Davey in *The Theatre*, I (n.s.), June 1880, p. 361.

Tanqueray ("*a young woman of about twenty seven: beautiful, fresh, innocent-looking*") enters dinnerless, having forgotten to order and having quarrelled with her cook, and dines instead on beautiful (and expensive) fruit. She can't bear unhappiness and declares she would be certain to kill herself "if anything serious happened to me." A feverish improvidence about material things, about money, dinners, and status, is somehow linked to a consumptive improvidence about life itself.

One of the curiosities for our time of a nineteenth-century artistic sensibility is the complete acceptability of the perfectly gratuitous deaths of so many sympathetic heroines who had gone astray. Bronson Howard supplies a resigned account of contemporary feeling in his *Autobiography of a Play:*

"In England and America, the death of a pure woman on the stage is not 'satisfactory,' except when the play rises to the dignity of tragedy. The death, in an ordinary play, of a woman who is not pure, as in the case of 'Frou-Frou,' is perfectly satisfactory, for the reason that it is inevitable. Human nature always bows gracefully to the inevitable. . . . The wife who has once taken the step from purity to impurity can never reinstate herself in the world of art on this side of the grave; and so an audience looks with complacent tears on the death of an erring woman."[9]

In *Frou Frou,* a mercurial decorative butterfly of a woman is married by a solid, soberly passionate man, and some years later circumstance and character conspire to make her run off with Another. Her lover is killed in a duel, and "Frou

[9] In *Papers on Play-Making,* Columbia University (New York, 1914), pp. 27-28 (originally delivered at Harvard, March 1886). Where the wicked woman was in fact the villain of the piece, as in Merivale and Grove's *Forget-Me-Not,* death was unnecessary. Also, where the sin or sins had occurred long before the start of the play, and the penance had been great and unreserved, and the playwright is consciously daring, as in Kotzebue's *Stranger* or Collins' *New Magdalen,* a reconciliation might occur without death.

Frou" dies at the end, without medical justification, but re-
pentant, reunited with her family, and (since she is dying)
forgiven by all. In *East Lynne*, Lady Isabel has been led astray
by an Iachimo-like tempter, who seduces her by making her
jealous. She dies, almost as gratuitously and even more pa-
thetically than Frou Frou, again in the bosom of her shattered family. In H. J. Byron's *Uncle Dick's Darling*, the
adulterous aberration of the heroine ends in her banishment
by both husband and seducer. Near death, she returns to her
childhood home where she is redeemed and forgiven by her
childhood lover and her old "Uncle" Dick (though fortunately the whole tragedy turns out to be a dream). Marguerite
Gautier, of course, dies of consumption and distress, and
Paula Tanqueray, feeling that something serious has happened
to her, flings her life away with reckless hand.

To these beautiful, careless, pathetic and sympathetic images, Shaw opposes the prospering, vulgar old woman who is
vital rather than feverish, and shrewd rather than careless.
Her apology is a justification, not a plea for forgiveness, and
she offers no bribe of gratuitous death for our kinder consideration. In the person of Mrs. Warren prostitution is presented
as a matter of economics and business organization, and not
of elegant and heedless sexual folly. "Mrs. Warren," Shaw
wrote, "is much worse than a prostitute. She is an organism
of prostitution—a woman who owns and manages brothels in
every big city in Europe and is proud of it."[10] She neither
languishes nor tempts. And she became a prostitute to live,
not to die.

The conventional courtesan (and domestic magdalen) was
usually a woman trying to "get back," in the language of
Wilkie Collins' Mercy Merrick. She wants to regain respectability, position, the comforts of society; and frequently this
effort is the entire action of the play. In *The New Magdalen*,
Mercy Merrick is a redeemed prostitute serving as a nurse in

[10] Letter of 4 Nov. 1895, *Advice to a Young Critic*, p. 41.

the Franco-Prussian war. When a young Englishwoman, Grace Roseberry, is seemingly killed, Mercy takes her identity and finds a place and a fiancé in a respectable English family. But of course Grace returns alive; and though the real Grace is unpleasant and generally disbelieved, Mercy's fundamental goodness wins out over her will to get back and she confesses the masquerade. Having resigned her fraudulently-acquired identity and character, Mercy can do nothing but return to the refuge which first reclaimed her. Those who had accepted her as Grace Roseberry and came to love her can at best forgive her and love her still, but they cannot keep her. In her own person, Mercy can't get back; indeed, she was only driven to her desperate venture by her earlier realization, "Society can subscribe to reclaim me; but Society can't take me back." However, there is always Providence. Julian Gray, a romantic Christian Socialist clergyman, loves her and offers her his name, though he takes it for granted that it means leaving England and giving up all his friends. Reviewing a revival of *The New Magdalen* in which it was billed as a problem play, Shaw wrote:

"The New Magdalen is no more a modern 'sex play' than Mercy Merrick is a real Magdalen, or, for the matter of that, a real woman. Mercy is the old-fashioned man made angel-woman. She is only technically a liar, an impostor, and a prostitute; for the loss of her reputation occurs through no fault of her own; and the fraud by which she attempts to recover her place in society is so contrived as to seem quite harmless when she enters on it. . . . Mercy Merrick and Tom Hood's drowned young lady 'fashioned so slenderly; young; and *so* fair' were not rebels against society: they were its victims, always conveying a faint suggestion that they were probably the daughters of distressed clergymen." (*OTN*, I, 231-34)

The sincere effort to get back implied an acceptance of

the standards of society. No one is severer upon the reclaimed Mercy Merrick than she herself. The same is true of Boucicault's Formosa even before reclamation, and in the end she gives away everything she has in the hope of making amends and regaining some shadow of acceptability. In T. A. Palmer's version of *East Lynne* (1874), the initial adultery is only incidental; all the drama and pathos is in the self-condemning heroine's sense of endless exile from family, home, and respectable domesticity. When her lover abandons her, the realization strikes Lady Isabel that she can't get back:

> My husband, my children!—Oh, never again to hear *him* say "Isabel, my wife!" Never again to hear *their* infant tongues murmur the holy name of *"mother!"* Lost, degraded, friendless, abandoned, and alone! Alone—utterly alone—for evermore!
>
> *Sinks on her knees despairingly as*
>
> ### THE CURTAIN FALLS
>
> *Music, "Home, sweet home." (French A. E.,* p. 29)

Eventually, battered and disguised, Isabel takes a position as a governess to her own children, in order to steal a little warmth from the domestic hearth; and only by dying can she almost "get back."

In Merivale and Grove's *Forget-Me-Not* (1879), a "wicked woman" play capitalizing on the glamour of the Courtesan genre, the entire intrigue is motivated by the desire of the beautiful and evil adventuress Stephanie de Mohrivart to transcend her past and achieve respectability. To reach this end, "Forget-Me-Not" (cf. "Camille") blackmails a respectable family into appearing in her company, introducing her, and indeed sponsoring her in society. She is finally forced to give up her wicked longing for undeserved respectability by being put in terror for her life. In Oscar Wilde's *Lady Windermere's Fan* (1892), the much more sympathetic Mrs.

Erlynne similarly attempts to blackmail her way back into society, and then gives up all she has gained to save another woman (her daughter) from suffering the pains of exile. ("You haven't got the kind of brains," she tells her daughter, "that enables a woman to get back.")

Noting the absence of genuine sexual interest in the so-called problem play, Shaw complained, "What is the usual formula for such plays? A woman has, on some past occasion, been brought into conflict with the law which regulates the relations of the sexes. A man, by falling in love with her, or marrying her, is brought into conflict with the social convention which discountenances the woman. Now the conflicts of individuals with law and convention can be dramatized like all other human conflicts; but they are purely judicial" (*Man and Superman*, p. ix). Shaw's formula exactly fits *The Second Mrs. Tanqueray* and applies almost as well to *La Dame aux Camélias*. In *Mrs. Tanqueray*, Aubrey marries Paula, and though marriage seems to open the approved gateway of respectability to Paula it in fact closes many avenues to her husband, and "getting back" in the end proves impossible. One of the messages of the play is that one can never say, with Aubrey Tanqueray, "We'll make our calculations solely for the future, talk about the future, think about the future" (p. 190), because the past must be paid for. In *La Dame aux Camélias*, Armand Duval is brought into conflict with the social conventions through his love for Marguerite Gautier, and Marguerite deliberately closes off the gateway to quasi-respectability because she loves Armand Duval too much to involve him in the inevitable ruin his father projects. (In Augier's counter-portrait, Olympe has been totally established, through marriage, as the Countess de Puygiron; but—Augier's point—she has a *nostalgie de boue* which brings her back to the mire, though there is everything to lose.)

Shaw's counter-portrait is more complex in respect of "getting back." Mrs. Warren is equipped with an older sister who has been in the same profession and made it her business to get back. She has had very little difficulty. "She's living down at Winchester now, close to the cathedral, one of the most respectable ladies there. Chaperones girls at the county ball, if you please" (*Mrs. Warren*, p. 210). In a similar vein Sir George Crofts, Mrs. Warren's partner, offers himself and his aristocratic position to Vivie Warren with the assurance, "There are no secrets better kept than the secrets everybody guesses. In the class of people I can introduce you to, no lady or gentleman would so far forget themselves as to discuss my business affairs or your mother's. No man can offer you a safer position" (p. 227). Moreover, when respectable Vivie learns Mrs. Warren's true history in very full detail, there is no horrified rejection, but rather a perfect reconciliation between erring mother and judging daughter. Mrs. Warren does not accept the social dictum that it would have been better to starve; on the contrary, she thinks it was too bad of society to offer her no better way to self-respect than prostitution, and Vivie adopts this point of view. Vivie cuts off her mother only when she learns that now when wealthy Mrs. Warren is still managing and expanding the business.

In the conventional image, the magdalen regretted her lost innocence, as symbolized by childhood, with bitterness or nostalgia. For example, at one of their crises Marguerite Gautier tells Armand, "For a moment I built a whole future on your love. I longed for the country. I remembered my childhood—one has always a childhood to remember whatever one may have become since; but it was nothing but a dream."[11] Similarly, Boucicault's "Formosa" periodically returns to her parents' inn near Oxford and pretends to be a simple country girl again. Though the most elegant courtesan in London, she hates the life she leads and keeps at least one suitor at bay (the lover who eventually makes an honest woman of her) to remind her of her lost innocence. One of Boucicault's villains

[11] *Camille*, in Stanton, ed., *Camille and Other Plays*, p. 133.

is even provoked to comment, "that girl has had a narrow escape from having been a virtuous woman."[12] In *Mrs. Tanqueray*, Aubrey and Paula quarrel over Aubrey's attempt to keep his daughter out of her way. He reminds Paula: "I know what you were at Ellean's age. I'll tell you. You hadn't a thought that wasn't a wholesome one, you hadn't an impulse that didn't tend towards good, you never harboured a notion you couldn't have gossiped about to a parcel of children." Now, Tanqueray continues, Paula's ordinary speech makes Ellean blush.

> P A U L A . Ellean—Ellean blushes easily.
> A U B R E Y . You blushed as easily a few years ago.
> P A U L A . . . . Well! Have you finished your sermon?
> A U B R E Y . (*With a gesture of despair.*) Oh, Paula! . . .
> P A U L A . (*To herself.*) A few—years ago! (*She walks slowly towards the door, then suddenly drops upon the ottoman in a paroxysm of weeping.*) O God! A few years ago! (pp. 142-43)[13]

When Shaw reviewed Fergus Hume's *The Fool of the Family* (1896), he commiserated with Gertrude Kingston, "condemned to impersonate that most exasperating of all the melodramatic impossibilities—the wicked woman who remembers what she once was, much as landladies are apt to re-

---

[12] Formosa is set in deliberate contrast with two minor courtesans, "Mrs. Dudley" and "Maud Leicester," who are vigorous, vulgar, and altogether unidealized, neither wounded angels nor tormented devils. They are much closer to the actual stage impression of the vigorous, vulgar, and unidealized Mrs. Warren than any leading-figure stage courtesan of the century. (Augier's Olympe, who is also unidealized, is presented as shallow, vicious, and artful, and belongs besides to a different order of character creation.)

[13] A parallel in domestic genre painting is Holman Hunt's notoriously popular painting "The Awakened Conscience" (exhibited 1854), in which a kept mistress is shown starting from the lap of her still thoughtless lover as the strains of "Oft in the Stilly Night" awaken some memory of innocent childhood. The tableau is acted out in Watts Phillips' *Lost in London* (1867).

member better days" (*OTN*, II, 40). The convention was particularly obnoxious to Shaw, and in an earlier article he objects specifically to Paula's sudden seizure when Tanqueray reminds her of her innocent youth. The terms of Shaw's objection suggest his own counter-portrait in Mrs. Warren:

"One can imagine how, in a play by a master-hand, Paula's reply would have opened Tanqueray's foolish eyes to the fact that a woman of that sort is already the same at three as she is at thirty-three, and that however she may have found by experience that her nature is in conflict with the ideals of differently constituted people, she remains perfectly valid to herself, and despises herself, if she sincerely does so at all, for the hypocrisy that the world forces on her instead of for being what she is. . . . [Paula] makes her reply from the Tanqueray-Ellean-Pinero point of view, and thus betrays the fact that she is a work of prejudiced observation instead of comprehension." (*OTN*, I, 47)

Shaw intended Mrs. Warren's Act Two apology as exactly the required eye-opener.

Mrs. Warren looks back to an innocent youth which made prostitution the least of many evils. She and her sister had two half sisters, "undersized, ugly, starved looking, hard working, honest poor creatures. . . . One of them worked in a whitelead factory twelve hours a day for nine shillings a week until she died of lead poisoning. She only expected to get her hands a little paralyzed; but she died" (p. 209). The other respectable sister of this paradigmatic family married a laborer and kept house on his eighteen shillings, until he turned to drink. Mrs. Warren herself was working fourteen hours a day for a pittance, washing glasses and serving drinks, when she was "rescued." Mrs. Warren doesn't feel she has betrayed her youthful self. As a child, she recalls, she bullied her respectable half sisters; and as a schoolgirl (the conventional time of recollected innocence), "I was more afraid of the whitelead factory than I was of the river . . ." (p. 210).

If Paula takes the "Tanqueray-Ellean-Pinero point of view" toward herself, Mrs. Warren remains "perfectly valid to herself." When Vivie asks her, "suppose we were both as poor as you were in those wretched old days, are you quite sure that you wouldnt advise me to try the Waterloo bar, or marry a laborer, or even go into the factory?" Mrs. Warren replies, "(*indignantly*) Of course not. What sort of mother do you take me for! How could you keep your self-respect in such starvation and slavery?" (p. 212). Unlike Paula Tanqueray, Mrs. Warren is ashamed of nothing but the hypocrisy the world demands. ". . . I cant stand saying one thing when everyone knows I mean another. Whats the use in such hypocrisy? If people arrange the world that way for women, theres no good pretending it's arranged the other way. No: I never was a bit ashamed really" (p. 213).

The final, and perhaps most important difference between the conventional magdalen and Shaw's counter-portrait is in this matter of shame, guilt, and responsibility. With nearly all previous magdalens, no matter how overwhelming the circumstances which led to their fall, the final guilt and responsibility was their own. In Boucicault's *Formosa*, though there are several villainous agents, the guilt for Formosa's profession is not shared at all. By later standards, Tom the hero is a scoundrel, for he wants to seduce, not only Formosa before he discovers her profession, but also the angelic ingenue who has fallen on evil days. Yet his credit as hero isn't tarnished in the slightest, and both angel and courtesan continue to adore him.

In Merivale and Grove's *Forget-Me-Not*, a change is apparently in process. In the course of her battle for social credit, Stephanie eloquently attacks Sir Horace Welby, a companion of her looser days who is now the accepted suitor for Alice Verney. Alice is the innocent and respectable young woman who is forced to accept Stephanie's company, much to the horror of Sir Horace. Stephanie asks:

> Is there no blight, no contamination, that a past like yours would throw upon the baby-innocence that you would link with it? Why may a man live two lives, while a woman must stand or fall by one? What was the difference between us two, Sir Horace Welby, in those bygone years, that should make me now a leper, and you a priest? that should give you the right to say to me, "You are Vice, and I am Virtue! sin on, or I damn you!" . . . There would be no place in creation for such woman [sic] as I, if it were not for such men as you! (*French A. E.*, p. 39)

Sir Horace is sorely shaken; but the uncertainty or caution of the authors in this extension of guilt is expressed in Alice's reassurance of Sir Horace:

> She has been blinding you with the old sophistries about men's vices and women's wrongs. They may blind men perhaps, but they never deceived a woman for a moment. Are we to set ourselves up as the objects of men's worship, and to be no more divine than our worshippers? It's as bad as the old Paganism. You are made of a metal whose virtue is its strength; ours shines by its purity. (p. 41)

Sir Horace is relieved, and remarks, "If your arguments are sophistries I like them better than hers."

In *The Profligate* (1889), Pinero had roundly condemned what he called "a man's life," and in *Mrs. Tanqueray* he continues the condemnation with no comforting equivocation on the different virtues of different minerals. When Tanqueray's world is falling about his ears, he curses Captain Ardale:

Curse him! Yes, I do curse him—him and his class!
Perhaps I curse myself too in doing it. He has only
led "a man's life"—just as I, how many of us, have
done! The misery he has brought on me and mine
it's likely enough we, in our time, have helped to
bring on other's by this leading "a man's life!" But
I do curse him for all that. My God, *I've* nothing
more to fear—I've paid *my* fine! And so I can curse
him in safety. Curse him! Curse him! (pp. 193-94)

Thus Pinero gives men who fall short of the ideal of sexual
conduct a full share of guilt. But the ideal of sexual conduct
is not examined. It is simply asserted vigorously, through
Paula, in her guilt and her recollection of innocence, as well
as through Tanqueray; and the inability of mankind to live
up to the ideal is deplored. Meanwhile, in the last words of
the play, merciful tolerance is asked for the specific victims,
the Paulas, who nevertheless remain the scapegoats for the
general inadequacy.[14]

In contrast, Shaw's play makes the guilt a social guilt
rather than a personal or inherent human guilt. Mrs. Warren
feels no shame because she tests her conduct by the world
as it is rather than by the world as it is pretended to be. On
the one hand, humanity is absolved from guilt, for it is the
ideals which are held to be inadequate to humanity, rather

[14] It is noteworthy that Pinero urges pity for the magdalen, but no forgiveness in the practical sense of total restoration to the rights and privileges of society. In *The Profligate*, the sympathetic heroine successfully
connives with Janet Preece, the magdalen, at a voluntary exile to Australia, though her brother and Janet have come to love each other, and
the exile causes unrelieved suffering all around. When Janet asks to be
let go, the heroine protests bewilderingly: "Let you go! You have come
into my life now, and your weakness and loneliness make it my task to
protect you. Put on your hat—quickly. . . . You mustn't re-enter this
house; you and my brother must never meet again. My poor brother!"
(*The Profligate*, London, 1898, p. 91). *Mrs. Tanqueray* is consistent with
this attitude. Paula cannot escape from what she has been; she *is* what she
has been, and there is no "getting back." Wilde, on the other hand, makes
a genuine plea for practical forgiveness, in the light of the mixed nature
of us all.

than the reverse; and on the other hand, everyone is implicated in guilt, for everyone is responsible for tolerating the vicious state of affairs. In Shaw's early view, human nature had to be accepted as the foundation of everything else. To feel guilt for human nature was unhealthy, but to feel social guilt was salutary, for social and economic institutions could be much more readily changed; and to tolerate the worse when the better was within reach was sin. Therefore, in Shaw's counter-portrait of the courtesan, she is the least guilty member of society, for it is she who has been forced to choose prostitution as the least damaging of the alternatives offered her by the social and economic state of affairs.

The actual effect of Shaw's counter-portrait was not to damage the Courtesan Play; indeed *Mrs. Warren* was not "publicly" performed in England until 1925,[15] and new plays varying the old conventions are still well received. But the conventions of the Courtesan Play served Shaw as a useful stalking horse and as a constant frame of reference, and Shaw expected anyone who saw or (after 1898) read his play to be implicated in the social guilt which it tries to demonstrate. To assign priority of intention to Shaw's assault on artistic convention or to his assault on society is impossible, but there is an obvious dependency between them. For example, Shaw could not make Mrs. Warren a conventional careless improvident who burns her candle at both ends and dies, because he wanted to show the cold logic of her economic choice in society as constituted; Mrs. Warren chooses prostitution not out of weakness, but through strength of mind, and she is successful because of shrewd native abilities. Similarly, Shaw's counter-portrait has no feverish sexual glamor, because Mrs.

---

[15] Its first presentation was in two "private" performances by the Stage Society, January 5 and 6, 1902. The Stage Society was technically a club, and the audience was technically its members. Consequently, its activities were exempt from the surveillance of the Lord Chamberlain's official censor.

Warren represents prostitution as a social and economic phenomenon rather than prostitution as forbidden fruit, personal temptation, and fall. There is no desperate, pathetic effort to "get back," because Mrs. Warren knew greater degradation in respectability. There is no nostalgic recollection of an innocent girlhood, because prostitution was her refuge from its bitterness. And finally, there is no tormenting shame, because the guilt is the spectators'.

7

ROMANTIC COMEDY

LORD SUMMERHAYS. . . . We shall now get the change of subject we are all pining for.

JOHNNY (*puzzled*) Whats that?

LORD SUMMERHAYS. The great question. The question that men and women will spend hours over without complaining. The question that occupies all the novel readers and all the playgoers. The question they never get tired of.

JOHNNY. But what question?

LORD SUMMERHAYS. The question which particular young man some young woman will mate with. (*Misalliance*, pp. 186-87)

S H A W ' S career-long exploitation of the conventions of nineteenth-century Romantic Comedy makes it clear that not all his methods of utilizing popular dramatic conventions were as aggressively simple as creating a genre anti-type, that the method of *Mrs. Warren* was in fact rather exceptional. In *Widowers' Houses* and *Pygmalion*, for example, Romantic Comedy conventions serve as theatrical points of departure. In each play Shaw seizes upon a familiar motif of the genre, involving conventional relationships between classes, persons, and generations. Shaw uses these conventional relationships to point out social and psychological realities, but at the same time he exploits the familiar motif for its normal theatrical appeal. (In the genre anti-type *Mrs. Warren*, it was precisely the normal theatrical appeal of the Courtesan Play which Shaw wished "to make an end [of] if I can.") In *Misalliance* and *Man and Superman* Shaw goes further in giving the conventions a formal as well as material function. *Misalliance* is a Discussion Play (and consequently will be discussed under that head); but it is the nature of the Discussion Play to depend upon an external genre-relationship for its cohering center of reference, so that *Misalliance* can be described in formal terms as a fantasia on themes of Romantic Comedy. *Man and Superman* uses elements of Romantic Comedy to provide the formal dramatic incarnation of a philosophy.

Since marriage and comedy are as companionable as death and tragedy, it is not surprising that other Shaw plays share in the courtship-romance characteristics though their fundamental allegiance is to another genre. These are: *The Philanderer, You Never Can Tell, Mrs. Warren, Arms and the Man, John Bull's Other Island, Fanny's First Play, Androcles, The Millionairess, Major Barbara*, and *Buoyant Billions*. These plays demand an occasional aside; but the principal business of this chapter will be with the plays centered on the conventions of Romantic Comedy: *Widowers' Houses, Pygmalion*, and *Man and Superman*.

Nineteenth-century Romantic Comedy had three characteristic story motifs. The first was misalliance between classes. The second, closely related to the first, was a Cinderella-Galatea motif of transformation and testing. The third was the opposition of youth and age. All three are traditional staples of comedy—youth and age in a love contest is surely Menandrian—but the nineteenth century imposed its own special forms upon them. A fourth traditional motif, the sex-duel, was rather less common in English drama than at any period since Elizabeth, and the earlier comedy which depended upon it had virtually disappeared from the repertory. The suitor, it seemed, was now either a vile seducer or a noble-hearted fellow who would blush to think of the sentimental heroine in an improper way. The ambiguity in the lover which makes the sex-duel possible had vanished. The duel was not extirpated, but it survived only under special conditions until Shaw revived it and gave it a philosophical turn.

WIDOWERS' HOUSES AND MISALLIANCE

Of the three standard story motifs in nineteenth-century Romantic Comedy, it is difficult to say which was more popular, misalliance or the opposition of youth and age. Frequently, of course, they were found together in the same play. Nineteenth-century Romantic Comedy took particular notice of the misalliances of the middle class, and a comprehensive case in point is Thomas and J. M. Morton's *All That Glitters Is Not Gold* (1851). The Plumbs, a rich cotton-manufacturing family, are here represented as making their alliances both up and down, with moneyless rank and with moneyless virtue. Frederick Plumb is matched with a Lady Valeria, whose mother, Lady Leatherbridge, is intensely disdainful of the connection, though she gladly makes the match for the money. Stephen Plumb falls in love with Martha Gibbs, a millhand, to the chagrin of his social-climbing father. The action of the play is simply to reconcile all classes and generations by revealing the common clay of the aristocrats and the superior metal of Martha Gibbs ("All That Glitters Is Not Gold").

Though the alliances between classes nearly always involved a barter of rank and money, the disdainful pride of the stage aristocrat often took the form of a scrupulosity about the origin of money. For example, the aristocratic Vavasours in Tom Taylor's romantic comedy *New Men and Old Acres* (1869) make a point of the "stigma" of trade, of the taint on money made in vulgar commerce. Shaw was to seize on this motif and exploit it, in *Mrs. Warren, Major Barbara*, and especially in *Widowers' Houses*, to present a vision of capitalist society in which all money was tainted, in which all hands that touched money received its taint, in which the pernicious alternatives were to receive the taint or perish.

Widowers' Houses began as a collaboration between Shaw and William Archer, with Archer supplying the scenario and Shaw working out the dialogue; but Archer withdrew from the partnership when Shaw brought back his well-made plot and "told him that I had finished up the renunciation and wanted some more story to go on with, as I was only in the

middle of the second act. He said that according to his calculation the renunciation ought to have landed me at the
end of the play. I could only reply that his calculation did not
work out, and that he must supply further material."[1] Archer's
original title for the play was *Rhinegold*, an allusion to the
theme of tainted money. In his review of the Independent
Theatre's two performances, Archer recounted the origins of
the play:

"I drew out, scene by scene, the scheme of a twaddling cup-
and-saucer comedy vaguely suggested by Augier's *Ceinture
Dorée*. The details I forget, but I know it was to be called
Rhinegold, was to open, as *Widowers' Houses* actually does,
in a hotel-garden on the Rhine, and was to have two heroines,
a sentimental and a comic one, according to the accepted
Robertson-Byron-Carton formula. I fancy the hero was to
propose to the sentimental heroine, believing her to be the
poor niece instead of the rich daughter of the sweater, or
slum-landlord, or whatever he may have been; and I know
he was to carry on in the most heroic fashion, and was ultimately to succeed in throwing the tainted treasure of his
father-in-law, metaphorically speaking, into the Rhine. All
this I gravely propounded to Mr. Shaw, who listened with
no less admirable gravity."[2]

After quoting Archer's review, Shaw retorted: "I most
strenuously deny that there is any such great difference between his *Rhinegold* and *Widowers' Houses* as he supposes. . . .
The Rhine hotel garden, the hero proposing to the heroine
in ignorance of the source of her father's wealth, the 'tainted
treasure of the father-in-law,' the renunciation of it by the
lover: all these will be found as prominently in the following pages as in Mr. Archer's description of the fable which
he persists in saying I did 'not even touch' " (p. xii).

[1] *Widowers' Houses* (Independent Theatre Edit.), p. xii.
[2] *Ibid.*, pp. x, xi; from *The World*, 14 Dec. 1892.

In Shaw's completed play, the situation presented is the matching of the wealthy daughter of a self-made man who derives his income from "the rental of a very extensive real estate in London" with a scantily endowed younger member of an aristocratic family. The girl's father has a great deal of suspicious pride and is concerned that Blanche, his daughter, be wholly accepted by the young man's family. He demands that a letter be written to Harry Trench's aunt, Lady Roxdale, and that gracious replies be exhibited before the match is concluded. When Trench tells Blanche, "I had to promise him not to regard anything as settled until I hear from my people at home," Blanche replies, " (chilled) Oh, I see. Your family may object to me; and then it will be all over between us. They are almost sure to." If the matter is unsettled, Blanche adds, let us break off the match immediately, and Trench declares " (intoxicated with affection) Blanche: on my most sacred honor, family or no family, promise or no promise—" when he is interrupted (Stand. Ed., p. 22).

The first act seems to present and prepare for two major class-representative figures of nineteenth-century Romantic Comedy. Lady Roxdale is potentially the aristocratic dowager-dragon, like Lady Leatherbridge in *All That Glitters*. Blanche's father is evidently the strong, proud, self-made titan of the middle class who flourished most characteristically in the guise of an "Ironmaster." The dowager-dragon appears as Lady Ptarmigant in Robertson's *Society* (1865); as the Marchioness (who will have nothing to do with the runaway match between her son George and a former actress until she thinks George dead and comes to claim her grandson) in Robertson's *Caste* (1867); and as Lady Matilda Vavasour in Tom Taylor and Augustus Dubourg's *New Men and Old Acres* (1869).

There is also an "Ironmaster" figure in *New Men and Old Acres* in the person of Samuel Brown, a Liverpool merchant who earns the disinterested love of an aristocrat (with whom

he has been venally matched) by his manly virtues and inherent nobility. Brown is typical in that he is not a pseudo-
aristocrat, like Bulwer Lytton's Claude Melnotte; his good
qualities are presented as those of his own rank and class
at its best. He remains, however idealized, a man of commerce, energetic, sober, virile, forthright, proud, and honorable as such. He appears in literature as Rouncewell, the
Ironmaster of *Bleak House*, and as Conolly, the workingman-
inventor-industrialist of Shaw's early novel *The Irrational
Knot*. He appears as the Ironmaster in T. W. Robertson's
Birth (1870), where he and an impecunious earl pair with
each other's sisters after a great deal of pride and antipathy
over the transfer of ancestral acres. He appears as Phillippe
Derblay in Georges Ohnet's *The Iron Master (Le Maître des
Forges)*, adapted by Pinero in 1884 and recalled by Shaw in
the next decade (*OTN*, I, 165), where he marries an aristocrat who repulses him on his wedding night and later sacrifices
her own pride to woo him out of his proud withdrawal.[3]

With the self-made Sartorius laying down the conditions
of marriage with his child (like Dickens' Rouncewell), and
the aristocratic Lady Roxdale threatening in the background,
the first act of *Widowers' Houses* seems to prepare for a conventional romance like *Caste* or H. J. Byron's *Our Boys*

[3] There also was a type of comically vulgar self-made man with sons
and daughters who marry above him, like Jasper Plumb in *All That
Glitters* and Perkyn Middlewick in *Our Boys*, and for that matter Burgess
in *Candida* and Malone in *Man and Superman*. Shaw uses and plays
upon both types rather frequently. Sartorius begins much closer to Plumb
than to Derblay; but between Shaw's original manuscript of *Widowers'
Houses* and the Standard Edition, many touches of vulgarity were removed. Sartorius no longer says, "my daughter is accustomed to a first
rate establishment"; he says "proper establishment" (cf. p. 75 of MS of
Acts I and II, p. 39 of Standard Ed.). He becomes smoother, more powerful, mesmeric in his effects, and the final Sartorius (like Undershaft)
resembles the heavy financier of Melodrama as well as the self-made man
of Romantic Comedy. Shaw's last word on the conventions of both the
Ironmaster and the heavy financier was Boss Mangan, Ellie Dunn's suitor
in *Heartbreak House*, who is turned inside out half a dozen times in the
course of the play (see below, pp. 319-20).

(1875) or Tom Taylor's *Babes in the Wood* (1860), where young people match, in defiance of their elders, across a class barrier ("family or no family, promise or no promise"), and after a period of tribulation are restored to grace and fortune. But the audience is deceived in its expectations. There is amazingly little difficulty put in the way of the lovers. Blanche is immediately accepted by Trench's aristocratic family and the dowager-dragon never appears. The objection comes from Trench himself, who refuses to accept her father's tainted money when he discovers it comes from tenement squeezing, only one level removed from the actual rent collecting. "Your family doesnt object," says Blanche, "Do y o u object?" "I do not indeed," Trench answers, "It's only a question of money" (p. 36). But Blanche refuses to live on Trench's own comparatively scanty seven hundred a year; and since Trench refuses to give the grounds of his objection she breaks off the match.

If Shaw wished to exploit the basic appeal of romantic comedy, in the end, despite all lover's crosses, Jack had to have Jill. Having quarrelled, the lovers had to be reconciled. "If the two young people had a lovers' quarrel in the presence of the audience, no power on earth could have convinced any man or woman in the house that they were not intended for each other by the eternal decrees of divine Providence."[4] In *Widowers' Houses* the imperative holds, but the usual atmosphere of the reconciliation is strangely transformed.

In the romance founded on misalliance, the action involves either a levelling up or a levelling down or both. The Bertram (of either sex) is reduced and the Helena exalted. In *The Lady of Lyons*, when Claude Melnotte, the son of a gardener, returns from war and apparent death loaded with wealth and glory, he finds the snobbish Deschappelles on the

[4] From Bronson Howard's illuminating account of his *Banker's Daughter, The Autobiography of a Play*, in *Papers on Play-Making* (New York, 1914), p. 40.

verge of ruin and Pauline, their daughter and once his bride, on the verge of a repulsive marriage to prevent her father's bankruptcy. Harry Trench, even before parting with Blanche, was devastated to discover that his own money, and indeed all the money of society was tainted, that he himself was a tenement-squeezer only two levels removed; but it was then too late to smooth over the quarrel. To effect a reconciliation in the last act, Blanche has to be informed of the extra-personal grounds of Trench's objection (which happens through a "well-made" contrivance: a parliamentary blue-book is introduced and left for her to encounter), and a meeting has to be brought about between the two lovers. The meeting is held under the auspices of Lickcheese, former rent-collector for Sartorius and currently devoted to municipal jobbery. Trench is called in to take a share of the risks and the profits in a scheme to swindle the public. His participation is undecided (though he seems to have no alternative) when Lickcheese proposes, "Why not Dr Trench marry Miss Blanche, and settle the whole affair that way? . . . I know Miss Blanche: she has her father's eye for business. Explain this job to her; and she'll make it up with Dr Trench. Why not have a bit of romance in business when it costs nothing?" (p. 61). Trench refuses to "have the relations between Miss Sartorius and myself made part of a bargain"; but he permits himself to be maneuvered into meeting her. She catches him on the verge of kissing her portrait, and after a brief passage-at-arms they are passionately reconciled. The syndicate returns immediately:

> LICKCHEESE (*on Trench's left, in a low voice*)
> Any noos for us, Dr Trench?
> TRENCH (*to Sartorius, on his right*) I'll stand in,
> compensation or no compensation. (pp. 64-65)

Compensation or no compensation, the romantic comedy ends with the "unpleasant" knowledge that the two young lovers

—·[167]·—

are sealing the mutual economic interests of their respective social classes.

In *Widowers' Houses,* Shaw has treated the conventions of courtship comedy with scant respect, but he has exploited them extensively. In the first act he set up a conventional plot of misalliance; in the second act, he turned his back upon it; in the third act, he returns to it for symbolic purposes. The conventional reconciliation and joyful union take place in the shadow of Lickcheese, the go-between. The notion of misalliance has been exploded, and the match is made to suggest the tacit alliance which Shaw believed existed in life between the aristocracy and the "rising" middle class: a piratical alliance of economic interest.

The misalliance motif receives explicit recognition in a number of other Shaw plays: in *Arms and the Man,* in *Major Barbara,* and in *Man and Superman.* In *Major Barbara,* the allusion to misalliance conventions points to the actual class-lessness of the foundling "Prince of Darkness," the professor of Greek, and the daughter of the foundling, who is also the granddaughter of an earl. In *Man and Superman,* the match between Violet and Hector Malone, Jr., deliberately inverts the conventions. By ordinary standards, Hector and Violet would be a very good match, but Hector Malone, Sr., a self-made millionaire, insists that his son marry a peer's daughter or a peasant's, so that there will be what he calls a social profit and what others would call misalliance. In another inversion it is Violet, not Hector, who insists on concealment because "You can be as romantic as you please about love, Hector; but you mustnt be romantic about money. . . . It is I and not you who suffer by this concealment; and as to facing a struggle and poverty and all that sort of thing I simply will not do it. It's too silly" (p. 64).[5]

[5] It is instructive to compare Violet with Belinda in Gilbert's *Engaged* (1877). Belinda declares: "Belvawney . . . I love you madly, passionately; I

Shaw doesn't perpetrate these inversions simply for the joke, but to make an urgently felt point about the social and economic realities masked by the conventions. There is a further inversion in the resolution of this subplot. Malone, Sr., has demanded a misalliance; but instead of finding out immediately that his son has married against his wishes, so that the young couple might struggle through the play to a final reconciliation as in *Our Boys*, Malone only finds out near the very end; and then, having offended Hector, he must plead to have his support accepted:

> M A L O N E (*pleading abjectly*) Dont be hard on me, Hector. I'd rather you quarrelled and took the money than made friends and starved. You dont know what the world is: I do. (p. 148)

He even begs Violet to intercede.

PYGMALION AND CINDERELLA

The misalliance motif of courtship comedy needs only a slight change of emphasis to become the Cinderella story of romance with its inevitable concomitants, a magical transformation and a fairytale test. When the lover himself prepares the transformation, he enacts the Pygmalion story; and it is therefore Shaw's own title which excused Beerbohm Tree's natural desire to end with a match instead of a mystery.[6]

---

care to live but in your heart, I breathe but for your love; yet, before I actually consent to take the irrevocable step that will place me on the pinnacle of my fondest hopes, you must give me some definite idea of your pecuniary position. I am not mercenary, heaven knows; but business is business, and I confess I should like a little definite information about the settlements." In his preface to *Man and Superman*, Shaw writes of Don Juan in a modern setting, "His former jests he has had to take as seriously as I have had to take some of the jests of Mr W. S. Gilbert" (p. xiv).

[6] ". . . for all Shaw's inflexibility as a stage manager, in the end the obstinate and clever Tree succeeded in circumventing the unromantic Irishman. By his insertion of the ingenious business of throwing flowers

T. W. Robertson's *School* (1869), a romantic comedy of courtship, presents a conscious and underlined Cinderella story, for it begins with Bella, an orphaned teacher-pupil, telling the Cinderella tale to other school-girls; it is punctuated throughout with music from *La Cenerentola*, and Bella herself loses a shoe in running away from a handsome lord. When Bella disappears it is generally thought she has gone off to a bad end with Lord Beaufoy; but interest in her revives with the news that she has become an heiress. Lord Beaufoy appears before all and admits he knows Bella's whereabouts. He declares he can't marry her—he is already married—and he attacks those who have mistreated Bella for their neglect and their previous pose of cynicism over her disappearance. "Bella is contented and happy. . . . She does not fetch or carry like a servant. She rings bells—she does not answer them" (p. 678). And then he presents his wife, Bella, dressed for the occasion in full bridal regalia. The Cinderella motif depends upon a poor orphan child marrying a dazzling prince. But it is like Robertson to make her an heiress after all.

Shaw's full title for *Pygmalion* is *Pygmalion; A Romance in Five Acts*. In his postscript Shaw writes, "Now, the history of Eliza Doolittle, though called a romance because the transfiguration it records seems exceedingly improbable, is common enough. Such transfigurations have been achieved by hundreds of resolutely ambitious young women since Nell Gwynne set them the example by playing queens and fascinating kings in the theatre in which she began by selling oranges" (p. 295). The transformation of Eliza, from flower girl to what Higgins calls "my creation of a Duchess Eliza," by learning to speak and to play the part of a lady, is in fact a staple of theatrical romance.

---

to Eliza in the very brief interval between the end of the play and the fall of the curtain, he achieved an instantaneous miracle of schizophrenia, transforming the disagreeable curmudgeon into the sympathetic lover . . ." (Henderson, *Man of the Century*, p. 685).

The theatrical antecedents of Shaw's *Pygmalion* are epitomized in Dion Boucicault's *Grimaldi; or The Life of an Actress* (London, 1862). Like Eliza, Violet in Boucicault's play is a Covent Garden flower girl. She is made over into an actress through patient education by Grimaldi, an old Utility, and in the end she becomes a duchess, not only, like Eliza, in metaphor and manner but in fact. Violet has the beginnings of a great triumph on the stage, interrupted by melodramatic machinations. In the last act, however, she appears as the great new sensation of the London theater at an aristocratic garden party, like the Ambassador's party in *Pygmalion*. We hear rumors of her forthcoming marriage to Lord Alfred Shafton and of her presentation to the Queen. The Countess of Beaumaris, Lord Alfred's dragon mother, objects and attempts to buy Violet off, but she is won over at last when Grimaldi, the old actor, turns out to be a duke and a former lover of the Countess in Naples, and Violet, the former flower girl, is adopted as heir to his title.

In a theatrical romance like *Grimaldi*, the more wonderful the transformation the better. It is better in *Grimaldi* that Violet be a flower girl turned duchess than a shopkeeper's daughter turned wholesaler's wife. But in a society where the duchess and the flower girl can be said to belong to two nations, a miraculous transformation is almost a necessary part of a match between the classes. Despite their beauty and their goodness, Cinderella and Galatea in the nineteenth-century romance had to be touched by the magic wand of an education.

A transformation, by education or otherwise, requires a test, a Cinderella's slipper. The candidate must prove her fitness to be the mate of the prince. In Bulwer-Lytton's *Money* (1840), a hidden act of charity finally traced to its true owner permits Arthur Evelyn to take the poor but good-hearted Clara as his bride. In *The Lady of Lyons* (1838), renunciation, heroic service, wealth, and rank in Napoleon's army, and the most honorable self effacement, enable Claude Melnotte to claim the bride he was presumptuous enough to marry.

A more comprehensive example is Tom Taylor's domestic romance, *An Unequal Match* (1857). While Claude Melnotte begins with all the appearance and qualities of an aristocrat, and his transformation requires simply a proving, Hester, Taylor's heroine, has not yet been transformed, and she has already married above her station. Her simple country virtues cease to charm her husband and he leaves her for a year; but meanwhile she becomes a lady according to her husband's precepts, follows him to the continent, and there charms a Grand Duke with her wit and accomplishments and mystifies the English colony. She also snubs her father and takes all things lightly, including her husband's jealousy. When he bemoans the artificial monster he has created, Hester has made her point, and she confesses that she is not really spoiled. In the end the simple virtues have been vindicated; but also (though this it not stated) Hester has been transformed from a blacksmith's daughter into a perfectly suitable wife for a peer. She has passed her test.

The transformation test-scene was an obvious high point in any drama based on the Cinderella-Pygmalion romance, and such a scene was the starting point of Shaw's *Pygmalion*. Its "obligatory scene," he himself declares, "the scene in which Eliza makes her successful début at the Ambassador's party was the root of the play at its inception. But when I got to work I left it to the imagination of the audience, as the theatre could not afford its expense and it made the play too long. Sir James Barrie spotted this at once and remonstrated. So when the play was screened, I added the omitted scene. . . ."[7]

When Higgins is bent on persuading Liza to submit to

[7] "How to Write a Play," an interview with Hayden Church, *Glasgow Evening Times*, 7 Feb. 1939; reprinted in Henderson, *Man of the Century*, p. 730.

his experiment, he dangles all sorts of prospects before her, including the fairy tale test:

> HIGGINS ... At the end of six months you shall go to Buckingham Palace in a carriage, beautifully dressed. If the King finds out youre not a lady, you will be taken by the police to the Tower of London, where your head will be cut off as a warning to other presumptuous flower girls. If you are not found out, you shall have a present of seven-and-sixpence to start life with as a lady in a shop. If you refuse this offer you will be a most ungrateful wicked girl; and the angels will weep for you. (p. 225)

This makes much more sense to Eliza than Higgins' earlier appeals to high romance ("you shall marry an officer in the Guards, with a beautiful moustache: the son of a marquis, who will disinherit him for marrying you, but will relent when he sees your beauty and goodness" [p. 224]); but she takes Higgins literally about the test, and objects to having her head cut off.

Even in the play-house version Shaw was evidently reluctant to do without a test scene altogether. He therefore introduces an intermediate test scene with inconclusive results. The whole of Act III concerns the trying-out of Eliza in Mrs. Higgins' drawing-room. Eliza passes the test in that she is not recognized by the Eynsford Hills, who had seen her in Covent Garden on the very night Higgins had picked her up (Act I). Eliza indeed makes a conquest of the younger Eynsford Hills; but while her voice, diction, and appearance are dazzlingly perfect, she speaks, with the tongue of angels, the small talk of a flower girl. Her exit line, the notorious "Not bloody likely," was in test-scene terms a catastrophe.[8]

[8] The effect of the line on its initial audiences was owing more to its dramatic circumstances (the test-scene) than to its intrinsic sensational-

Eliza's real test, the Ambassador's party, was a public debut in "society," and that is precisely the form of the test in *Grimaldi* and in Morton's *All That Glitters Is Not Gold*. In *Grimaldi*, Violet's theatrical debut, like Eliza's preliminary test, was abortive, and her final test is at an aristocratic garden party. In *All That Glitters*, Martha the millgirl can marry Stephen if she can live in the Plumb family for three months without committing an impropriety. The final test is a fancy-dress ball, comprising most of Act II, in which Jasper Plumb sets a watch on Martha like that of the Hungarian phoneticist on Eliza:

> It's now two months since I promised that unhappy boy of mine, Stephen, that I would transfer this uneducated girl, Martha Gibbs, from the factory to the saloon; to-night she makes her first curtsey in a ball-room—surely there *can* be but one result; her head *must* turn giddy with her sudden elevation, her vulgarity be exposed, perhaps, her integrity shaken, and Stephen be cured of his infatuation. I'll set this fellow to watch her. . . . watch her closely, and if you perceive the slightest levity of manner, or the most trifling want of decorum in her conduct, inform me instantly. (*French A. E.*, pp. 20-21)

Naturally Martha's behavior is admirable, though there are

---

ism. Another factor was the no doubt calculated restraint Shaw placed upon his audience by a protest, inserted in the program, against laughter during the performance. In a letter to his wife giving an account of the first performance, Shaw wrote: "The house was of course crammed; and the people behaved very well. My protests had been read and though there was plenty of laughing, it was kept in hand and the play listened to practically without serious interruption until the ends of the acts, when the applause was serious and sustained. But in the third act the effort to keep quiet was less successful; and when 'Not bloody likely' came, the performance was nearly wrecked. They laughed themselves into such utter abandonment and disorder that it was really doubtful for some time whether they could recover themselves and let the play go on" (letter of 12 April 1914, B. M. Add. MS 46506, f. 103).

suspenseful moments when it is open to grave misunderstanding.

Shaw helps himself to this test motif in other plays besides *Pygmalion*. In *The Millionairess* Epifania's father, like Portia's, has instituted the test of worthiness. "I was like a princess in a fairy tale offering all men alive my hand and fortune if they could turn my hundred and fifty pound cheque into fifty thousand within six months" (p. 149). On the other hand, the mother of the man she wants as her second husband has instituted a test also: any aspirant to the hand of her son must earn her living alone and unaided for six months, with nothing more than the clothes on her back and two hundred piastres. Of course Shaw uses these tests to make a philosophical and social point: Epifania's first husband passes the test because "ninety per cent of our selfmade millionaires are criminals who have taken a five hundred to one chance and got away with it by pure luck. Well, Alastair was that sort of criminal" (p. 138). On the other hand, Epifania herself goes out into the world with her two hundred piastres and builds a small empire because she is one of those few people with a genius for organization, management, and the making of money.

Grimaldi's transformation of Violet the flower girl into Violet the actress in a spirit of paternal benevolence was designed to provide her with a vocation and a way of life. But in *Pygmalion*, Mrs. Higgins sees the education of Eliza beyond her station or opportunities as " (*unconsciously dating herself by the word*) A problem" (p. 258). It seems incredible to everyone that Higgins should have "created this thing out of the squashed cabbage leaves of Covent Garden" (p. 282) without any motive, either acquisitive or benevolent, that bore upon Eliza as a person; and in the seduction scene of the second act, presented in the pattern of the poor-but-good girl who has been picked up off the streets and tempted with furs and chocolates by the wealthy rake, everyone suspects

Higgins' designs. His housekeeper ventures to say, "Mr Higgins: youre tempting the girl. It's not right. She should think of the future" (p. 224). Eliza herself fears the seducer's opiate: "Ive heard of girls being drugged by the like of you" (p. 223). Even Colonel Pickering, Higgins' fellow phonologist, asks "Excuse the straight question, Higgins. Are you a man of good character where women are concerned?" (p. 228). Doolittle comes in a pose of "wounded honor and stern resolution" to "rescue her from a fate worse than death"—or to settle the matter for five pounds. For his interest in a girl so far beneath him, Higgins is as suspect as Lord Beaufoy in *School*, though his interest (however perverse in its limitations) is strictly artistic and scientific.

The difference between *Pygmalion* and *Grimaldi* is in Shaw's serious concern with the nature of the barrier between the "two nations" and with the real difference between a lady and a flower girl. The barrier may be largely a technical matter, as Higgins believes; but it is not the real difference, as Shaw points out, in the intermediate test scene, and in the scenes of Eliza's rebellion. Eliza declares that by becoming a lady she has been disqualified from making a living in any way but by selling herself in marriage. Moreover, she credits her transformation not to Higgins and his techniques, but to Colonel Pickering, who treated her like a lady and behaved like a gentleman. But Higgins' defense, that he treats duchess and flower girl alike, that he believes in behaving "as if you were in Heaven, where there are no third-class carriages, and one soul is as good as another" (p. 288), is a radical attack on the very concept of the lady, on the social and economic structure it presupposes, and is the dialectical destination of the play.

For all the passing unconventionalities in his rehandling of the Cinderella-Pygmalion motif, Shaw relies so heavily on its fundamental appeal throughout *Pygmalion* that his refusal to end with a match between Higgins and Eliza was considered mere perversity. Actually Shaw took care to make the ending perfectly ambiguous on the stage, and was provoked into writing the long final note for the reader which now ends the play only by the ingenuity of the actors in finding ways to resolve the ambiguity.[9] The film version and the musical-comedy version succeed in implying the romantic resolution, though Shaw himself wrote the additions to the script of the film and worked closely with the entire production. In a number of ways the original ambiguity is preferable to the alternative resolutions provided for readers and spectators. The point of the ending is not Eliza's marriage, but her casting loose, her achievement of independence. Almost to the very end Higgins always speaks of having made a duchess of a flower girl; but after her assertion of independence and equality he cries "By George, Eliza, I said I'd make a woman of you; and I have" (p. 294). The deliberately unresolved ending tells much about the art of a play whose social and intellectual heterodoxies flourish in a traditional setting of orthodox popular appeal.

MAN AND SUPERMAN AND THE DUEL OF SEX

The duel of sex was not common in nineteenth-century English comedy before Wilde and Shaw. However, in its long decline from its Restoration dominance, it never altogether disappeared; it simply became less witty, less verbal, more at home in farce than in courtship comedy. Where it survives in the nineteenth century with some suggestion of its old

[9] In his account to his wife of the first performance, Shaw was particularly violent over "the raving absurdity of Tree's acting," and full of praise for Mrs. Patrick Campbell. Though he never saw Tree toss flowers at Mrs. Campbell, Shaw's most specific complaint concerned the distortion of the ending. "I had particularly coached him at the last rehearsal in the concluding lines, making him occupy himself affectionately with his mother, & throw Eliza the commission to buy the ham &c, over his shoulder. The last thing I saw as I left the house was Higgins shoving his mother rudely out of his way and wooing Eliza with appeals to buy a ham for his lonely home like a bereaved Romeo" (12 April 1914, *ibid.*).

flavor, there is usually some exceptional circumstance. For example, it survives in Boucicault's *London Assurance* (1841), a play which in many respects of style and theme belongs to the eighteenth century. It survives in H. T. Craven's *Meg's Diversion* (1866), on condition that the duellists are not the destined lovers. It survives in S. Theyre Smith's *My Uncle's Will* (1870), where the stakes are not sexual conquest and marriage, but the gain or loss of an inheritance. It survives finally in the comedies of James Sheridan Knowles, in consequence of their debt to Shakespeare; so that in *The Love Chase* (1837) there is an obvious Beatrice and Benedick couple, Constance and Wildrake, who plague each other endlessly until Trueworth maneuvers a discovery of mutual love and a match. (There is also a sentimental couple, Young Waller and Lydia, a ladies' maid who meets Waller's attempts to seduce her with stiff resistance and honorable love until, hopelessly outgeneralled, he is reduced to marriage, and is assuaged with the discovery that the maid is really a lady.)

Implicit in the sex duel is the woman's desire to have the man on her own terms. In nineteenth-century farcical comedy, this becomes the reversed love chase. Shaw suggests Shakespeare's aggressive heroines as his antecedents for the pursuit in *Man and Superman*; but after *The Wild Goose Chase* the situation is a stock motif, though in the nineteenth century it seems to have dropped out of "serious" comedy. It appears, however, in Gilbert's farces and burlesques, in his race of middle-aged maiden contraltos, and in such heroines as Caroline Effingham in *Tom Cobb* (1875), who, resorting to breach of promise proceedings, kneels at Tom's feet "*kissing his hand as she places the writ in it.*" The reversed love chase appears in more characteristic form in Charles Selby's "Musical Interlude" *The Bonnie Fish Wife* (1858), in which Miss Thistledown disguises herself as Maggie Macfarline, a fishwife, in order to lure and catch Wildoats Heartycheer, the young blade who fled from her as the bride designated by his father. Tom Taylor's "Comedietta" *Nine Points of the Law* (1859) tells how the widow, Mrs. Smylie, uses her wit and artfulness to secure both a cottage whose title is in dispute and a good husband. The widow is far cleverer and more determined than any male character, most of whom patronize and "protect" her, or pretend to. Candida, Ann Whitefield, and, to some extent, Lady Cicely Waynflete are Shaw's women in this line.

Shaw presents straightforward instances of the reversed love chase in *The Philanderer, Man and Superman, Misalliance, The Village Wooing,* and *The Millionairess,* and it is undoubtedly his most common dramatic approach to the relation between the sexes. In *Misalliance* he shows the heroine actually chasing her prey off stage, and then being chased by him back on. In *The Philanderer* and its complement, *You Never Can Tell,* the duel of sex is revived in terms of modern movements and the New Woman. Despite his name, the Philanderer, like Shaw's Don Juan, is more pursued than pursuing, but he uses the new fashions to win the duel and evade capture successfully. Valentine, "the Duellist of sex" in *You Never Can Tell,* also like Shaw's Don Juan, is caught when a force beyond himself, a Life Force in fact, seizes him in the midst of flirtation and sweeps him into marriage.

In *Major Barbara* Shaw uses conventions of the love chase, but transposed to another key. Though the drum-carrying Cusins is "the very unusual *jeune premier* of the play" his pursuit of Barbara gives way for a time to her pursuit of Bill Walker. In a note to the American press on the production of *Major Barbara,* Shaw wrote, "The possibility of using the wooing of a man's soul for his salvation as a substitute for the hackneyed wooing of a handsome young gentleman for the sake of marrying him had occurred to Bernard Shaw many years before. . . ."[10] And though Bill Walker belongs to

---

[10] "To Audiences at *Major Barbara*" (1915-16), in *Shaw on Theatre*, pp. 118, 121.

the line Dickens distilled into Bill Sikes, Shaw insisted on another occasion that he was not to look "like a murderer in a nightmare or melodrama. He should be clean and good looking enough to make the scene in which Barbara breaks down his brutality—which is a sort of very moving love scene—look natural, which it will not do if Bill is disgusting physically and sanitarily."[11] It is this hidden ground of the love chase which should make Barbara's passion over the loss of Bill's soul emotionally convincing to the audience.

In *Man and Superman, A Comedy and a Philosophy*, the reversed love chase is the governing action of the entire play. In keeping with its nineteenth-century farcical associations, the chase is given a most literal physical embodiment in a motorized race across Europe. In the first act, the audience is made elaborately acquainted with the antagonists and with the chase as it proceeds in its covert stages. John Tanner, the descendant of Don Juan Tenorio, even inflicts a mild defeat on Ann, his pursuer, by his persistent unconsciousness in their flirtation. But in the second act, Tanner is enlightened by his less visionary chauffeur and the literal stage of the chase begins. The act builds to a striking close written in the vein of melodramatic farce and, for sensational realistic effect with the latest thing (in 1903), worthy of a Dion Boucicault or an Augustus Harris. An automobile planted before the eyes of the audience through the entire act spectacularly drives off the stage.

Some of the apparent paradoxical novelty in *Man and Superman* arose from Shaw's invocation of the Don Juan legend and his presentation of the arch-pursuer of all time as (in modern dress) the arch-pursued. Actually, Mozart and Da Ponte were beforehand in this respect, and a shrewd observer such as Max Beerbohm was more impressed by the obvious conventionality of *Man and Superman* than by its

[11] Letter to Miss Theresa Helburn, 10 Nov. 1928, in Henderson, *Playboy*, p. 808.

seeming novelty: "Mr. Shaw, using art merely as a means of making people listen to him, naturally lays hands on the kind that appeals most quickly to the greatest number of people. There is something splendid in the contempt with which he uses as the vehicle for [his] thesis a conventional love-chase, with motors and comic brigands thrown in. He is as eager to be a popular dramatist and as willing to demean himself in any way that may help him to the goal, as was (say) the late Mr. Pettitt [one of the leading writers of hack melodrama]."[12]

There is an essential relationship, however, between Shaw's conventional love chase and his thesis, so that he might have argued with Beerbohm that, far from demeaning himself with the love chase, he alone had managed to give it its proper philosophical due. In Shaw's creative-evolutionary philosophy, the love chase became a metaphor for the relation of male and female principles in the universe. In the detachable third act of *Man and Superman*, John Tanner becomes his ancestor Don Juan, the male principle, the projective imagination of the Life Force. Ann Whitefield becomes Doña Ana, the female principle, the generative vital instinct. Both are ruthless in their way, and their appearance in the third act establishes a cosmic theater for the combat and love chase of Tanner and Ann. In the epistle which prefaces the play Shaw offers his rationale for his translation of the sex duel, the love combat between men and women to have each other on their own terms, into the impersonal and universal:

". . . we observe in the man of genius all the unscrupulousness and all the 'self-sacrifice' (the two things are the same) of Woman. He will risk the stake and the cross; starve, when necessary, in a garret all his life; study women and live on their work and care as Darwin studied worms and lived upon sheep; work his nerves into rags without payment, a sublime

---

[12] *Around Theatres* (New York, 1930), I, 345.

altruist in his disregard of himself, an atrocious egotist in his disregard of others. Here Woman meets a purpose as impersonal, as irresistible as her own; and the clash is sometimes tragic." (p. xx)

The results of the clash in *Man and Superman* are conventionally comic rather than tragic. With the help of brigands, Ann's car catches Tanner's in the mountains of the Sierra Nevada, and in Granada she brings him to bay: *"He makes an irresolute movement towards the gate; but some magnetism in her draws him to her, a broken man"* (p. 160). From this point, though the struggle rises to an intense climax, Tanner cooperates in his own defeat. "The Life Force. I am in the grip of the Life Force" (p. 161). When Ann nears exhaustion and loses her courage to go on, Tanner insists on continuing the struggle. When she compromises him by declaring "I have promised to marry Jack," he says aside to his friend and rival Tavy, "I never asked her. It is a trap for me" (p. 164); but he never says so publicly.

In the last encounter Shaw gives a vitalist impersonality to the conflict. Much talk of the Life Force, Tanner's behavior even in embracing Ann as if he were in the grip of an electric current, Ann's behavior as if she were undergoing the pains of birth, all contribute to the sense of extra-personality. The forces involved in the conventional duel of sex are made explicit, and it is made quite plain that there is an ambivalence in the happiness of the conventional comedy ending. Marriage for Tanner, the ineluctably free male spirit and man of creative intellect, is biological subjection, is "apostasy, profanation of the sanctuary of my soul, violation of my manhood, sale of my birthright, shameful surrender, ignominious capitulation, acceptance of defeat" (p. 160). But both sides of the inherent ambivalence of the conventional ending are essential parts of its philosophical usefulness, its functioning as a philosophical metaphor. The lover's defeat is also a victory and an occasion for happiness; and the marriage ending of *Man and Superman* is an emblem of the ultimate identity of the two aspects of the Life Force: its generative vital impulse and its projective intellectual aspiration to knowledge of itself. The genre conventions of the comedy of romance and courtship were generally useful to Shaw as theatrical points of departure and sources of dramatic appeal; but in *Man and Superman* the two chief characters in one of the basic relationships of the genre are raised to symbolic significance, so that the Comedy becomes a parable for a Philosophy.

8

MELODRAMA

W H E N William Terriss, actor-manager of the Adelphi, approached the creator of *Arms and the Man* for "a strong drama" for his theater, Shaw wrote to Ellen Terry: "I seriously think I shall write a play for him. A good melodrama is a more difficult thing to write than all this clever-clever comedy: one must go straight to the core of humanity to get it, and if it is only good enough, why, there you have Lear or Macbeth."[1] In consequence, Shaw wrote *The Devil's Disciple*, though Terriss did not live to play in it, having been melodramatically assassinated in the alley of his own theater.

Shaw had written *Arms and the Man* to embarrass permanently at least one of the chief divisions of melodrama: military romance. But the experience (and relative success) of *Arms and the Man* seems to have suggested to Shaw that melodrama was perhaps better adapted to his style and purposes than most other popular genres. Shaw greatly preferred working with broad strokes and strong coloring; and some months before Terriss made his approach Shaw had written in one of his weekly criticisms, "There is no reason why all the attractive features of the Drury Lane displays should not be retained as integral parts of a genuine drama . . ." (*OTN*, I, 207).[2] Yet the decisive reason for Shaw's turn to melodrama was neither its broad techniques nor its vast popularity, but, of all things, its philosophical possibilities.

In Shaw's time, a melodrama was essentially a play whose action embraced matters of life and death, where the focus was not on suffering (as in tragedy or "drama") but on peril.

[1] 26 March 1896, *Ellen Terry and Bernard Shaw*, p. 21.
[2] Under the management of Augustus Harris, Drury Lane was as closely identified with spectacular Melodrama as the Adelphi.

Such a description could apply almost as it stands to the allegory of John Bunyan, whom Shaw greatly loved and declared a great dramatist, "far too great a dramatist for our theatre" (*OTN*, III, 1). Shaw observed allegorical qualities in melodrama that made it all the more suitable for stories presenting the Bunyanesque perils, conversions, instructive adventures, and pilgrim's progresses of the soul. When Shaw set out to define a good melodrama, he wrote:

"It should be a simple and sincere drama of action and feeling, kept well within that vast tract of passion and motive which is common to the philosopher and the laborer, relieved by plenty of fun, and depending for variety of human character, not on the high comedy idiosyncrasies which individualize people in spite of the closest similarity of age, sex, and circumstances, but on broad contrasts between types of youth and age, sympathy and selfishness, the masculine and the feminine, the serious and the frivolous, the sublime and the ridiculous, and so on. The whole character of the piece must be allegorical, idealistic, full of generalizations and moral lessons; and it must represent conduct as producing swiftly and certainly on the individual the results which in actual life it only produces on the race in the course of many centuries." (*OTN*, I, 93)[3]

[3] Shaw's last requirement is an obvious translation into creative-evolutionary terms of the idea that the workings of Melodrama should reproduce the workings of an exacting Providence. A remarkable expression of the morality aspect of Melodrama was *Seven Sins; or, Passion's Paradise* (1874) by George Conquest and Paul Merritt, two of the notable creators of "minor-theater" Melodrama. The characters are listed as Inspector Peacock Sleuth (Pride), Captain Tempest (Rage), Nero Morath (Cruelty), Boozey (Intemperance), Lounge (Idleness), Clinch (Avarice), Hemlock (Envy)—though there are suggestions of the unmentionable Luxuria about the last. The heroine is named Faith Morath and she suffers many trials, including seven years in prison for a murder her father committed. In the end she is both vindicated and saved from Cruelty, who sets the house afire and attempts her murder. There is a revealing coincidence of humour and line: Rage is the hot-tempered but virtuous hero; Cruelty is the villainous heavy; Intemperance is the low-comic drunkard;

In writing *Arms and the Man*, Shaw found that melodrama was not simply a form to be ridiculed, but one to be converted and saved. *The Devil's Disciple, Captain Brassbound's Conversion*, and *The Shewing-Up of Blanco Posnet* are the results of this discovery. By examining the four plays in chronological order, in relation to particular conventions and types of melodrama, we can follow Shaw's discovery of the possibilities of the genre in *Arms and the Man*, his exploitation of these possibilities in *The Devil's Disciple* and *Captain Brassbound's Conversion*, and, perhaps, his exhaustion of the possibilities for his own talent and interests in *The Shewing-Up of Blanco Posnet*.

THE BRAVE AND THE FAIR

Arms and the Man was subtitled "A Romantic Comedy" on its first program, and "An Anti-Romantic Comedy" in subsequent publications, evidently because original audiences had tended to enjoy the fun and miss the serious concerns. The play was particularly concerned with love and heroism. It was a comedy whose point of departure was not Romantic Comedy, but Romantic Drama, and particularly Military Melodrama.[4]

The conventions of heroism in melodrama (Shaw inveighed against their catastrophic potential twenty years before the World War) presented an idyllic picture of war in which all wounds were chest-high and the brave acquired the fair. *The Daughter of the Regiment*, as an opera by Donizetti and as an operatic drama by Edward Fitzball (1843), was quintessential military romance in its fusion of love and

---

Idleness is the languid stage swell; Avarice is the miserly Old Man; and Envy, with lust implicit, is the wicked heavy female.

[4] Military Melodrama as such was often provided with an exotic setting, and several specimens considered below in connection with *Captain Brassbound*, such as J. T. Haines's *The French Spy*, and Boucicault's *Relief of Lucknow*, are examples of the military type. Both of these present Shaw's particular point of assault in *Arms*: the connection between romantic love and romantic heroism.

heroism. In Fitzball's version, Madelaine has been found, a baby, on the battlefield of Marengo and adopted by the gallant and sentimental Twenty-first Hussars. She falls in love with a young Tyrolean, Andreas, who joins the regiment as a private to win her hand; but her noble birth is discovered and she is taken in charge by a Marchioness. In the second act, a marriage for Madelaine is being prepared with a strange captain. Andreas returns as a private in the regiment, and Madelaine declares her willingness to run off with him. Andreas reappears as the captain, and all is explained:

> Yes, dearest Madelaine, driven to despair at your loss, I rushed into the thickest of the fight—was distinguished by the Emperor, and rapidly promoted. Wishing to know whether you had forgotten me, I came hither, disguised like one of my brave comrades, whose troop I have just rejoined. You loved me for myself alone—and now, as the captain of your old regiment, I place at once my laurels and my heart at your disposal. (*Baker*, p. 24)

The soldier made brave by a lover's joy or a lover's despair was the typical hero of military romance. W. S. Gilbert burlesques him in Caroline Effingham's picture of her unknown lover in *Tom Cobb* (1875): "He was a poet-soldier, fighting the Paynim foe in India's burning clime—a glorious songster, who swept the lute with one hand, while he sabred the foe with the other!" Raina, who, like the audience of *Arms and the Man*, is to be re-educated, has doubts of the reality of such an ideal; but Sergius magnificently plays up to it, with the help of an error in supply. "Cant you see it, Raina," cries Catherine, her mother: "our gallant splendid Bulgarians with their swords and eyes flashing, thundering down like an avalanche and scattering the wretched Serbs and their dandified Austrian officers like chaff. And you! you kept Sergius waiting a year before you would be betrothed to him. Oh, if you have a drop of Bulgarian blood in your veins, you will worship him when he comes back" (pp. 4-5). "Oh, to think that it was all true!" cries Raina: "that Sergius is just as splendid and noble as he looks! that the world is really a glorious world for women who can see its glory and men who can act its romance! What happiness! what unspeakable fulfilment!" (p. 5).

Popular Melodrama presented a picture of war as gloriously ennobling. In Tom Taylor and Charles Reade's *Two Loves and a Life* (1854), Sir Gervase Rokewood, a Jacobite rebel, paints such a picture of battle to instruct a nominal man of peace:

> You are a priest, father, and a priest has never a soldier's heart. O, if you knew what it is to stand out in the sunlight, and stake all upon the sword, as our Scottish brethren are doing! The ranks move towards each other like two thunder clouds. Every cheek pale, every brow bent, every eye bright. The next moment the trumpets peal along the line, and amidst smoke and dust, and the great music of drum and cannon, man and horse and steel clash together in the grapple for death or glory. (*Spencer*, p. 26)

This is not far different from the charge envisioned by Catherine and Raina. Bluntschli's contrasting picture is the cavalry charge, "like slinging a handful of peas against a window pane: first one comes; then two or three close behind him; then all the rest in a lump." The leader reins madly, because his horse is running away; the young soldiers are wild and slashing; the old ones come huddled up to present the smallest possible target.

In T. W. Robertson's *Ours* (1866), the Crimean War forms the background of Act III, and the ladies of the piece have come adventuring to the battlefield by yacht.[5] The conven-

[5] In Robertson's *Principal Dramatic Works*, II. "Ours" is a term of affectionate reference to a regimental organization.

tions of military melodrama are present but, as is usual with Robertson, played down with whimsical comedy. Nevertheless, Angus, the romantic lead, captures the Russian colors, and the effect of war is to invigorate the melancholic, bored, and idle, to precipitate romances, and to rouse latent nobility. "Battle elevates as well as brutalises us" (p. 485). No one is killed; ". . . they never do get killed in 'Ours' " (p. 481). There are several glamorous though lightly treated wounds. These are offered as "the realities . . . the horrors of war" (p. 472).

Ours is a Comedy. In his drama *War* (1871), Robertson is more actively concerned to achieve battlefield realism. A note in the printed text suggests, by contrary admonition, the usual splendid mounting of Military Melodrama: "Anything like uniform or accoutrement seen in this Act must be stained, dusty, muddy, and exhibit the signs of severe use. Nothing sparkling, tinselly, or patent-leathered" (p. 766). The play makes some pretensions to thought, and two viewpoints are presented: the suffering of war (through Lotte and her father, a peace-loving German professor); and the glory and nobility of war (through Oscar and his father, a chauvinistic French colonel). The Shavian view, the non-heroism of war, drops between.

In *Arms and the Man*, Shaw makes a catalogue of non-heroism: the professional soldier carries chocolate instead of cartridges; having been under fire for three days, his nerves are shattered and he will weep like a child if he is scolded; his friend is ingloriously burned to death in a woodyard; the battle was lost through a mistake, and won through an absurdity; the war is full of paperwork and prosaic routine.

But though Shaw methodically rebutted some of the conventions of Military Romance in *Arms and the Man*, he uses others with straightforward effect. For example, he continues the custom of exploiting the special appeal of a recent real war. The Indian Mutiny (1857) inspired Boucicault's *Jessie Brown; or, The Relief of Lucknow* (1858). The Crimean War

(1853-1856) had a long currency, and was still providing useful background at the Grecian Theatre in 1876 in Pettitt and Conquest's *Neck or Nothing*. Gordon's campaign in the Sudan and the belated relief of Khartoum (1884-1885) was instantly immortalized with a cheerful outcome in Pettitt and Harris's *Human Nature* (1885). The audience, wrote a contemporary critic,

". . . follow with interest the career of Captain Temple in the Soudan campaign, watch him at the head of his men storming the gates of Khartoum, applaud him when he is merciful to the man who has done him the deepest injury, and naturally welcome him to Charing-cross at the head of his men, the fever of battle over, and the victory supposed to have been won. It is easy to see what the dramatists intended here, but fate was against them. They worked on the full understanding that Gordon would be rescued, and that the object of the campaign would be accomplished. What a theme for a dramatist to work upon! What a brilliant stage picture that rescue would have been! But as events turned out otherwise . . . heroic Gordon or his counterpart dropped out of the story, but still the germ of the original idea was faithfully retained."[6]

Shaw gives a cool notice to *Human Nature*, already a solid success, in one of his earliest review articles on the drama. He mentions "A fiendish Frenchman, whom the audience insisted upon identifying with the late M. Olivier Pain," and other accepted correspondences between the dramatic events in the Sudan and those at Drury Lane.[7]

As for *Arms and the Man*, Shaw admitted that "The first version of the play had no geography—nothing but a war with a machine gun in it. It was Sidney Webb who suggested

[6] *Illustrated London News*, 87 (19 Sept. 1885), p. 291. The same issue reports and illustrates the return of the Guards from the Sudan (pp. 295-96).

[7] "Art Corner" in *Our Corner*, VI (Nov. 1885), p. 314.

the Servo-Bulgarian war. However, I adapted it to the historical & social facts of the time very carefully."[8] To the critics, nevertheless, the use of a "real" war, in *Arms* as in straightforward Melodrama, was a Crummles effect for creating interest. Archer, who was particularly struck by the Opera Bouffe qualities of the play, pointed out with amusement that "Instead of presenting an episode in the great war between the realms of Grünewald and Gerolstein, or in the historic conflict between Paphlagonia and Crim Tartary, he places his scene in the (more or less) real principality of Bulgaria, dates his action to the year and day (6th March 1886), and has been at immense pains to work-in Bulgarian local colour in the dialogue, and to procure correct Bulgarian costumes and genuine Balkan scenery."[9] Archer found Shaw's local "realism" paradoxical; but it was no more than a standard practice of military romance.

No less conventional was the motif of love overcoming the antipathies of war. Shaw particularly appreciated among later Melodramas William Gillette's *Held by the Enemy; An American Drama* (London: 1887). Like much Civil War Melodrama, the play presents the distresses of love and honor between enemies. It begins with an occupation situation—a Northern garrison in a Southern town. Colonel Prescott and Rachel McCreery are in love, but she is betrothed to a gallant Southern cousin who appears inopportunely, fleeing from capture as a spy. Capture, trial, and prolonged struggle over the body of the spy interfere with the romance until the prisoner is finally put out of the way. But in the end, love triumphs over picket-lines. The war also ends, and the union of Rachel and Prescott is held up as an emblem for the country at large.

In reviewing the origins of *The Chocolate Soldier*, Shaw recalled that when he was confronted with the libretto of the

[8] MS letter to Siegfried Trebitsch, 16 Jan. 1905.
[9] Review of 25 April 1894 in William Archer, *The Theatrical 'World' of 1894* (London, 1895), p. 111.

opera, he replied to the author that "if none of my dialogue was used I did not think I could appeal to the courts successfully to stop the performance, because (a) parodies and travesties of standard serious works are privileged by custom, (b) I had clearly no rights in the Servo-Bulgarian war as a dramatic subject, and (c) the incident of a fugitive soldier taking refuge in a lady's bedroom was too common to be patented by me or anyone else."[10]

The incident of the fugitive soldier had appeared previously (for example) in Thomas Morton's "Serio-Comic Drama" of the French revolution, *The Angel of the Attic* (1843). The fugitive in Morton's play finds himself in a triangle very like that in *Arms and the Man*. A young nobleman who has been pursuing Mariette, a milliner, comes to her room wounded and in flight from the revolutionary soldiers. Like the women in *Arms and the Man*, Mariette protects her helpless enemy. She hides him in her bedroom while Michael, her revolutionary fiancé, visits her after the day's fighting. (Quite the same situation occurs in the "Prologue" of Sardou and Moreau's *Madame Sans-Gêne* [Paris: 1893]; see below, p. 356).

In *Arms and the Man* it is simply a strange soldiery who threaten the fugitive in Raina's bedroom; her Bulgarian lover's part in the tensions of concealment and discovery belongs to a later act. In both *The Angel* and *Arms*, however, a good deal of suspense and mildly risqué farcical activity center on the bedroom situation and the threat of discovery, and the combination of Melodrama and Comedy, neither Burlesque nor pure Farce, strengthens the dramatic resemblance.

The incident of the fugitive soldier in a lady's bedroom appears again, with resemblances to *Arms and the Man*, in Tom Taylor's historical melodrama, *Lady Clancarty; or, Wedded and Wooed. A Tale of the Assassination Plot, 1696* (1874). Lord and Lady Clancarty have been married as chil-

[10] Letter to Golding Bright, 17 Oct. 1925, *Advice to a Young Critic*, p. 204.

dren, and have not seen each other since. Act Three presents
Lady Clancarty's bedchamber. She hears that the conspirators
against the King are being hunted through the streets that
night, and that her stranger-husband is among them.

> BETTY . . . (*a shot without*) Hark! What's that?
>
> LADY C. (*Starting up*) A shot! (*another*) Another!
> Oh, mercy! Those arrests! . . . Look out! Look
> out!
>
> BETTY. (*opening window*) The snow blinds me.
> I can see nothing; but all seems quiet again. Ha!
> she is fainting! (*Runs down, leaving window open,
> and busies herself with* LADY CLANCARTY)
>
> LADY C. Nay, 'tis nothing; but a sudden and sick-
> ening fear. (LADY BETTY *goes back to shut the
> window*)
>
> BETTY. I'll close the window.
>
> LADY C. Leave it; the fresh air revives me.
>
> (*French S. D.*, p. 46)

Both here and in *Arms*, the dramatist wishes to call attention to the window, and to excuse its penetrability. In *Arms*,
Louka, the servant, enters the bedroom with news of possible
shooting in the streets. Raina asks her to leave the shutters
open, but Catherine, her mother, forbids it; Louka then
secretly informs Raina that the bolt is gone, and the shutters
will open at a push. Left alone, Raina hears shots in the street,
and hurries into bed. There is a fusillade, the shutters open,
and a strange man in silhouette comes silently through the
window. *Clancarty* presents a similar culmination, though it
sacrifices sinister effect for a clap-trap entrance:

> LADY C. . . . (*a noise at the window*) What's that?
>
> BETTY. But the tapping of a branch against the
> balcony. No! (*with cry of alarm*) See—a man in
> the branches! He climbs the balustrade!

—·[193]·—

And a fugitive (Clancarty) enters spectacularly through the window.

Though Shaw exploits the drama of the incident at least as wholeheartedly as Tom Taylor, he is not content to leave it at that. Before the play closes he has Bluntschli confess to an incurably romantic disposition, and gives as an example, "I climbed the balcony of this house when a man of sense would have dived into the nearest cellar" (p. 68). Similarly, he might have pointed out that, though Raina falls out with her dashing lover and makes her alliance with the nominally prosaic Bluntschli, the relationship of the fugitive to his savior is intrinsically far more romantic than that of the formal fiancé to his formally betrothed.

How is the conventionality of action and setting in *Arms and the Man* to be explained? Shaw ostensibly wrote *Arms and the Man* to explode the conventions of military romance and replace them with a much more common-sensical view of war and women. But he did not simply paint a stark and grim contrasting picture of war. His method was to confront the conventional attitudes and actions with this common-sense point of view, and to make his drama out of their conflict. In the process, we get an exterior action filled with the conventions of Military Romance and an interior action presenting the disillusionment and conversion of the heroine of that romance to the exalted common sense embodied by Bluntschli. The artistic success with which Bluntschli, Sergius, and Nicola embody philosophical points of view and the success, despite misunderstanding, with which the play embodies a drama of spiritual discovery undoubtedly inclined Shaw toward his further experiments in Melodrama.

REBELS AND REDCOATS

When Max Beerbohm passed judgment on *The Devil's Disciple* for *The Saturday Review*, he took the line of friendly bewilderment:

"What scorn would Mr. Shaw have not poured down these columns on such a play? How he would have riddled the hero, the sympathetic scapegrace (called, of course, 'Dick') who, for all his wickedness, cannot bear to see a woman cry, and keeps a warm corner in his heart for the old horse Jim and the old servant Roger, and wishes to be hanged by the English in the place of another man, and tries to throttle the major for calling a lady a woman! What scathing analysis Mr. Shaw would have made of this fellow's character, declaring that he, 'G.B.S.,' refused to see anything noble in a man who, having lived the life of a wastrel and a blackguard, proposed to commit suicide by imposing on the credulity of a court-martial!"[11]

Though Beerbohm also reported that the end of the play "suddenly tumbled into wild frivolity," Shaw intended no such last-minute apology. When he had just written the play he reported to Ellen Terry that "this thing, with its heroic sacrifice, its impossible courtmartial, its execution . . . its sobbings and speeches and declamations, may possibly be the most monstrous piece of farcical absurdity that ever made an audience shriek with laughter. And yet I have honestly tried for dramatic effect."[12] In another spirit (incensed at the actor Richard Mansfield for preferring *The Devil's Disciple* to *Caesar*) Shaw declared that "The D's D is a melodrama, made up of all the stage Adelphi tricks—the reading of the will, the heroic sacrifice, the court martial, the execution, the reprieve at the last moment. Anybody could make a play that way."[13]

It is clear that *The Devil's Disciple* was meant to be taken wholeheartedly for what its subtitle proclaims it: "A Melodrama." The audience would feel on familiar ground when

[11] *Around Theatres* (New York, 1930), I, 51.
[12] 30 Nov. 1896, *Ellen Terry and Bernard Shaw*, p. 97.
[13] Letter to Mrs. Mansfield, 3 May 1899, in Henderson, *Man of the Century*, p. 473.

the attractive scapegrace appeared, chaffed his brother, the Comic Countryman, probed the hidden vices of the meanly respectable, and flushed with instinctive anger at the neglect of an orphan child. Yet, even in the first act, there were grounds for uneasiness in Dick's unfeeling treatment of his mother (a tender regard for a usually distant mother normally helped redeem a disreputable hero). The audience would find familiar dramatic values through the rest of the play: the hero was full of rousing dash; Judith Anderson, the heroine, was pretty and distressed; the situations were thrilling and suspenseful. Yet, the hero is subject to the same criticism that Lady Britomart levels at that other Devil's Disciple, Andrew Undershaft: he always does the right thing for the wrong reasons. Dick Dudgeon puts his head in a noose for his own sake, he claims, not for the sake of Judith or her husband. He flatly denies that he loves Judith or that he is moved by a spirit of heroic sacrifice.

Shaw never undercuts Dick's familiar predicaments; but the melodramatic crises are converted into crises in spiritual history. In the course of the play Richard finds his true vocation as a martyr-saint in the cause of humanity, while Anderson, the priest, finds his as a warrior. Other personages become allegorical challenges to the progress of the hero. Shaw wrote to Ellen Terry soon after completing the play: "Burgoyne is a gentleman; and that is the whole meaning of that part of the play. It is not enough, for the instruction of this generation, that Richard should be superior to religion and morality as typified by his mother and his home, or to love as typified by Judith. He must also be superior to gentility: that is, to the whole ideal of modern society."[14] General Burgoyne is meant to appear to Dick's puritan spirit as Mr. Worldly Wise-man. The vigorous situations of the physical drama are meant to body forth the edifying situations of a spiritual contest.

[14] 13 March 1897, *Ellen Terry and Bernard Shaw*, p. 124.

For a contemporary theater-going audience, *The Devil's Disciple* would call up a number of specific associations. For example, melodramatists had long been accustomed to use a patriotic rebellion to justify a hero in wholehearted opposition to the symbols of orthodox authority. They did not favor the American revolution, perhaps because the rebellion was successful and the authority English, but nineteenth-century Ireland was a favorite setting for the perils of a fugitive from red-coated martial law.[15]

The best of the Irish Melodramas using a rebel and garrison situation is Boucicault's *Arrah-na-Pogue* (1864). Its close resemblance to *The Devil's Disciple* in a number of specific details simply emphasizes Shaw's transfer of the Irish sub-genre as a whole to America. Like Dick Dudgeon, Shaun the Post (Boucicault's own part, the "Irish Character Lead") makes a false confession to the authorities and is imprisoned in place of a hunted rebel, Beamish McCoul (the dashing Romantic Lead). As in *The Devil's Disciple*, there is a question of a heroic sacrifice for love. Shaun confesses for the sake of his own just-wed bride, who he thinks has bestowed her love elsewhere, to save her from prison and the scandal of unchastity. His trial is a court-martial, similar to Dick Dudgeon's in conduct and appearance.[16] In both *Arrah-na-*

[15] Examples are Samuel Lover's *Rory O'More* (1837), Edmund Falconer's *Peep o' Day* (1861), and Dion Boucicault's *Arrah-na-Pogue* (1864), *The Shaughraun* (1875), and *The Rapparee* (1870). See below, "Irish Romance." Not all plays presenting fugitive heroes at odds with military authority had Ireland for a background. Tom Taylor and Charles Reade's *Two Loves and a Life* (1854) is set in the Jacobite rebellion of 1745, and Tom Taylor's *A Sheep in Wolf's Clothing* (1857) uses Monmouth's Rebellion. The latter play is similar to *The Devil's Disciple* in that it presents a rebel hiding from a Redcoat garrison with a pretense to be kept up on the part of the fugitive's wife. Anne Carew allows herself to be wooed by Colonel Percy Kirke in order to save her husband who is given out as dead. When her husband is discovered hiding in the house, rescue comes in the person of Lord Churchill, an embryonic Burgoyne, cool and gentlemanly, who softens the reign of terror.

[16] See Allardyce Nicoll, *A History of English Drama 1660-1900* (Cambridge, 1959), V, 90-91.

Pogue and *The Devil's Disciple* the discourse is chiefly between the innocent accused and two officers, one gentlemanly and sympathetic, the other pompous and military-minded. Shaun's peasant wit in his responses is surprisingly close in language and idea to Dick's *diablerie*.

The association, in situation, character, and action, between Shaw's rebel-and-redcoat play and revolutionary Irish Melodrama gave the deceptive comfort of a familiar setting to Dick Dudgeon's rebellious heterodoxies. But these were not the heterodoxies of the conventional gallant, if misguided, patriot-hero. The Devil's Disciple is a rebel, not against armies, rulers, or parties, but against ideas: against religion and morality, romantic love, and "the whole ideal of modern society."

The most recognizable situation in *The Devil's Disciple* presents Sydney Carton's heroic sacrifice for love from *A Tale of Two Cities*. The novel was notably dramatized by Tom Taylor in 1860 (with the help of Dickens himself) and by numerous lesser playwrights in the course of the century.[17] Tom Taylor's Sydney Carton is a Devil's Disciple with a puritan conscience, an impulse toward sacrificial martyrdom, and a sentimental fixation on another man's wife. On his first entrance, Carton announces himself:

> I'm an incurable idler. . . . For your offer of attentions—I don't think our tastes would suit. I'm fond of low company, late hours, loose haunts, and strong wine.
>
> DARN[AY]. Hardly the tastes I fear, to make life either very pleasant or very profitable!

[17] See S. J. Adair Fitz-Gerald, *Dickens and the Drama* (London, 1910), pp. 269-85. Fitz-Gerald mentions eight different dramatic versions of the novel. He also treats the similarity of *A Tale* to Watts Phillips' play *The Dead Heart* (1859); Dumas *père*'s play *Le Chevalier de la Maison Rouge* (1847), adapted as *Genevieve; or, The Reign of Terror* by Dion Boucicault (1853); and Bulwer-Lytton's romance *Zanoni*. All four works culminate in a similar self-sacrificing substitution during the reign of terror.

CART[ON]. What the devil do you know about it?
(*French A. E.*, pp. 16-17)

But Carton cancels out this fine assertion of diabolical allegiance, for unlike Dick Dudgeon, he is altogether ashamed of himself and his way of life.

As in *The Devil's Disciple*, a high point in Tom Taylor's play is a trial scene, in which Darnay is condemned. Motivated entirely by love for Lucie Manette and by a sense of his own worthlessness, Carton drugs Darnay and takes his place. The trading of coats is a most important piece of business in the play, as it is in *The Devil's Disciple*. The last scenes also show some correspondences, the one play presenting Carton in a tumbril, the other Dudgeon on a cart with a rope on his neck. The plays are thus similar not only in their central action but even in their scenes and devices.

There is a telling resemblance between the rather famous poster for the Rev. Freeman Wills's later adaptation of Dickens' novel, *The Only Way* (1899), showing Martin Harvey as Sydney Carton at the guillotine and photographs of the last scene in the first London production of *The Devil's Disciple* (1907), directed by Shaw himself (see Figures 11, 12). An earlier version of Wills's final tableau may be found in Watts Phillips' *The Dead Heart* (1859), revived by Irving and knowledgeably mentioned by Shaw.[18] Robert Landry (the "Dead Heart,") was buried in the Bastille in the course of a romantic rivalry, and became a revolutionary power after his liberation. In the end he substitutes himself on the scaffold for the aristocratic son of the woman he has always loved:

TABLEAU.—Back of stage opens and discovers a view of the guillotine, guarded by GENDARMES and SECTION-AIRES, surrounded by MOB. The tall old houses of quaint architecture are just touched by the light of early morning, which covers with a crimson glow

[18] *How to Become a Musical Critic*, p. 180.

the tower of Notre Dame. In the extreme background, upon scaffold, stands ROBERT LANDRY, prepared for the fatal axe. He extends his arms in direction of COUNTESS, as curtain slowly falls. (*French
A.E.*, p. 58)

In reproducing this much-used scene, as in echoing the
trial scene, the changing of coats, and the hero's diabolic
pose, Shaw exploits the familiarity of the sacrifice for love
in its standard theatrical embodiment. Shaw has Judith conceive of Dick Dudgeon's action in Sydney Carton terms in
order to make his own point all the more vigorously: Dick
Dudgeon is superior to the romantic love and the romantic
self-hatred which provoke Sydney Carton and Robert Landry
to the sacrifice.

In an undated letter to Hesketh Pearson, Shaw wrote of
The Devil's Disciple, "The play was written round the scene
of Dick's arrest, which has always been floating in my head
as a situation for a play."[19] Scenes of arrest were frequently
and naturally conjoined with a heroic substitution in both
Melodrama and Melodramatic Farce, and some of these
scenes are remarkably suggestive of *The Devil's Disciple* in
making the presence of the wife or fiancée of the fugitive an
essential part of the action. For example, in J. R. Planché's
A Peculiar Position (1837—an adaptation of the *comédie
vaudeville, La Frontière de Savoie* by Scribe and Bayard)—
the Countess de Novara shuffles the passport of her fugitive
husband with that of Champignon, a greengrocer, and then
persuades Champignon to play the Count while her husband
gets away. Champignon is arrested as the Count, and he puts
on the Count's morning-gown to confirm his false identity.
Similarly, Dick Dudgeon is arrested as the minister (because
he is found in apparently intimate circumstances, at tea in

[19] Hesketh Pearson, *Bernard Shaw*, p. 200. See also Henderson, *Table-
Talk of G. B. S.* (London, 1925), p. 75.

his shirtsleeves, with the minister's wife in the minister's house), and he puts on the minister's characteristic coat to confirm his mistaken identity. Later, to lull the suspicions of the arresting sergeant, Dudgeon and Judith are obliged to show affection for each other. The same "peculiar position" provides most of the comedy in Planché's play.[20]

Conventionally, the man replaced on the scaffold contested the sacrifice, unless carefully reduced to impotence or unconsciousness by the skillful playwright. In *Arrah-na-Pogue*, Beamish McCoul gives himself up immediately, as soon as he hears of Shaun's arrest in his place. The conventional action similarly occurs in T. W. Robertson's adaptation from Scribe and Legouvé, *The Ladies' Battle* (1851), where an amorous countess conceals a reputed Bonapartist leader in post-Empire France among her servants, and induces a hopelessly devoted lover to put on her livery and draw the searching police off the track. The plot succeeds and the real fugitive escapes; but when he learns that his substitute is to be summarily shot in his place, he returns to give himself up.

In *The Devil's Disciple*, when Judith finally tells her clerical husband that Dick Dudgeon has been arrested in his place, she fully expects him to hurry to English headquarters, and Dick himself had some apprehensions that this would be the minister's honorable action. Expecting and dreading the heroic gesture, Judith is sorely disillusioned when the clergyman jumps into his boots and rides away. Here Shaw is deliberately invoking a convention (articulated through Judith,

---

[20] More farcical versions of the arrest scene, utilizing some of the same elements, occur in J. M. Morton's *Your Life's in Danger* (1848), and in his *Steeple-Chase; or, In the Pigskin* (1865). The latter was a favorite play with J. L. Toole, who himself was a favorite in Dublin. Toole played Mr. Tittums, a hapless victim of error, and at one point, when a sheriff's officer is carrying him off to jail as another man, that other man's wife throws herself upon him to confirm the error and keep her husband safe. For another view of Shaw's use of *A Peculiar Position* and *The Ladies' Battle* (discussed below), see Stephen S. Stanton's introduction to *Camille and Other Plays*, New York, 1957, p. xxxviii.

who has all the audience's expectations); but his purpose is not merely to ridicule or, like Gilbert in *The Mikado* with his "Lord High Substitute," to burlesque this convention. The action at this point of *The Devil's Disciple* dramatizes Anderson's discovery of his true vocation. Surrender and self-sacrifice should come naturally to a Christian minister; instead, he finds his way in resistance and violence.

The last act of *The Devil's Disciple* is divided into three increasingly public scenes: the confrontation of Richard and Judith, where she offers her love and he rebuffs her; the court-martial; and the execution and delivery. Far from wishing the play to tumble into wild frivolity in the last act, Shaw was anxious to guard against it. He wrote Siegfried Trebitsch to instruct an Austrian Judith that she must weep at the end of the first scene "in a really heartrending way; and all through the court martial she must not let the audience lose the sense of the horror with which she listens to the deadly jesting of Burgoyne & Richard. All the rest is easy."[21] He was particularly concerned that productions exploit the proper melodramatic qualities of the scene of execution. He wrote Trebitsch that it was "very important to get the last scene well stage managed, with a big surging crowd."[22] And he complained to Mrs. Mansfield, who played Judith to her husband's Richard in New York:

"I quite understand that the last scene is so arranged that nobody watches Judith, and that the spectacle of Richard Dudgeon making Sidney Carton faces keeps the theatre palpitatingly indifferent to everything else. And that's just what I object to: it's all wrong: the audience ought to see everything—the frightful flying away of the minutes in conflict with the equally frightful deliberation of Burgoyne and the

[21] MS postcard, 17 Feb. 1903.
[22] MS postcard to Siegfried Trebitsch, 9 Aug. 1902. The last scene of *The Devil's Disciple* is as thoroughgoing a crowd-sensation scene as Shaw ever wrote.

soldierlike smartness of the executioner: they ought to long for a delay instead of that silly eagerness to see whether the hanging will really come off or not and so on."[23]

The justice of Melodrama is providential; and therefore the greater the peril, and the more ingenious the circumstances of virtue's escape and vice's unmasking the greater the audience delight. When Sweet William, the simple, handsome, true-blue, universally loved and Billy Budd-like sailor in Douglas Jerrold's *Black-Ey'd Susan* (1829) is about to be hanged from the yard-arm for striking his captain, his situation seems altogether hopeless. The villain Doggrass has just been drowned fortuitously, with the paper which could save William's life fast in his pocket. Suspense grows as the execution approaches and the action plays up the pathos and hopelessness. Then, the hand of Providence shows itself: ever so naturally, but unexpectedly because the audience was too preoccupied to think ahead to the ritual of execution, William is saved. The ritual cannon sounds, and, conforming to popular lore, the body of Doggrass rises to the surface with pockets intact.

Even when the audience had become more sophisticated (and less talented authors could not contrive so ingenious a rescue), Shaw felt it was the writer's obligation in Melodrama to cultivate the sense of wonder and peril. Reviewing *The Girl I Left Behind Me* by Franklin Fyles and David Belasco (1895), Shaw points out:

"The third act . . . is an adaptation of [Boucicault's] the Relief of Lucknow, which, as a dramatic situation, is so strong and familiar that it is hardly possible to spoil it, though the authors have done their best. The main difficulty is the foreknowledge of the hopelessly sophisticated audience that Mr Terriss will rush in at the last moment, sword in hand, and rescue everybody. The authors' business was to carry us on

[23] Letter of 1 Jan. 1898, in Henderson, *Man of the Century*, p. 450.

from incident to incident so convincingly and interestingly as to preoccupy us with the illusion of the situation sufficiently to put Mr Terriss out of our heads." (*OTN*, I, 96)

To put Anderson and the Springtown messenger sufficiently out of our heads, Shaw arranges the last scene's marching and music, Judith's suffering, Dick's recapitulated rejection of religion, gentlemanliness, and love, and the final scare to the audience when it hears that the time for redemption has elapsed:

> BURGOYNE. Have you anything more to say, Mr Dudgeon? It wants two minutes of twelve still.
>
> RICHARD (*in the strong voice of a man who has conquered the bitterness of death*) Your watch is two minutes slow by the town clock, which I can see from here, General. (*The town clock strikes the first stroke of twelve. Involuntarily the people flinch at the sound, and a subdued groan breaks from them.*) (p. 72)

Earlier, information has been planted that the town clock is always fast; and later, Burgoyne declares that he should never dream of hanging a gentleman by an American clock. But meanwhile, the audience has been given a turn.

The final catastrophe is averted, as it is so often in Melodrama, by Providence in the form of a legal technicality. As Sweet William escapes hanging because he was technically out of the Navy when he struck his captain, so both Dick and Anderson escape hanging because Dick was to be hanged only if Anderson failed to present himself by twelve noon, and Anderson came armed with Burgoyne's own safe-conduct. Moreover, the clock was fast.

The straightforward Melodrama of *The Devil's Disciple*, for which Shaw was so concerned in his letters and in his dramaturgy, is more than just an attractive container for the inner drama of ideas. Rather, in the economy of the play, the same familiar devices which serve the dramatic action serve the dramatic idea. Thus, the changing of coats, besides justifying Dick's arrest in the action, functions as an extended dramatic symbol of conversion. Initially there is simply an elaborate and exciting business with ironic overtones as the Devil's Disciple puts on the minister's coat under the eye of the sergeant. Then, when the Reverend Anthony Anderson learns what has happened, and *"the man of peace vanishes, transfigured into a choleric and formidable man of war"* (p. 45), he buckles a pistol belt over Dudgeon's coat, and significantly declares: "If they took him for me in my coat, perhaps theyll take me for him in his" (p. 46). Later, having rescued Richard with the cooperation of the British War Office, he tells Burgoyne:

> Sir: it is in the hour of trial that a man finds his true profession. This foolish young man . . . boasted himself the Devil's Disciple; but when the hour of trial came to him, he found that it was his destiny to suffer and be faithful to the death. I thought myself a decent minister of the gospel of peace; but when the hour of trial came to me, I found that it was my destiny to be a man of action, and that my place was amid the thunder of the captains and the shouting. . . . Your mother told me, Richard, that I should never have chosen Judith if I'd been born for the ministry. I am afraid she was right; so, by your leave, you may keep my coat and I'll keep yours.
>
> (pp. 73-74)

The exchange of coats is a visual metaphor for the twofold discovery and conversion which has taken place, for the accomplishment of a pair of spiritual destinies. In making this the true inner action of the play, Shaw has not departed a hairsbreadth from the understood ethos of Melodrama. In his

"Art of Dramatic Composition," Dion Boucicault, perhaps the most accomplished melodramatist of the century, explained the providential wonders, technicalities, and coincidences of his art as follows:

"Life is profluent; all human actions are directed to some desired object, and Providence produces what, as they happen, we call accidents, but when past we perceive to be necessary results. And this should be the process of the fictitious providence of which a spectator is the witness, that he may be led to believe that he is watching the accomplishment of a destiny."[24]

ADVENTURE

Captain Brassbound's Conversion is subtitled "An Adventure," though the original subtitle of the play, when performed for copyright purposes, was "a Melodramatic Comedy."[25] The later subtitle relates to the setting. It evokes an entire sub-genre of Melodrama, characteristic of an Empire-conscious age, a sub-genre presenting the perils of Europeans in a barbarous, heathen clime.

North Africa was a favorite setting for Adventure Melodrama because of recent French and English imperial exploits in the region and also, no doubt, because of the popularity of Ouida's much-dramatized romance, *Under Two Flags* (1867). But Shaw had immediate practical reasons for choosing this setting. He wrote *Captain Brassbound* specifically for Ellen Terry when she had already turned fifty; and when Siegfried Trebitsch questioned the stage-worthiness of the play, Shaw replied by pointing out its "unique" practicality for an actress like the Austrian Odilon, who "is getting too old to stand the competition of pretty young women side by side with her

[24] *North American Review*, 126 (1878), p. 45.

[25] Henderson, *Man of the Century*, p. 562n. Shaw originally called *Buoyant Billions* "An Adventure and a Discussion." The "Adventure" part is set in a South-American jungle.

on the stage." In *Brassbound*, however, she had "a great part, and no other woman in the play, the want of bright costumes (usually supplied by the women's dresses) being supplied . . . by the costumes of the Arabs."[26]

Shaw was not the first playwright to see the usefulness of a North African setting for a woman star at a competitive disadvantage. An early crude and pungent Adventure Melodrama, also designed as a one-actress vehicle, was J. T. Haines's *The French Spy; or, The Siege of Constantina* (1837), in which the heroine, Mathilde de Meric, is dumb, doubtless because she was played all over the English-speaking world by the (then) French-speaking Madame Céleste. The costumes were abundantly colorful, and Madame Céleste had no vocal female competition.[27]

The Arabs in *The French Spy* were, as usual, cunning villains, and, as usual, they presented a sexual threat to the European heroine. Mathilde, the beautiful and mute fiancée of a French colonel, arrives disguised as a recruit while the French forces are besieging Constantina. She is sent re-disguised as a mad Arab boy into Constantina; but meanwhile the Arabs raid the French camp and carry off the colonel and others. In Constantina, Mathilde comes before Achmet Bey, Dey of Algiers, and by interpreted signs deludes him with a vision of victory. In the course of spying (she sends vital information to the French lines with a burning arrow) Mathilde is challenged and becomes a veritable superwoman,

[26] Typescript letter to Trebitsch, 7 Oct. 1903.

[27] An earlier version of *The French Spy* had been one of the staples of Céleste's repertory during the period from 1827, when the dancer made her debut as an actress, to Christmas 1837, when she ventured on her first speaking part. Céleste was extremely successful, both in the silent and speaking phases of her long career (Shaw saw her in Dublin; *OTN*, I, 138). Among the many plays tailored to meet her special talents and requirements during the earlier period were W. B. Bernard's *The Wept of Wish-ton-Wish* (1831) based on Cooper's novel, in which the heroine's power of speech is restored only at the moment of death; J. T. Haines's *The Wizard Skiff; or, The Tongueless Pirate Boy* (1831); and J. R. Planché's *The Child of the Wreck* (1837), featuring Maurice, the dumb boy.

hurling men left and right and disarming the chief heavy after "*a desperate sword encounter.*" But the discovery of her sex unmans her. She is clothed in a gorgeous harem dress, and the wily Achmet presents a villainous choice to the Colonel: tell all or suffer your love to be dishonored; and to Mathilde: yield, or suffer your love to die. Finally, the axe is about to fall on the Colonel:

> ACHMET. Do you consent?
> COL. No, "Vive la France!"
> ACHMET. Now strike!
> *(Music—Explosion of a mine in centre—walls and towers fall—red fire and crash—French troops rush in, headed by* GENERAL DAMREMONT *and* CAPTAIN DIDIER—*Damremont bearing the French flag . . .)*
> (*French S. D.*, p. 24)

A Military Melodrama as well as an Adventure, *The French Spy* contains much glorious rhetoric on bravery, honor, and battle. A spectacular military rescue, with red fire and flag, is the typical high point of the piece. The virtue of the Europeans and the villainy of the Arabs are never doubted for a moment. The European heroine defeats all threats, by force of arms as well as by ingenuity. And when Achmet bargains for her chastity with the Colonel's life, she steadfastly refuses to yield, unlike her Shavian counterpart, Lady Cicely, who has stayed with six cannibal chiefs in her time and is perfectly delighted that the Sheik Sidi el Assif "offered to swop Sir Howard for me."

An important aspect of Adventure Melodrama, more essential than even the sensational rescue, the sexual threat, and the glorious rhetoric, was its patriotism. In *The French Spy* with its French star, France rather than England was the object of patriotic emotion. More typical of the English theater was Dion Boucicault's *Jessie Brown; or, The Relief of*

1. Types and Stereotypes: Poster for *The Lancastershire Lass* (1867)

2

3

ACTORS, STYLES, AND PARTS

2. Dion Boucicault as Conn in *The Shaughraun*
3. Frédéric Lemaître as Robert Macaire
4. Barry Sullivan as Hamlet
5. Charles Wyndham as Robert Sackett in *Brighton*

6. Adelaide Ristori as Maria Stuart
7. Lillah McCarthy as Mercia (Charles Dalton as Marcus) in *The Sign of the Cross*
8. Mrs. Patrick Campbell and George Alexander as Paula and Aubrey Tanqueray in *The Second Mrs. Tanqueray*

4

5

7

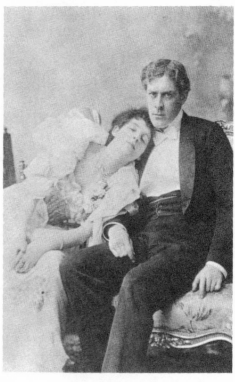

8

9

10

THE FALLEN WOMAN

9. Poster for *East Lynne*, Lady Isabel and her husband
10. *Mrs. Warren's Profession*, Mrs. Warren and her daughter

THE HEROIC SACRIFICE

11. Poster for *The Only Way* (1899), Martin Harvey as Sydney Carton
12. *The Devil's Disciple*, Matheson Lang as Dick Dudgeon

12   11

13

ADVENTURE: Stock posters for *Freedom*

13. The native rebellion
14. The rescue foiled (or Constance in the harem)
15. The gunboat arrives

14

15

16

THE KEY OF MELODRAMA

16. Bill Walker (Conway Tearle) and Jenny Hill (Mary Nash) in *Major Barbara* (New York, 1915)
17. Stock poster; Bill Sikes and Nancy in *Oliver Twist*

THE PANTOMIME ANIMAL

18. *Androcles and the Lion*; O. P. Heggie and Edward Sillward, 1913
19. *Puss in Boots*; Charles Lauri, Jr., and Miss Wadman, Drury Lane, 1888

17

18

19

20

POLITICAL
EXTRAVAGANZA
20. *Geneva*
21. J. L. Shine and A.
Ross's *Joan of Arc* (1891)
with Arthur Roberts as
Lord Randolph Churchill
22. *The Apple Cart*

21

22

Lucknow (1858), set in India during the Sepoy Rebellion. As a matter of course Boucicault contrives to make the leader of the rebellion fall in love with one of the heroines. There are also sensational battle scenes, a hanging (the villain, Achmet, is put in his own noose and whisked off through the flies), and a classic last-minute rescue of the entire garrison. But the rescue, the sensation, and the sexual threat concern an English garrison, an English relief column, and an English heroine.

In his criticism, Shaw was frequently acid over the quite literal flag-waving of Military and Colonial Melodrama, and he particularly deplored the crude jingoism of Sir Augustus Harris's Drury Lane drama. Therefore, it is particularly instructive to find all the adventure elements of *Captain Brassbound* in *Freedom* (1883), by George Fawcett Rowe and Augustus Harris, with an essential difference: in *Freedom* the adventure elements flourish in their integrity, with all their chauvinistic values ablaze. The politics of Empire is translated into Melodrama. English force becomes the heroic defender of freedom, and native resistance becomes the villainous partisan of slavery.

The play is set in Egypt. Constance Loring, the daughter of an English banker in Cairo, is coveted by Mohammed Araf Bey, a powerful chieftain. But Constance is betrothed to Ernest Gascoigne, Commander of H. M. Dispatch Boat "Arrow" and Araf's hated enemy.

> ARAF. I have yet to know by what right you make this claim here! Is this city yours—who are you?
>
> ERN. Who am I? Look at the uniform I wear— look at the blue-jackets around me! You should surely know, sir, that the broad seas are Britain's heritage—that there is hardly an inch of the blue waters where we have not carried our colours to

vindicate the rights of liberty. I am an Englishman,
and these are English tars.

(*Sailors "Hurrah!"*)[28]

The sailors of the Pinafore could say no less.

Under cover of a revolt against the Europeans, Araf carries off Constance to his harem. Ernest comes to rescue her and is captured, but Suleima, Araf's dark, passionate wife, helps them to escape. Later Ernest is recaptured by the Arabs and marched in a slave caravan. Just as he is about to be shot, the gunboat steams up the river on stage, and tars jump off to the rescue for the spectacular close. The play also featured real camels, dancing girls, and a whimsical stage-American, the stereotype ancestor of Shaw's Captain Kearney (Figures 13, 14, 15).

Shaw took the materials of Adventure Melodrama—the European woman; the fanatical Arab chieftain; the hero who has gone adventuring, like Captain Temple in *Human Nature* or Bertie Cecil in *Under Two Flags*, because he is "wounded to the quick"; even the gunboat rescue—and constructed a parable for Imperialism. He tried to convey as much to Ellen Terry:

"I accordingly give you a play in which you stand in the very place where Imperialism is most believed to be necessary, on the border line where the European meets the fanatical African, with judge on the one hand, and indomitable adventurer-filibuster on the other, said I. A-F. pushing forward 'civilization' in the shape of rifles and pistols in the hands of Hooligans, aristocratic *mauvais sujets* and stupid drifters. I try to shew these men gaining a sense of courage and resolution from continual contact with and defiance of their own fears. I try to shew you fearing nobody and managing them

[28] *Freedom: An Original Drama in Four Acts, Printed,* Not *Published . . . Produced under the Direction of Augustus Harris, At Theatre Royal, Drury Lane, on August 4, 1883* (William Seymour Theatre Collection, Princeton University), p. 19.

—·[210]·—

all as Daniel managed the lions, not by cunning—above all, not by even a momentary appeal to Cleopatra's stand-by, their passions—but by simple moral superiority."[29]

Shaw dramatically convinces us that the last-minute rescue of Lady Cicely from the thoroughly awed Sheik Sidi is perfectly unnecessary, since we have just seen her overwhelm the filibuster, and she has already begun managing the Arabs. The rescue itself departs from convention. The rescuers are the Arab Cadi of the region and his many followers. The warship and the gallant tars are American and stay comfortably off stage until the last-act court-martial. However, the rescue is perfectly conventional in that it uses fear and the threat of revenge, military and judicial; whereas Lady Cicely has demonstrated Shaw's point: that if civilization has any claim to moral superiority (the rationale of Imperialism), it cannot act by the laws of the Atlas Mountains.

Though Captain Brassbound has served with Gordon in breaking up the slave caravans of the Sudan, most of his whole adult life has been devoted to the hope of revenge for his mother's wrongs. In his parable on Imperialism, Shaw introduces the plot motif of a personal revenge to illuminate the primitive force and retributive justice used in the name of civilization. Revenge is the theme of Captain Brassbound's conversion.

In nineteenth-century Melodrama, revenge was not associated with justice, though there were exceptions like Boucicault's *Corsican Brothers* (1852), but rather with a Heavy's passionate vindictiveness. Revenge is presented as criminal even when the revenger has been bitterly wronged (in the past). For example, in Tom Taylor's *Retribution* (1856), "Count Priuli's" web of revenge against the seducer of his wife is unhallowed and destructive. His brother dies to prevent it, and the Count cries in the end, "And for this I have

[29] Letter of 8 Aug. 1899, *Ellen Terry and Bernard Shaw*, p. 248.

dared usurp Heaven's work of retribution! . . . I have sowed the wind, and round me lies the whirlwind's harvest." In H. J. Byron's *Lancashire Lass; or, Tempted, Tried and True* (1867), the passionate villain Redburn haunts the heroine and hero everywhere, even as far as Australia, seeking revenge for having been foiled in a nearly successful seduction.

Captain Brassbound is a melodramatic heavy hero bent on revenge, and he looks and acts his part. But Shaw establishes an equivalence between the law of England and the law of the Atlas Mountains, between the justice of Brassbound, the revengeful filibuster, and the justice of Sir Howard Hallam, the judge (". . . this fellow who puts on ermine and scarlet and calls himself Justice").

> BRASSBOUND (*raging*) He did not spare my mother—"that woman," he calls her—because of her sex. I will not spare him because of his age. (*Lowering his tone to one of sullen vindictiveness*) But I am not going to strike him. (*. . . Brassbound continues, with an evil glance at Sir Howard*) I shall do no more than justice.
>
> SIR HOWARD (*recovering his voice and vigor*) Justice! I think you mean vengeance, disguised as justice by your passions.
>
> BRASSBOUND. To many and many a poor wretch in the dock you have brought vengeance in that disguise—the vengeance of society, disguised as justice by its passions. Now the justice you have outraged meets you disguised as vengeance. How do you like it? (p. 243)

After Lady Cicely has reduced Captain Brassbound, or, rather, effected his conversion by destroying his purpose of revenge, the rescue takes place and the situation is reversed. The reformed revenger is now at the mercy of justice. Having thwarted the law of the Atlas Mountains, it is now up to

Lady Cicely to thwart the law of civilization, whose first action will be to set up a court and a courtroom. In the strong second act closing (to which Shaw was addicted though it was a mark of the well-made play) Brassbound and his men are seized by the rescuing Arabs preparatory to the curtain tableau:

> SIR HOWARD (*drily*) I told you you were not in a strong position, Captain Brassbound (*Looking implacably at him*) You are laid by the heels, my friend, as I said you would be.
>
> LADY CICELY. But I assure you—
>
> BRASSBOUND (*interrupting her*) What have you to assure him of? You persuaded me to spare him. Look at his face. Will you be able to persuade him to spare me? (p. 259)

Fortunately, Lady Cicely is as successful in taming the justice of the court as she was in taming the vengeance of Captain Brassbound. But meanwhile, Shaw has made a complete equivalence between unhallowed revenge and civilized justice, not merely in the dialogue but in the action.

The turning of Captain Brassbound from his dark and damnable purpose by the influence of a good woman follows a classic motif of Melodrama. It appears, for example, in Boucicault's *Colleen Bawn* (1860) and in mythic form in *Vanderdecken* (1846, 1878), the legend of The Flying Dutchman, who will be released from his cursed wanderings when he finds a pure woman who will love him above life. It would have been typical Melodrama if Lady Cicely had softened Brassbound by patient suffering, by returning good for evil, by faithfulness unto death. She does in fact reply to his murderous intentions by mending his coat. But Lady Cicely chiefly converts Brassbound by managing and frustrating him and helpfully disillusioning him. Instead of evoking tender recollections of maternal solicitude (a formula for softening burlesqued in Grosvenor's appeal to his rival in Gilbert's *Patience*), Lady Cicely reminds Brassbound that his childhood was a hell and his mother unbearable, and that he failed in kindness and forbearance during her lifetime (after he asserts, "I am doing my duty as a son"). Finally she points out that if his uncle is no better than a filibuster, Brassbound is no better than a judge. Brassbound is converted and, indeed, redeemed, insofar as he is freed from his obsession with revenge.

One of Shaw's reasons for the title *Captain Brassbound's Conversion* was that he had decided to include the play in a book called *Three Plays for Puritans*.[30] But the conversion metaphor runs through the entire play. Rankin is a missionary, in Africa to make converts. Drinkwater undergoes several conversions for prudential reasons. The Arabs are presented as religious fanatics. Brassbound himself experiences three conversions in the course of the play: he gives up his vengeance; he (temporarily) changes from his own clothing and puts on the formal surface of English civilization; and he stumbles onto the clue to the world which restores him, he says, to power and purpose at the end of the play. Like Dick Dudgeon in an earlier play, and Blanco Posnet in a later play, Captain Brassbound makes a Pilgrim's Progress.

Shaw began with a genre devoted to exotic adventure, where the civilized and Christian European met the fanatical and uncivilized heathen and overcame him by superior violence (British pluck) and the threat of national retaliation. In these dramas, the sight of a British flag was often enough to strike terror into the hearts of the menacing natives.[31] Shaw deliberately uses this form, devoted to the most sanguine chauvinism, to embody a parable for Imperialism, in which

[30] Letter of 1 Aug. 1899, *Ellen Terry and Bernard Shaw*, p. 243.
[31] See, for example, "*British Born*," *A New and Original Drama of National and Domestic Interest* (1872), by Paul Merritt and Henry Pettitt, where a British flag and nothing else protects the hero from a native firing squad during a revolt in Bolivia.

all the British pluck is concentrated into his non-violent, non-revengeful civilized heroine, and in which the judge and the filibuster, the ordinary agents of Empire, are simply burdens to her. At the same time, Shaw embodies an analogous moral drama in the physical drama, in which the hero is tested and converted from a romantic worship of violence and retaliation to a truer and morally superior vision of the world.

BARBARIAN MELODRAMA AND MELODRAMATIC FARCE

The Shewing-Up of Blanco Posnet: A Melodrama (1909) was subtitled originally "A Sermon in Crude Melodrama." In his preface, devoted to the censorship and its disallowance of the play, Shaw calls it "A religious tract in dramatic form." The play is only one act long, but, like its melodramatic predecessors, it presents a drama of spiritual discovery.

Its briefness and bareness (it is literally a sermon embedded rather than embodied in Melodrama) and its rather farcical tone suggest that Shaw may have reached a point in his exploitation of Melodrama where it no longer answered his purposes. At this time Shaw was writing his Discussion Plays, and it may be that the ideas he wished to present were too discursive in their nature, too ramifying in their concerns, to lend themselves to the simplicities of melodrama. At any rate, the melodrama in *Blanco Posnet* is treated in cavalier fashion, and the evolutionary answer to the problem of evil is presented as undraped doctrine.

The tone of *Blanco Posnet* is closer than any of Shaw's earlier melodramas to the vein of Farcical Melodrama, or Melodramatic Farce, associated with the great French actor Frédéric Lemaître. Lemaître's masterpiece in this vein was his grotesque creation, Robert Macaire in the *Aubèrge des Adrets*. The part was brought into English by Charles Selby in *Robert Macaire; or, The Two Murderers* (1835) and by Stevenson and Henley in *Macaire; A Melodramatic Farce* (published in 1885). G. H. Lewes reported that Macaire was a "picture of ideal blackguardism. For the peculiarity of Robert Macaire is the union of a certain ideal grace and *bonhomie* with the most degraded ruffianism and hardness . . ."[32] Lemaître describes his own initial appearance, "with a swaggering stare, his crownless hat on one side of his head, his green coat flung back, his red trousers covered with patches and darns, his black bandage over one eye, his lace cravat and dancing shoes,—the effect was overwhelming."[33] (Figure 3.)

The opening situation of *Blanco Posnet* presents a familiar dramatic pair, the sympathetic scapegrace and his respectable brother. Blanco, the scapegrace ne'er-do-well, is about to be hanged as a horse thief with scraps of poetry on his lips. He also swears and blasphemes and mocks law, virtue, and respectability. Shaw describes his first appearance:

> *Blanco is evidently a blackguard. It would be necessary to clean him to make a close guess at his age; but he is under forty, and an upturned red moustache, and the arrangement of his hair in a crest on his brow, proclaim the dandy in spite of his intense disreputableness. He carries his head high, and has a fairly resolute mouth, though the fire of incipient delirium tremens is in his eye.* (p. 430)

No one knows that Blanco is the brother of Elder Daniels, and no one knows that Blanco "distrained upon" the horse (which actually belonged to the sheriff) because he thought

[32] *On Actors and the Art of Acting*, p. 74. Lewes writes "A common melodrama without novelty or point became in [Lemaître's] hands a grandiose symbolical caricature; and Robert Macaire became a type, just as Lord Dundreary has become one in our own day."

[33] Quoted by Constant Coquelin in *Art and the Actor*, in *Papers on Acting*, 2nd Ser., II (New York, 1915), p. 49. The most recent incarnation of the elegant ruffian Macaire and his simple-minded accomplice Bertrand is that villainous pair in Walt Disney's *Pinocchio*, the fox and the cat.

it belonged to his hypocritical brother. Blanco only came for what he himself calls "a damned piece of sentimentality"; "for mother's old necklace with the hair locket in it. You wouldnt give me that: you wouldnt give me anything. So as you refused me my due I took it, just to give you a lesson" (p. 434).

In reviewing *The Rogue's Comedy* (1896) by Henry Arthur Jones, Shaw dignifies Punch by making him the protagonist of all "philosophic comedy."

"A safe rule for the dramatist is, 'When in doubt, revive Punch and Judy.' Mr Henry Arthur Jones . . . has fallen back on Punch and Judy, the eternal rogue's comedy, tempting the business dramatist by its assured popularity, and fascinating the artist dramatist by its unlimited depth, which yet involves no obligation to fully fathom it or else fail. . . . At the street corner, with a deplorable Judy, an infant thrown out of the window, a dog Toby, and a few assorted types of law and order culminating in a hangman and a devil, the great issues of the comedy can be ribaldly touched to the music of pipes and drum. At the other end of the range, Mozart's Don Giovanni, the world's masterpiece in stage art, is only Punch on a higher plane. . . . Between the two lies all philosophic comedy, high and low, with its Faustuses, its Robert Macaires, its Affable Hawks [*The Game of Speculation*, by G. H. Lewes], its Jeremy Diddlers [*Raising the Wind*, by James Kenney], its common Joeys [pantomime clown] with red-hot poker and sausages, its Pierrots, and, since last Tuesday night, its Mr Bailey Prothero." (*OTN*, II, 104)

Later Shaw adds Richard III as "the prince of Punches: he delights Man by provoking God, and dies unrepentant and game to the last" (*OTN*, II, 285).

All of Shaw's best heroes are Punch in this sense. They are at odds philosophically—that is, on principle or by nature—with assorted types of law and order, especially the

—·[217]·—

hangman and Shaw's Devil of Romance. Like Richard III, Dick Dudgeon and Blanco Posnet fly in the face of conventional respectability and morality, and are prepared to die game to the last. But we cannot find in them the attractive freedom from scruple and conscience that we enjoy in Punch or Don Juan. Their wickedness is all a sham. In fact, they fly in the face of law and respectability because they have too much conscience for the wickedness of society.

Nevertheless, the Disreputable Hero and the Engaging Villain are akin in that their challenging relation to society is the same. Stevenson and Henley's Macaire, a magnificent, indomitable, flamboyant creation, looks and acts like Shaw's Mendoza, but thinks and philosophizes like John Tanner and Andrew Undershaft. "Dreams, dreams!" he rattles to Bertrand,

> We are what we are; and what are we? Who are you? who cares? Who am I? myself. What do we come from? an accident. What's a mother? an old woman. A father? the gentleman who beats her. What is crime? discovery. Virtue? opportunity. Politics? a pretext. Affection? an affectation. Morality? an affair of latitude. Punishment? this side the frontier. Reward? the other. Property? plunder. Business? other people's money—not mine, by God! and the end of life to live till we are hanged.

> .   .   .   .

> The honest man, Bertrand, that's God's noblest work. He carries the bag, my boy. Would you have me define honesty? the strategic point for theft. Bertrand, if I'd three hundred a year, I'd be honest tomorrow. . . . Bertrand, I will bet you my head against your own—the longest odds I can imagine—that with honesty for my spring-board, I leap through history

like a paper hoop, and come out among posterity
heroic and immortal.[34]

Stevenson and Henley's Macaire is a Punch who manages to
articulate the issues of "philosophic comedy." But his challenge to society is heroic and delightful only because in the
final analysis it is not to be taken seriously. Blanco Posnet,
like John Tanner and Andrew Undershaft, is an inversion of
Macaire and the typical philosophic rogue because his challenge to law and respectability *is* to be taken seriously. When
the framework of law and society is genuinely doubted, the
philosophic rogue becomes Shaw's favorite hero, the heretic-
saint.[35]

Blanco's challenge to law and respectability takes the
form of a trial, in which he is satisfactorily defiant and in-
sulting to the dubiously good people and questionably legal
processes that are determined to hang him. Trials and court-
martials were among the most familiar events in Melodrama
(Shaun the Post was tried by court-martial, and Gillette's
Held By the Enemy presents a most thrilling and irregular
court-martial); and in a review of a Military Melodrama
based on the Dreyfus case, Shaw wrote: "A trial scene is the
last resource of a barren melodramatist: it is so safe an ex-
pedient that improvised amateur attempts at it amused even

[34] *The Works of Robert Louis Stevenson*, Pentland Ed. (London, 1907),
XIV, 229, 243.

[35] There is a further important difference between Stevenson's Macaire
and Shaw's Blanco and Don Juan. In Shaw's psychology of ideological
types (outlined in *The Quintessence of Ibsenism*) , his heretic-saint was
distinguished by the vivid consciousness of inner realities. Cynicism,
purely negative, was the mark of the disillusioned romantic "idealist."
Macaire is a cynic in his heresies, and it is no accident that his rhetoric
is echoed precisely by Shaw's prince of romance and cynicism, the Devil
(himself a seedier version of the romantic brigand Mendoza): "Man measures his strength by his destructiveness. What is his religion? An excuse
for hating me. What is his law? An excuse for hanging you. What is his
morality? Gentility! an excuse for consuming without producing. What is
his art? An excuse for gloating over pictures of slaughter. What are his
politics? Either the worship of a despot because a despot can kill, or
parliamentary cock-fighting" (*Man and Superman*, pp. 102-3).

the doomed aristocrats in the Paris prisons during the Terror" (*OTN*, I, 287). Nevertheless, trial scenes are prominent in *The Devil's Disciple* and *Captain Brassbound's Conversion* (to name only Melodramas), while *Blanco Posnet* is in effect a primitive and therefore revealingly honest trial scene from beginning to end. The inner drama of *Blanco Posnet* is not, however, in the legal struggle over the hero's neck. It is in the struggle over his soul, the story of his conversion from "the rotten game" of selfish vindictiveness, of being strictly out for yourself, to "the Great Game" of working for Life, of doing the Lord's work. Blanco initially appears as the dashing cynical rogue very much battered; he ends as a vitalist preacher delivering a sermon.

Blanco's true story is revealed gradually in the course of the trial. He denies having stolen the horse (he was apprehended on foot), and Feemy Evans, a reckless young prostitute, is brought as a witness against him. The witness for him is a strange woman who arrives in town with a horse and a dead child, who tells a story of a bad man who swore and wept and gave her the horse to take her dying child to a doctor when "it got its little fingers down his neck and called him Daddy and tried to kiss him . . . He said it was a little Judas kid, and it was betraying him with a kiss, and that he'd swing for it" (p. 450). Feemy is touched, and so is Sheriff Kemp; Feemy forswears herself and the hanging is called off. Blanco declares he was treacherously hounded out of his tough take-care-of-yourself attitude and trapped into softness. He admired the sunset, and he heard God's voice, "Now I've got you," and there was the good woman, with her child, dying of the croup, who put its fingers down his neck. The desperate badman, the disreputable woman, and the gruff, bullying sheriff have all been touched in their hearts of gold.

The setting and persons of *Blanco Posnet* belong to a particular type of American melodrama that occasionally

travelled to London, with leading characters modelled on
Bret Harte's good-bad mining-camp ruffians.[36] Shaw demon-
strated his familiarity with the strain in his comments on
Barbarian Melodrama (*OTN*, III, 364-65) and in his review
of David Belasco's *Girl I Left Behind Me* (*OTN*, I, 92-97).
The progenitor of the type was Augustin Daly's *Horizon*
(New York, 1871), and it appeared in London in Joaquin
Miller's *The Danites* (Sadlers Wells, 1880) and Bartley Campbell's *My Partner* (Olympic, 1884). Both of the later plays
presented ruffianly types softened and transfigured by love.
English melodramatists took up the strain, and *The Fatal
Card* (1894) by Haddon Chambers and B. C. Stephenson presented a play to Adelphi audiences in which the scoundrel
is rescued, like Blanco, from a Colorado lynch mob in the
very first act. Bret Harte himself, with T. Edgar Pemberton,
presented *Sue* to London (1898), and Annie Russell in the
title part made it something of a sensation. The second act
was that staple of the species, a Vigilante trial scene, with a
hanging in the offing. The genre transcended itself in Moody's
Great Divide (London, 1909), but was epitomized in an
earlier play, Belasco's *Girl of the Golden West* (New York,
1905), which inspired the libretto of Puccini's opera. Belasco's
play had a leading trio of an outlaw hero, a saloon-owning
heroine, and a powerful sheriff to match Shaw's rough and
reluctantly sentimental trio, Blanco, Feemy, and Sheriff
Kemp. The heroine, who has lived virtuously, falls in love
with the outlaw hero and saves him several times over, finally
from a semi-official lynch mob. The outlaw is touched and
ennobled by "the Girl's" pure love, as are the boys of the

[36] See "The Drama of the Frontier" in Arthur H. Quinn, *A History of
the American Drama from the Civil War to the Present Day* (New York,
1937), esp. p. 108. Lady Gregory was reported to have said, at the time
of the *Blanco Posnet* controversy in Dublin, "I did not like *Blanco Posnet*
at first, but now I think it very powerful and effective, a sort of Bret
Harte" (Michael J. O'Neill, "Some Shavian Links with Dublin as Recorded in the Holloway Diaries," *Shaw Review*, II, May 1959, p. 4).

mining camp. The dialect is close to the dialect of *Blanco Posnet*, and there is at least one verbal parallel to Blanco's sermon on the "Great Game" and the "rotten game."

> SONORA . . . Girl . . . the boys an' me ain't per-
> haps reelized jest what Johnson stood for to you,
> Girl—an', hearin' what you said, an' seein' you
> prayin' over the cuss—
> RANCE. Damned cuss!
> SONORA. Yes, the damned cuss, I got an idee may-
> be God's back of this here game.[37]

The softening effect of an infant child was of course common in literature and drama; but an audience which had seen plays in the particular vein of *The Girl of the Golden West* would doubly expect little fingers to affect ruffians as they did in *Blanco Posnet* (particularly since Bret Harte's best known single piece was "The Luck of Roaring Camp"). What an audience would not expect was the creative evolutionary doctrine of Blanco's sermon, where Blanco declares that God made mistakes, such as the croup, and "He made you and me to fight the croup for him." As with Dick Dudgeon's heroic substitution, as with Lady Cicely's melting of Brassbound, Shaw takes a sentimental convention of Melodrama and gives it a fresh rationale. The difference is that in *Blanco Posnet* Shaw doesn't bother to devalue the sentiment; he simply adds a leavening of deliberate farcical hyperbole, and makes the sentiment itself the vehicle of his philosophy.

All Shaw's melodramatic plays, even *Arms and the Man* which was a deliberate effort to discredit some of the conventions of Melodrama, present a philosophical progress, a conversion, a dramatic discovery by a leading personage of his own real nature and the meaning of life. The broad style

---

[37] David Belasco, *Six Plays* (Boston, 1929), p. 402.

of Melodrama, its vivid, generalized personages, its essential character as a story of perils and providential fulfillments—in short, all the qualities Shaw found in Melodrama which made it seem Bunyanesque—also made it seem a natural vehicle for the drama of ideas, or the drama of persons who embodied ideas. After explaining *The Rhinegold* as an allegory in *The Perfect Wagnerite* (1898), Shaw admonished his readers:

". . . do not forget that an allegory is never quite consistent except when it is written by someone without dramatic faculty, in which case it is unreadable. There is only one way of dramatizing an idea; and that is by putting on the stage a human being possessed by that idea, yet none the less a human being with all the human impulses which make him akin and therefore interesting to us. Bunyan, in his Pilgrim's Progress, does not, like his unread imitators, attempt to personify Christianity and Valour: he dramatizes for you the life of the Christian and the Valiant Man. Just so, though I have shewn that Wotan is Godhead and Kingship, and Loki Logic and Imagination without living Will (Brain without Heart, to put it vulgarly); yet in the drama Wotan is a religiously moral man, and Loki a witty, ingenious, imaginative and cynical one." (p. 188)

Similarly Burgoyne is a Gentlemanly man, Sergius a dashing Romantic one. Judge Hallam is not Law, but a man "with a legal mind, proceeding on the fundamental legal error."[38] And the dramatic conflicts in which they are moved are the conflicts of incarnated ideas.

[38] Shaw's characterization of Wagner's Fricka in a letter to Henry Arthur Jones, 8 Jan. 1899 (D. A. Jones, *Taking the Curtain Call*, p. 115). Shaw continues, "this is the only way in which an allegory can become a drama."

9

DOMESTIC COMEDY

GENRE RELATIONS

IN a classification of Shaw's plays according to genre foundations, *Candida* and *The Doctor's Dilemma* fall under Domestic Comedy; *The Philanderer, You Never Can Tell, Fanny's First Play, Overruled,* and *Getting Married* under Farce. Shaw exploits the Domestic Comedy foundations of the one group and the Farce foundations of the other in radically different ways; nevertheless, the two genres were closely related in the nineteenth-century theater, both in history and subject matter. They differed considerably in tone and moral atmosphere; but that very climate of indecorous irresponsibility which distinguished Farce fostered its alternative, Domestic Comedy.

Domestic ties and romantic longings were the subject matter of Domestic Comedy. Marital infidelity and sexual adventure are the staple subject of Farce, and were so in the Victorian theater after the early eighteen-seventies. One authority states that in modern times the word "farce" is applied "to a full-length play dealing with some absurd situation hinging generally on extra-marital relations—hence the term bedroom farce."[1] And Shaw declares in the preface to his brief farcical comedy *Overruled,*

"The stage has been preoccupied by such affairs ['the gallantries of married people'] for centuries, not only in the jesting vein of Restoration Comedy and Palais Royal farce, but in the more tragically turned adulteries of the Parisian school

---

[1] *Oxford Companion to the Theatre*, ed. Phyllis Hartnoll, 2nd ed. (London, 1957). For a critique of the *Companion's* article on Farce, see Eric Bentley's "The Psychology of Farce," in *Let's Get a Divorce! and Other Plays* (New York, 1958).

which dominated the stage until Ibsen put them out of countenance and relegated them to their proper place as articles of commerce. Their continued vogue in that department maintains the tradition that adultery is the dramatic subject *par excellence*, and indeed that a play that is not about adultery is not a play at all." (pp. 158-59)

It is true that adultery, and the possibility of adultery, was a leading dramatic subject in the nineteenth century and that the theater was heavily stocked with studies in a "tragic" vein. The overwhelming piety, morality, and sentimentality of the traduced household angels and despairing magdalens of Melodrama and Domestic Drama called aloud for an extreme relief. "Palais Royal farce," in which sexual immorality was only slightly less comic than sexual morality, brought such relief to France, and (somewhat tempered) eventually to England. However, during the sixties and early seventies, when Shaw sat in the Dublin audience, only a small percentage of the Farce abounding in the bills contained a suggestion of domestic irregularity, and even such Farce, by the most finicky standards, was remarkably chaste.

While avoiding sexual irregularity in the irresponsible vein of Farce, the English mid-century theater beheld it freely in the vein of Domestic Comedy. Domestic Comedy was an intermediate kind of play which lacked the frightening amorality of Sex Farce and still supplemented with lighter tones the more "tragically turned" studies of sexual misadventure. In the plays of this middle range, a domestic triangle invariably ends in the defeat of the lover by the husband. Domestic Comedy is, in a sense, the obverse of the domestic magdalen play, for the adultery is always unconsummated, though the possibility provides the interest and the intrigue. It is in a sense the reverse of Sex Farce, for domesticity triumphs and morality reigns.

Most of the plays which took it upon themselves to provide

a treatment of domestic infidelity that was lighter than Domestic Drama, but less irresponsible than Palais Royal Farce, were of French origin or inspiration, since the French theater of the time provided not only the tragic and farcical extremes of sexual misadventure but the whole range between. The connection between *Candida* and these plays is fairly straightforward. The connection with *The Doctor's Dilemma* is less simple, but no less essential. In both cases, Shaw uses the conventions of Domestic Comedy to say something not only about the nature of domesticity but also about the relation of the artist to ordinary life.

CANDIDA

A fundamental convention of Domestic Comedy was the triangle composed of a romantic wife, a seemingly prosaic husband, and a seemingly poetic lover. For example, in Tom Taylor's *Still Waters Run Deep, A Comedy in Three Acts* (1855), Mrs. Mildmay, a shallow young woman with romantic yearnings, finds her husband all too mild and sensible, especially when compared with the glittering Captain Hawksley. Captain Hawksley is a heavy villain—a swindler and a blackmailer; but he cultivates a romantic exterior and speaks of Seville, love, the duel. He affects a cool imperturbability, but shakes and starts conventionally and twice, according to stage directions, even gnashes his teeth. John Mildmay is by contrast quiet and undemonstrative. He is the "Still Waters," and when his wife, seeking romance, is half entangled in the toils of Hawksley, she finds true love and true passion in the depths of Mildmay. In the last act, when everyone else is powerless, Mildmay takes command and defeats the villain with great dash and practicality.

The lover's bait was always his romantic glamour. He stressed his poetic sensitivity, in contrast to the husband's commercial coarseness, and in consequence he was sometimes epitomized as an artist or a poet. In Tom Taylor's *Victims*

(1857), Mr. Merryweather is a wealthy stockbroker, and Mrs. Merryweather, his sensitive, languid wife who keeps a salon for intellectuals, feels herself tragically mismated. She is deeply impressed by Mr. Herbert Fitzherbert, a genuine poet, who makes a poetic appeal and pretends to appreciate her properly. After coming upon his wife and Fitzherbert in a compromising attitude, Merryweather complains, "I don't know what to think. That's the worst of these fine sentiments; they're like the mirage eastern travellers write about; seen through their medium, sin looks heroic, and duty despicable." However, Mrs. Merryweather learns in time that Fitzherbert has a wife whom he treats badly and that he is really interested in money. She comes to appreciate her unpoetic husband, with whom she is reconciled.[2]

In Sardou's *Nos Intimes!* (Paris, 1861) the wealthy and middle-aged Caussade, with a young wife and a country villa, has a folly about friends, whom he acquires by the score. The triangle consists of Caussade, Cécile, his young wife, and Maurice, one of the "friends." Cécile allows herself to be drawn to Maurice, who makes the usual appeal of the romantic lover: he holds up the prosaic insensibility of the husband in contrast to his own poetic sensitivity and capacity for appreciation. In their first presented conversation, Cécile and Maurice talk of the husband:

[2] The poet-lover is farcically presented in Gilbert's *Patience*, of course, and also in T. J. Williams' *On and Off* (1861), in which the recently married Laetitia, who has quarrelled with her husband, is courted by Mr. Alphonso de Pentonville, "a youth, with 'Poetical tendencies.'" Alphonso speaks in an elevated, tragic manner of his blighted existence, his crushed young hopes, and love's young dream dispelled. He is described on his first appearance: "Enter Pentonville R., romantic make up—long hair, turn down collar, moustache and pointed beard." Though Laetitia tolerates him, she is really only concerned with her husband, and she treats Alphonso's poetry as disrespectfully as Candida treats Eugene's in the poetry-reading scene, when she too has other things on her mind. Eventually the married couple come to an understanding, and the poet is banished comically and cruelly.

CECILE. Il est si bon!

MAURICE, *vivement*. Oh! excellent! . . . mais un peu prosaïque... peut-être!...

CECILE. Peut-être!

MAURICE, *un peu railleur*. Voyons, entre nous ...il ne faut pas lui demander le sens de tout ce qui est delicat, artistique... et fin!

CECILE, *souriant*. Oh! jamais! mais il est si bon!...

MAURICE. Oui, madame...mais la bonté...la bonté!...

CECILE. Oh! assez d'éloges![3]

Cécile later finds she has gone too far, and she rejects Maurice. But first her poetic lover subjects her to a nightmarish siege in which he will attend to nothing she can say or do on the logically irrefutable grounds that in her heart she really loves him. Thus Cécile gets romance and high sentiment enough to frighten her, and almost to compromise her, and she learns to value her prosaic but good-hearted husband.

In *Divorçons* (Paris, 1880), an altogether admirable comedy by Sardou and Emile de Najac which hovers on the edge of farcical irresponsibility,[4] Cyprienne Des Prunelles writhes under the injustice which deluded her into marrying, while inexperienced, a man exhausted by his previous gallantries. Des Prunelles falls far short, in his mild embraces, of her novelistic notions of passion and romance. She therefore intrigues

[3] *Nos Intimes! Comédie en Quatre Actes* (Paris: Calmann Lévy, 1884), pp. 18, 19. Adapted as *Peril* (1876) by B. C. Stephenson and Clement Scott (not published), and knowledgeably mentioned by Shaw along with their *Diplomacy* (Sardou's *Dora*), H. J. Byron's *Our Boys*, Merivale and Grove's *Forget-Me-Not*, and Tom Taylor's *Clancarty, New Men and Old Acres*, and *Still Waters Run Deep*, as "the plays which were regarded as dramatic masterpieces in the eighties" (*OTN*, I, 164).

[4] Adapted as *The Queen's Proctor* (1896) by Herman Merivale, and reviewed as such by Shaw (*OTN*, II, 149 ff). However, Shaw refers familiarly to effects obtained in the original version by the French actress Chaumont, and the play had been brought to England by Réjane, Duse, and others. For a fuller account of the plot, see below, pp. 265-66.

with an apparently romantic young philanderer, Adhémar, who is ultimately out-maneuvered by an inspired Des Prunelles. By casting Adhémar in the role of husband and himself in the role of lover, Des Prunelles proves that the romantic-poetic glamour of the lover and the prosaic dullness of the husband lie in the office, not in the persons. *Divorçons* has an important resemblance to an earlier play, adapted by Charles Dance as *Delicate Ground*, in which Sangfroid has a romantic wife, Pauline, who dreams over an old lover whom she thinks dead. Alphonse appears, a fugitive from the revolution; but Sangfroid coolly procures him a passport; and since this was in the early days of the Republic when divorce was easy, he pushes Alphonse and Pauline together. Sangfroid so maneuvers, however, that the lovers shy at the prospect of being man and wife, and Pauline learns the value of her uneffusive spouse. The "auction scene" in *Candida*, in which the husband resigns his conjugal rights and places himself on an equal footing with the lover, had precedent in these two plays.[5]

From one point of view, the triangle situation and its outcome in *Candida* is a simple anti-romantic treatment of the Tristan and Isolde, Launcelot and Guinevere theme of romantic literature. Instead of joining Eugene in sublime adultery and transcendent sin, Candida "pitches in her picture of the home, the onions, and the tradesmen, and the cos-

[5] Ibsen's *The Lady from the Sea* (1888; Eng. trans. 1890) has a significant resemblance to the plays of this group, but it is in itself an exploitation of the materials of the genre, like Shaw's *Candida*. Huneker (p. 14) points out the parallel between Shaw's "auction scene" and Wangel's release of his wife Ellida so that she may choose freely between himself and the stranger, between domesticity and the wild unknown. (This release from all claims, which Ellida craves, Candida resents acutely, because it shows Morell's ignorance of the gift she has bestowed upon him.) Given her freedom, Ellida chooses her husband. The similarities between *Candida* and *The Lady* are generic similarities. The uses to which Ibsen and Shaw put the materials of the genre are radically different.

setting of the big baby Morell,"[6] reminds Eugene she will be fifty when he is thirty-five, and sends him about his business, out into the night. All the plays we have been considering are, in this sense, equally anti-romantic, but Shaw's play is something more. The conventions Shaw is playing upon directly are not those of the drama of romantic adultery, but of the genre which had simply inverted these conventions in the interests of domesticity and sometimes philistinism— the plays like *Still Waters Run Deep, Victims,* or *Divorçons,* in which the prosaic husband rather than the poetic lover turns out to be the better man.

Candida herself, in motive if not in action, is the antithesis of the conventional foolishly romantic wife of Domestic Comedy, who is tempted by romance and held back by duty and respectability. Candida is tempted, not by romance, but by the poet's need. She is a practical realist, with no illusions about herself, her husband, or her poet-lover. On the other hand, she is as free from the claims of duty and respectability as from romantic illusion, and she would give up purity and goodness for Eugene "as willingly as I would give my shawl to a beggar dying of cold, if there were nothing else to re-strain me" (p. 117). Shaw spoke of her variously, even as "the Virgin Mother and nobody else";[7] but he insisted upon this dual freedom, from romance and respectability, in her conception:

"Candida is as unscrupulous as Siegfried: Morell himself sees that 'no law will bind her.' She seduces Eugene just ex-actly as far as it is worth her while to seduce him. She is a woman without 'character' in the conventional sense. With-out brains and strength of mind she would be a wretched

---

[6] Shaw in a letter to James Huneker, printed in his essay "The Quin-tessence of Shaw," in *George Bernard Shaw,* ed. Louis Kronenberger (New York, 1953), pp. 18-19.

[7] Letter of 6 April 1896, *Ellen Terry and Bernard Shaw,* p. 23. Part of the visible iconography provided by the single setting is "*a large autotype of the chief figure in Titian's Assumption of the Virgin.*"

slattern or voluptuary. She is straight for natural reasons, not for conventional ethical ones. Nothing can be more cold-bloodedly reasonable than her farewell to Eugene: 'All very well, my lad; but I don't quite see myself at fifty with a husband of thirty-five.' It is just this freedom from emotional slop, this unerring wisdom on the domestic plane, that makes her so completely mistress of the situation."[8]

If Candida is an inversion of her counterpart in the conventional triangle, Morell is both an inversion and an exposure. Usually the conventional play disclosed progressively the hidden strengths and hidden virtues of the prosaic husband. Morell, on the other hand, is presented initially as a man of magnetic personality and ostensible strength, but in the course of the play Eugene's absurd prediction that he shall shake Morell to his foundations comes true. "Now the whole point of the play," Shaw wrote to Siegfried Trebitsch, "is the revelation of the weakness of this strong and manly man, and the terrible strength of the febrile and effeminate one." Candida finally declares that she gives herself, not to the better or stronger man, but "to the weaker of the two," and Eugene, divining her meaning and at that moment discovering his strength, whitens, we are told, *like steel in a furnace*" (p. 138).[9]

[8] Letter to Huneker in "The Quintessence of Shaw," p. 18.

[9] See MS letter to Trebitsch, 7 Jan. 1903. The Reverend James Mavor Morell might even be supposed to start with some of the automatic romantic aura previously reserved to the artist and the junior officer. This audience attitude is in fact reflected in "Prossy's complaint," her infatuation with the clergyman. Maurice Willson Disher writes of the importance of the Reverend Julian Grey in *The New Magdalen*: "The hero who had the right to preach as well as the right to fall in love was a new inspiration to the drama. To be photographed in a 'dog-collar' was every actor's ambition at this sudden blossoming of Episcopalian romance—Belasco was rarely photographed out of it. W. S. Gilbert's 'pale young curate,' whom maidens of the noblest station, forsaking even military men, would gaze upon while rapt in admiration, was no figment of idle thought but a shrewd caricature of the times (and the parson in Shaw's *Candida* needs this as reference)," *Melodrama; Plots that Thrilled*, London, 1954, pp. 110-11. In his review of *The New Magdalen*, Shaw himself

In the end, it is Morell's prosaic dependence and Eugene's exalted independence which are made manifest. Eugene rises superior to "happiness," to domesticity, and embraces his "nobler" destiny, dark at the moment, lonely, and demanding ("The night outside grows impatient"), but neither stifling nor circumscribed. To a play-reading society at Rugby, puzzled by "the secret in the poet's heart," Shaw wrote:

"The secret is very obvious after all—provided you know what a poet is. What business has a man with the great destiny of a poet with the small beer of domestic comfort and cuddling and petting at the apron-string of some dear nice woman? Morell cannot do without it: it is the making of him; without it he would be utterly miserable and perhaps go to the devil. To Eugene, the stronger of the two, the daily routine of it is nursery slavery, swaddling clothes, mere happiness instead of exaltation—an atmosphere in which great poetry dies. To choose it would be like Swinburne choosing Putney. When Candida brings him squarely face to face with it, his heaven rolls up like a scroll; and he goes out proudly into the majestic and beautiful kingdom of the starry night."[10]

The final effect of *Candida* is to reject the measuring of a poet by the virtues of the domestic sphere and to distinguish his sphere, the kingdom of the starry night, from the "greasy fool's paradise"[11] of domestic happiness.

An outline of *Candida*, presenting the apparent character relationships and the outer action, would read like the outline of *Candida*'s conventional predecessors. A wife is tempted by a young and romantic poet to leave her engrossed and

---

wrote, "Where Wilkie Collins really struck the new movement was in his sketch of the Reverend Julian Grey, who might have been a stagey forecast of the Reverend Stewart Headlam, though he was probably a reminiscence of some earlier pioneer of Christian Socialism" (*OTN*, I, 232). Morell is of course a strenuous Christian Socialist.

[10] On several postcards, 8 March 1920, in George A. Riding, "The Candida Secret," *The Spectator*, 185 (Nov. 17, 1950), p. 506.

[11] Letter to Huneker in "Quintessence of Shaw," p. 18.

relatively prosaic husband; the poet claims that he can understand and appreciate the wife, while the husband cannot; in the crisis, sanctioned domesticity wins out over lawless romance. But the inner action, the action of motives and ideas which culminates in spiritual discovery, shows that into the mould of the conventional drama of unconsummated adultery Shaw has poured the first of his parables on the artist's relation to ordinary life.

The conventional triangle and the conventional action that is reinterpreted in *Candida* is burlesqued in Shaw's brief farce, *How He Lied to Her Husband*, written for Arnold Daly, who had played the poet in *Candida*. Here again, the romantic poet-lover is presented not as a designing seducer, but as a hopeless idealist, in this case worshipping a woman *"hopelessly inferior in physical and spiritual distinction to the beautiful youth"* (p. 184). Nevertheless, the poet draws the conventional contrast between himself and Bompas, the husband, to whom he declares in his final bitterness, "I told her that you were a sordid commercial chump, utterly unworthy of her; and so you are" (p. 198). The comedy of the piece lies in the poet's disillusionment with Aurora, the very vulgar and commonplace Candida, and his utter bewilderment in the strange (to the poet) world of West Kensington. The farce hinges on the husband's unexpected delight with the love-poems obviously written to his wife, and his violent truculence when the poet gallantly declares he would never dream of writing poems to Mrs. Bompas.

THE DOCTOR'S DILEMMA

Like *Candida*, *The Doctor's Dilemma* is preoccupied with the artist's relation to common life, and, like *Candida*, it is rooted in the seemingly remote comedy of unconsummated adultery. The reasons for this unlikely conjunction lie in the usefulness of the convention which brought an instrusive artistic sensibility into the sphere of prosaic domesticity. The opposition between lover and husband in the conventional triangle of Domestic Comedy was already a symbolic conflict between apparent lawlessness, romance, and poetry, and apparent prudence, prose, and propriety.

Drawing upon the materials of Domestic Comedy, *The Doctor's Dilemma* varies the conventional triangle unexpectedly. Having presented the artist as lover in *Candida*, Shaw now presents him as husband; and the middle-aged sober and respectable professional man, who would ordinarily be the husband, serves as the extra-domestic lover. The reason for this reversal is a reversal in emphasis.

In *Candida* Shaw takes seriously the romantic concept of the artist as an alien creature. The artist is out of place in ordinary life, and the idea of happy domesticity functions (in *Candida* as in *Man and Superman*) as the sum and symbol of ordinary life. The artist-lover in *Candida* is thus spiritually as well as legally an intruder into domesticity, and the point of the play is his fundamental alienation. On the other hand, the emphasis in *The Doctor's Dilemma* is on the artist as ordinary citizen, and the difference between alienation and bohemianism. Only a year after *The Doctor's Dilemma*, Shaw wrote, with reference to the play, ". . . it is idle to demand unlimited toleration of apparently outrageous conduct on the plea that the offender is a genius, even if by the abnormal development of some specific talent he may be highly skilled as an artist."[12] Nevertheless, the last thing in the world Shaw wanted to do was to deny the artist's specialness or to offer a pat formula for dealing with his unorthodoxies. Shaw varies the conventional triangle and presents the artist as husband, first of all, because his emphasis is on the artist in ordinary life, and secondly, because he is raising questions. A conventional rascally artist-intruder and a respectable physician-

[12] "The Sanity of Art," Pref., 1907, in *Major Critical Essays*, p. 289.

husband would have called up an automatic response. No such response was likely with the respectable physician as lover, and the rascally artist as husband commanding his wife's fullest, most gratifying domestic adoration.

The play is oddly constituted, for the story is the doctor-lover's, and the artist is simply presented in his ambivalent relation to common life. Yet the play is subtitled "A Tragedy" more for the artist's sake than the doctor's. However, "tragedy" and "comedy" are deprived of their ancient antinomy in this play. Shaw wrote to Archibald Henderson:

"*The Doctor's Dilemma* was called a tragedy partly for the absurd reason that Archer challenged me to write a tragedy, and partly for the much better reason that its theme: that of 'a man of genius who is not also a man of honor,' is the most tragic of all themes to people who can understand its importance. Even the comedy which runs concurrently with it: the comedy of the medical profession as at present organized in England, is a tragic comedy, with death conducting the orchestra. Yet the play is funnier than most farces. The tragedy of Dubedat is not his death but his life; nevertheless his death, a purely poetic one, would once have seemed wholly incompatible with laughter."[13]

This conflation of, on the one hand, the comic tragedy of the artist-scoundrel and, on the other, the tragic comedy of the Doctor's romantic dilemma, reflects a division in the antecedents of the play which deserves elucidation.

The situation of *The Doctor's Dilemma* is that of a greying bachelor who, at the moment of scientific and social recognition, falls in love with a woman who comes to beg him

[13] 8 March 1918, Henderson, *Playboy*, pp. 616-17. Shaw was ever anxious to write pathetic comedy and to draw laughter in which there were tears. In the same letter, Shaw declares Ibsen to be "the first great dramatic chemist" in the fusion of comedy and tragedy. In *The Wild Duck*, in place of an Elizabethan alternation of comedy and tragedy, "every moment of it is at once tragic and comic."

to save her artist husband from consumption. Unlike the unscrupulous artist-lover of convention (and artist-husband of the play) Sir Colenso Ridgeon is too honorable to make love to another man's wife, and too scrupulous to refuse a cure in the hope of making the wife a widow. He has power to save ten lives, and he must decide on the value of the man himself. The choice is ultimately given full embodiment: it lies between the artist-husband, Louis Dubedat, and Ridgeon's sympathetic friend, Dr. Blenkinsop.

Louis Dubedat is thoroughly amoral and totally unscrupulous with money and women, but he is a gifted and devoted artist with most of his painting life ahead. Blenkinsop is totally without genius or importance, but he is exceedingly scrupulous (especially with money) and exceedingly good. The doctor's dilemma is stated at the end of two (out of five) acts: "its a plain choice between a man and a lot of pictures"; and a good case is made for both.

Dubedat's destiny is finally decided through his relation with his wife. Jennifer Dubedat is extravagantly devoted to her husband, whom she passionately idealizes. His carelessness with money, and even with women, she attributes to his transcendent superiority to ordinary life. He, on the other hand, exploits her unconscionably, using her attractiveness to coax money out of interested men, using even her unreserved love for him as a basis for a scheme of blackmail.

In Tom Taylor's domestic comedy *Victims*, the poet-lover Fitzherbert also has a wife whom he exploits outrageously, who has great faith in his genius and his superiority to herself and all men, and who is wholly naïve about his moral limitations. Mrs. Merryweather paints the lot of this artist's wife (not knowing that Fitzherbert is the husband) in terms of the City ideal of marriage:

> Imagine, then, a woman, young, beautiful, accomplished, married to a man too idle to turn his powers

to account . . . but not too proud to incur debts which he cannot pay. . . . Conceive this young wife toiling in secret to procure for this husband means to indulge his costly tastes, and luxurious appetites— employing her lonely nights—for he is absent at his pleasures—to earn that paltry pittance with which the selfish rich reward the vigils of the poor— . . . And through all this, not one murmur, not one regret; but the tenderness of an angel, the heroism of a martyr, the self-denial of a saint (*French S. D.*, pp. 38-39).

Fitzherbert is not a do-nothing like his relation Harold Skimpole. His genius is not put in question, but his morality and his ultimate value to society are. His weaknesses are used to reveal and set off the stock-brokerly virtues of Merry-weather. In the end he is found out, and he confesses in shame and remorse. Fitzherbert's claim to special treatment is never taken seriously in the play, and the claims of domestic virtue overwhelm the claims of art.

The questions which did not exist or were answered by an application of philistine principles in *Victims* are the very questions Shaw's play wishes to raise. "I know no harder practical question," wrote Shaw, "than how much selfishness one ought to stand from a gifted person for the sake of his gifts or on the chance of his being right in the long run."[14] When Ridgeon's choice is put to him, as between "a man and a lot of pictures," he says, "I'm not at all convinced that the world wouldnt be a better world if everybody behaved as Dubedat does," and he adds, "It's easier to replace a dead man than a good picture" (pp. 127-28). But his temporary antagonist has as much to say for saving the man rather than the picture "in an age that runs to pictures and statues and plays and brass bands because its men and women are not good enough to comfort its poor aching soul. . . ." For Shaw,

[14] "The Sanity of Art," *Major Critical Essays*, p. 288.

Dubedat is a problem which extends beyond the question of what a society should do with the man who is valuable in one respect and intolerable in another, to the question of what a society should do with its heretics. Shaw believed that all progress and evolution began as heresy but that few heresies ended in progress and evolution. Much heresy was in fact regressive or futile. From heresy in action society had to protect itself; yet how could it distinguish those heresies which were the expression of the evolutionary appetite from others which were quite pernicious, when both were equally subversive of orthodoxy and order? It is in the light of this problem that Ridgeon suggests his uncertainty as to whether Dubedat's egotistical amorality might not be a better thing for the world than the current orthodoxy.

The doctor resolves his dilemma by avoiding it. He chooses finally, not between the man and the paintings, but between enshrining an illusion and shattering it. By willfully allowing Dubedat to be treated by an incompetent, and by supplying a dangerous treatment, Ridgeon intends to preserve her hero for Mrs. Dubedat. Consequently, Ridgeon becomes a figure of comedy, not by making the wrong choice (practically speaking, perhaps it was the right one), but by choosing on irrelevant grounds. He assumes the quack's pose of omniscience and omnipotence while losing sight of the real dilemma in vapors of romance. In the light of Ridgeon's *hubris* in presuming to act as Providence, the ending takes on its irony. Dubedat dies splendidly, and Jennifer's hero is preserved to her; in fact he is twice magnified. Jennifer's feelings for Dubedat never depended on ignorance of fact, as Ridgeon had assumed; but now all hints of mortality are erased, and beside the sanctified splendor of the dead artist the physician seems old and absurd, his actions mean and envious and, of all things, immoral. Following Dubedat's dying recommendation, Jennifer has already remarried, and

Ridgeon can't even buy any pictures. The lover, as usual, has been defeated by the husband.

The doctor's comic tragedy has yet another antecedent besides the conventional Domestic Comedy of frustrated adultery. It also belongs to a drama of the professions, and though no such contemporary genre was recognized, there is justification for the naming of such a dramatic type. Shaw wrote in the preface to *Mrs. Warren's Profession*, "A man's profession only enters into the drama of his life when it comes into conflict with his nature. The result of this conflict is tragic in Mrs Warren's case, and comic in the clergyman's case (at least we are savage enough to laugh at it) . . ." (pp. 168-69). By the time of Shaw's comment, clergymen as clergymen had become serious leading figures in plays, from Wilkie Collins' *The New Magdalen* (1873) to Henry Arthur Jones's *Michael and His Lost Angel* (1896). Lawyers had been gradually promoted from stock villains in Melodrama to honest men whose profession might have some interesting relation to their lives.[15] Even doctors had been turned to dramatic account. In 1897, Shaw reviewed a play by Henry Arthur Jones called *The Physician* (*OTN*, III, 90-96) and based on a triangle in which, as in *The Doctor's Dilemma*, a conflict exists between a doctor's profession and his passion. Dr. Lewin Carey has been cast into a modern despair of the meaning and purpose of life by a disappointment in love. He is roused by a young country girl, Edana Hinde, who comes to his consulting rooms (like Jennifer to Ridgeon's) to get him to restore the extraordinary man with whom she is in love. Carey himself falls in love with Edana and agrees to look into the case. He discovers, however, that Walter Amphiel,

[15] For example, *Her Advocate*, by Walter Frith (1895), a courtroom drama in which the lawyer-leading-man falls in love with his elsewhere-attached client. Reviewed by Shaw (*OTN*, I, 207-10). Satire of the professions belongs, of course, to a far older tradition, and the satirical aspect of *The Doctor's Dilemma* has more in common with Molière than with later drama.

whom Edana loves for his passion and greatness as a Temperance reformer, is a hopeless alcoholic whose periodic debauches stem from a tormented conscience. Amphiel once "ruined" a young woman who has since sunk into depravity. Doctor Carey, like Doctor Ridgeon, is asked to cure this unworthy possessor of the woman he loves. "This situation," Henry James reported in words which sum up Jones and anticipate Shaw, "is the doctor's predicament, his dilemma; call it, if we will, his temptation, his struggle and his resistance. He is so mad to possess the girl that an easy way stares him in the face: he has only to reveal to her the private turpitude of her lover and she will infallibly fall into his arms. She does so, of course, in the last act, but by ways remarkably devious."[16] However Shaw may have come by his title, he used essentially the same predicament as the basic situation of *The Doctor's Dilemma*.

With great passion, Carey attempts to cure Amphiel, and he has some success. The difference between Carey's decision and Ridgeon's was in the disease: to cure Amphiel's physical disease was also to cure his moral disease, for the two were inseparable; whereas to cure Dubedat's tuberculosis would have affected his vigor but not his character. As a good man Carey had no real choice, since curing Amphiel was working for the happiness of the woman he loves; whereas Ridgeon, in contrast, persuades himself that killing Dubedat is the only way to prevent a great unhappiness for Jennifer. Fortunately for Carey, Amphiel proves incurable and Edana learns the truth before his death, so that, unlike Ridgeon, Carey secures Edana without the awkward problem of a shameful revelation.

Doctor Carey's dilemma is simpler than Doctor Ridgeon's. His profession comes into conflict with his nature only in the sense that to cure Amphiel is to lose Edana. Doctor Ridgeon's profession, which pretends to scientific objectivity,

---

[16] *The Scenic Art* ("The Blight of the Drama," 1897), p. 300.

—·[240]·—

comes into conflict with his nature when he must choose on moral and social grounds, between genius and goodness, and on personal grounds, between genius and the wife of genius. As a man of professional honor, Doctor Carey has no alternative to attempting the cure of Amphiel. But Ridgeon has only alternatives, and no clear course at all. In the upshot, he cannot and does not choose with the inhuman objectivity which his scientific professionalism demands. But he also evades the moral and social issue, and following his passional obsession chooses on grounds sentimentally irrelevant and unrealistic. The doctor is in conflict with the man, and the result is his comic tragedy.

In writing *The Doctor's Dilemma*, Shaw drew upon the materials of Domestic Comedy, drama of the professions, and dramatic satire of the professions, and the result is reasonably unified. Shaw's unembarrassed fusion of these materials is characteristic of the period of his Discussion Plays (see below), in which he freely invoked the conventions of the particular genre associated with the subject of discussion. In *The Doctor's Dilemma*, when considering the artist in relation to common life, Shaw called upon the conventional triangle of Domestic Comedy, as he previously had in *Candida*, because the genre was associated with the subject. But, because he wished to reverse the emphasis of *Candida*, he reversed the roles of the romantic lover and the prosaic husband. The final importance of conventional Domestic Comedy as an antecedent of *The Doctor's Dilemma* corresponds to the importance of the consideration of the artist in the total scheme of the play. In both *Candida* and *The Doctor's Dilemma*, a conventional genre (Domestic Comedy) furnishes the fundamental relationship (the artist-inclusive triangle) and the fundamental metaphors (domesticity and the romantic intruder) by which the idea of the artist's relation to common life is made flesh.

—·[241]·—

10

FARCE

W H I L E Domestic Comedy went about its work of providing some little relief from the "more tragically turned" dramas of adultery, Farce was by no means banished from the stage. In fact, on the evidence of titles, there was more Farce to be seen in the mid-century English theater than any other kind of play. This was partly because the contemporary Farce was brief and theatrically simple, partly because it formed an expected part of every evening's long and varied bill. But such Farce, on the whole, was careful to avoid the subject-matter of sexual impropriety. Eventually there was a change, and as the ordinary evening at the theater shortened, the Short Farce began to disappear. At the same time a longer Farcical Comedy appeared, thoroughly devoted to the hitherto avoided subject-matter.

The change was marked by the extraordinary success of James Albery's *Pink Dominos* in 1877. By 1885, a Conservative party reviewer, looking for signs of national degeneration in the wake of Liberal government, was able to point to the change in the form of Farce as evidence of a decadence in dramatic taste. "The fact is both patent and notable that for some time past the old form of farce has practically disappeared, and has given place to the 'farcical comedy' (a stupid and contradictory title), which is really a farce, well or ill written, occupying three acts instead of one, and forming the staple of an evening's dramatic entertainment."[1] While scoffing at the reviewer's identification of the theatrical with the political revolution, William Archer nevertheless grants the apparent theatrical change: "The decline, or rather the dissolution, of cup-and-saucer comedy, with the correlative de-

---

[1] W. H. Pollock, "A Glance at the Stage," *National Review*, V (July 1885), 646.

velopment of farce—an apparent increase in quantity, a real improvement in quality—is one of the salient facts of the past four years."[2] Ten years later Shaw was able to write, "One of the strongest objections to the institution of monogamy is the existence of its offspring, the conventional farcical comedy" (*OTN*, II, 118).

Shaw drew upon both the earlier and later Farce forms. Many of his "playlets" and "tomfooleries" (such as *Augustus Does His Bit: A True-to-Life Farce*) belong to the earlier Farce type, or to the cognate music-hall skit, while *The Philanderer, You Never Can Tell*, and *Fanny's First Play* belong to the developed genre of three-act Farcical Comedy. But materials and devices from the Farce of both periods are to be found throughout the canon. In the succeeding sections, I shall treat "Dublin Farce" and Farcical Comedy in the order of their theatrical succession, in order to show, first, that Shaw's dramaturgy has a living connection with the particular devices and atmosphere of farce of his Dublin period; and second, that *The Philanderer, You Never Can Tell, Fanny's First Play, Overruled*, and *Getting Married* are a connected series of essays in the longer Farcical Comedy.

DUBLIN FARCE

Farce in the Dublin repertory between 1868 and 1876 tended to situations of extravagant absurdity, exploiting the comedy of tramp and policeman, or, in Shaw's terms, the comedy of clown and ringmaster.[3] A typical example is John Maddison Morton's *Grimshaw, Bagshaw, and Bradshaw*

[2] William Archer, "Are We Advancing? (1882-1886)," *About the Theatre* (London, 1886), p. 18.

[3] Shaw wrote to Alan S. Downer (with reference to an article on Granville-Barker), "My technique is that of the first circus clown cheeking the first ringmaster, a technique rampant in Le Bourgeois Gentilhomme. Barker's was that of the first strolling poet who lived by reciting his verses at the street corner. These primitive techniques have developed. The solitary mendicant tragedian and the circus couple have combined and made Twelfth Night possible" (Typescript letter, 12 Nov. 1947).

(1851), set in a lodging house with many doors and even a sliding panel. Towzer, a sheriff's officer, takes Grimshaw for Bradshaw, who has run off with his niece, and then for Bagshaw, who has defaulted on a tailor's bill. Grimshaw, of course, is a simple victimized innocent. In another favorite, Morton's *Slasher and Crasher* (1848), an irascible old man who is about to bestow his sister and niece on the seemingly fierce Slasher and Crasher instead banishes the men on suspicion of cowardice. To prove their courage, Slasher and Crasher plan a false duel. The comedy climax arrives when Slasher, the greater coward, gets drunk and fierce and pursues Crasher over the stage. In Morton's classic, *Box and Cox* (1847), the basic situation is the encounter of a hatter and a printer, of whom one works by day and one by night, so that their landlady has been able to rent the same room to both of them without having been found out.

Even more popular than J. M. Morton in the Dublin theater of the sixties and seventies was Thomas J. Williams, a specialist in Farce. Williams, no less than Morton, provided a robust fare that generally avoided the intrigues of married life. For example, in *My Wife's Maid* (1864), Tootles, a young clerk in romantic dress and makeup ("I'm all poetry, romance, and gush unspeakable") and Barbara Perkins, a lady's maid, meet in the park and pretend to other names and stations than their own. Tootles ("De Ravensbourne") comes unhappily to the home of the bride his parents have chosen for him and there finds Barbara ("Evelina Mountpaddington") in cap and apron, the servant who opens the door. In *Who Is Who; or, All in a Fog* (1869), a new manservant and a prospective son-in-law arrive at a country house at the same time and are mistaken for each other. And they in turn mistake the maid and the mistress. In *The Trials of Tompkins!* (1863), a mercenary bachelor discovers that his eccentric prospective father-in-law has devised a series of tests for him, and accordingly plays the part of a paragon. He carries it off bravely, until he discovers that the duel with a young officer, which he believed to be part of the test, was altogether in earnest, and fought with real bullets.

A platoon of farce writers supplied the Dublin audience with its scores of repertory favorites; but the plays of J. M. Morton and T. J. Williams were typical. As the most notable suppliers, they wrote exceptionally characteristic rather than otherwise exceptional plays.

When Shaw modulates into the key of Farce, as he does constantly throughout the body of his work, both tone and device often suggest the exuberant Farce of the Dublin period. Sometimes he adopts a farcical device for a relatively serious purpose, but even then the device brings with it something of its native farcical atmosphere. In *Heartbreak House*, when Ellie Dunn discovers, by a coincidence, that the dashing "Marcus Darnley" is none other than the tame domestic animal Hector Hushabye, the scene reproduces, with some of its farcical flavor, the confrontation of Barbara Perkins and young Tootles in *My Wife's Maid*. However, Ellie is denied the fantastic imperviousness of farcical character, and she is genuinely "heartbroken" by the workings of the farcical mechanism.

The farcical encounter against all likelihood is a favorite device of Shaw. In his hands, it ranges from relative sobriety, in the meeting between Mrs. Lutestring and the Archbishop (formerly parlor-maid and curate) in *Methuselah*, Part III, to relative extravagance, in the appearance of the real Billy Dunn (as the burglar) in *Heartbreak House*, to sheer fabulousness, in the encounter between the lion and the tailor in *Androcles*. Shaw wrote about this last encounter, in a souvenir booklet of the original production: "Given such a pair, there is nothing incredible in the story except the theatrical coincidence of the meeting of the two in the arena. Such coincidences are privileged on the stage, and are the special delight of this particular author. And really, when one considers how many men met lions in the arena from first to last, it is not too much to ask you to believe that just for once they turned out to be old friends."[4]

Again, in *Methuselah* III, Shaw echoes a farcical device he had enjoyed in *Box and Cox*. After the two lodgers of the older play come to some understanding of the nature of their joint tenancy, they discover that Box has been engaged to the very widow who has since made Cox her only joy. On the basis of his experience, Box advises Cox: faced with a breach of promise suit, "I took a desperate resolution—I left my home early one morning, with one suit of clothes on my back, and another tied up in a bundle under my arm. I arrived on the cliffs—opened my bundle—deposited the suit of clothes on the very verge of the precipice—took one look down at the yawning gulf beneath me—and walked off in the opposite direction" (*French A. E.*, p. 15). Earlier he declares, "I've been defunct for the last three years! . . . Do as I did. . . . Drown yourself!" When Shaw's Archbishop in *Methuselah* III began to have trouble with the pension authorities because of his evident disposition to live for three hundred years, he chose the same solution. He is told that he should have killed himself: "I did kill myself. It was quite easy. I left a suit of clothes by the seashore during the bathing season, with documents in the pockets to identify me. I then turned up in a strange place, pretending that I had lost my memory, and did not know my name or my age or anything about myself. . . . I have had several careers since I began this routine of life and death" (p. 108).

Farce of the Dublin period was filled with violent physical action and with the comedy of physical terror. Shaw frequently uses distinctly farcical violence, as in the scene in *The Apple Cart* where Orinthia wrestles Magnus to the floor; the scene in *Misalliance* where Lina slings Bentley over her

[4] Mander and Mitchenson, p. 151.

shoulder and carries him off; the scene in *Too True To Be Good* where the supposed invalid springs out of bed to defend her necklace and hurls burglar and accomplice about with compelling vigor. Adrian in *The Millionairess*, the Dauphin in *Saint Joan*, Drinkwater in *Captain Brassbound*, even John Tanner in *Man and Superman*, are all made to present the spectacle of comic terror. The most "heightened" example occurs in *Androcles and the Lion*, when at the peak of a quarrel, Megaera announces:

> Then I'll make my way through the forest; and when I'm eaten by the wild beasts youll know what a wife youve lost. (*She dashes into the jungle and nearly falls over the sleeping lion*). Oh! Oh! Andy! Andy! (*She totters back and collapses into the arms of Androcles, who, crushed by her weight, falls on his bundle*).
>
> ANDROCLES (*extracting himself from beneath her and slapping her hands in great anxiety*) What is it, my precious, my pet? Whats the matter? (*He raises her head. Speechless with terror, she points in the direction of the sleeping lion. He steals cautiously towards the spot indicated by Megaera. She rises with an effort and totters after him*).
>
> MEGAERA. No, Andy: youll be killed. Come back.
> *The lion utters a long snoring sigh. Androcles sees the lion, and recoils fainting into the arms of Megaera, who falls back on the bundle. They roll apart and lie staring in terror at one another.* (p. 106)

Later in the play, the terror of the epicene Lentulus as the massive Ferrovius prepares to teach him to turn the other cheek is equally farcical. Lentulus falls on his knees and cries for his mother and finally faints dead away. The scenes between Androcles, the Emperor, and the lion exploit the same vein to the very end.

When the would-be murderer in *Misalliance* conceals himself in a portable steambath and pops his head in and out of the hole at the top while Hypatia is making love to Joey Percival, Shaw reproduces the action of one of the commonest situations of farce. In Alfred Bunn's *My Neighbour's Wife* (1833), for example, a set of concealed husbands who are trespassing with adulterous intent watch from a closet while their neighbor seems to make love to their own wives. Their heads bob in and out as they fluctuate between outrage and prudence and teeter on the extremest edge of discovery. Shaw goes beyond this predecessor in abstract heightening and sheer extravagance; for he caps the headbobbing with the entrance of Tarleton, weary from unwonted exercise:

> (. . . *He dabs his brow with his handkerchief, and walks stiffly to the nearest convenient support, which happens to be the Turkish bath. He props himself upon it with his elbow, and covers his eyes with his hand for a moment. After a few sighing breaths, he feels a little better, and uncovers his eyes. The man's head rises from the lunette a few inches from his nose. He recoils from the bath with a violent start.*)
> Oh Lord! My brain's gone. (p. 162)

Though *My Neighbour's Wife* was a better farce than many of those played at the Theatre Royal and the Gaiety, Dublin, it was too extravagantly indecorous on a marital theme to appear in the programs of either of those reputable houses during the years of Shaw's attendance. Limited in the direction of its irresponsibilities, Farce of Shaw's Dublin period was all the more given to physical buffoonery, superhuman embarrassments, and other forms of exaggerative absurdity. These made a firm impression on Shaw's own dramaturgy. The exaggerative principle apparent in his playwriting, along with his neglect of commonplace verisimilitude, sets Shaw as much among the writers of extravagant farce as in the company of the heroic and poetic dramatists.

FARCICAL COMEDY

The advent of three-act Farcical Comedy with the characteristic subject-matter of sexual misadventure was identified with Charles Wyndham (largely in consequence of the success of *Pink Dominos*) and with the Criterion Theatre, which Wyndham actor-managed until the end of the century. The most important review of *Pink Dominos* helped arouse a lively public interest by opening with the declaration, "All who know anything of the Parisian stage are aware of the kind of pieces usually associated with the Palais Royal, and everybody desirous of maintaining the purity of the drama in this country must have regretfully noticed that a theatre in Piccadilly has seemed lately anxious to emulate the distinction acquired by that establishment."[5] Another reviewer noted that "*The Pink Dominos* . . . bears a strong family resemblance to its popular predecessors here [at the Criterion], *The Great Divorce Case* [by Clement Scott and Arthur Matthison, 1876], *Hot Water* [by H. B. Farnie, 1876], and *On Bail* [by W. S. Gilbert, 1877]. The characters and incidents in all are very similar, though the motives are differently actuated, and the results differently arrived at, marital incontinency being the basis of the plot of each."[6]

For Shaw, Charles Wyndham was permanently associated with *Pink Dominos* and its numerous successors. "Pink Domi-

[5] *Daily Telegraph*, 5 April 1877, given in entirety in *Dramatic Works of James Albery*, ed. Wyndham Albery, II, 205. The notice was written by E. L. Blanchard, though "universally attributed" to Clement Scott (see T. Edgar Pemberton, *Sir Charles Wyndham, A Biography* [London, 1904], p. 118).

[6] *Illustrated Sporting and Dramatic News*, 7 April 1877. The germinal piece was actually, not *Pink Dominos*, but Bronson Howard and Frank Marshall's *Brighton*, with which Wyndham first established himself as a star, and which he brought to London in 1874. Having found his vein, Wyndham asked Albery to adapt *Les Dominos Roses* by Hennequin and Delacour (Pemberton, *Charles Wyndham*, pp. 85, 101-16).

nos is memorable," he recalled in the nineties, "not for it-self, but for the performances of Wyndham and [John] Clarke [who played Brisket, the comic head-waiter]" (*OTN*, II, 120). And years later Shaw wrote of a renaissance of farcical comedy during the first World War that it pleased, among those re-turning from the field, even "Men who had just read the news that Charles Wyndham was dying, and were thereby sadly reminded of Pink Dominos and the torrent of farcical comedies that followed it in his heyday until every trick of that trade had become so stale that the laughter they provoked turned to loathing" (*Heartbreak House*, p. 31).

Wyndham played the farcical hero in *Pink Dominos* and its successors in a characteristic style, very much suited to the medium. When Wyndham revived Bronson Howard and Frank Marshall's *Brighton* in 1880, a reviewer noted, "The piece is signalized by its eccentricity, and prevails on account of its absurdity. The interest is centered on its hero, Robert Sackett, who makes love to every woman with whom he be-comes acquainted, a character which exactly suits Mr. Charles Wyndham, who, by his volatile manners, reconciles the spec-tator to the incoherence both of word and act."[7] Wyndham's volatile style, as the complement of a fantastic atmosphere, became the *sine qua non* of the farcical-comedy hero for Shaw. Reviewing an indifferently-acted Farcical Comedy by Feydeau and Desvallières, done into English as *A Night Out*, Shaw wrote that since *A Night Out* "is essentially the same as previous nights out," the question is one of acting, and as such "we had better start by making certain allowances . . . for the homeliness of our English attempts to volatilize our-selves sufficiently to breathe that fantastic atmosphere of moral irresponsibility in which alone the hero of farcical comedy,

[7] Unidentified review of 24 Jan. 1880 in the Enthoven Collection, Vic-toria and Albert Museum. *Brighton* was originally *Saratoga* in the version Wyndham played through America.

like Pierrot or Harlequin, can realize himself fully" (*OTN*, II, 121).

Charteris ("The Philanderer"), and Valentine, the aptly named hero of *You Never Can Tell*, behave very like Robert Sackett and embody the irresponsible volatility proper to the atmosphere of Farce. It is revealing testimony on the origins and atmosphere of both plays that Shaw persistently thought of Charteris and Valentine as Charles Wyndham parts.

Shaw wrote *The Philanderer* for Grein's Independent Theatre; "But even before I finished it, it was apparent that its demands on the most expert and delicate sort of high comedy acting went beyond the resources then at the disposal of Mr Grein. I had written a part which nobody but Charles Wyndham could act, in a play which was impossible at his theatre . . ." (*Plays Unpleasant*, p. xi). Similarly, Shaw wrote *You Never Can Tell* for Cyril Maude at The Haymarket in 1895-1896, and one of the parts proved impossible for the company. To Mrs. Mansfield, who was interested in the play for New York, Shaw wrote in 1899: "There is no difficulty about You Never Can Tell except the difficulty of getting it acted. The end of the second act requires a consummate comedian; and that comedian has never been available. At the Haymarket here we rehearsed the play for some time; but that scene beat us; and finally I told the management that they must give it up . . . You would find the same obstacle—no Valentine. . . . John Drew, or Wyndham (20 years younger) could manage Valentine; but they are out of your reach."[8]

In 1907, Shaw wrote to the business manager of the Court-Savoy enterprise, "I wish we could secure [Robert] Loraine for the autumn at the Savoy. He could do Barker's new play, also Bluntschli & Charteris & Valentine & what not?" Some weeks later, he noted: "Loraine's line in paying work is

[8] Letter of 21 October, in Henderson, *Man of the Century*, pp. 474-75. John Drew was an Anglo-American actor who played romantic-comedy leads. Shaw refers to "his grace of style and apologetic humor" (*OTN*, I, 166).

Wyndham's line. Ten years ago he might have been able to pull off dramatic heroism; but now he knows too much . . ."[9]

Though the moral irresponsibility of the atmosphere in which the farce-comedy hero realized himself was usually, more particularly, a sexual irresponsibility, there is little in the actual texts of the long farcical comedies to justify a reputation of extravagant naughtiness, even with an audience more sensitive to what was said out loud or thought in common in places of public entertainment. However, William Archer offers an explanation. Writing about F. C. Burnand's adaptations of French Farce, with particular reference to *Boulogne* (1879) and *Betsy* (1879), he declares, "the Bowdlerizing process is carried on by means of a sort of cipher to which every one has the key. When Mr. Burnand introduces us to a variety actress or a female acrobat, we all know what was the lady's profession in the original French; and that elastic and convenient term 'flirtation' covers a multitude of sins, but covers them in a very gauzy fashion."[10] Shaw himself notes that the printed text, and the text as submitted to the censorship, was a poor guide to the propriety of a play, and he cites as examples what popular comedians have done with the line, "Might I speak to you for a moment, miss?" and a play in which the principal actress, "between two speeches which contained no reference to her action, changed her underclothing on the stage!" (*Blanco Posnet*, p. 394). There is a difference, of course, between sexual impropriety as deed and as subject matter; but in either form it was the mark of the genre whose standard-bearer in England was *Pink Dominos*.

The comedy of *The Philanderer*, like that of the conventional long farcical comedy, is based upon sexual intrigue and its surroundings of subterfuge rather than upon the joys and sorrows of courtship. The pervasive indignity of Farce

[9] MS letters to J. E. Vedrenne, 10 June 1907 and 16 Aug. 1907, in the Enthoven Collection of the Victoria and Albert Museum.
[10] *English Dramatists of Today*, p. 102.

and the sense of furiously insane operation, like a motor racing in a turned-over car, are in this play the consequences Shaw wishes us to connect with the obsolescence of the social institutions governing the relations between the sexes and with the attempt of "advanced" people to ignore them. The initial situation stems clearly from contemporary Farce: Charteris is visiting with one woman when another breaks in on him in a jealous rage. "Julia!" he cries, "The Devil!" That Julia should possess herself of the humours of an outraged wife, though she has not that official position, adds to Shaw's social point as well as to his comedy. Charteris is the conventional irresponsible and volatile hero of farcical comedy in the guise of a radical Ibsenist thinker, and much of the comedy comes, conventionally enough, from the inability of the other characters to cope with him (particularly the philistines and idealists, but also the so-called emancipated persons). What is not conventional is that the "fantastic atmosphere of moral irresponsibility" in which Charteris flourishes exists in the play in order to be judged unsatisfactory.[11]

Marriage and libertinism are the unsatisfactory antagonistic possibilities in *The Philanderer*; similarly, sexual bondage and sexual freedom are the ambivalent and unsatisfactory competing ideas in *You Never Can Tell*. In the latter play, Mrs. Clandon's rebellion, in which she gathered up her children and abandoned their father, was against the domestic and sexual tyranny of a husband. Many years later the issues are still alive. Meanwhile her daughter Gloria, who has been bred up in the ideal of emancipated womanhood, discovers to

[11] Shaw subtitled *The Philanderer* "A Topical Comedy," though in a mood of dislike he calls it "a combination of mechanical farce with realistic filth which quite disgusted me" (28 Aug. 1896, *Ellen Terry and Bernard Shaw*, p. 33). Though he never subtitled a three-act play "farce" or even "farcical comedy," for reasons which will appear below, he sometimes used the category "topical farce," to which *The Philanderer* properly belongs. (See, for example, Shaw's preface to the Independent Theatre edition of *Widowers' Houses*, p. xviii.)

her agony that she is no longer (not even physically) her own mistress when she is caught in the web of physical attraction Valentine spins for her. In *You Never Can Tell*, the basic issues of Farce are developed in terms of a woman's point of view.

Though *You Never Can Tell* and *The Philanderer* are related in subject matter, and Valentine belongs to the same line of farcical-comedy hero as Charteris, the two plays are critically different in that *You Never Can Tell* was conceived as a humanization of Farce rather than as an invidious exploitation of its atmosphere. In Shaw's most general consideration of Farce in *Our Theatres in the Nineties*, he wrote that "to laugh without sympathy is a ruinous abuse of a noble function; and the degradation of any race may be measured by the degree of their addiction to it." After discoursing on conditioned responses and "galvanic tricks" of acting, he continues, "I shall now, perhaps, be understood (if not, no matter) when I class the laughter produced by conventional farcical comedy as purely galvanic, and the inference drawn by the audience that since they are laughing they must be amused or edified or pleased, as a delusion" (*OTN*, II, 118-20).

In the preface to the *Pleasant Plays* (p. ix), Shaw speaks of *You Never Can Tell* as a response to requests by managers in search of fashionable comedies for West End Theatres. "I had no difficulty in complying, as I have always cast my plays in the ordinary practical comedy form in use at all the theatres; and far from taking an unsympathetic view of the popular preference for fun, fashionable dresses, a little music, and even an exhibition of eating and drinking by people with an expensive air, attended by an if-possible-comic waiter, I was more than willing to shew that the drama can humanize these things as easily as they, in the wrong hands, can dehumanize the drama." If the material which is thus humanized is drawn from farcical comedy, Shaw avoids the term, though his contemporaries in the theater made the identification easily.

Shaw objected to the billing of *You Never Can Tell* as a farce or a farcical comedy because the words suggested to him "galvanic" laughter and a neglect of the very aspects which made the difference between the inhumanly mechanical world of Farce and the world of his play. Following Archer's notice in the *Tribune* (July 1906), Shaw wrote to him in reproof: "And you still talk about 'a farce.' The thing is a poem and a document, a sermon and a festival, all in one."[12] On receiving reports of a provincial production, Shaw wrote to the management at the Court, "Indignant letters from disciples in the country and a chance press cutting reveal the fact that Trevor Lowe has announced Y.N.C.T. as a farcical comedy, and has cut Mrs. Clandon's speech out of the first act. Kindly obliterate Trevor Lowe from the book of life and tell him not to accept any further dates. If he wants to be a waiter in a farcical comedy, let him try Pink Dominoes [*sic*]."[13]

To benefit from Shaw's humanization of the materials of Farce, an audience had to recognize in Crampton, for example, not only the conventional crusty old curmudgeon but also the tactless and bad tempered human being, soured by marriage to a woman who didn't love him—the man who is most in need of affection because he lacks the art of making himself agreeable. Similarly, it was important to recognize more than the bluestocking in Mrs. Clandon, more than the haughty feminine prig in Gloria, more than the usual comic waiter in "William," since all these figures were similarly humanized, that is, psychologically and philosophically rationalized. But Shaw evidently found that interpreters and audiences could be blind to the modifications and see only the underlying materials. Theatrically sophisticated, they recognized the volatile, amoral hero bent on sexual conquest; the comic waiter; and the initial situation in which a family from

[12] 10 July 1906, in Charles Archer, *William Archer*, p. 295.
[13] 28 Oct. 1908, *Letters to Barker*, pp. 137-38.

—·[255]·—

Madeira with three grown children, who are totally ignorant of their father's identity, engage to have lunch with him (through an outrageous coincidence) in the gardens of a seaside hotel. Even apart from the situation, the hero, the waiter, and the setting were the manifest emblems of farcical comedy.

Nothing identified nineteenth-century Farce and farcical comedy as inevitably as the setting and the comic waiter. In the earlier variety, where errors carried the burden of the comedy, the favorite setting seems to have been the lodging house. In later farce-comedy, where extra-marital adventures loomed larger, it was, for an act at least, the publicly-private place, the hotel restaurant or pleasure garden. Shaw wrote of the three-act farcical comedy,

"I first learnt the weariness of it from Pink Dominos, although that play had an excellent third act; and I have been wearied in the same way by every new version. For we have had it again and again under various titles. Act I, John Smith's home; Act II, the rowdy restaurant or casino at which John Smith, in the course of his clandestine spree, meets all the members of his household, including the schoolboy and the parlormaid; Act III, his house next morning, with the inevitable aftermath of the complications of the night before: who that has any theatrical experience does not know it all by heart?" (*OTN*, II, 120)

In *Pink Dominos*, two wives try their husbands by giving them anonymous rendezvous in masks at the Cremorne Gardens, a pleasure ground on the Thames (providing music and dancing, nightly fireworks, a circus and a theater, temples, chalets, refreshment rooms and private dining rooms), which became the classical setting for extra-marital adventure adapted to English conditions. Rebecca, a seemingly innocent maid, complicates the action by going also, in a pink domino matching that worn by her mistress. The second act is set in a gallery at Cremorne, with doors to private supper rooms all around. The prime comic figure, presiding deity, and general master of confusion, is Brisket, a cool, rascally headwaiter who measures his customers knowingly and cheats them assiduously.[14]

In Boucicault's *Forbidden Fruit* (1880), which Shaw bracketed with *Pink Dominos* (*OTN*, II, 121), Cato Dove is persuaded by his law partner to have a night out with Zulu, the Female Cartridge, one of the star attractions at Cremorne. Dove invents a trip to Nottingham to cover his adventure, but meanwhile Mrs. Dove's long-absent brother from India appears and takes her to Cremorne. The comic waiter and king of confusion here is Swallbach, a German. Dove, of course, is jealous, and disguises himself as the waiter. After much sprinting between rooms, and some fearful lying, all are reconciled.

By the time of Pinero's notable success *The Magistrate* (1885), Cremorne had been closed by a licensing dispute for some seven years and other haunts had taken its place in the popular imagination. The second act of *The Magistrate* presents the usual "private room," the usual comic waiter, and the usual outrageous coincidences, now at the metropolitan "Hotel des Princes." The waiter remained a constant of the convention once he had become familiar.

While farcical form and fashion changed, the archetypal seaside hotel remained a standard Farce setting, no doubt because it combined the dramatic advantages of the later pleasure garden and the earlier lodging house. J. M. Morton's *Steeple-Chase* (1865) takes place at a Southampton inn. Bronson Howard and Frank Marshall's *Brighton* is set, by acts, in the

[14] Earlier imports from France had also used the public masked ball as a setting. For example, in J. R. Planché's *The Follies of a Night* (1842), a vaudeville comedy of errors and farcical intrigue, a husband and wife belonging to the highest nobility both sneak off to a masked ball and there become entangled. J. M. Morton's *Lend Me Five Shillings* (1846), a farce of jealousy and mistaken identity, is similarly set at a ball, and includes a comic waiter.

Aquarium, Brighton; the Hall of the Grand Hotel, Brighton; Brunswick Park, Brighton; and an Apartment in the Grand Hotel, Brighton. Charles Mathews' *My Awful Dad* (1875) has its second act (of two) take place in the "General room in the Sea View Hotel, Scarborough, opening on a terrace, with a view of the sea and the Spa." Here Cruets, a comic headwaiter, reigns, and here a remarkable family encounter takes place, between a son accompanied by his intended in-laws and a father with two music-hall ladies. W. S. Gilbert's *Randall's Thumb* (1871), a mixture of courtship comedy, farce, and melodrama, is similarly set: "Gardens of Beachington Hotel. Entrance to Hotel L.; garden table and two chairs, R.; table and chair, L. . . . entrance to hotel garden, C.; sea view." W. E. Suter's *The Lost Child* (1863), a one-act Farce with a comic waiter, is set in the "Garden of a Sea-side Hotel at ————, the house supposed to be on an eminence fronting the sea . . . vessels sailing; bathing machines, &c., in the distance; garden chairs and small tables scattered about the gardens, which is [*sic*] tastefully laid out."

An audience of the nineties could not have overlooked the farcical derivation of Shaw's second-act setting for an unusual family encounter (on the terrace of the generically named "Marine Hotel") or of his extraordinary genius of a comic waiter (who unobtrusively manipulates everyone through the whole of the second act), or of even the masked ball with which the play ends (an extravagant harlequinade bringing with it a fantastic atmosphere, like the festival-dance at the end of the old play when Jack hath his Jill). It is illuminating to compare Shaw's description of his setting with some of those above, remembering that Shaw translated his settings and stage directions, for publication, out of what he considered to be the barbarous jargon of acting editions:

> *On the terrace at the Marine Hotel. It is a square flagged platform, glaring in the sun, and fenced on*

*the seaward edge by a parapet. The head waiter
[facing the audience], busy laying napkins on a
luncheon table with his back to the sea, has the hotel
on his right, and on his left, in the corner nearest
the sea, a flight of steps leading down to the beach.
When he looks down the terrace in front of him he
sees, a little to his left, a middle aged gentleman sitting on a chair of iron laths at a little iron table with
a bowl of lump sugar on it . . . At the hotel side of
the terrace, there is a garden seat of the ordinary
esplanade pattern. Access to the hotel for visitors is
by an entrance in the middle of its façade. Nearer
the parapet there lurks a way to the kitchen, masked
by a little trellis porch.* (p. 219)

Photographs of the Court Theater production (1906) show
sea and sky beyond the parapet as in *My Awful Dad, Randall's Thumb*, and *The Lost Child*.

To note the farcical origins and associations of *You Never
Can Tell* is by no means to deny the humanization of these
materials. In fact, the rationalization of character and action
becomes all the more significant in the light of the play's irrational farcical antecedents. But it was this rationalization,
on which the humanization depends, which a theater-wise
audience found so comparatively pale, and so easy to ignore.

Though Shaw frankly declared it a potboiler, *Fanny's First
Play* attempts a similar humanization of the materials of
farcical comedy. The play is in three acts, framed by an induction and an epilogue, and the frame, which puts on the stage
five of the leading dramatic critics of the day, belongs to the
tradition of *The Rehearsal* and *The Critic*. The inner three
acts, however, are "Fanny's play" properly speaking, and have
been performed alone. After the play had achieved some success, Shaw wrote to the editor of the *Play Pictorial*, in the
person of the least intelligent of Fanny's critics, that "Know-

ing Shaw's fearless nature, I could not conceive he would pen a satiric (at the expense of me and my distinguished colleagues) Induction and Epilogue merely as his *apologia* for writing a Shavian version of a Palais Royale farce, minus its entertaining bustle."[15]

In his comment, "Flawner Bannal," the critic, has missed everything except the most superficial aspects of the play; and about those he is right. He misses Margaret Knox's earnest passion and her mother's quiet suffering; the ideas on innocence and experience, on parents and children; and the "humanization" of the farcical materials. He has noticed, however, the resemblance to plays such as F. C. Burnand's *Betsy* (1879), in which Adolphus Birkett, a huge young man of twenty-one, is babied, spoiled, and sheltered, like Shaw's Bobby Gilbey, because his mother considers him still a child. Adolphus is given a private tutor, like Bobby, and a study with a private door; but he uses both for nocturnal adventures, like Bobby, and for seeing a forbidden young lady. However, the characteristic ambiguous young woman (whom another stage-critic, "Gilbert Gunn," declares the author has dragged into Fanny's Play) is not really ambiguous at all; Juggins the butler describes her as "a daugher of joy." Also, the characteristic midnight escapade with the police and the sojourn in the lock-up, which provides so much of the comedy in Pinero's *The Magistrate*, is painted as an experience of considerable brutality. Nevertheless these elements, as well as the post-escapade explanations between the principal persons, the easy juggling of the couples, and the unembarrassed transformation of Juggins into a duke's brother so that the matches might be made up, all stem from the devices of Farce and bring the ambiance of Farce to *Fanny's First Play*.

[15] *Play Pictorial*, 19 (1911), 50. In the same issue of *Play Pictorial* (devoted to *Fanny's First Play*), the editor, B. W. Findon, asks, "What can be more genuinely farcical than the basis of the plot and characterisation of 'Fanny's First Play?'" (p. 52).

Overruled, "A Demonstration" of what a farcical comedy treating extra-marital adventures ought to be, is also set in *"the lounge of a seaside hotel. It is a summer night: the French window behind them stands open. The terrace without overlooks a moonlit harbor"* (p. 169). Shaw wrote of *Overruled*, "The little piece which follows this preface . . . takes the form of a farcical comedy, because it is a contribution to the very extensive dramatic literature which takes as its special department the gallantries of married people" (p. 158). Cast in the Short Farce form, it treats the materials more commonly put on the English stage by the later three-act form. Of Shaw's plays thus far considered, its relationship to Farce is least equivocal. Nevertheless, it has a specific connection with a play which strictly speaking lies outside the area of Farce or farcical comedy.

In his first theatrical criticism for *The Saturday Review* (5 Jan. 1895), Shaw reviewed Sydney Grundy's *Slaves of the Ring*, a play in which, he noted gratefully, there was "a quadrille of lovers instead of a pair." The "ring" of the title is, of course, the marriage ring, and the lovers love out of its bounds. The central scene of the play is the discovery by wife A of her husband and wife B declaring their passion for each other. "It happens," wrote Shaw, "that the plot devised by Mr Grundy to bring off his one scene has all the potentialities of a capital comedy plot" (*OTN*, I, 5).

Shaw used the cross-partnered quadrille and the discovery for *Overruled*, his short play treating the same subject: what people do and how they feel when they love out of marriage. However, a number of devices in *Overruled* stem directly from earlier Farce, as, for example, the mutual and distressing discovery by Gregory Lunn and Mrs. Juno that the other is currently married. And the cross-partnered married quadrille, while not common in serious drama, was not Grundy's invention. A similar situation occurs in Hubert Lille's Farce *As Like as Two Peas* (1854), featuring couples named Richards and Pritchards. Mr. Richards, a lawyer, reveals to the audience that he has made up a "double" to cover his extra-marital expeditions to Cremorne and expresses interest in a young widow. By coincidence, Mrs. Pritchards, the "young widow," comes to consult him about a separation from her husband, and she and Richards discover (like Lunn and Mrs. Juno) that they have been deceiving each other and that they are both married. Further complications follow, and, after a harmless duel between Richards and Pritchards, both couples are reconciled.

There were two points to Shaw's "demonstration" in *Overruled*. First, he held that the contemporary farcical comedy, no less than the contemporary drama of adultery, merely professed a subject-matter of sex, and presented instead only legal dilemmas and plot puzzles. "Duels are not sex; divorce cases are not sex; the Trade Unionism of married women is not sex" (*Overruled*, p. 160). In a section of his preface titled "Farcical Comedy Shirking its Subject," Shaw declares, "Conventional farcical comedies are always finally tedious because the heart of them, the inevitable conjugal infidelity, is always evaded" (p. 165). To remedy this shortcoming, Shaw puts before the audience of *Overruled* a genuine scene of sex—genuine, that is, within the limits of the art: "There is, of course, a sense in which you cannot present sex on the stage, just as you cannot present murder. . . . But the feelings of a murderer can be expressed in a certain artistic convention." In a similar way, he says, in *Tristan and Isolde* (unlike *Romeo and Juliet*), "the curtain does not . . . rise with the lark: the whole night of love is played before the spectators" (p. 161). By using the Tristan convention in "the key of farce," Shaw intends to write the scene that all of nineteenth-century farce teasingly evaded. In the arms of Mrs. Juno, Gregory Lunn cries:

> I protest to the last. I'm against this. I have been
> pushed over a precipice. I'm innocent. This wild

joy, this exquisite tenderness, this ascent into heav-
en can thrill me to the uttermost fibre of my heart
(*with a gesture of ecstasy she hides her face on his
shoulder*); but it cant subdue my mind or corrupt
my conscience, which still shouts to the skies that
I'm not a willing party to this outrageous conduct.
I repudiate the bliss with which you are filling me.

MRS JUNO. Never mind your conscience. Tell me
how happy you are.

GREGORY. No: I recall you to your duty. But oh,
I will give you my life with both hands if you can
tell me that you feel for me one millionth part of
what I feel for you now. (p. 176)

The second point of the "demonstration" in *Overruled* is
a grappling with essentials in causes and consequences. "I
want the unfaithful husband or the unfaithful wife in a
farcical comedy not to bother me with their divorce cases or
the stratagems they employ to avoid a divorce case, but to
tell me how and why married couples are unfaithful. I dont
want to hear the lies they tell one another to conceal what
they have done, but the truths they tell one another when they
have to face what they have done without concealment or
excuse" (p. 166). Shaw's adulterers, in deed or in intention,
are amazingly aware and articulate as to their motivations and
hidden desires (an awareness which contributes to the fantastic atmosphere), and they finally behave in the way Shaw
feels most married people really behave: they make the best
of it. After the discovery, half-way through this play which
Shaw offers as "a model to all future writers" (p. 166), the
four characters settle down into a discussion.

FARCE AND DISCUSSION

There is a special relation between the genre of Farce and
the genre of Discussion. The Discussion Play (see below,

Chapter 12) is marked by a general loosening of the elements of orthodox dramaturgy and by a particular abandonment of all economy of action and situation. Action is asked to dramatize dialectic, to keep pace with thought. Broadly sketched situations, reversals, dilemmas and solutions, are heaped up as fuel to keep the intellectual pot bubbling. Probability is ignored, and the action takes on a quality of extravagant improvisation. The external characteristics, apart from the dialectic, are the external characteristics of Farce.

Stark Young begins an admirable review of *Candida* by declaring, "the theatre's very essence consists in the heightening of its material. Heightening that is free, fluent, almost abstract, unless it has the restrictions of character and rational measure, floats off into farce; which is thus closer to poetic drama and serious tragedy than to plain everyday prose realism." The usual condition for Farce, he goes on to say, "is the lack of strict connection, or the racing ahead of the plot with regard to the characters." *Candida* is "a kind of cerebral farce," a "farce of ideas," because of a peculiar detachability of motive and explanation from the immensely heightened characters.[16] *Candida* was by no means a true Discussion Play like *Getting Married, Misalliance,* or *Heartbreak House.* However, it culminates in a discussion, and as such was an approach to the genre, the genre of cerebral farce, of farce of ideas.

Getting Married; a Disquisitory Play has an immediate relation to Farce and Domestic Comedy in addition to those generic resemblances to Farce which it shares with *Misalliance* and *Heartbreak House.* First of all, its subject of discussion is marriage and the relations of the sexes in relation to marriage, a subject as native to the traditions of Farce and Domestic Comedy as it is foreign to those of Romantic Comedy. Secondly, the encompassing situation of the play is a last-minute reluctance of both the bride and bridegroom to submit to the

[16] *Immortal Shadows: A Book of Dramatic Criticism* (New York, 1948). p. 193.

ceremony for which the guests are assembled and the preparations made. Wedding-day complications (a still-active inspiration to farcical comedy) were the subject of one of the best-known farces of the century, *Le Chapeau de Paille d'Italie* of Labiche, or *The Wedding March* of W. S. Gilbert (1873). Finally, Collins, the ubiquitous stage-managing green-grocer, is an extension of the waiter in *You Never Can Tell*.

The most illuminating resemblance subsists between *Getting Married* and Sardou and de Najac's comedy of ambiguous genre, *Divorçons*, whose English adaptation, *The Queen's Proctor*, might have been reasonably titled "Getting Divorced." In *Divorçons*, despite the Domestic Comedy plot, an atmosphere of farcical absurdity embraces a brilliantly controlled and admirably underplayed discussion of marriage and a reasonable divorce law. The play opens on the eve of legislative consideration of a divorce law, and the point is nicely made, several times over, that with the passage of a divorce act "On a tué la galanterie!" Cyprienne, who has begun an intrigue with young Adhémar decides that, since there would be no recourse for her husband except violence under current conditions, she will not become Adhémar's mistress until divorce makes it possible for her husband to seek and find other redress. Adhémar, who plans to make his conquest and decamp, sends himself a false telegram stating that divorce has been passed, and Cyprienne prepares to rush to him. But Des Prunelles, her husband, unexpectedly calls a conference and declares for an amicable divorce. He gives his wife to Adhémar (who is charmed at the extent of her fortune), on the condition that his honor be temporarily respected. Then Des Prunelles assumes the air of a bachelor, arouses his wife's jealousy, and maneuvers her into coming to dinner with him, in a private room in an elegant, if shady, cabaret, while Adhémar, who was to dine at home with Cyprienne, is sent a false message. Consumed with jealousy, Adhémar rushes in pursuit, follows many false scents through the rain, and reveals (to Cyprienne) his stupidity, stuffiness, insensibility, and lack of romance. The married couple are on the point of "deceiving" Adhémar in their private room when he brings the police to have them arrested.

The parallels to *Getting Married* are not only in the overall fusion of Farce with a genuine discussion of marriage and divorce, but in particulars and details. In Shaw's play, the wedding plans are upset by tracts on marriage which have come into the hands of the bride and groom on the day of the ceremony, so that both lock themselves into their rooms, the groom with a copy of Belfort Bax's essays on Men's Wrongs, the bride with a pamphlet called "Do You Know What You Are Going To Do? By a Woman Who Has Done It." Similarly, in *Divorçons*, part of the first act is devoted to Cyprienne's passionate interest in a pile of books—*On Divorce, About Divorce, Divorce!*—which have thoroughly aroused her to her wrongs. In *Getting Married* Rejjy (the bride's uncle) and his pretty young wife, Leo, have arranged a collusive divorce in which Rejjy struck Leo before a witness and went off with a lady to Brighton. Leo is thus freed to marry the young and clever St. John Hotchkiss. Similarly, in *Divorçons*, the interested parties agree to contrive a divorce by blows so that Cyprienne will be free to marry Adhémar. In both plays the divorcing couples are finally reconciled, partly through the wife's recognition that the substitute husband would be, as husband, just as prosaic and perhaps less comfortable. Shaw's Bishop points out to Leo that "A man is like a phonograph with half-a-dozen records. You soon get tired of them all; and yet you have to sit at table whilst he reels them off to every new visitor. In the end you have to be content with his common humanity . . . Marry whom you please: at the end of a month he'll be Reginald over again" (pp. 281-82).

The history of Shaw's significant uses of Farce is complicated, like the history of his exploitation of Melodrama. It is perfectly plain that Shaw disliked Farce. *The Philanderer*, an "unpleasant" play designed to disturb and disconcert an audience, attempts to identify a social situation with an atmosphere of fantastic immorality, mechanical inhumanity, and pervasive indignity. The mechanical laughter of Farce, Shaw felt, when extended through three acts, simply puts us out of sorts with ourselves and with the world. In *The Philanderer*, Shaw was not attempting to reform Farce or to destroy it; he was using it as a tarbrush.

You Never Can Tell was conceived as an attempt to rescue farce from itself, to replace "galvanic" laughter with "human" laughter, that is, to provide "that proximity of emotion without which laughter, however irresistible, is destructive and sinister" (*Pen Portraits*, p. 287). However, to humanize Farce was in a sense to destroy it, and, where Shaw brings pathos and explanation into *You Never Can Tell* or *Fanny's First Play*, the farcical atmosphere vanishes.

Overruled, in contrast, was not an attempt to negate Farce, but to reveal it to itself, to make it set forth plainly what Shaw observed to be its quintessential concerns. These concerns were sexual adventure, or libertinism, and the marriage bond (softened in Domestic Comedy into romance and domesticity). But the extravagant, sometimes heroic irresponsibility also fundamental to Farce is transferred in *Overruled* from the sexual level to the cerebral. The errant couples are anything but thoughtless. As soon as they discover their infidelities, they sit down to dissect their motives and analyze their positions with an objectivity detached from their simultaneous buffoonery, and with immensely heightened powers. The more volatile of the two husbands, the proper farcical hero, is shown troubled acutely in mind and spirit (much more so than the relatively carefree spokesman for conventional morality) though he ought to be congenitally devoid of both. *Overruled* is a play that could have no successors in Farce, though it claims to be a demonstration for future writers, but only in more Discussion Plays like *Getting Married.* Ultimately, just as Shaw found in Melodrama a basic action and a mode of characterization for his drama of impassioned ideas, he found techniques and an atmosphere for his drama of discussion in Farce.

11

IRISH ROMANCE

John Bull's Other Island is a discussion of the realities of Irish life and character in terms of their theatrical conventions. It belongs to that group of plays, including *Arms and the Man* and *Mrs. Warren's Profession*, which makes direct attacks upon the fundamental romantic elements of a particular dramatic genre, elements which Shaw considered pernicious and illusory. But *John Bull's Other Island* follows the tendency of Shaw's later dramaturgy, and accordingly conventions are invoked chiefly to provide points of reference and to illustrate a discussion. For its wholeness, connection, and rational interest, the play depends upon a dialectically pursued argument on the nature of Irish Reality; for its background materials, and points of departure, it draws upon the conventions of Irish Romance. The discussion of Irish Reality and the disintegration of Irish Romance thus proceed simultaneously.

Shaw's dramatic attack upon the Irish Romance might have been tolerably sketched in advance from his review in 1896 of a revival of Dion Boucicault's germinal play, *The Colleen Bawn* (1860). Under the acid title "Dear Harp of My Country," Shaw told his readers:

"When I imply . . . that the Irishmen in The Colleen Bawn are not real Irishmen, I do not mean for a moment to challenge the authenticity of Mr Richard Purdon, who succeeds Dion Boucicault as Myles. Nor do I even accuse him of demonstrating the undeniable fact that the worst stage Irishmen are often real Irishmen. What I mean is that Dion Boucicault, when he invented Myles, was not holding the mirror up to nature, but blarneying the British public precisely as the Irish car-driver, when he is "cute' enough, blarneys the

English tourist. To an Irishman who has any sort of social conscience, the conception of Ireland as a romantic picture, in which the background is formed by the Lakes of Killarney by moonlight, and a round tower or so, whilst every male figure is 'a broth of a bhoy,' and every female one a colleen in a crimson Connemara cloak, is . . . exasperating . . . The occupation of the Irish peasant is mainly agricultural; and I advise the reader to make it a fixed rule never to allow himself to believe in the alleged Arcadian virtues of the half-starved drudges who are sacrificed to the degrading, brutalizing, and, as far as I can ascertain, entirely unnecessary pursuit of unscientific farming. The virtues of the Irish peasant are the intense melancholy, the surliness of manner, the incapacity for happiness and self-respect that are the tokens of his natural unfitness for a life of wretchedness. His vices are the arts by which he accommodates himself to his slavery—the flattery on his lips which hides the curse in his heart; his pleasant readiness to settle disputes by 'leaving it all to your honor,' in order to make something out of your generosity in addition to exacting the utmost of his legal due from you; his instinctive perception that by pleasing you he can make you serve him; his mendacity and mendicity; his love of a stolen advantage; the superstitious fear of his priest and his Church which does not prevent him from trying to cheat both in the temporal transactions between them . . . Of all the tricks which the Irish nation have played on the slow-witted Saxon, the most outrageous is the palming off on him of the imaginary Irishman of romance." (*OTN*, II, 28-29)

The details of this outline of the Irish stage romance are nearly all put to account in *John Bull's Other Island*. The contrasts are made explicit, as shall be shown below, between the Stage Irishman and the real peasant, with his real virtues and vices; between the "colleen" as she is imagined by the Englishman and the "colleen" as she is; between Ireland as romantic picture, with moonlight and a genuine round tower in the background, and Ireland as reality. Yet Shaw was not concerned to enlighten the "slow-witted Saxon" alone, for the Englishman was not the only one who had succumbed to the illusion. Shaw wrote *John Bull's Other Island* in 1904 "at the request of Mr William Butler Yeats, as a patriotic contribution to the repertory of the Irish Literary Theatre" (*JBOI*, p. 13). His first experience of the atmosphere and appeal of *The Colleen Bawn* had taken place, not in London, but in Dublin.

"The worst of it is," complains Shaw of the imaginary Irishman of romance, "that when a spurious type gets into literature, it strikes the imagination of boys and girls. They form themselves by playing up to it; and thus the unsubstantial fancies of the novelists and music-hall song-writers of one generation are apt to become the unpleasant and mischievous realities of the next" (*OTN*, II, 29-30). The stage Irishman, who had been a welcome favorite in Dublin long before *The Colleen Bawn*, became an institution after. Irish Romance, which could claim exoticism as an excuse for its appeal in England, was evidently not compromised by the proximity of the reality in Ireland; and, indeed, the romance was even paraded as the genuine reality. When Falconer's *Eileen Oge* (1871) opened in Dublin, it was announced in advertisements as "A Drama illustrative of Irish Character and the Romance of Life in the Land of the Shamrock" (*D.E.M.*, 29 April 1872). The Stage Irishman was so sure to be popular that when Joseph Jefferson brought the Gaiety audience his Rip Van Winkle, by all testimony one of the great character creations of the century, "One of the managers (I think it was Mr. Michael Gunn) seemed to have a presentiment of my failure; for, after witnessing the rehearsal, he asked my agent if he thought I could be prevailed upon to make *Rip Van Winkle* an Irishman. I thought at first that this suggestion was meant as a joke; but upon asking Mr. Gunn if he were serious he assured me that he was, adding that he was quite certain that the audience would understand and appreciate the character more fully if I would give the performance a Hibernian coloring instead of a Dutch one. I told him that if I did this, in order to make an harmonious entertainment it would be necessary to alter the entire play—lay the scene in Ireland, and change the names of all the characters; that poor *Rip* would have to be called *Misther O'Winkle*; and to me these alterations would be very absurd. The manager argued that such violent changes were not necessary, and he only suggested that I should act the part with just a 'shlight taste of the brogue.' "[1] Michael Gunn no doubt perceived in Rip's whimsical, drunken, good-hearted humours the elements of the Stage Irishman, and a better chance of success. Dublin, Jefferson reports, was one of the very few places in the world where Rip in a Dutch accent flatly failed.

Complementing the Gaiety's partiality to a stage-Irish hero, the Theatre Royal refused to accept a stage-Irish villain if he were not offset, as in Buckstone's *Green Bushes* (1845), by an abundance of Irish virtue. A vigorous disturbance occurred, for example, over Mulhowther, a low-comedy Irish villain in T. W. Robertson's *M.P.* (1870). When the play was presented in Dublin for the first time by "Richard Younge's celebrated London Comedy Company," Younge found it necessary "to come before the curtain and beg of the audience to allow the piece to proceed without interruption, stating that it was an author's right to pourtray any character he pleased, and that Mr. Canninge was merely fulfilling to the best of his ability the part assigned him" (*D.E.M.*, 29 Aug. 1871). Later in the week, it was reported that "the Irish character of 'Mulhowther' . . . has been entirely changed" (*D.E.M.*, 1 Sept. 1871). A low comedy auxiliary villain was a regular

---

[1] *The Autobiography of Joseph Jefferson* (New York, 1890), p. 378. Jefferson's only visit to Dublin took place in the fall of 1876, some months after Shaw had left for London.

feature of Irish Romance, but he was generally made an Ulsterman or Scot.

The term "Stage Irishman," as Shaw used it, meant something other than the Irishman put on the stage. It implied a stereotype, a developed body of conventions forming a vigorous dramatic mask, instantly recognizable and easily distinguished from the limited number of other dramatic masks. Tim Haffigan, Shaw's Stage Irishman, flaunts the type insignia, both visual and verbal. He presents a bullet head, a red nose, *"a show of reckless geniality and high spirits, helped out by a rollicking stage brogue"* (*JBOI*, p. 73). His first words are "Tim Haffigan, sir, at your service. The top o the mornin to you, Misther Broadbent." He rattles off, in a single breath, all the other tell-tale phrases: "More power to your elbow! an may your shadda never be less! for youre the broth of a boy intirely" (p. 76). He seems warmhearted, impulsive, and whimsically witty, with a weakness for drink. He acts the stereotype, and Broadbent accepts him (p. 77) as "a thorough Irishman, with all the faults and all the qualities of your race: rash and improvident but brave and good-natured; not likely to succeed in business on your own account perhaps, but eloquent, humorous, a lover of freedom, and a true follower of that great Englishman Gladstone." Broadbent is incredulous when his partner tells him that Haffigan was born in Glasgow, and was never in Ireland in his life.

> BROADBENT. But he spoke—he behaved just like an Irishman.
>
> DOYLE. Like an Irishman!! Man alive, dont you know that all this top-o-the-morning and broth-of-a-boy and more-power-to-your-elbow business is got up in England to fool you, like the Albert Hall concerts of Irish music? No Irishman ever talks like that in Ireland, or ever did, or ever will. But when a thoroughly worthless Irishman comes to England

> . . . he soons learns the antics that take you in. He
> picks them up at the theatre or the music hall.
> Haffigan learnt the rudiments from his father, who
> came from my part of Ireland. (p. 81)

Irish character parts were not unusual on the stage before the nineteenth century, from Shakespeare's slave of passion, Captain Macmorris, to Sheridan's whimsical gentleman, Sir Lucius O'Trigger; but only in the nineteenth century did the Stage Irishman develop the importance and consistent individuality to become more than a specialty by which certain actors (like "Irish" Johnstone) were best known. John Brougham and Tyrone Power and, in the golden age of Irish drama, Dion Boucicault and Edmund Falconer wrote plays for themselves that raised the Stage Irishman to "leading business." Only in the nineteenth century did a distinct genre develop with a Stage Irish lead and a setting that was Ireland itself.

The Stage Irishman was fairly launched into the nineteenth century, with many of his identifying humours complete, by George Colman the Younger's *John Bull; or, The Englishman's Fireside* (1803). The influence of Dennis Brulgruddery, Colman's whimsical innkeeper, on the stereotype matched the great popularity of the play and its long continuance in the repertory. *John Bull* invites comparison with *John Bull's Other Island*, not only because the former begins a line that the latter wishes to terminate, and not only because of the suggestive similarity in the two titles, but because both plays contrast and compare persons deliberately designed to represent the national characters of England and Ireland. Colman's Job Thornberry, his "John Bull," corresponds to Shaw's Tom Broadbent; his Dennis Brulgruddery corresponds to Shaw's Larry Doyle. Job Thornberry emerges as an honest tradesman, warmhearted and open-handed, but strong in his hatred of what strikes him as not fair play. Peregrine, a mysterious stranger who pulls all the wires, summarizes the contrast between Job and Dennis: he comments on the Irishman, "'tis national in him to blend eccentricity with kindness. John Bull exhibits a plain, undecorated dish of solid benevolence, but Pat has a garnish of whim around his good nature; and if, now and then, 'tis sprinkled in a little confusion, they must have vitiated stomachs who are not pleased with the embellishment" (IV, i; *Cumberland*, p. 57). Peregrine's presentation and summary of Irish and English character are not far from Tom Broadbent's views. There is particular likeness in the air of patronizing benevolence toward the Irishman's eccentricity and incapacity; a benevolence which Shaw found vicious in its effects.

Colman's characterization of his innkeeping Stage Irishman was substantially that employed through the rest of the century. However, though the overwhelming tendency was toward presenting the Stage Irishman as a man of modest rank, a menial, an artisan, or a minor tradesman, a particular social position was not an incorporate feature of the nineteenth-century stereotype before *The Colleen Bawn*. In James Kenney's *Irish Ambassador* (1831), Sir Patrick is not only a Stage Irishman as Peregrine describes him but a gentleman as well, who is mistaken, in a foreign court, for a master diplomatist with a secret and delicate mission. Sir Patrick is open, joyous, tactless, happy-go-lucky and charming, with a gift for talking nonsense. He accomplishes his unknown mission through luck and confusion, and produces a reputation for himself—comic because so undeserved—of closeness, discretion, and diplomatic tact.

Between *John Bull* and *The Colleen Bawn*, the Stage Irishman, like Sir Patrick, was most frequently found in Comedy or Farce, where the type continued in the pattern Peregrine had laid down for it. For example, in Rodwell's *Teddy the Tiler* (1830), Teddy is a roofer mistaken for a lost heir. Teddy is good-natured, whimsical, gallant, garrulous, and the comedy depends upon his unsophisticated reactions among his snobbish "relatives," and his parody of gentility. Tom Moore in Buckstone's Farce, *The Irish Lion* (1838), is a journeyman-tailor with the same leading qualities. He has literary pretensions and accepts the mis-delivered invitation of a lady-lion-hunter to Tom Moore the poet. Andy Rooney in W. R. Floyd's comedy *Handy Andy* (1860, based on Lover's novel of 1842) is similarly whimsical and bumbling, a servant who happens to end as a peer. Comedy and Farce were the usual vehicles for the Stage Irishman at this period; but such pieces as Samuel Lover's *Rory O'More: A Drama in Three Acts Founded on [Lover's] Romance of that Title* (1837) anticipated the fusion of melodramatic romance with Stage Irish humours characteristic of Boucicault and Falconer. Rory O'More is a glib, gay, and honorable Stage Irishman with an elaborate brogue and endless resources, acting against a background of the rebellion of 1798.

The Colleen Bawn (1860) made a great theatrical success of the union of romantic action and peasant humours manufactured by the Irish novelists of the previous half-century. Based on Gerald Griffin's novel *The Collegians* (1829), it brought the Stage Irishman permanently back to Ireland. In the impoverished gentlemen like Sir Lucius O'Trigger or humorous servingmen generically named Teague who were the Irishmen of fiction and drama before the nineteenth century, Irishness and eccentricity were outlandish; they took their point from a non-Irish setting.[2] But the Stage Irishman of Irish Romance was a peasant on his native turf, like Bryan O'Farrell, the "Low Comedy Lead" in Falconer's *Eileen Oge* (1871), whose class like his costume was part of the fundamental stereotype: "O'Farrell.—Irish peasant, homespun, gray mixed coat, red waistcoat, black neckerchief, gray calico shirt, gray stock-

[2] "Teague" appears in Howard's *The Committee; or, The Faithful Irishman* (1662), in Farquhar's *Twin Rivals* (1702), in Mrs. Centlivre's *A Wife Well Managed* (1715), in Frederick Reynolds' *Notoriety* (1791), and elsewhere.

ings, greased brogues, fustian breeches, hat."[3] Teague the serving man was the ancient mask of the "clever servant" adapted to English conditions. His Irishness was chiefly local coloring, though his locale was England, not Ireland. Bryan had many of Teague's characteristics; but in Ireland, the local variety of a universal comic servant could become a supposed quintessential peasant. In Ireland, in a milieu of romantic action, the quintessential peasant could be thoroughly idealized. It was this form of the stereotype that Shaw found particularly damnable.

Despite his inclusion in a native habitat of spectacular melodrama and romance, the later nineteenth-century Stage Irishman was not much changed in his characteristic humours. More was made of his immoderate goodness of heart and his reckless courage, but he still belonged, as in Farce, to the province of "Low Comedy," even as the star of a play in which virtue was imperilled and innocence betrayed and traduced. Myles-na-Coppaleen, the Stage Irishman in *The Colleen Bawn; or, The Brides of Garryowen*, who kills one villain and prevents the drowning of the loving and faithful wife of another, is a romantic, drink-distilling, poaching ne'er-do-well, with great charm, a good heart, and a ready tongue, comically evasive on all occasions, and faithfully devoted to his friends. Myles as acted by Boucicault fixed the character of the Stage Irishman, as *The Colleen Bawn* fixed the genre of spectacular, melodramatic, Irish Romance, for the rest of the century.

Edmund Falconer soon followed in the wake of Boucicault with *Peep o'Day; or, Savourneen Deelish: An Irish Romantic Drama* (1861), having seized the essential combination of romance, sensational melodrama, and the humours of the cottage-bred Stage Irishman, here named Barney O'Toole. And the Stage Irishman remains a supposed peasant in the succeeding representatives of the genre, as, for example, in

[3] Costume list of the acting edition issued by the Dramatic Publishing Co. [n.d.].

Boucicault's *Arrah-na-Pogue; or, The Wicklow Wedding: An Irish Drama* (1864) and *The Shaughraun* (1875), where Shaun the Post and Conn the Shaughraun are peasants very much idealized. They are faithful, daring, and whimsical, full of spirits (literal and figurative), of blarney, and mother-wit, and given to misunderstandings with the law. One reviewer noted of Conn, "It may be premised that the term 'shaughraun' means a ne'er-do-well, and is the generic appellation given to those types of an idle, good-natured Irish peasant, overflowing with humour, reckless of danger, inexhaustible in his ingenuity and wit to counteract and defeat villainy, and faithful to death to those he holds dear—types so amusingly and so frequently portrayed in the pages of Lever, Banim, and other Irish novelists."[4]

In Falconer's *Eileen Oge; or, Dark's the Hour Before the Dawn: An Irish Drama* (1871), Bryan O'Farrell is quite typically the peasant "foster brother" of the gentleman hero, in this case Patrick O'Donnell. Bryan was played by Edmund Falconer himself; however, he has almost nothing to do with the plot or the significant action in an ordinary tale of traduced and vindicated innocence. Bryan's own love affairs follow the fortunes of those of his foster brother; he appears once in the nick of time (like Myles-na-Coppaleen) to save the heroine from villainy; and he leads "the bhoys" against the police with no significant results. His seeming superfluity in the play in which he stars is the measure of the indispensability of the peasant Stage Irishman in the genre of Irish Romance.[5]

Shaw is not content just to present a counterfeit Stage Irishman in *John Bull's Other Island*; he also presents a gallery

---

[4] *Illustrated Sporting and Dramatic News*, III (18 Sept. 1875), 590.

[5] In spite of its imperfections and its poor success, *Eileen Oge* is an interesting play, for one or two characters, for certain structural techniques, and for a deliberate effort to utilize Irish folk customs. The last act of the play recapitulates the first, and in both the formal ritual of "calling for the bride," with its prescribed questions, actions, and responses, plays an essential part.

of true Irish types, set in deliberate contrast with the romantic stereotypes. Shaw's true Irish peasant is no attractive, ebullient Conn the Shaughraun, all play and no work; he is Matthew Haffigan, Tim Haffigan's genuine Irish uncle, ugly, morose, and brutalized, with *"a surliness that is meant to be aggressive, and is in effect pathetic"* (p. 118). When Broadbent expresses surprise at the possibility of an industrious Irishman, Doyle replies, "Industrious! That man's industry used to make me sick, even as a boy. I tell you, an Irish peasant's industry is not human: it's worse than the industry of a coral insect. An Englishman has some sense about working: he never does more than he can help . . . but an Irishman will work as if he'd die the moment he stopped" (p. 119). After making a farm out of "a patch of stones on the hillside," and losing it when the landlord put a rent upon it to fit its new value, Haffigan has finally become a small peasant proprietor in his own right, tenacious, greedy, inefficient, and worked out. "The real tragedy of Haffigan," cries Larry Doyle "is the tragedy of his wasted youth, his stunted mind, his drudging over his clods and pigs until he has become a clod and a pig himself—until the soul within him has smouldered into nothing but a dull temper that hurts himself and all around him. I say let him die, and let us have no more of his like" (pp. 170-71).

If Matthew Haffigan embodies most of the "virtues" of the real Irish peasant as Shaw had sketched them in his review of *The Colleen Bawn*, most of the "vices" are embodied in Patsy Farrell, the worthless and seemingly witless young man whom Haffigan is anxious to exploit and keep down. Patsy is described as having *"an instinctively acquired air of helplessness and silliness, indicating, not his real character, but a cunning developed by his constant dread of a hostile dominance . . . Englishmen think him half-witted, which is exactly what he intends them to think"* (p. 97). Barney Doran, a third member of Shaw's gallery, presents Shaw's view of the high spirits and abundant humor which, in the Shaughraun, shows in Conn's enjoyment of the grief at his own wake. Barney Doran leads the mirth over the catastrophe which ensued when Broadbent took Haffigan's pig for a drive. Doran is described as stout bodied, middle-aged, *"with an enormous capacity for derisive, obscene, blasphemous, or merely cruel and senseless fun, and a violent and impetuous intolerance of other temperaments and other opinions, all this representing energy and capacity wasted and demoralized by want of sufficient training and social pressure to force it into beneficent activity and build a character with it"* (pp. 122-23).

Shaw has literally analyzed the Stage Irishman by splitting him into his various aspects: peasant, ingratiating incompetent, and humorist. In addition to this analysis, Shaw brings other elements of the conventional Irish Romance into his discussion: the colleen and the "Irish heiress"; the Irish priest; and the romantic appeal of the Irish scene for Englishmen.

Boucicault's Irish plays generally provided a feminine lead, a "Character Lead," for Agnes Robertson (Mrs. Dion Boucicault), who played both Eily O'Connor (the "Colleen Bawn") and Arrah-of-the-Kiss (*Arrah-na-Pogue*). Shaw later judged that in these parts she "was always hopelessly ladylike," and in *The Colleen Bawn*, "usually made Hardress Cregan's complaints of her rusticity ridiculous by being more refined than he" (*OTN*, II, 32). Shaw is here less than fair, for that Eily O'Connor's natural gentility made her husband's complaints absurd was very much to the point of the play. Moreover, unlike the characteristics of the later Stage Irishman, those of the ideal Irishwoman of Irish Romance were independent of social position. Heiress or peasant, the colleen of Irish Romance had a fine sensibility, a quick apprehension, and, above all, a charming voice and manner. Also, like Claire Ffoliott, the Irish-gentlewoman lead in *The Shaughraun*, she had a special spirited independence of mind, tongue, and action associated with her Irishness. Furthermore, an Irish heiress

was an heiress indeed. In Falconer's *Peep o'Day*, the English
Captain Howard neatly asserts the two chief qualities of the
Stage Irish heiress when someone says of Mary Grace that she
has a brogue: "It is not brogue, but a softening of the harsher
accents of our speech, which colors our language more bright-
ly, and makes music of her dullest sayings. As for her other
charms, she will have ten thousand pounds from her father"
(*Sergel*, p. 16).

When Broadbent first hears of Nora Reilly, his partner tells
him, "Nora has a fortune."

> BROADBENT (*keenly interested*) Eh? How much?
> DOYLE. Forty per annum.
> BROADBENT. Forty thousand?
> DOYLE. No, forty. Forty pounds.
> BROADBENT (*much dashed*) Thats what you call
> a fortune in Rosscullen, is it?
> DOYLE. A girl with a dowry of f i v e pounds calls
> it a fortune in Rosscullen. Whats more, £ 40 a
> year is a fortune there. (*JBOI*, pp. 90-91)

Nevertheless, when Broadbent meets Nora Reilly under the
round tower in the moonlight, he finds himself swept away
by "the magic of this Irish scene, and—I really dont want to
be personal, Miss Reilly; but the charm of your Irish voice."
When Nora, used to polite gallantry, asks in friendly fashion,
"Is it making love to me you are?" Broadbent replies, "If you
say that to me again I shant answer for myself: all the harps
of Ireland are in your voice" (pp. 110-11). But later, when
Broadbent confesses to Larry Doyle, "Her voice has a most
extraordinary effect on me. That Irish voice!" Larry replies,
sympathetically, "Yes, I know. When I first went to London
I very nearly proposed to walk out with a waitress in an
Aerated Bread shop because her Whitechapel accent was so
distinguished, so quaintly touching, so pretty—." Broadbent

finds Nora delicate and ethereal as compared to English women; but Larry indelicately asks, "Do you know what Nora eats?" and details a diet largely composed of tea and bread-and-butter. "The difference is not a difference of type: it's the difference between the woman who eats not wisely but too well, and the woman who eats not wisely but too little" (p. 122). In truth, Nora, the Irish heiress, is frail and low spirited, with an occasionally peevish sensibility. The charm of her fortune is not apparent out of Ireland, as the charm of her voice is not apparent in it. She is neither vigorous nor independent enough to resist such strength of purpose as lies in Broadbent's wooing, and she is swept off in the tide of his superior vitality.

The Catholic priest of Irish Romance was almost as much a stereotype as the Stage Irishman himself. That he developed the external insignia of a stereotype is suggested in the costume note for the Reverend Mr. Mahoney in *Eileen Oge*: "Catholic priest. Black, broad felt hat, eye-glass, as usual; cane." As to character, Father Dolan in *The Shaughraun*, like the priest in *The Colleen Bawn*, is shrewd and kindly, close to the people and part of their life. He even has a tendency to take a drop more than he ought. His sympathetic instincts often threaten to get out of hand, and they reduce his priestly admonitions to mere dutiful gestures, gravely but not seriously regarded. As chaplain to the governed rather than to the powers of the land, he is something of a Friar Lawrence, counselling prudence and abetting imprudence. Falconer's priests are very much the same as Boucicault's. O'Clary in *Peep o'Day* ("First Old Man" in the cast list of the acting edition) is humorous and sympathetic, with vigorous touches of the old Adam. He knocks down Black Mullins, the "Second Heavy," with a cane wielded as a shilelagh. In *Eileen Oge*, when a villainous rent-agent is about to "insult" Norah O'Donnell " (*Music, forte.*)," the priest enters just in the nick of time:

M A H O N E Y (*to* NORAH). Run away! (*exit* NORAH,
   R. MAHONEY *knocks* MACLEAN *down with his cane
   as the latter rushes to follow* NORAH) Leave me to
   deal with this ruffian!

M A C L E A N (*rises on his elbow, as if stunned*). The
   priest!

M A H O N E Y. Yes. There are some occasions on
   which the church must be militant. This is one of
   them. (*Sergel*, p. 23)

Shaw's Father Dempsey is no chaplain of the oppressed and
powerless; he is not troubled by a division between his function and his instincts; and he has no need to assert the mili-
tancy of the church with a vigorous secular arm. Father Dempsey presides over the meeting which is to choose the local
member of parliament, and Larry Doyle declares, "he's the
most powerful man in Rosscullen. The member for Rosscullen
would shake in his shoes if Father Dempsey looked crooked
at him. (*Father Dempsey smiles, by no means averse to this
acknowledgment of his authority*)" (*JBOI*, p. 131). In point
of fact, Father Dempsey has the temper and manner of the
old Stage Priest, affable, shrewd, and worldly, transformed by
affluence and authority. He is introduced as "*a priest neither
by vocation nor ambition, but because the life suits him. He
has boundless authority over his flock, and taxes them stiffly
enough to be a rich man. The old Protestant ascendency is
now too broken to gall him. On the whole, an easygoing,
amiable, even modest man as long as his dues are paid and
his authority and dignity fully admitted*" (p. 102). Other
qualities also found in the Stage Priest of Irish Romance—his
humorous eccentricity, unsettling sympathies, and the manner
of the chaplain rather than of the priest—are transferred to
Peter Keegan, Shaw's unfrocked priest and visionary Irish
saint.

The "conception of Ireland as a romantic picture, in which

—·[283]·—

the background is formed by the lakes of Killarney by moonlight, and a round tower or so" is by no means dismissed as a baseless invention in *John Bull's Other Island*. It is ironically modified, of course, by the story of Matt Haffigan and by the pointed insensibility of Haffigan, the elder Doyles, Barney Doran, and Father Dempsey to anything like the beauty of a landscape. Nevertheless, Shaw asks his scene makers for both magic landscape and the round tower by. moonlight. Doyle in England remembers "that soft moist air, on those white springy roads, in those misty rushes and brown bogs, on those hillsides of granite rocks and magenta heather. Youve no such colors in the sky, no such lure in the distances, no such sadness in the evenings" (*John Bull's Other Island*, p. 84). Here, says Larry Doyle, is the cause of the Irishman's endless dreaming. Though Larry has been away from Ireland for eighteen years and might, therefore, be subject to an enhancement of memory the first view of Island offered to the audience is:

> *Rosscullen. Westward a hillside of granite rock and heather slopes upward across the prospect from south to north. A huge stone stands on it in a naturally impossible place, as if it had been tossed up there by a giant. Over the brow, in the desolate valley beyond, is a round tower. A lonely white high road trending away westward past the tower loses itself at the foot of the far mountains. It is evening; and there are great breadths of silken green in the Irish sky. The sun is setting.*
>
> *A man with the face of a young saint, yet with white hair and perhaps 50 years on his back, is standing near the stone in a trance of intense melancholy, looking over the hills as if by mere intensity of gaze he could pierce the glories of the sunset and see into the streets of heaven.* (p. 95)

Though no Peter Keegan, Tom Broadbent also is affected

by the landscape. The magic of the tower by moonlight has a great deal to do with his infatuation for Nora, and he has at least a guidebook interest in the sunset scene which strikes so deeply into Keegan's soul. But Broadbent's sensibility is not disabling. He has the Englishman's strange power, as Keegan puts it, "of making the best of both worlds," the power to "Let not the right side of your brain know what the left side doeth" (p. 150). Having swept up Nora Reilly, Broadbent comes by the very scene where, the evening before, Keegan had stared at the sunset, and where he himself had first seen the old tower, and where *the grasshopper is again enjoying the sunset by the great stone on the hill.*"

> BROADBENT (*stopping to snuff up the hillside air*) Ah! I like this spot. I like this view. This would be a jolly good place for a hotel and a golf links. Friday to Tuesday, railway ticket and hotel all inclusive. I tell you, Nora, I'm going to develop this place. (p. 164)

As a final comment on the matter, the statement and counterstatement of the two scenes on the hill are brought together in an emphatic cadence. The difference between Keegan's vision and the romantic appeal of the Irish scene for the Englishman is made manifest in Broadbent's innocent reply to Keegan's rueful irony:

> KEEGAN . . . you have promised me that when I come here in the evenings to meditate on my madness; to watch the shadow of the Round Tower lengthening in the sunset; to break my heart uselessly in the curtained gloaming over the dead heart and blinded soul of the island of the saints, you will comfort me with the bustle of a great hotel, and the sight of the little children carrying the golf clubs of your tourists as a preparation for the life to come.

BROADBENT (*quite touched, mutely offering him a cigar to console him . . .*) Yes, Mr Keegan: youre quite right. Theres poetry in everything, even (*looking absently into the cigar case*) in the most modern prosaic things, if you know how to extract it (*he extracts a cigar for himself and offers one to Larry, who takes it*). (p. 168)

The end of *John Bull's Other Island* is a resolution of the discussion, illustrated by the events and characters of the play, on the nature and differences of Englishmen and Irishmen. Thus Shaw's play finally goes behind the Irish Romance to plays like Colman's *John Bull*, Macklin's *Love à la Mode*, and even Shakespeare's *Henry V*, where national types are created to be valued and understood in terms of one another.[6]

The final division between Irishman and Englishman in Shaw's play is that between the Thinkers and the Doers. In terms of character creation, Broadbent of Broadbent and Doyle (like Henry Higgins in *Pygmalion*) is supremely unconscious of his true nature, his true motives, even of his true sentiments. Consequently, he is impervious to satire and takes himself and the world most seriously. He acts promptly and efficiently, never doubting the morality or the disinterest of his most interested behavior. Doyle, in contrast, is extremely conscious of his nature, his motives, and the nature and motives of others. He is aware of the gap between the dream and the reality which, in Shaw's psychology, makes idealists into cynics. He is aware even of his awareness of the gap, and its paralyzing nature. Consequently he has become an Anglophile,

[6] When reviewers deplored the lack of construction, Shaw replied, "Consider my characters—personages who stalk on the stage impersonating millions of real, living, suffering men and women. Good heavens! I have had to get all England and Ireland into three hours and a quarter. I have shown the Englishman to the Irishman and the Irishman to the Englishman, the Protestant to the Catholic and the Catholic to the Protestant," etc. (From an interview in *The Tatler* [16 Nov. 1904], quoted in Henderson, *Man of the Century*, p. 619n).

a willful admirer of Broadbent's blind efficiency. But Keegan
asks near the end,

> Come, Mr Doyle! is this English sentiment so much
> more efficient than our Irish sentiment, after all?
> Mr Broadbent spends his life inefficiently admiring
> the thoughts of great men, and efficiently serving the
> cupidity of base money hunters. We spend o u r lives
> efficiently sneering at him and doing nothing. Which
> of us has any right to reproach the other? (p. 174)

Broadbent, finding that something must be done, does
what lies to his hand; but this is building luxury hotels in "a
hungry land, a naked land, an ignorant and oppressed land."
Doyle, finding that dreaming can be deadly, leaves off sneer-
ing idleness at any cost and by a reflex of cynical despair
seizes on the gospel of Broadbent. Keegan passes judgment:
"Standing here between you the Englishman, so clever in your
foolishness, and this Irishman, so foolish in his cleverness, I
cannot in my ignorance be sure which of you is the more
deeply damned; but I should be unfaithful to my calling if I
opened the gates of my heart less widely to one than to the
other" (pp. 175-76). For Keegan, after all, is a Creative Evolutionary priest and believes in the unity and divinity of life;
in the creative power of imagination ("Every dream is a
prophecy: every jest is an earnest in the womb of Time");
in the presence of hell and the possibility of heaven on earth.

If Shaw ended by counselling Ireland against imitating
England's capitalistic ways, he took care all along to ridicule
and reduce the opposite course, a retreat into the mists of
Irish Romance. He scorns Celticism,[7] laughs at the idea that

[7] "BROADBENT . . . Of course you have the melancholy of the Keltic race—
"DOYLE (*bounding out of his chair*) Good God!!! . . . When people talk
about the Celtic race, I feel as if I could burn down London. That sort of
rot does more harm than ten Coercion Acts. Do you suppose a man need
be a Celt to feel melancholy in Rosscullen? Why, man, Ireland was peo-

—·[287]·—

Irish heroic legend has any meaning for anyone but the English tourist armed with a guidebook (p. 103), and exposes the Stage-Irish idealized peasant as an altogether contemptible fraud. *John Bull's Other Island* would have had an interesting place in the history of the Irish theatre had it reached the Abbey stage, where Yeats and Lady Gregory were drawing upon Irish legend, and where Synge was transforming the speech and humours of Boucicault's idealized stage Irishmen into poetry. But Shaw's play was not produced in Dublin, because, he writes, it was "at that time beyond the resources of the new Abbey Theatre," and also for another reason: "It was uncongenial to the whole spirit of the neo-Gaelic movement, which is bent on creating a new Ireland after its own ideal, whereas my play is a very uncompromising presentment of the real old Ireland" (*John Bull's Other Island*, p. 13).

Shaw's presentation was fundamentally an attack upon the conventions of Irish Romance; but further, the conventions attacked became propositions in a discussion of Irish reality. In the discussion, Tom Broadbent constantly propounds a conventional view and Larry Doyle exposes the reality, while persons like Tim Haffigan, Matt Haffigan, Barney Doran, and Patsy Farrell illustrate the discourse. Ultimately, however, Shaw had more in mind than simple illustration. Nora Reilly, the Irish Heiress, poor, proud, and undernourished, appears to Larry Doyle as *"an incarnation of everything in Ireland that drove him out of it"* (p. 99). She is nevertheless all charm itself to the conquering Englishman, and she becomes his prize. Other illustrative personages are equally broad "incarnations" by virtue of the stereotypes whose place they fill, and they speak for a group or a point of view in the forum of ideas.

On the highest level of the drama of ideas in *John Bull's Other Island*, underlying the national and the economic de-

---

pled just as England was; and its breed was crossed by just the same invaders" (*John Bull's Other Island*, p. 83).

bates, is the debate between Action and Thought as embodied in Tom Broadbent, the Englishman, and Larry Doyle, the Irishman. For all the partnership of Doyle and Broadbent, there is also a grave separation, and the man of realistic imagination can only alternate between the acceptance of thoughtless action and the torments of helpless thought. "I wish I could find a country to live in," Doyle says, "where the facts were not brutal and the dreams not unreal"; but he doesn't believe in such a country. The union of vision and action is asserted by Peter Keegan, who is, he declares, "a Catholic. My country is not Ireland nor England, but the whole mighty realm of my Church" (p. 175). To both the man of thought and the man of action he reveals his vision of the Trinity, in which opposites are reconciled and dreams become reality. Peter Keegan is one of Shaw's visionary realists raised to sanctity and the reputation of madness. In preaching his own religion, Shaw was more and more given to proclaiming the ultimate harmony of vitality and thought; and Peter Keegan, whose Church was the Church of the Life Force, harmonizes the debate between action and imagination, England and Ireland, in his prophetic dream of a heaven on earth which ends the drama of ideas:

> In my dreams [heaven] is a country where the State is the Church and the Church the people: three in one and one in three. It is a commonwealth in which work is play and play is life: three in one and one in three. It is a temple in which the priest is the worshipper and the worshipper the worshipped: three in one and one in three. It is a godhead in which all life is human and all humanity divine: three in one and one in three. It is, in short, the dream of a madman. (p. 177)

12

DISCUSSION PLAY

T H E Discussion Play is a genre in its own right, amenable
to positive definition. It may be, however, that to make the
claim is to fall into a trap for obsessive criticism; for there
is no question but that Shaw used the term "Discussion" to
flaunt his impatience with constricting academic definitions.
The view of the academic purists is satirized in *Fanny's First
Play* when Fanny speaks to the critic Trotter (a genial caricature, in Academy dress, of A. B. Walkley) about the avant-
garde repertory-theater play:

> T R O T T E R (*emphatically*) I think I know the sort
> of entertainments you mean. But please do not beg
> a vital question by calling them plays. . . .
>
> F A N N Y . The authors dont say they are.
>
> T R O T T E R (*warmly*) I am aware that one author,
> who is, I blush to say, a personal friend of mine,
> resorts freely to the dastardly subterfuge of calling
> them conversations, discussions, and so forth, with
> the express object of evading criticism. But I'm
> not to be disarmed by such tricks. I say they are not
> plays. Dialogues, if you will. Exhibitions of char-
> acter, perhaps: especially the character of the au-
> thor. Fictions, possibly . . . But plays, no. I say
> NO. Not plays. (p. 261)

The initial reviews of *John Bull's Other Island* had found
it particularly discursive, formless, and "not a play."[1] Shaw

---

[1] For example, "E. F. S.," in *The Sketch*, called *John Bull's Other Island* "Mr. Shaw's goodness-knows-what. . . . To me the play was vastly
entertaining, despite its excessive length and total lack of form . . . of
course, much of it is irrelevant . . . and of course, it was plotless" (9 Nov.
1904, p. 122). The reviewer in *The Illustrated London News* declared:
"It is not a play . . . no, it is not a play, but something much more inter-

accordingly called his next major effort *Major Barbara, A Discussion in Three Acts.* Alone, *Major Barbara* would not have established a genre; but by the time Shaw dramatized Trotter's complaint in *Fanny's First Play*, he had added *Getting Married, A Conversation* (later called *A Disquisitory Play*) and *Misalliance, A Debate in One Sitting.* When these plays are taken together, it is evident that the Discussion Play is a distinct genre with defining characteristics and that it was a realization and culmination of tendencies evident in Shaw's earlier work, dating particularly from just after the period of the melodramas. *John Bull's Other Island* and the detachable third act of *Man and Superman* were discussion plays without the name. *Major Barbara* was a deliberate experiment in the potentialities of the genre. *Getting Married* and *Misalliance* were its mature fruits. *Heartbreak House*, as. I shall try to show, was alchemically speaking its perfection and sublimation.

The joke in Shaw's substitution of the terms "discussion," "conversation," and "debate" for "drama," or "comedy," or "play" is that there was no joke. In his expansion of the early *Quintessence of Ibsenism* ("Completed to the Death of Ibsen" after *Misalliance* and before *Heartbreak House*), Shaw constructs a poetics of modern drama in which he offers "the discussion" as "a new technical factor in the art of popular stage-play making" which every considerable playwright has been using for a generation:

"Formerly you had in what was called a well made play an exposition in the first act, a situation in the second, and unravelling in the third. Now you have exposition, situation, and discussion; and the discussion is the test of the playwright. . . .

---

esting—a series of loosely connected, almost disconnected scenes, in the progress of which the dramatist, through the mouths of his characters, expresses his views on a multitude of topics connected with the distressful country and it problems and its various classes of people and its predominant partner" (125 [19 Nov. 1904], p. 719).

The discussion conquered Europe in Ibsen's Doll's House; and now the serious playwright recognizes in the discussion not only the main test of his highest powers, but also the real centre of his play's interest." (*Quintessence*, p. 135)

Once introduced, the discussion did not remain a simple feature of an otherwise ordinary play. Shaw offers, as the primary technical novelty of the Ibsen and post-Ibsen plays, "the introduction of the discussion and its development until it so overspreads and interpenetrates the action that it finally assimilates it, making play and discussion practically identical" (*Quintessence*, p. 146). In Shaw's developmental view of Ibsen's innovation, the discussion in *A Doll's House* was only the beginning; the Discussion Play proper was, in effect, the end.

Shaw's view of the role of the discussion in his own work was similarly developmental. In a later "dialogue" constructed from his answers to a written questionnaire, Shaw speaks again of the birth of the Discussion Play at the end of *A Doll's House*, where Nora says, "We must sit down like two rational beings and discuss all this that has been happening between us":

"But the discussion, though at first it appears as a regularly placed feature at the end of the last act, and is initiated by the woman, as in *A Doll's House* and *Candida*, soon spreads itself over the whole play. Both authors and audiences realise more and more that the incidents and situations in a play are only pretences, and that what is interesting is the way we should feel and argue about them if they were real. . . . In *A Doll's House* and *Candida* you have action producing discussion; in *The Doctor's Dilemma* you have discussion producing action, and that action being finally discussed. In other plays you have discussion all over the shop. Sometimes the discussion interpenetrates the action from beginning to end. Sometimes, as in *Getting Married* and *Misalliance*, the whole play, though full of incident, is a discussion and nothing else."[2]

In its fully developed form, the Discussion Play was marked by the total subordination of incident to discussion, even though, as Shaw remarks, the given plays might be full of incident. As a matter of fact, *Getting Married* and *Misalliance* are remarkably crowded with incident because they have been freed so completely from that restraining logic which required an "unravelling" of all the ingenious circumstances of the ingenious situation in the well-made play. Instead, incident can now be used as point of departure, as illustration, or as emphatic resolution of some crisis of the argument. Action is governed by thought. Though the logic of dialectic is different from that of "construction," it is no less strenuous; but from the point of view of orthodox dramaturgy, there had been a great loosening of elements, giving that quality of crowded and extravagant improvisation more generally found in Farce (see above, pp. 263-64).

The subordination of incident to dialectical exigencies is the fundamental formula of the mature Discussion Play. On this foundation other qualities rest, and a descriptive definition of the genre must take into account the following technical characteristics: a central subject of discussion, as in the Platonic dialogues and Shaw's own prefaces, but a free resort to the entire intellectual universe of G.B.S.; a familiar center of reference in a genre associated with the subject of discussion, but a freely improvisatory handling of the basic conventions of that genre; a systematic use of representative social types in addition to representative figures embodying values and points of view. These common features are realized in *Major Barbara, Getting Married, Misalliance,* and *Heartbreak House.* They inhere in a full-fledged genre, as characteristic of

[2] Archibald Henderson, "George Bernard Shaw Self-Revealed," *Fortnightly Review*, 125 (1926), 434-35.

Shaw's "middle period" as Melodrama of the early period and Extravaganza of the late.

MAJOR BARBARA

Major Barbara only partly suits Shaw's description of the fully-developed Discussion Play, for the centrality and seriousness of Barbara makes her story, her passion, dominate the other elements in the first half of the play. Up to the point where she cries, "My God: why hast thou forsaken me?" *Major Barbara* is not a full-fledged Discussion Play; but thereafter it is entirely so, even though Barbara finds a second vocation, experiences a second spiritual upheaval schematically equal to the first. In the last scenes, where incident is fully subordinated to discussion, Shaw carefully takes the primary attention off Barbara's story. (In the early shelter scenes, Barbara's struggle for her soul was direct. In the late arms-factory scenes, it is managed through a surrogate, for Undershaft is apparently engaged in seducing, not Barbara, but her affianced lover, Adolphus Cusins.) Nevertheless, the schematized movement of *Major Barbara* culminates in, first, Barbara's conversion from Christianity, and, second, equally important, her conversion to the Gospel of Andrew Undershaft. Her fall is only the prelude to her redemption, so that we have, not a discussion tacked on to an action, but an entire action treated first in one key, with an interest in persons and events dominating discussion, then in another key, with an interest in discussion dominating persons and events. It is noteworthy that in the succeeding Discussion Plays there is no character as central as Barbara. Instead there is always the sense of a group whose total interplay is valued for itself, rather than for the way it affects any particular individual.

The central subject of discussion is religious and social morality, and characters like Barbara, Lady Britomart, Stephen and Andrew Undershaft, Peter Shirley and Bill Walker are spokesmen for moral points of view. The genre principally invoked to supply a theatrical frame of reference for the discussion is that best suited to the subject, Melodrama. Shaw had already tried the usefulness of Melodrama to present the temptations, perils, and spiritual discoveries of a Bunyanesque pilgrim. Like the Devil's Disciple and Captain Brassbound, Major Barbara undergoes conversion and finds a true vocation, a valid morality, or what amounts to the same thing for her, a valid religion.

Major Barbara shows two of the observable common characteristics of the Discussion Play in possessing a central subject of discussion (Christian and un-Christian moralities) and a familiar genre appropriate to the subject as a center of theatrical reference. It shows a third characteristic in making use of representative social types in addition to characters speaking for values and moral points of view. Lady Britomart, in addition to being "the incarnation of morality," represents an unreconstructed aristocracy; Undershaft, the foundling, represents an essentially classless plutocracy. That Barbara is her aristocratic mother's as well as her foundling father's daughter when she marries the philosopher is as important to the philosophical-political resolution of the play as Plato's suggestion, "that society cannot be saved until either the Professors of Greek take to making gunpowder, or else the makers of gunpowder become Professors of Greek" (*Barbara*, p. 334). Peter Shirley and Snobby Price represent, between them, the working class. Peter Shirley is conscientious, profitable (to his employers), and honest, "and what av I got by it?" (pp. 288-89). Snobby Price, who has none of these virtues, describes himself as "an intelligent workin man. . . . In a proper state of society I am sober, industrious and honest: in Rome, so to speak, I do as the Romans do" (pp. 266-67). He speaks not for himself only but for a social contingent. In the Discussion Plays which followed *Major Barbara*, this technique was to become increasingly important until *Heartbreak House*, in which there is a fusion of the subject of discussion and these representative social types.

In the course of composition, Shaw summarized the first part of *Major Barbara* as follows:

"[Barbara] is a religious young pusson, who has been a wonderful success in the Salvation Army, making converts in all directions, and, as to violent and brutal roughs who beat women on the stage in the most melodramatic manner, she stands them on their heads as if they were naughty children. . . . Her father, who is fond of her (he meets her for the first time practically in the first act) has a most terribly wicked religion of his own, believing only in money and gunpowder; and he finally gets her turned out of the Army as an enemy of religion in a very subtle and very simple way."[3]

The melodramatic associations of *Major Barbara* cluster around the relationship between Barbara and her father, though there are other reminiscences of Melodrama which contribute to the generic reference, such as the stagey asides that pass between Cusins and Undershaft in the presence of Barbara, the question of the inheritance, and the familiar motif of the foundling heir.[4] But fundamental to the melo-

---

[3] Eleanor Robson Belmont, *The Fabric of Memory* (New York, 1957), p. 39. (Letter dated 4 July 1905.)

[4] Shaw inverts the last device, for Cusins is obliged to prove he is a foundling before he can qualify as the true heir. (Stephen, the legitimate son, is kept out of the inheritance, on principle.) Examples of straightforward use of the foundling heir are in Edward Fitzball's *Daughter of the Regiment* (1843), where Madelaine has been found on the battlefield of Marengo, and is identified long after as the niece of a Marchioness; in T. J. Lynch's *Rose of Ettrick Vale* (1829; based on Scott), where Albert, a foundling is really the heir of the Leonards, and recovers his inheritance from the usurping Red Ronald; and in Tom Taylor's *The Serf* (1865), where Ivan is thought to be, at best, the illegitimate son of the old Count and the hated serf of the new, and turns out to be the legitimate son and true heir after all. J. R. Planché, in *The Brigand, A Romantic Drama in Two Acts* (1829), anticipates with romantic seriousness Gilbert's burlesque of the privileges of orphanhood in *The Pirates of Penzance*. In *The Brigand*, Albert, who has been captured, requests to be let go to fetch his own ransom: "Let the belief in your generosity which has in-

dramatic reference of the play is the conventional relationship between the passionate, designing "heavy"[5] and the fair, spiritual heroine who is protected by the aureole of her innocence as Barbara feels she is protected by her uniform. Like Jacob M'Closky in Boucicault's *Octoroon*, like the tormented, passionate Meadows in Reade's *It's Never Too Late To Mend*, like the lawyer-agent Coyle in Tom Taylor's *Our American Cousin*, like the gentlemanly Loftus in Falconer's *Eileen Oge*, Undershaft plans first to beggar his victim, by cutting her off from existing supports, and then to get her into his power. M'Closky ruins the Peytons, Zoe's protectors, and buys her as a slave in the forced sale of the plantation; Loftus has Eileen's lover transported and wins her through his power to ruin or save her father. And like these heavy lawyers and rent-agents of Melodrama whose dark passions disqualify them for straightforward wooing, Undershaft realizes he must capture Barbara by indirection. In the scene in which he plots her downfall, he tells Cusins, Barbara's lover, "My friend: I never ask for what I can buy."

> CUSINS (*in a white fury*) Do I understand you to imply that you can buy Barbara?
> UNDERSHAFT. No; but I can buy the Salvation Army. (p. 288)

In this preliminary project he is, from Barbara's point of view, successful. By paying to the Salvation Army a few thousand pounds, and emphasizing that these are the devil's profits in misery, he cuts Barbara off from her external resources. In

---

spired so novel a proposition, be the pledge of the sincerity with which it is made. That, and his oath, are all a poor foundling has to offer. (MASSARONI, *affected, drops gun. Brigands advance a little, listening.*) MAS. (*starting.*) A foundling? abandoned by your parents? (*A pause.*) Enough, I will trust you . . ." (*French S. D.*, p. 14).

[5] Shaw spoke of the role as "the enormously difficult and heavy part of Barbara's father" (Belmont, *Fabric of Memory*, p. 49).

effect he robs and beggars her in order to offer her the sinister comforts of his home.[6]

Having bought away the Army in the first part of the play, Undershaft buys away Cusins in the last. Having turned Barbara out of her old religion, he tempts her with the splendors and comforts of his new one. And having seen Undershaft's heavenly city, Barbara, like her mother, "felt I must have it—that never, never, never could I let it go; only she thought it was the houses and the kitchen ranges and the linen and china, when it was really all the human souls to be saved" (p. 339).

Though Barbara has not the innocent sanctity of the conventional melodramatic heroine, she is intended as Shaw's equivalent in the line. He wrote to Eleanor Robson, "You see, the priest Keegan in John Bull was an immense success (I mean inside myself, though he did very well on the stage); and now I want to see whether I can make a woman a saint too."[7] But Barbara's sanctity is no more conventionally passionless than it is conventionally innocent. It is not the divinity hedging the usual pure-minded heroine of Melodrama which enables Barbara to subdue the brutality and violence of Bill Walker. Rather it is force of will and confidence in oneself and one's mission. Barbara's foil, the more conventionally virginal Jenny Hill, has no such protection when Bill Walker behaves in the style of Bill Sikes (Figures 16, 17) or Danny Mann drowning Eily O'Connor in *The Colleen Bawn*. Bill strikes down old Rummy Mitchens and seizes Jenny Hill by

---

[6] Of course Undershaft lusts for Barbara's soul ("I shall hand on my torch to my daughter. She shall make my converts and preach my gospel—" p. 287); but Shaw uses Cusins, who thinks in terms of Greek tragedy, to reconcile Undershaft the father with Undershaft the seducer:

    CUSINS. Have you, too, fallen in love with Barbara?
    UNDERSHAFT. Yes, with a father's love.
    CUSINS. A father's love for a grown-up daughter is the most dangerous of all infatuations. I apologize for mentioning my own pale, coy, mistrustful fancy in the same breath with it (p. 286).

[7] *The Fabric of Memory*, p. 39.

the hair *"so violently that she also screams."* He holds Jenny *"writhing in his grasp . . . she screams again as he wrenches her head down"*; she asks God for strength, Bill meanwhile *"striking her with his fist in the face."* No providential retribution like that which overtook Sikes or Danny Mann saves Jenny Hill, though the subject of retribution is not ignored and the melodramatics of the scene create an appropriate background for a consideration of the ethics and efficacy of vengeance. Barbara's handling of Bill gains much from the contrast with his treatment of Jenny; and the difference between her sanctity and that of the conventional innocent heroine is rendered unmistakable.

Undershaft has other associations with the villainous heavies of Melodrama besides those related to his designs on Barbara. He is given the manner and force of the conventional heavy (see Shaw's instructions to the actor, pp. 32-33 above); he has the mesmeric power of the type, and when *"He suddenly reaches up and takes Barbara's hands, looking powerfully into her eyes,"* she answers *"hypnotized"* (p. 327). He also recalls the merciless bankers and ruthless financiers most notably represented by Gideon Bloodgood in Boucicault's *Streets of London* (*Poor of New York*, N.Y., 1857), who ruins others in the first act, "The Panic of 1837," and profits malevolently in the second, "The Panic of 1857." Like Undershaft, Bloodgood will cheat, steal, and attempt to kill rather than be poor, and he does all these things successively. Bloodgood, however, is a villain because he is a villain, whereas Undershaft deliberately adopts the style. Undershaft one day decided "that nothing should stop me except a bullet, neither reason nor morals nor the lives of other men. I said 'Thou shalt starve ere I starve'; and with that word I became free and great. I was a dangerous man until I had my will: now I am a useful, beneficent, kindly person. That is the history of most self-made millionaires, I fancy. When it is the history

—·[299]·—

of every Englishman we shall have an England worth living in" (*Barbara*, p. 330). Undershaft makes a principle of Bloodgood's lack of principle.

The conventional stage villain, however, was not content merely to act villainously; he also professed villainy, as a code. He was not, like Sartorius in *Widowers' Houses*, a man convinced that his actions were reasonable, decent, and inevitable in the light of circumstances; he was consciously wicked and malevolent, hardening himself against the conscience which still caused him to start and shake, and occasionally uttering the devilish sentiments which were to call down upon him the wrath of heaven. Undershaft, preaching the devil's gospel of money and gunpowder, plays upon this convention for all it is worth, to the great scandal of Lady Britomart. In a "drama of unsettled ideals," Lady Britomart's conventional morality is given no initial advantage over Undershaft's heterodox morality; but to absolutists like Stephen, who believe that "Right is right; and wrong is wrong; and if a man cannot distinguish them properly, he is either a fool or a rascal" (pp. 250-51), Undershaft's self-conscious turpitude is that of Richard Crookback, Macaire, and Spider Skinner, the gentlemanly scoundrel and master criminal in Jones and Herman's *Silver King*.

The Silver King (1882) was an expert Melodrama presenting an ideal division of the elements which are concentrated in the figure of Andrew Undershaft. It is a story of traduced and vindicated innocence, in which Wilfred Denver, who flees from a crime he mistakenly thinks his own, goes to Nevada and becomes the "Silver King." Meanwhile the true villain, Spider Skinner, has also been prospering, without qualm or conscience. He is impervious to the pleas of his own wife when he decides to evict Denver's temporarily destitute "widow" and "orphans" from their miserable cottage:

OLIVE. But it isn't her fault she is poor.

—·[300]·—

SKINNER. Fault! It's no fault in England to be
poor. It's a crime. That's the reason I'm rich.[8]

Undershaft uses the very language of Spider Skinner; and if
Skinner is a master-thief and a murderer, Undershaft is a
capitalist and a maker of aerial battleships, which to Shaw
was the social equivalent. But Undershaft leaves no room for
Olive's retort ("Rich? When I think how our money is got,
I grudge the poorest labourer's wife her crust of bread and
drink of water"):

CUSINS. Do you call poverty a crime?
UNDERSHAFT. The worst of crimes. All the
other crimes are virtues beside it: all the other dis-
honors are chivalry itself by comparison. Poverty
blights whole cities; spreads horrible pestilences;
strikes dead the very souls of all who come within
sight, sound, or smell of it. What y o u call crime
is nothing: a murder here and a theft there, a blow
now and a curse then: what do they matter? they
are only the accidents and illnesses of life . . .
(p. 329).

The paradoxical inversion of crime and disease, crime and
misfortune, is originally Erewhonian. But to propound it as
a gospel in a play, Shaw creates Undershaft in the image,
not of Butler's conscientious traveller, but of the Prince of
Darkness and his melodramatic counterparts.

Skinner's principles, or rather, his articulate lack of principle, do not spare him from working hard at his "profession"
for his money. He is rich, but not so rich as Undershaft, who
can afford to relax into the role of the beneficent, kindly millionaire, who creates a heavenly city for his workmen in England's green and pleasant land, resulting incidentally in "a
colossal profit, which comes to me." The benevolent million-

[8] H. A. Jones and Henry Herman, *The Silver King*, in *Representative
Plays by Henry Arthur Jones* (Boston, 1925), I, p. 45.

aire in *The Siver King* is Wilfred Denver, whose money came
to him without effort and without stain; who

> . . . Went to bed one night a common miner, and
> the next a millionaire.
> SELWYN. I've heard so. They call him the Silver
> King.
> BAXTER. Gives a lot of money away, doesn't he?
> SELWYN. His whole life is spent in doing good.
> He's as noble and generous as he is rich. (p. 69)

Denver even speaks of the city in Nevada that he, like Undershaft, has built, "where every man would shed his blood for
me, and every child is taught to reverence the name of John
Franklin [Denver's pseudonym]."

The diabolism of Skinner, the anti-social villain, and the
humanitarian paternalism of Denver, the benevolent millionaire, are the nicely distinguished melodramatic references for
Andrew Undershaft, humanitarian diabolist and self-declared
mystic bent on making power for the world, who would have
every man do as he had done and become dangerous, and
whose vocation in the end is the same as Barbara's: the saving of souls.[9]

The difference between the use of Melodrama in *The
Devil's Disciple* and in *Major Barbara* is in the integrity of
the stage world that the genre conventions create. In *The
Devil's Disciple*, Melodrama provided a form and a method,
and the play is a demonstration of what can be done within

[9] Shaw looked upon Blake as the great visionary poet-prophet of moral
and social revolution and of creative evolution, and in these respects, his
own direct ancestor. Undershaft's diabolism is Blake's diabolism, as Shaw
understood it: the form taken by Blake's rejection of encrusted and perverted idealities. Dick Dudgeon in *The Devil's Disciple* similarly dramatized the rejection of his mother's puritanism with a dash of brimstone;
but the melodramatic course of events reveals to him that his seeming
irreligion is a higher religion. Undershaft is of course aware of the two
sides of his gospel, the destructive and the visionary. It is up to Barbara
and the others to discover the visionary, creative side if they can.

the genre. In *Major Barbara*, Melodrama provides a center of suggestive associations, and the form and method of the play belong outside the genre. The conventions of Melodrama are used casually, impressionistically. In the long run, however, Melodrama with its broad effects, strong narrative interests, and ideal types, though easily harnessed to project its own form of the Drama of Ideas, was scarcely compatible with the subtly analytical and discursive techniques of the Discussion Play. That *Major Barbara* falls into two distinct halves, two distinct keys, suggests that it should be regarded (presumably without disparagement) as "experimental" or as "transitional" between two mature modes, between *The Devil's Disciple, Captain Brassbound,* and the Melodrama of Ideas, and *Getting Married, Misalliance,* and the Discussion.

GETTING MARRIED

Getting Married, Shaw's next play in the genre, is a discussion of marriage in its legal, social and psychological bearings. It exploits the conventions of Farce as the genre chiefly associated with the subject (see above, pp. 264-66).[10] Character and incident are fully subordinated to the discussion, so that the various personages are used systematically to illustrate attitudes toward the subject, and the various incidents to initiate stages of the argument. There is no action issuing out of the discussion; there is simply a clarification. Lesbia can find no way to an alliance that is honorable in her own

[10] The generic connections of *Getting Married* set forth in the chapter on Farce by no means exhaust the subject. Innumerable details of action and dialogue are farcical in "key," that is, executed with broad comic exaggeration. For example, when the General enters, formidable and resplendent in his uniform, he catches sight of the wedding cake and flees weeping into the garden, crying, "I cant bear it." When Hotchkiss, the snob, is driven frantic by his overwhelming passion for the wife of a coal merchant, he lapses suddenly into burlesque melodramatics (a frequent comedy technique of nineteenth-century farce). "Fatal woman," he cries, "if woman you are indeed and not a fiend in human form"; and later he announces, "It's Fate. Ive touched coal; and my hands are black; but theyre clean."

eyes; Leo can find no way to have her Sinjon and simultaneously look after her Rejjy; and Edith and Gerald find no workable alternative to the regular marriage contract with all its legal horrors. Lesbia stays single, Leo has to settle for Sinjon or Rejjy, and Edith and Gerald insure themselves as best they may and get married anyhow.

The subordination of other elements to discussion results in the striking if somewhat disingenuous note which precedes the play, in which Shaw points out he has returned "to unity of time and place as observed in the ancient Greek drama." "I find in practice," Shaw writes, "that the Greek form is inevitable when drama reaches a certain point in poetic and intellectual evolution. Its adoption was not, on my part, a deliberate display of virtuosity in form, but simply the spontaneous falling of a play of ideas into the form most suitable to it, which turned out to be the classical form" (*Getting Married*, p. 180). Shaw is here referring to the "unities"; but his note is at least as suggestive of the Socratic discussion as of classical Greek drama, and *Getting Married* has more in common with the *Symposium* than with the Euripidean tragedies which just recently had been alternating with Shaw's plays at the Court.[11]

The discussion in *Getting Married* proceeds dialectically, as in a Socratic conversation, by the testing of propositions. Alternatives to the institutions of English marriage are proposed and debated until they collapse in evident impossibility. At this crisis of the argument its structure is underlined:

> SYKES. It's certainly rather odd that the whole
> thing seems to fall to pieces the moment you touch
> it.

[11] Granville-Barker produced Gilbert Murray's translations of Euripides' *Hippolytus* (1904), *The Trojan Women* (1905), *Electra* (1906) and *Medea* (1907). Murray appears in *Major Barbara* as Cusins, and recites from his translation of *The Bacchae*. For the Barker-Murray correspondence on the production of the translations, see C. B. Purdom, *Harley Granville Barker*, London, 1955.

THE BISHOP. You see, when you give the devil
fair play he loses his case. He has not been able to
produce even the first clause of a working agree-
ment; so I'm afraid we cant wait for him any
longer. (p. 316)

At this point in the discussion, it is more than ever apparent
that English marriage is painfully inadequate; but it is
equally apparent that no radical transformation of the institution is possible without the unstated moral and economic
transformation of the entire society. As in *Major Barbara* and
the Unpleasant Plays, society is shown to be all of a piece,
and it is not possible to redeem an isolated area from the
general blight. The argument leads to the conclusion that
without the great transformation there is no local remedy,
merely local alleviation.

COLLINS. Cant nothing be done, my lord?
THE BISHOP. You can make divorce reasonable
and decent: that is all.
LESBIA. Thank you for nothing. If you will only
make marriage reasonable and decent, you can do
as you like about divorce. (p. 316)

Characters in *Getting Married* are marshalled by the argument, and systematically embody attitudes toward marriage
or illustrate its workings. For example, we hear of Mrs. Collins, the ideal wife, wholly absorbed in her home, her husband, and her children (who consequently run away), "such
an out-and-out wife and mother that she's hardly a responsible
human being out of her house, except when she's marketing"
(p. 264). She is contrasted with Collins' sister-in-law, the Lady
Mayoress "Mrs. George," whose variety of experience outside
respectable domesticity "made her wonderful interesting. . . .
and gave her a lot of sense" (p. 263). Later in the play Mrs.
George goes into a trance, and freed from time and person
speaks for Woman in general.

—·[305]·—

Other women who embody aspects of the discussion are Lesbia Grantham and Leo Bridgenorth. Lesbia speaks for the old maids of England who would bear children if they could do so on honorable terms. She wants children but not a husband; "The law will not allow me to do that; so I have made up my mind to have neither husband nor children" (p. 268). In contrast, Leo wants many husbands. She is a *femme moyenne sensuelle* with moods and personality-needs unsatisfied by marriage as constituted. Among the men are Soames, the Bishop's chaplain, who condemns marriage from the point of view of Pauline celibacy; and the General, the Man of Sentiment, whose vision of marriage reduces, in the debate with Lesbia Grantham, to "calls of nature" and the "natural appetites." Finally, there is St. John Hotchkiss, the classical enemy of marriage, an aristocratic libertine who loathes "the whole marriage morality of the middle classes with all my instincts"; who is nevertheless "not a man of sentiment, but a man of honor," and is bound by the marriage bond "as it never seems to bind the people who believe in it, and whose chief amusement it is to go to the theatres where it is laughed at" (pp. 350-51).

In addition to their function of representing attitudes and aspects of the debate on marriage, a number of the personages of the play have a representative social function as well. The Bridgenorths are in fact presented as an archetypal governing-class family. There are three brothers, in the Land, the Church, and the Army. Reginald declares "I take it that we Bridgenorths are a pretty typical English family of the sort that has always set things straight and stuck up for the right to think and believe according to our conscience. But nowadays we are expected to dress and eat as the week-end bounders do, and to think and believe as the converted cannibals . . ." (p. 285). The third estate is represented as well. The General, who wears his resplendent uniform despite army customs, sends Collins, the catering greengrocer, for his Aldermanic gown. "The Bishop's apron, my uniform, your robes: the Church, the Army, and the Municipality" (pp. 269-70). Given a basis in costume, the representative function of the wearers is reinformed in the dialogue. For example, the General later announces to his brother the Bishop, as Collins enters in his robes, "Alfred: I'm not equal to this crisis. You are not equal to it. The Army has failed. The Church has failed. I shall put aside all idle social distinctions and appeal to the Municipality" (p. 302).

The many needs, temperaments, institutional representatives, and points of view among the persons of *Getting Married* serve not only to illustrate the central subject but to permit its complex, discursive, and elaborate investigation. No single character is possessed of more than a corner of the whole truth, and the argument only threads the multiplicity; it does not include it. The dialectical results are not even stated, though they are evident enough and are given lengthy exposition in the preface. There is no Socrates in the play, though the Bishop perhaps gives a sense that he could say more if he wished; consequently there is no sense that a discussion has been driven to a prearranged conclusion. Moreover Mrs. George's sibylline speaking, "as if it was the whole human race giving you a bit of its mind," and the provoking interruption which prevents her from answering the last question of the play, leaves a sense that the debate is alive, and that there is truth in each progressive moment of the discussion on the stage, and not merely in the ultimate conclusion; for the subject is not closed.

MISALLIANCE

Misalliance, A Debate in One Sitting also shows the characteristics of the Discussion Play genre fully developed. Its subject, which follows from that of *Getting Married*, is "Parents and Children" (the title of the preface), with particular reference to upbringing—the care and training of the young—

and its reciprocal influence upon social organization. The genre which furnishes the discussion with its play-house associations is Romantic Comedy, whose conventions are handled with such dash, such impressionistic extravagance, that the atmosphere verges on that of Farce. *Misalliance* touches on all three of the characteristic story motifs of nineteenth-century Romantic Comedy: the transformation and testing of Cinderella, misalliance between classes, the opposition of youth and age.

The test motif receives only a glancing allusion, though it is important as a familiar reference for the opening situation. Johnny Tarleton reminds Bentley Summerhays, who is courting his sister, "The match isnt settled yet: dont forget that. Youre on trial in the office because the Governor isnt giving his daughter money for an idle man to live on her. Youre on trial here because my mother thinks a girl should know what a man is like in the house before she marries him" (p. 110). Conventionally, the test was applied to a Cinderella figure being raised to a higher station. But it is Bentley, not Johnny's sister, who belongs to the aristocracy. The convention is reversed.

The misalliance motif is more significantly used in *Misalliance*, though the convention itself receives only perfunctory acknowledgement. The motif is used as an excuse for presenting the virtues and qualities of the classes and the classless, and the difficulties which rise in the way of the match between Bentley and Hypatia Tarleton have nothing to do with class frictions. The match was not to be a conventional barter of money and rank in the first place, but a union of brains and vitality. (From Shaw's social viewpoint such a union was not a misalliance; it was the alliance desperately needed for the governing of England.) The money convention is not ignored, for eventually the manufacturer's daughter asks her father to buy someone else for her, someone with brains and body, in place of her original Bentley. And Bentley, before he is swept away by a vitality eclipsing Hypatia's, inverts the convention of misalliance by pretending shock at some of the views of his prospective manufacturer father-in-law: "And mind you, this is the man who objected to my marrying his daughter on the ground that a marriage between a member of the great and good middle class with one of the vicious and corrupt aristocracy would be a misalliance. A misalliance, if you please!" (p. 126). Aside from the title, there is no other explicit reference to the convention, though class characteristics are studied at length.

Romantic Comedy is invoked as a center of reference for the sake of the third characteristic motif of the genre, the opposition of youth and age. The subject of Shaw's discussion is "Parents and Children," youth and age; and the triumph of youth, life, and spring over wintry opposition apparently lies at the very roots of the comedy that ends in a marriage-feast. The contest of youth and age took two forms in nineteenth-century Romantic Comedy: in one, free, attractive, and regardless young love was opposed by the prejudice, prudence, tyranny, and venality of parents; in the other, there was an actual competition of January and June for the hand of May.

The plot of parental opposition to lovers' inclinations found a generic title in Dion Boucicault's *Old Heads and Young Hearts* (1844). In this commonest of motifs, the parental relation was always subordinate to an interest in the love relation, though occasionally the former was treated at some length. In H. J. Byron's *Our Boys* (1875), the relations of parents and children are the substance of a bare-faced Terentian borrowing. There are two fathers, Sir Geoffrey Champneys, a snobbish stage aristocrat with an iron policy toward his son, and Perkyn Middlewick, a retired butterman with a permissive policy toward his son. Neither system has the desired result, for when the sons return from touring the continent, they follow their wills and upset their fathers' designs by switching matches. Interest and sympathy as usual are with the lovers. In *Misalliance*, Shaw invokes the convention and reverses it. He also presents two fathers, an aristocrat and a manufacturer of underwear, whose designs and inclinations are boisterously brushed aside by the younger generation. But interest and sympathy, for a change, are with the parents. Old hearts are shown to be sensitive, young heads are shown to be tough.

The direct competition of youth and age for the same hand was a less frequent and less biting motif in the nineteenth century than in earlier drama. It occurs with some of its earlier flavor in Boucicault's *London Assurance* (1841), a play which in many respects of style and theme belongs to the eighteenth century. In *London Assurance*, Sir Harcourt Courtly, a decayed fop who has taken to cosmetics, finds competition for Grace Harkaway in his own son Charles. Sir Harcourt loses, and in the end is converted to the doctrine of Nature's Gentleman. In Charles Mathews' more typical *Married for Money* (1855—"altered from *The Wealthy Widow* by John Poole" [1827]), Sir Robert Mellowboy is advanced as a suitor to the nineteen-year-old Matilda by her dragonish mother, and is beaten out by the much younger Bob Royland. Sir Robert is presented as a nice old man, gentle and bruisable, though a trifle odd. In Andrew Halliday's *Daddy Gray* (1868), a benevolent sixty-year-old rescues a maiden's family from ruin and defends her lover from criminal prosecution with the best legal assistance though he knows that to win the case is to lose the girl. In the end he loses both the case and the girl. For all his benevolence, Daddy Gray's marital aspiration is presented as an unhallowed thing, half-comic and half-evil. It turns young Jessie Bell's filial love for him into unconcealed repugnance.

In *Misalliance*, Lord Summerhays, in particular, constantly reverts to the theme of the delicacy of age as compared with the ruthless coarseness of youth. The retired governor of a colony of the empire, Lord Summerhays has come at the command of Hypatia Tarleton, to whom his son is engaged. Shaw teases the audience by retrospectively revealing a situation which would have made a splendid obligatory scene in a well-made play:

> And then, what a situation it was! Just think of it! I was engaged to your son; and you knew nothing about it. He was afraid to tell you: he brought you down here because he thought if he could throw us together I could get round you because I was such a ripping girl. We arranged it all: he and I. We got Papa and Mamma and Johnny out of the way splendidly; and then Bentley took himself off, and left us—you and me!—to take a walk through the heather and admire the scenery of Hindhead. You never dreamt that it was all a plan: that what made me so nice was the way I was playing up to my destiny as the sweet girl that was to make your boy happy. And then! and then! (*She rises to dance and clap her hands in her glee*).
> LORD SUMMERHAYS (*shuddering*) Stop, stop. Can no woman understand a man's delicacy?
> HYPATIA (*revelling in the recollection*) And then —ha, ha!—you proposed. You! A father! For your son's girl! . . .
> LORD SUMMERHAYS . . . How callous youth is! How coarse! How cynical! How ruthlessly cruel!
> (p. 138)

Hypatia was not repelled by Summerhays' proposal; in fact she nearly married him for it; but she has no patience with his shuddering sensibilities. The ultimate reference of Shaw's title is not to marriage as such, but to the consorting of those incompatibles, youth and age, which is part of the human condition.

In addition to a central subject of discussion and a suitable generic reference, *Misalliance* also shows the Discussion Play's characteristic generalizing on society by the use of representative persons. Tarleton's house at Hindhead is the middle-class equivalent of Heartbreak House, with Tarleton and his son respectively presenting the vitality and the smug inertness of the middle class as Summerhays and his son present aspects, past and present, of the aristocracy. Another representative figure is Julius Baker, the underpaid clerk whose mind is a garish mixture of romance, anarchism, and socialism, who declares "I'm a problem. . . . Ive read more than any man in this room . . . Thats whats going to smash up your Capitalism. The problems are beginning to read" (p. 185). Julius Baker reveals the tendency of the discussion: from issues of youth and age, parents and children, the education and breeding up of the young, to the problems of right rule and the Good Society. The Tarletons and the Summerhayses together form the ruling class. Of the younger generation, Bentley Summerhays lacks vocation and training, and Johnny Tarleton lacks imagination and intellect, for he sees all social action in terms of what is good for Tarleton's Underwear. Both are as unfit to rule as Julius Baker is to be ruled; for as Lord Summerhays points out, "to make Democracy work, you need an aristocratic democracy. To make Aristocracy work, you need a democratic aristocracy. Youve got neither, and theres an end of it" (p. 129).

The development of the Discussion Play was always toward a freer handling of the elements, and consequently the clear line of argument which runs through *Getting Married* is missing from *Misalliance*. Instead there is a more casual verbal exploration of the subject, in which aspects are stated and developed at each recurrence, like musical themes, and brought to some sort of consummation in a final ordering of all the elements—an ordering sufficient unto the day, but pregnant with the necessity of radical transformation. For example, the theme of the inevitable misunderstanding between parents and children is stated first in a conversation between Tarleton's son and Lord Summerhays: "I wish youd talk to [my father] about it. It's no use my saying anything: I'm a child to him still" (p. 116). At the next recurrence of the theme, we learn that the elder Tarleton knows nothing of what is on his daughter's mind either. (She has shown herself on the verge of explosion from the ennui of her upbringing, whereupon Tarleton declares to Lord Summerhays, "I think my idea of bringing up a young girl has been rather a success. Dont you listen to this, Patsy: it might make you conceited." Immediately thereafter the two fathers discourse at great length on the unnaturalness of the relation between parent and child and "the fearful shyness of it" [pp. 141-43].) The theme is further developed in the scenes with Julius Baker, who knew nothing about his mother until she was dead. And it reaches a climax (which is indeed the emotional high point of the play) in the scene between Patsy—Hypatia—and Tarleton where she indelicately asks him to buy her a husband. Tarleton is shocked and offended, and distressed at Patsy's evident alacrity to give up her father for a stranger, and Patsy is incapable of understanding his pain. Tarleton is *"almost in hysterics"* and *"broken with emotion,"* and when Lord Summerhays advises him to calm his nerves by reading something, he declares, "I'll read King Lear."

> TARLETON . . . Parents and children! No man should know his own child. No child should know its own father. Let the family be rooted out of civilization! Let the human race be brought up in institutions!
>
> HYPATIA. Oh yes. How jolly! You and I might be friends then; and Joey could stay to dinner. (p. 194)

In the economy of the play the theme is not a product of this incident, but the incident consummates and illustrates the theme. The incidents are particular illustrations of a general aspect of the discussion, and the thematic development of several such aspects provides the organization of the play. The free handling of the themes, which correspond to basic motifs of Romantic Comedy, would have justified Shaw in subtitling *Misalliance* "A Fantasia on Courtship Themes in the Disquisitory Manner." Such a subtitle would have helped to explain *Heartbreak House*, which is not unique in Shaw's canon, but the culmination of a long development with many extraordinary resemblances in form, manner, and content to its immediate predecessor in the line, *Misalliance*.

HEARTBREAK HOUSE

Heartbreak House was first called "A Dramatic Fantasia" and later "A Fantasia on English Themes in the Russian Manner."[12] "Dramatic Fantasia" is in some ways much more apt than "discussion," "conversation," and "debate." It seizes upon such essential qualities of the genre as the allusive and spontaneous handling of conventional dramatic forms and materials and the tendency to treat subject matter and ideas as if they were freely developed musical themes. "Fantasia" is a musical term, and Shaw used it to describe what he looked upon as a particularly music-like play.[13] The Fantasia is de-

[12] The early designation is reported by F. E. Lowenstein in *The Rehearsal Copies of Bernard Shaw's Plays* (London, 1950), p. 21. Of a "first-print" of *Heartbreak House*, he writes: "One copy of this issue the author corrected and used as 'copy' for the 1919 edition which gives a much shortened version. The copy bears (in his hand) 'Rough Proof. Unpublished' on the front cover, and this handwritten addition to the title page: 'A Dramatic Fantasia.'"

[13] Writing to Edward Elgar (12 Aug. 1929) on the idea of an overture to *The Apple Cart* for the first summer dramatic festival at Malvern (1929), Shaw adds: "I demanded overtures to Caesar, to Methuselah (five preludes), and a symphonic poem to Heartbreak House, which is by far the most musical work of the lot." *Letters of Edward Elgar and Other Writings*, ed. Percy M. Young (London, 1956), p. 327.

DISCUSSION PLAY

fined by standard authority as "A piece of instrumental music owning no restriction of formal construction, but the direct product of the composer's impulse. . . . The term is also applied to works built on already existing musical themes." Its family includes the "fantasie" which, according to the Elizabethan musician Thomas Morley, results "when a musician taketh a point [fugal subject] at his pleasure, and wresteth and turneth it as he list, making either much or little of it according as shall seeme best in his own conceit. In this may more art be showne than in any other musicke, because the composer is tide to nothing but that he may adde, deminish, and alter at his pleasure."[14] Applied to a play, the term "fantasia" suggested, above all, a lack of plotted "construction" and an organization around a subject rather than on an action. It was so used by William Archer, who, writing to Gilbert Murray on the *Troades* of Euripides, declared, "It is a fantasia on the theme 'Fuit Ilium.' It might have served Aristotle for the model of the episodic play—perhaps it did, for aught I know."[15] In this sense of organization around a subject, *Heartbreak House* is a fantasia on the theme of England Before the War.

At first glance *Heartbreak House* seems devoid of that other common characteristic of the Discussion Play as earlier defined, a familiar center of reference in a genre associated with the subject of discussion. There is a great deal in *Heartbreak House* that grows out of the nineteenth-century theater, but apparently out of no particular dominating form. For example, Ellie Dunn, the Ingenue, Hector Hushabye, the Romantic Lead, Boss Mangan, the ominous Heavy, Captain Shotover, the eccentric Old Man, Nurse Guiness, Comic Old Woman, Hesione and Ariadne, Heavy Heroine and somewhat sophisti-

[14] *Grove's Dictionary of Music and Musicians*, 5th edit., ed. Eric Blom (London, 1954), "Fantasia" and "Fantasy."
[15] Letter of 18 Oct. 1904 in Charles Archer, *William Archer*, p. 276. The letter followed upon the reading of Murray's translation in typescript.

cated Soubrette, all rest on stereotypes common to many genres.[16] The plot of the innocent maiden who "is going to marry a perfect hog of a millionaire for the sake of her father, who is as poor as a church mouse" (*Heartbreak House*, p. 50) belongs to Melodramatic Romance. The meeting of Ellie Dunn and Hector Hushabye belongs to Farce (see above, p. 245), as does the successful burlesque of Hector's romantic disposition:

> Hector, left alone, contracts his brows, and falls into a daydream. He does not move for some time. Then he folds his arms. Then, throwing his hands behind him, and gripping one with the other, he strides tragically once to and fro. Suddenly he snatches his walking-stick from the teak table, and draws it; for it is a sword-stick. He fights a desperate duel with an imaginary antagonist, and after many vicissitudes runs him through the body up to the hilt. He sheathes his sword and throws it on the sofa, falling into another reverie as he does so. He looks straight into the eyes of an imaginary woman; seizes her by the arms; and says in a deep and thrilling tone "Do you love me!" The captain comes out of the pantry at this moment; and Hector, caught with his arms stretched out and his fists clenched, has to account for his attitude by going through a series of gymnastic exercises. (p. 74)

Captain Shotover has numerous anticipations, from Grandfather Whitehead (1842) in Mark Lemon's play of that name (a doddering old man, trusting, naïve, and troublesome—a key role in the stereotype); and Admiral Guinea (1884) in the

---

[16] For the "line" of Ellie Dunn and Hesione, see Shaw's letter to Siegfried Trebitsch above, pp. 20-21. Ariadne (Lady Utterword) is characterized on her first entrance as "*a blonde . . . very handsome, very well dressed, and so precipitate in speech and action that the first impression (erroneous) is one of comic silliness*" (*Heartbreak House*, pp. 45-46).

play by Stevenson and Henley (a rigid and fierce old sea dog given to preaching and prophecy); to King Lear.[17] The closest anticipation was in the play by Octave Feuillet, adapted as *The Romance of a Poor Young Man* by Pierrepont Edwards and Lester Wallack, and (the version played in Dublin) as *A Hero of Romance* by Westland Marston. In this play, Captain Laroque is an ex-privateer in a stage of impressive and eccentric senility. Like Captain Shotover, he is the head of an aristocratic country house dominated by women (two of them middle-aged, with a contrasting ingenue) and is in closest sympathy with the Ellie-like young girl. Like Captain Shotover, Laroque has created the country home and its civilized inmates, and like him he has a guilty secret. Shotover was supposed to have sold his soul for power when he took a black wife at Zanzibar; Laroque betrayed the French fleet for his fortune. Even Shotover's farcical business of mistaking Mazzini Dunn for someone from the past is anticipated in Captain Laroque's senile mistaking of the rightful heir of the stolen fortune for that heir's remote ancestor.

Despite all these connections, the genre reference Shaw offered for *Heartbreak House* was not drawn from the familiar

[17] There is a reminiscence of Cordelia and the broken Lear in Shotover dozing on the shoulder of Ellie, to whom he has been mystically joined. In *Shakes Versus Shav*, Shaw's late puppet play, Shakes asks "Where is thy Hamlet? Couldst thou write King Lear? SHAV. Aye, with his daughters all complete. Couldst thou/Have written Heartbreak House? Behold my Lear. *A transparency is suddenly lit up, shewing Captain Shotover seated, as in Millais' picture called North-West Passage, with a young woman of virginal beauty.*"
The resemblance between *King Lear* and *Heartbreak House* was not just Shaw's afterthought. Besides a Cordelia in Ellie, who also is fresh, loving, dowerless, heartbroken, and strongminded, Shaw's old daughter-troubled man has his Goneril and Regan. Hesione and Ariadne are modern embodiments of the wicked sisters' sexuality and worldliness. Their husbands, the wife-dominated Hector, the bamboo-wielding Utterword, are reminiscent of Albany and Cornwall. Hector even echoes Albany. His cry to the heavens, "Fall and crush," at the end of the second act of *Heartbreak House*, repeats Albany's similar gesture and cry, "Fall and cease," near the end of *King Lear*. Compare also Mangan's symbolic attempt to take off his clothes with Lear's.

forms of the nineteenth-century theater, but from relatively exotic sources. Consequently the genre is plainly indicated (for the first time) in both the preface for the reader and the subtitle for the playgoer. The first words of the preface declare the central subject and the associated theatrical species:

"HEARTBREAK HOUSE is not merely the name of the play which follows this preface. It is cultured, leisured Europe before the war. . . . A Russian playwright, Tchekov, had produced four fascinating dramatic studies of Heartbreak House, of which three, The Cherry Orchard, Uncle Vanya, and The Seagull, had been performed in England. Tolstoy, in his Fruits of Enlightenment, had shewn us through it in his most ferociously contemptuous manner." (p. 3)

The subtitle in its final form, "A Fantasia in the Russian Manner on English Themes," is pithier, but somewhat misleading; for the "manner" of *Heartbreak House* is not Tchekovian, while a number of the themes are. The preface itself affirms a connection with the Russians in subject matter and attitude, but not in dramatic method. Even the subject matter was one Shaw had been long pursuing. The capabilities, possibilities, and responsibilities of the aristocracies of money and power had been prominent themes in *Major Barbara, Getting Married*, and *Misalliance* (Lina finds and rejects a stifling amoristic domesticity in Tarleton's house, which has correspondences with the characteristic atmosphere of Heartbreak House). The "themes" of *Heartbreak House* were in evidence through the whole group of the Discussion Plays; the "manner" is even more distinctively that of the Discussion Plays.

Though Shaw used Tchekov and Tolstoy to give a genre reference to *Heartbreak House*, there is a sense in which the genre of the Discussion Play here provides its own frame of reference. It is a noteworthy feature of *Heartbreak House* that a major technique of the Discussion Play—the use of representative social types—is transformed into the central subject of the play. *Getting Married* and *Misalliance*, playing on the conventions of other genres, had secured to the Discussion Play its own distinct character as a genre. In seeming confirmation of its maturity, the conventions of the Discussion Play are themselves played upon in *Heartbreak House*. The conversion of techniques to themes is both the fulfillment and the transcendence of the form.

The discussion in *Heartbreak House* is organized as a progressive stripping away of pose and illusion from the wretched and often unsightly truth. Insofar as it takes on thematic importance and in itself becomes matter of discussion, the progressive stripping is the "sublimation" of an ordinary discussion-play technique. The culmination of the process is Boss Mangan's cry near the end of the play, "Look here: I'm going to take off all my clothes . . . Weve stripped ourselves morally naked: well, let us strip ourselves physically naked as well . . ." (pp. 129-30). Mangan himself first appears in the conventional clothes of the masterful captain of industry. He plans to marry Ellie Dunn, who accepts him as the benefactor of her family, but he turns out to have been its oppressor and exploiter. Then Mangan, who "never made up my mind to do a thing yet that I didnt bring it off," "this slavedriver, who spends his life making thousands of rough violent workmen bend to his will and sweat for him: a man accustomed to have great masses of iron beaten into shape for him by steam-hammers!" —Mangan is revealed as weaker than Ellie; he is successful, not because he is stronger or more intelligent or more determined than most men, but because his interests and his passions are more exclusively concentrated upon money. "He doesnt know anything about machinery. He never goes near the men: he couldnt manage them: he is afraid of them. I never can get him to take the least interest in the works . . . People are cruelly unjust to Mangan: they think he is all rugged strength just because his manners are bad" (p. 88).

Finally Mangan, the successful industrialist so reduced and redefined, is revealed as only a sham front, like Dickens' Merdle. He has no money of his own. He lives off his reputation as "an industrial Napoleon," plus "Travelling expenses. And a trifle of commission." He is not even a great swindler, like Merdle, but a stereotyped mask of the conventional Ironmaster, exploited by his faceless, corporate masters and himself. Mangan is peeled layer by layer, like the onion in *Peer Gynt*. When the layers are off, there is nothing left, and he literally disappears.

The other persons and classes and Heartbreak House itself are similarly laid bare by stages. The apparently reckless penetration through the decent fictions of life and personality which takes place in Heartbreak House horrifies a barbaric outsider like Mangan; but the intelligence and courage to find and face unpleasant truth is held up in the play as one of the virtues of the inhabitants. "In this house," says Hector Hushabye, "we know all the poses: our game is to find out the man under the pose" (p. 117). That the game inhered in the Discussion-Play mode is suggested by Shaw's account, as far back as 1897, of "the root objection to Ibsen's people":

"They will not keep up appearances. They come out with our guiltiest secrets so coolly that we feel that if there were such a thing as a hospital for ailing doctors, and a layman were put into a bed there by mistake, the illusionless conversation in the wards might make him feel as we feel when the old people in Ibsen, long finished with chivalry and sentiment, tell each other the frozen truth about their symptoms." (*Pen Portraits and Reviews*, p. 142)

The range of representative social types, which was also a technical feature of the Discussion Play, becomes in *Heartbreak House* an attempt to draw the portrait of a whole civilization. Heretofore, the civilization as a whole was an implicit subject of the discussion, the consideration to which the dialectic led. Now it is objectified as Heartbreak House itself. There are at least thirty pregnant allusions, great and small, to "the house," which give cumulative reminder of its emblematic nature. The persons of the play are either projections of Heartbreak House as the home of cultured and leisured England before the War, or of Heartbreak House as the ship of state drifting perilously toward the rocks. The sets are built to remind one of a ship; and the Captain discourses on "this ship that we are all in . . . This soul's prison we call England." The two aspects of Heartbreak House are joined in the problem of "navigation," the problem of getting the government into the hands of the "most advanced, unprejudiced, frank, humane, unconventional, democratic, free-thinking" class in England, and out of the hands of Mangan and Utterword, the one a "practical man of business" who "may not know anything about my own machinery; but I know how to stick a ramrod into the other fellow's"; and the other the imperial product of "Horseback Hall," who would save the country at the price of "your ridiculous sham democracy" with "a good supply of bamboo to bring the British native to his senses" (pp. 138, 135, 128, 129).

Into the house of Captain Shotover come Lady Utterword, the spokesman for Horseback Hall; Boss Mangan, the dubious representative of plutocracy; Mazzini Dunn, the child of nineteenth-century poetry and liberal idealism; and Billy Dunn, the thief. With the past embodied in Captain Shotover, the present in "my daughters and their men living foolish lives of romance and sentiment and snobbery," and the future in Ellie Dunn, "you, the younger generation, turning from their romance and sentiment and snobbery to money and comfort and hard common sense," we are offered a social, intellectual, and temporal microcosm of England. The end of the play, which moves from portraiture to prophecy, presents both a mystical union of the past and the future, and the day of reckoning for the nineteenth century, which for Shaw was the first World War.[18] Captain Shotover cries "Stand by, all hands, for judgment" (p. 140) as a bomb falls in the gravel pit, purging the society and wrecking old certitudes:

> MAZZINI (*sitting down*) I was quite wrong, after all. It is we who have survived; and Mangan and the burglar—
>
> HECTOR. —the two burglars—
>
> LADY UTTERWORD. —the two practical men of business—
>
> MAZZINI. —both gone. And the poor clergyman will have to get a new house. (p. 142)

The play of discussion is thus ended with a punctuating action, a brief and hopeful allegory embodying the implicit point of the earlier discussions (the need for a redeeming transformation), and suggesting dramaturgic developments to come. The end caps the tendency of the whole, both play and genre, for in order to transform the technical feature of a range of representative types into the substance of *Heartbreak House*, Shaw gave his ensemble and its setting a quality of symbolic inclusiveness. Heartbreak House is not simply representative of or typical of England; it *is* England. The subject of the discussion is given present and actual embodiment, and the drama takes on qualities of parable and fable. Thus, the raising of techniques to subject-matter in *Heartbreak House* is the prelude to *Back to Methuselah*.

Though Shaw continued to use highly discursive techniques in succeeding plays, *Heartbreak House* was the culmination and completion of the clear and vigorous line of dramatic development which found a form in the Discussion Play. The Discussion Play was extraordinary in Shaw's work for the theater in being the closest thing to a genre of his own inven-

[18] See the preface to *Heartbreak House*, "Nature's Long Credits." The tone is apocalyptic, with a bitterness and an absence of any attempt to humor the reader practically unexampled in Shaw.

tion or discovery, though even here, let it be noted, a recognizable reference to an established genre was an essential part of the dramaturgy. In *Heartbreak House*, Shaw was already reaching out of the Discussion Play genre to the last of the three major crystallizations of his drama of ideas: the philosophical extravaganza. The step was from an illustrative and discursive dramatic technique to one that tries to give analogical form to the matter under discussion; from a drama concerned with ideas set in a more or less real, contemporary, country-house world, to a drama concerned with the contemporary world set in an altogether fantastic realm of embodied ideas; from the dramatic Fantasia to the dramatic Fantasy.

13

CHRISTIAN MELODRAMA AND CHRISTMAS PANTOMIME

"A Salvationist pantomime—that defines the show. There ought really to be a harlequinade, in which Marcus Superbus, transformed into the Clown, should throw dust in the eyes of the clergyman, who would of course, for the nonce, replace the policeman of tradition."—WILLIAM ARCHER'S review of *The Sign of the Cross*.

S H A W subtitled *Androcles and the Lion* "A Fable Play" to indicate that it was after all a purposeful whole with an integrity and character of its own. But he recognized that there was an ambivalence in his inspiration, with respect to recognized modes and genres, which led "hardened playgoers" astray. In a program note for the first New York production of *Androcles* (1915), Shaw declared:

"It is not a comedy: it is precisely what the author calls it, A Fable Play: that is, an entertainment for children on an old story from the children's books, which nevertheless contains matter for the most mature wisdom to ponder. In England . . . The children were delighted. But the hardened playgoers did not know what to make of it. At first they settled down to a Christmas pantomime, with low comedians and a comic lion, and began to laugh very good-humoredly. Then they suddenly found their teeth set on edge by a scene of the sort of satirical comedy they most dread and dislike: that is, the comedy that satirizes the kind of thing they are accustomed to accept as extremely correct, official and high-toned. . . .

"But worse remained behind. No sooner had the old playgoers readjusted themselves, with a disagreeable effort, to the episode of satirical comedy, than they found themselves plunged without a moment's preparation into the deepest realities of religion, the most unbearable of all subjects for the purely theatrical public, as it is the most enthralling for the real national public at which the author always aims. And before the playgoers had recovered from their consternation, or decided whether they ought to be scandalized or not, they were back in pantomime fun again. And so it went on, getting more and more bewildering ... until the fun, the satire, the historical study of manners and character, and the deadly deep earnest, were all on the stage at the same moment, many of the audience being so torn one way by laughter and the other way by horror, besides being quite upset by pure shock, that they did not know where they were, and left the theatre rending their garments (metaphorically) and crying Blasphemy, whilst the deeper people for whom the play was written proclaimed that a great movement in religious drama had been inaugurated."[1]

Unquestionably, *Androcles and the Lion, A Fable Play* is a satisfying and original whole, and the playgoers who rejected it as an unpalatable hash were misled by their accumulated knowledge of theater and drama into considering the play only in its variety and not in its unity. No one wishes to excuse the hardened playgoer of 1913 for not recognizing that Shaw was preaching his best truths while apparently engaged in exploiting the charm of one familiar genre and ridiculing the idealistic solemnities of another. Nevertheless, the audience experience which identified *Androcles* first as a Christmas Pantomime, then as an irreverent mockery of pious Melodramas like *The Sign of the Cross*, was perfectly sound and is

---

[1] Quoted in its entirety by Henderson, *Man of the Century*, p. 594n. Supported by this note, Henderson writes of *Androcles*, "It is a Shavian species of Christmas pantomime, an English holiday festivity not found in the American theater. . . . Had it come fifteen years earlier, this play might perhaps have been taken—or mistaken—for a satire on *Quo Vadis* or *The Sign of the Cross*" (p. 593).

worth recovering; it tells much about the making and the meaning of the play.

There is a further dimension to *Androcles*, which was not available to its early audiences, but which appears from the standpoint of Shaw's later plays: *Androcles* was a radical experiment in the direction of the Philosophical Extravaganza, Shaw's last development in the creation of his drama of ideas.

CHRISTMAS PANTOMIME

The English Christmas Pantomime, which still survives in reduced circumstances, was an annual entertainment which, for a time, occupied the nation's theaters from "Boxing Night" (December 26) often to the end of March. It was ostensibly an occasion for children in the theater, and, accordingly, Shaw speaks of *Androcles* as a play for children.[2] The entertainment itself has had a complex history and character, testified to by its misleading name (in its later stages, Christmas Pantomime was totally devoid of dumbshow). However, its leading features were fairly set when Shaw made his first trip to the theater in 1863-1864 to see the "New Grand Christmas Comic Pantomime . . . *Harlequin Puss in Boots!*" Among these, the features which contributed to the making of *Androcles* were the following: the arrangement of the spectacle, the Pantomime story, the Pantomime animal, and the Harlequinade conclusion. Each of these will be considered separately.

Christmas Pantomime was above all spectacular. When William Archer damned *The Sign of the Cross* as a "salvationist pantomime," he meant to call attention to the grossly spectacular aspects of this fountainhead of Christian Melodrama. When the leading impresario of opera in England

---

[2] Shaw makes this assertion, not merely in the program-note quoted above, but also in a remark, cited in Mander and Mitchenson, p. 152, that *Androcles* "was written as a sample of what children like in contrast to Barrie's 'Peter Pan,' which seemed to me a sample of what adults think children like, and is the only play of Barrie's that bored me."

made a similar criticism of Wagner, Shaw found a certain justice in the remark and wrote, "The late Sir Augustus Harris's description of Wagner's Das Rheingold as 'a damned pantomime' was, on its own plane, a thoroughly sound one." For suppose, Shaw asks, the stage had been completely given over to drawing-room drama of the Robertson-to-Pinero school: "Das Rheingold would in that case have been impossible: nobody would have known how to work the changes, to suspend the Rhine maidens, to transform Alberich into a dragon, to assemble the black clouds that are riven by Donner's thunderbolt, or to light up Froh's rainbow bridge" (*OTN*, III, 22). Curiously enough, the whole later history of Christmas Pantomime was a tale of flamboyant hypertrophy of spectacular elements, nowhere reaching a greater elaboration than in the amazing presentations of Sir Augustus Harris at Drury Lane.

Androcles has its share of the spectacle which was almost the only common ground between Pantomime and Christian Melodrama, and which also played so important a part in the music drama of Wagner and his successors; indeed, Shaw recognized the importance of all these spectacular affinities. With the last word of *Androcles* scarcely set down, he informed Siegfried Trebitsch that he had written a new play unlike anything he had done before. "It would make quite a good opera book for [Richard] Strauss. One of the principal characters is a lion. The rest are Christian martyrs and gladiators and Roman emperors. The final scene is in the Coliseum and requires a revolving stage. Reinhardt had better build a big circus and produce it."[3]

The spectacular aspects of Christmas Pantomime, though abounding in invention, conformed, nevertheless, to a traditional scenic arrangement. This arrangement is reflected in *Androcles*, with its "dark opening" in the glooms of the forest and its final "transformation" of the stage into the Colosseum.

[3] Typescript letter to Siegfried Trebitsch, 7 March 1912.

The traditional "dark opening" of pantomime presented a storm, a forest, or a gloomy cavern.[4] The Surrey Theater's pantomime of 1843, *Lindley Murray's Grammar; or, Harlequin A.E.I.O.U. and Y.* began in "The Halls of Gloom." The Adelphi pantomime of 1850, *Nell Gwynne; or, Harlequin Merry Monarch*, began in the "Serpentine Laboratory of Scorpions." The Marylebone pantomime of 1850, *Alfred the Great, the Magic Banjo and the Magic Raven*, began in the "Mystical Playground of Despair." The Olympic pantomime of 1852, *Romeo and Juliet; or, Harlequin and Queen Mab in the World of Dreams*, began with a dark witching scene between Mischief, six sprites, and two deadly poisons, Prussic Acid and British Brandy.[5] A reviewer of *Harlequin Puss in Boots and the Fairies of the Gossamer Grove*, Shaw's first pantomime at the Theatre Royal, Dublin, mentions the "established rule" of the opening (by "burlesque" it must be here understood that part of the Pantomime which precedes the Harlequinade; see below, "Extravaganza," p. 389n.):

"The opening scene, according to the established rule of burlesque, is a dark and gloomy vault, the 'Haunt of the Rats beneath the Old Mill.' This is succeeded by a slowly-elaborated and magnificent fairy tableau, representing the 'Gossamer Groves.' As its name implies, this scene is semi-transparent, the wild depths of the forest appearing in a weird and ghastly manner through the waving pillars, golden arches, gauzy columns, and floating *bouquets* of the Elfin Haunt." (*D.E.M.*, 28 Dec. 1863)

Albert Rothenstein's original forest setting for the dark opening of *Androcles* is almost a fusion of these first two scenes of *Harlequin Puss in Boots*.[6]

[4] See Thelma Niklaus, *Harlequin Phoenix; or, The Rise and Fall of a Bergamask Rogue* (London, 1956), pp. 141-42.

[5] From the programs reported in A. E. Wilson, *King Panto: The Story of Pantomime* (New York, 1935), pp. 130-32.

[6] See the photographs in Mander and Mitchenson, p. 153.

Shaw's revolving-stage magic at the end of *Androcles*, where the Colosseum's green-room becomes the arena, reflects the spectacle-climax of Christmas Pantomime. The succeeding buffoonery, between Androcles, the Lion, and the Emperor, reflects its concluding "harlequinade." The spectacular "transformation scene" of Christmas Pantomime was originally brought about by the good fairy when the hero and his friends were finally inextricably entangled in the nets of villainy. A few touches of the wand brought into play all the available stage machinery, and transformed the actors into the personages of the "harlequinade." The transformation scene was expected to outshine all previous spectacle. The initial reviewer of *Harlequin Puss in Boots* reported of that fairly typical Pantomime, "The transformation scene is entitled 'Leafy Gems of Morning.' It is highly effective. Much of its brilliancy is due to the pyramidal arrangement of the fairies in the background, and the play of the coloured light on their bright dresses. The comic business [the Harlequinade] is very good." A second notice (*D.E.M.*, 19 Jan. 1864), evoked by an unusual success, reflects on the spectacular nature of the whole entertainment: "The secret of this great success is to be found in the magnificence of the scenery, and its singular appropriateness to the story which it illustrates." The reviewer then follows an appreciation of the Gossamer Grove and its "fairy ballet" with a summary of the rest of the pantomime. It is noteworthy that the account is primarily of scenes and spectacle and that all other qualities are matter for an afterthought:

". . . the fortunes of the miller's son, destined to become by feline aid a wealthy lord and a successful lover, are followed from the quaint old mill which his churlish brother inherits into the splendid halls of King Pumpkin, and thence through the pleasant cornfields, which the mendacious puss has claimed as her master's into the Ogre's castle, with which the ingenuity of his faithful attendant has enriched him. Fairy aid being again invoked, the splendours of the transformation scene gradually unfold, and disclose a vista of giant flowers and leafy shrubs, where the fairies rest among the quivering foliage. While the scenery is justly praised as the chief attraction, it would be inconsiderate to pass over without acknowledgment the vivacity with which Mrs. Burkinshaw impersonates Puss in Boots, and the graceful acting of Miss Montague as Ralph, the disinherited son of the miller. The comic business passes over wonderfully well."

During the 1860's, the Pantomime story became more and more confined in character and subject under the sustained influence of J. R. Planché's "fairy extravaganzas." Earlier such bizarre notions as *Harlequin A.E.I.O.U. and Y.* and the other titles mentioned above were not unusual; but by the time of Shaw's theatrical nonage, the Pantomime subject was generally a story from Perrault (e.g. Red Riding Hood, Puss in Boots), or the Countess d'Aulnoy (the Yellow Dwarf, Goldilocks, The White Cat), or *The Arabian Nights* (Ali Baba, Aladdin, Sinbad); or it had to be a popular tale like Dick Whittington, the Babes in the Wood, or Robinson Crusoe.[7] Between 1863 and 1876, the Theatre Royal, Dublin, used all the above as Pantomime subjects, as well as Beauty and the Beast, The House that Jack Built, Jack and the Beanstalk, Bluebeard, and Valentine and Orson, stories of similar character, largely from the same sources. However, the Pantomime subject was not so much limited during this period as defined in character, and less popular tales of similar character were often pressed into service, including an occasional "Androcles and the Lion."[8] The original tales were always treated with considerable freedom, usually in a style of broad farce. Shaw's fable was in-

[7] A. E. Wilson, *King Panto*, p. 161.
[8] For example, Nicoll records an *Androcles and the Lion* at Bristol (26 Dec. 1893), by S. Planché.

stantly recognizable as a legitimate Pantomime subject, legitimately treated.

Puss in Boots, Dick Whittington's Cat, Ali Baba's mule, and Goldilocks' bears were the most notable representatives of a numerous and distinct race of Pantomime animals. One nostalgic historian of the pantomime writes of them, "in a particular sense animals have always belonged to the pantomime. They appeared in Rich's earliest creations and he himself acted a famous impersonation of a chicken. . . . I must confess to a deep affection for pantomime animals. Knowing, affectionate, self-willed, sublimely amoral, they transcend the normal creation."[9] There was no attempt to pretend that the pantomime animal was a genuine animal, or anything less than a talented clown. It is in this spirit that the lion in *Androcles "yells with pain, and shakes his paw wildly"* when the thorn comes out, nods his head intelligently, *"responds by moans of self-pity,"* and holds his tail (like a lady's train) and waltzes with the tailor. It is instructive to compare the photographs of Edward Sillward as the absurd stage lion in the original production with stills from the film made in 1952, where the lion appears in all respects like a superb specimen from the zoo (Mander and Mitchenson, pp. 154-56). Shaw's original conception is made perfectly explicit in a letter to Archibald Henderson on the modern mixture of comedy and tragedy (8 March 1918), where Shaw writes of *Androcles*, "Here I take historical tragedy at its deepest: a point reached only by religious persecution. And the thing is done as if it were a *revue* or a Christmas pantomime, the chief figure being a pantomime lion" (Figures 18, 19).[10]

[9] V. C. Clinton-Baddeley, *All Right on the Night* (London, 1954), p. 227.
[10] Quoted in Henderson, *Playboy*, p. 617. Shaw's production visit to the lions at the zoo should not be misconstrued as the desire for sober naturalism. The effective parodist must also study his subject. Lillah McCarthy reports, "We went back to rehearsals of 'Androcles' and told Edward Silwood [*sic*], who was to play the Lion; but he knew all about lions. Edward Silwood had been on the stage for sixteen years without ever speaking a word—he was a stage menagerie in his gifted self . . ." (*Myself and My Friends*, p. 171).

Androcles was accompanied on its original bill by *"The Harlequinade,* Contrived by Dion Clayton Calthrop and Granville-Barker, Music by Morton Stephenson."[11] The piece featured Clown, Harlequin, Pantaloon, Columbine, and presented, in the form of a Harlequinade, the history of the Harlequinade, from Olympus to the present and into the future. A souvenir program entitled "Notes on Granville Barker's Productions at the St. James's Theatre, September 1st, 1913 with a few portraits" seems to suggest that the piece opened with Harlequin dancing on stage; then Columbine; then "A tremendous shout of 'Here we are again!' and Clown with Pantaloon come into the picture." This was of course the traditional mode of their appearance in Christmas Pantomime.

The presence of *The Harlequinade* on the same bill with *Androcles* would serve to reinforce the Pantomime, children's-play associations of Shaw's drama. The Harlequinade was a traditional part of the Christmas Pantomime and once its leading feature. But with the adoption of the long fairy extravaganza for the Pantomime opening, and with the ballooning of the spectacular elements, the Harlequinade, which was now quite unrelated to the Pantomime story, dwindled and deteriorated, and sometimes disappeared.[12] The Harlequinade nevertheless persisted, though much changed. Reviewing a *Cinderella* at Her Majesty's Theatre in January 1890, Shaw noted the change from the "string of definite incidents" he recalled from Dublin days, in which "The policeman still plotted, the clown counterplotted, the pantaloon muddled everything he attempted, and the harlequin at least danced. At Her Majesty's I found to my astonishment that all this has dwindled to a single scene, lasting about twenty minutes, dur-

---

[11] Notice in the London *Times,* 2 Sept. 1913, p. 6.
[12] See V. C. Clinton-Baddeley, *All Right on the Night,* p. 214. "Harlequinade" was something of a misnomer, for since the days of Joseph Grimaldi, whose memoirs Dickens edited, the clown who sang "Hot Codlins" rather than the Harlequin was the leading figure.

ing which two clowns, two pantaloons, two policemen, and a crowd, without distinct functions, improvise random horse-play."[13] However, in a later review of the Oscar Barrett-Augustus Harris *Aladdin* (January 1897), Shaw notes:

"Mr Barrett does not consider the transformation scene and harlequinade out of date. His transformation scene is very pretty; and the harlequinade is of the kind I can remember when the institution was in full decay about twenty-five years ago: that is, the old woman and the swell have disappeared; the policeman has no part; the old window-trap, through which everybody jumped head foremost except the pantaloon (who muffed it), is not used; the harlequin and columbine do not dance; and the clown neither burns people with a red-hot poker nor knocks at the baker's door and then lies down across the threshold to trip him up as he comes out. But there *is* a clown. . . . And there is a pantaloon." (*OTN*, III, 27)

The spectacle, the story, the lion, and the *Harlequinade* would all have suggested to *Androcles'* early audiences the atmosphere of a Christmas Pantomime. And they would have found the conjunction of Christmas Pantomime and Christian Melodrama a comment in itself. However, though Shaw used Christmas Pantomime, he was by no means an enthusiast of its long traditions and its long decay. In *Fanny's First Play*, he has the Count O'Dowda, a man of taste, heap scorn upon the genre. The Count tells Savoyard, an impresario, that Fanny's play will be like "a Louis Quatorze ballet painted by Watteau," with Columbine, Harlequin, Pantaloon, and a Punchinello or Mascarille or Sganarelle. Savoyard misunderstands:

SAVOYARD. I see. That makes three men; and
the clown and policem[a]n will make five. Thats
why you wanted five men in the company.

[13] *London Music in 1888-89*, p. 291. Shaw declares he has "not been to a pantomime for fourteen years at least" (p. 289), which would carry him back to his last winter in Dublin.

THE COUNT. My dear sir, you dont suppose I mean that vulgar, ugly, silly, senseless, malicious and destructive thing the harlequinade of a nineteenth century English Christmas pantomime! What was it after all but a stupid attempt to imitate the success made by the genius of Grimaldi a hundred years ago? (p. 253)

The Count is by no means Shaw, but Shaw had much more stinging things to say about the Christmas Pantomime in his own person. After complimenting a provincial *Cinderella* in comparison with a stupendous London Pantomime on the same theme, Shaw wrote, "If I were forced to choose which of the two I should sit out again on pain of death, I should choose death" (*London Music*, p. 294). But when writing a modern play whose nearest parallel, one perceptive reviewer pointed out, was "one of those old miracle plays in which buffoonery and religion were mixed pell-mell together,"[14] Shaw used this nineteenth-century spectacle for children for atmosphere, material, and form.

CHRISTIAN MELODRAMA

The First Act of *Androcles* (following the "Prologue" in the vein of Pantomime) begins in a heroic setting of triumphal arches, with bugles, Roman soldiers, and Christians on the road to martyrdom. However, contrary to the stage associations of such a scene, *"the soldiers are dogged and indifferent, the Christians lighthearted and determined to treat their hardships as a joke"* (p. 108). The Roman centurion sets the tone with the admonition, as the marchers wait for the captain to come up, "Now then, you Christians, none of your larks." "A few years ago," wrote the *Times* reviewer, "it would have been an invaluable antidote to *The Sign of the Cross*" (2 Sept. 1913, p. 6).

[14] Desmond MacCarthy, *Shaw* (London, 1951), p. 102.

The sixteen years between Shaw's own review of *The Sign of the Cross* and the writing of *Androcles* (1912) distracted attention not only from Wilson Barrett's play as an inspiration to *Androcles* but from the entire genre to which *The Sign of the Cross* belonged, and of which it was the classic specimen. It was this genre Shaw had in mind as "the kind of thing [playgoers] are accustomed to accept as extremely correct, official and hightoned."[15]

The advent of Barrett's Religious Melodrama in the nineties was complicated by the long history of controversy between religion and the stage. There was a traditional sensitivity in England about the "mingling" of the two, so that audience, critics, and people of the theater, while willingly risking their own persons, were anxious not to contaminate

[15] Religious Melodrama on the stage was by no means obsolete in 1912, and it early became a staple of the film. The new medium perhaps provided an immediate impetus for Shaw's dramatic comment on the genre. He wrote to Mrs. Patrick Campbell in August, 1912, "Do you ever study the cinema? I, who go to an ordinary theatre with effort and reluctance, cannot keep away from the cinema. . . . all these Dramas are dramas of *Bella Donna* in one version or another. Twice I have seen a version called *The Judgment of Solomon* . . ." (*Bernard Shaw and Mrs. Patrick Campbell*, p. 39). In an article called "What the Films May Do to the Drama," Shaw declared, "I have never seen Max Linder in the flesh; nor have I even been within miles of the American Vitagraph company of players. Yet I am as familiar with their persons and their acting as I was in my youth with Buckstone's Haymarket Company or later on with Augustin Daly's Company" (*Metropolitan*, 42 [May 1915], 54). The lists in *The Film Index: A Bibliography*, ed. Harold Leonard (New York, 1941), under the categories "Religion" and "Spectacle," show an international fashion in Biblical and early Christian subjects beginning in 1909 and reaching a numerical peak in 1910 and 1911. Contemporary periodicals reflect the fashion in discussions of Religion and the Films. Among the film listings in Leonard's *Index* obviously in the vein of *The Sign of the Cross* are: *The Christian Martyrs* (U.S. 1910), in which a noble Roman loves a Christian slave whom the Empress consigns to the lions; *St. Paul and the Centurion* (France 1910), in which the daughter of a centurion is converted by a Christian slave, whereupon her father leads a band of soldiers against the Christians, but they too are converted; *The Way of the Cross* (U.S. 1909), in which "A Roman soldier is converted to Christianity by his sweetheart, and both are thrown to the lions by Nero's soldiers" (p. 494). The last film, apparently a direct borrowing from Barrett's play, was produced by Vitagraph, the company Shaw mentions above.

the truths of religion by exhibiting them in a place so un-sanctified. Even so cosmopolitan a thinker as George Henry Lewes spoke of the Oberammergau mystery play as "a mimic presentation of the most solemn and affecting of stories—a story so sacred that to Protestant feeling there is something shocking in the idea of its being brought into the remotest relation with anything like amusement, especially theatrical amusement." Lewes also reports on a *Paradise Lost* in Paris, in which "Eve tries to awaken the better feelings of Cain, and appeals to him as a *bourgeoise* mother would appeal to her refractory son (on the stage), recalling the early years of maternal solicitude and maternal anguish." "With us," Lewes declares, "the Lord Chamberlain would not even permit the title to appear on the bills; and even if there were no licenser of plays, the public would tear up the benches at the opening scene of the fall of the Angels, so profound would be the agita-tion of horror at the sight of what would seem this daring desecration of things sacred."[16]

By the 1890's, however, the way was opening for some sort of compromise. Acting as a profession had become more re-spectable, and clergymen were now portrayed on the stage with relative frequency.[17] Nevertheless, the habitual antag-onism between the men of the theater and the guardians of public morality flared briefly and violently in 1893, following the licenser's refusal to sanction Wilde's *Salomé* on the issue of "The Bible on the Stage." *The New Review* published a three-cornered debate under that title, between Alexandre Dumas *fils*, F. W. Farrar (canon of Westminster and chaplain to the House of Commons; later Dean of Canterbury), and Henry Arthur Jones. Dumas claims to be at a loss to differ-entiate theater and religion, and he enumerates various dra-

---

[16] *Actors and the Art of Acting*, pp. 209, 204, 207.

[17] Clergymen appear significantly in Collins' *The New Magdalen* (1873), Wills's *Olivia* (1878—Irving as the clergyman), H. A. Jones's *Saints and Sinners* (1884), *Judah* (1890), *The Tempter* (1893).

matic spectacles with religious content. He believes that *Salomé* would have received much kinder treatment in France (as indeed it did, shortly after) and suggests, "It may be that the theatre is destined to save the Church: it is quite possible. This would be a truly Christian revenge, for the Church has always done its uttermost to destroy the theatre." Farrar declares himself opposed to representing sacred history "amid the inevitable surroundings of the stage." He suggests that questions of literary taste, success, criticism, dress, and amusement would all "be an invasion of the reverence which belongs of right to everything which pertains to the religious life." Jones, as a playwright, claims the privilege of every painter, poet, and musician. He shudders, however, at the thought of the consequences if "our great religious public took to saving their souls through the medium of religious melodrama as they now save them through lithographs of the Crucifixion and serial stories in the *Sunday at Home.*"[18]

The success of *The Sign of the Cross* with the great religious public is in part a testimony to its shrewdness as a compromise. Without touching on Biblical narrative, or even quoting scripture, it managed to capture enough of the Doré Bible, the popular chromo-lithograph, and the *Sunday at Home* to wrap an atmosphere of profound religiosity around a splendid and sensational melodrama. In spite of Barrett's caution, he was attacked (much to Shaw's delight) for profaning holy text and the mysteries of religion; but numerous clergymen rushed to the defense with their testimony as to the edifying religiosity of the play and with their physical presence during its performance.[19] Archer wrote, in intellectual

[18] "The Bible on the Stage," *The New Review*, VIII (1893), pp. 183, 185, 188. The controversy was vigorously continued in "The Bible and the Stage," *Spectator*, 70 (4 Feb. 1893), pp. 155-56.

[19] Delighted to convict the attackers of ignorance of the very scriptures they defended from contamination, Shaw wrote (*OTN*, II, 12) "I can assure the public that the text of The Sign of the Cross is essentially original; and if Mr Wilson Barrett writes to the papers to assure us, in the usual terms, that so far from his having taken his play from the

and non-conformist disgust, that the play was "a combination of the penny dreadful with the Sunday-school picture-book"; a "salvationist pantomime";

"[a] series of tawdry tableaux, with their crude appeal to the shallowest sentiments and lowest instincts of the mob. The thing is an astute and apparently successful attempt to make capital out of that half-hearted hankering after the stage which has of late become an almost inseparable characteristic of your liberal-minded cleric. . . . Having no reasonable standards of comparison, the simple-minded padres, like children at their first pantomime, do not recognise the pretentious puerility, the hideous vulgarity of the whole thing, and set to work dutifully to beat the 'pulpit, drum ecclesiastick' at the door of Mr. Barrett's booth."[20]

With clerical support, Barrett easily overwhelmed the unregenerate puritan opposition (the criticisms of the intellectuals were embarrassed by enmity to censorship) and spectacular religious melodrama was established, for the vast body of playgoers, as most correct, religious, and high-toned.

In creating the setting and atmosphere of *The Sign of the Cross*, Barrett was not an absolute innovator. Persecuted Christians in a pagan Roman world of circuses and debauchery had appeared before, even on the English stage. But in no previous case was the "Christianity" of the play paramount. Barrett had precedent for his setting, for example, in Soumet's *Le Gladiateur*, brought to England by Salvini in 1875, in which a gladiator finds and must slay his Christian daughter in the arena, to the accompanying roar of the beasts and

---

Bible, he has never even read that volume, I am quite prepared to believe him." Barrett went out of his way to avoid quoting scripture to such an extent that in a Christian prayer-meeting the leader reads a paraphrase of the Sermon on the Mount. Barrett even substitutes the word "Chrystos" for "Christ," as the less familiar form of the name, and therefore less likely to give offense.

[20] *Theatrical 'World' of 1896* (London, 1897), pp. 9-10.

the crowd. Joseph Knight in his review compared it to Bulwer-Lytton's *Last Days of Pompeii*,[21] dramatized by Edward Fitzball (1835), J. B. Buckstone (1834), John Oxenford (1872), and eventually made into George Fox's *Nydia* (1892), an opera climaxing (like *Androcles*) in a gladiatorial combat and a providential salvation from the jaws of a lion. Shaw reviewed *Nydia* as a music critic:

"In prison [the hero] shared his cell with a Nazarene, who strove hard, not without some partial success, to make him see the beauty of being eaten by a lion in the arena. Next came the amphitheatre, with a gladiator fight which only needed a gallery full of shrieking vestals with their thumbs turned down to be perfectly *à la* Gérome. Then the hero, kept up to the mark by the Nazarene, was thrown to the lion, whereupon Vesuvius emitted clouds of spangles and red fire. A scene of terror and confusion in the streets followed, the crowd standing stock-still, with its eyes on the conductor, and the villain falling, slain by lightning, and then creeping off on all-fours behind the calves of the multitude.

"Finally the clouds parted; and we had a pretty pictorial composition of the hero and heroine at sea in a galley with the blind girl, who presently took a deliberate header into the waves, to the intense astonishment of everybody except the hero, who, without making the smallest attempt to save her, set up a thundering Salve eternum just as I was expecting him to break into

> Rosy lips above the water,
> Blowing bubbles soft and fine;
> As for me, I was no swimmer,
> So I lost my Clementine."
>
> (*Music in London*, II, 94)

Off the stage, *The Last Days of Pompeii*, Cardinal Wiseman's *Fabiola* (1854), Lew Wallace's *Ben Hur* (1880), the

[21] *Theatrical Notes* (15 May 1875), p. 39.

novels of Marie Corelli, and the hack-work serials of the *Sunday at Home* undoubtedly prepared the way for *The Sign of the Cross*; and in fact Barrett was seriously charged with plagiarizing another novel in the vein, *Quo Vadis?* by Henryk Sienkiewicz.[22] Dramas, and later films, made from nearly all of these constituted the genre of Christian Melodrama.[23]

The classic situation in Christian Melodrama, cautiously varied and endlessly repeated, was the difficult redemption through love of a pagan hero by a Christian heroine who is under the threat of martyrdom. It was doubtless with this situation in mind in January of 1912 that "Shaw wrote to Pinero that he had begun a religious sketch something like *The Sign of the Cross* and asking whether he knew anyone who could play the lion."[24] Years before, in his review of *The Sign of the Cross*, Shaw had already suggested the points to be confuted in *Androcles*. Seizing upon the contrast between pagan and Christian, and the relationship between hero and heroine, Shaw assured his readers that Barrett's play was really Ibsenist in inspiration:

"[Barrett] has drawn a terrible contrast between the Romans . . . with their straightforward sensuality, and the strange, perverted voluptuousness of the Christians, with their shuddering exaltations of longing for the whip, the rack, the stake, and the lions. The whole drama lies in the spectacle of the hardy Roman prefect, a robust soldier and able general, gradually falling under the spell of a pale Christian girl, white and worn with spiritual ecstasy, and beautiful as Mary Ander-

---

[22] See Disher, *Melodrama*, "Sex and Salvation," p. 124. Barrett wrote the novel version of *The Sign of the Cross* after the initial success of his play, a rather unusual proceeding for the times.

[23] *Quo Vadis* reached the English stage in 1900, and a one-reel *Ben Hur* was produced as early as 1907. Spectacular stage versions of *Ben Hur* could be seen at Drury Lane in 1902 and 1912.

[24] Rattray, *Bernard Shaw: A Chronicle*, p. 183. Rattray describes the letter no further.

son. As she gradually throws upon him the fascination of suffering and martyrdom, he loses his taste for wine; the courtezans at his orgies disgust him; heavenly visions obsess him; undreamt-of raptures of sacrifice, agony, and escape from the world to indescribable holiness and bliss tempt him; and finally he is seen, calm and noble, but stark mad, following the girl to her frightfully voluptuous death." (*OTN*, II, 12, 13)[25]

Androcles parallels *The Sign of the Cross* in persons and their relationships and in scenes and their arrangement. It is in deliberate contrast with *The Sign of the Cross* in its view of early Christianity as an influence on these persons and in its view of the conflict between paganism and Christianity. (The last element was the foundation of Religious Melodrama's claim to edifying seriousness.)

The counterparts of Barrett's obsessed Roman prefect, Marcus Superbus, and his pale Christian girl, the beautiful Mercia, are Shaw's self-contained Roman captain and the vital Lavinia. Lavinia, like Mercia, is a Christian slated for martyrdom, and like Mercia she chooses martyrdom over the love and comfort pressed upon her by an attractive Roman aristocrat. Lavinia, however, escapes martyrdom and her lover escapes conversion. Unlike Barrett's leading couple, Lavinia and the Captain never lose their pride or their sanity, and their end is not a union but a treaty. It is no accident that Shaw wrote the part of Lavinia specifically for Lillah Mc-

[25] Barrett himself played Marcus Superbus, the Roman Prefect; but, like Bottom, he was evidently anxious to try his hand at playing the other parts, and he followed his success in *The Sign* with *The Daughters of Babylon* (1897). There Barrett played Lemuel, a prophet who, like John the Baptist, resists the advances of Ishtar, the "Improper Person of Babylon" (in Shaw's phrase). The play was not a success, since the melodramatic conventions of male and female virtue are not the same. Shaw reports (*OTN*, III, 47), "When Lemuel decided to let his sweetheart, himself, and all his faithful confederates be baked in the fiery furnace sooner than accept [Ishtar's] proffered affection, the sympathy of the audience departed from him forever."

Carthy, who had played Mercia when *The Sign of the Cross* went on tour (see above, p. 111). She was Barrett's leading lady after 1900 and played opposite him in *Quo Vadis?* as well.[26] (Lygia in *Quo Vadis?* is a Christian princess loved, like Mercia, by a pagan Roman patrician, Marcus Vinitius. Vinitius also pursues his beloved lustfully, is foiled, and is converted. Vinitius, however, eventually escapes with Lygia after she has been saved from martyrdom.)

Other conventional personages of Christian Melodrama have their counterparts in *Androcles*. Shaw's Emperor parallels Barrett's (and Sienkiewicz's) Nero; Shaw's Spintho, a criminal and a coward among the Christians, parallels Barrett's Servillius, a spy and a coward unwillingly martyred (and Sienkiewicz's Chilo, a spy and informer, who in despair of his great crimes is baptized by Paul of Tarsus and led to redeeming martyrdom); Shaw's Ferrovius, a Pauline Christian whose irascible spirit so overcomes him in the arena that he massacres the gladiators, parallels Barrett's Melos (and Sienkiewicz's Ursus, guardian of Lygia, who, when Lygia is stripped and tied to the horns of a raging bull, loses his Christian resignation and breaks the bull's neck).

With respect to scenes and their arrangement, the Act I opening of *Androcles* is a direct parallel and comment upon the opening of *The Sign of the Cross*. The latter also presents a street in Rome and an arch, and Christians being conveyed to martyrdom. "*Soldiers cross from L.1.E. to R.U.E. guarding two men in chains and poor garments. They seem faint and weak, one totters for a moment and one of the soldiers strikes him with the butt of his spear he staggers and the crowd laugh and jeer at the men, who struggles on* [sic] *and Exits with soldiers.*"[27] The last act of *Androcles* similarly parallels and plays upon the end of *The Sign of the Cross*. Barrett sets

[26] *Who's Who in the Theatre*, ed. John Parker, 8th ed. (London, 1936).
[27] From a typed MS in the Library of Congress, *The Sign of the Cross, A Play in Four Acts by Wilson Barrett*, Act I [p. 1].

the scene in *"A dungeon off the Amphitheatre. Heavy brick and stone arches. Large double swinging doors R.C. which when opened show the circus arena beyond bathed in sunshine. Doors R & L. Grouped round stage are men and women of all ages on their knees singing the following hymn . . ."* (III, iii; p. 13). Shaw turns the dungeon into a theatrical green-room and allows his expectant martyrs a variety of moral attitudes, but the physical arrangement is the same: *"Behind the Emperor's box at the Coliseum, where the performers assemble before entering the arena. In the middle a wide passage leading to the arena descends from the floor level under the imperial box. . . . On the west side of this passage . . . the martyrs are sitting on the steps. Lavinia . . . thoughtful, trying to look death in the face. . . . Androcles consoles himself by nursing a cat. Ferrovius . . . his eyes blazing, his figure stiff with intense resolution. . . . Spintho . . . full of horror at the approach of martyrdom"* (p. 125). The gladiators stand near as fellow performers, and there are mirrors and a call boy to call out each "turn." In *The Sign of the Cross*, Tigellinius, the villain, and his guard enter the dungeon to sort out those for the lions from those for the gladiators. Stephanus, a boy (played by an actress) who has broken under torture and trembles at death is left with the women for the lions. There is a similar parting in Shaw's play, and Androcles, declining the combat, tells the Editor (or stage-manager), "I'm to be thrown to the lions with the lady." Finally, in *Androcles*, the Captain appears in the greenroom to make his last unsuccessful offer to Lavinia, paralleling the final confrontation of Marcus and Mercia in the climactic ending of *The Sign of the Cross*.

The conflict of Christianity and paganism as embodied in Mercia and Marcus Superbus is pure melodramatic convention. Like Hardress Cregan of *The Colleen Bawn*, Marcus is a man of fierce passions reduced and redeemed by the power of virtuous innocence as manifested in a good woman. Marcus

calls Mercia "the better part of me—that killed the worser
moiety—lifted my soul from filth and degradation—made me
abhor evil and strive for good" (IV, i; p. 9).[28] Mercia, at her
very first appearance, manifests herself as the power of innocent purity distilled from dramatic generations of virtuous
heroines. As a mob chases in one Favius, shouting *"Death to
the Christians," "Mercia Enters from R.U.E. and stands between Favius and the Crowd. She is in pure white. She stands
calmly with outstretched hands—The crowd fall back and
gaze with awe at her as if at some spirit"* (I, i; p. 7). Marcus,
while still unregenerate, declares "She's in the clouds and if
I do not exercise my will she'll drag me after her—If I do not
make a Pagan of her—she will make a Christian of me—On
some level we must meet—Bah—In her Heaven there is no
place for me—I'll bring her back to earth" (II, iii; p. 24). Accordingly, at the end of Act III, the audience is prepared for
a rape. Marcus is mad with passion; Mercia begs; Marcus
pleads; she swoons in his arms and the struggle is apparently
over. Then, at the last possible moment (Figure 7):

The Christian Hymn is heard off R.

MERCIA. (*Starting up transfigured.*) A sign—the
Master has called me—He is here—you cannot harm
me now.

*Mercia stands in C. holding up the Cross and
Marcus sinks down on his knee down R. The Hymn
swellsup* [sic] *and the Curtain slowly falls.* (III, iii;
p. 32)

At the end, Marcus comes to the dungeon to propose marriage
and safety, and Mercia almost wavers. She won't renounce her
faith, but she confesses that she has always loved Marcus—
next to the Master. Marcus then confesses he has had strange

[28] Other conventional types which greatly contributed to the Melodrama
though they have little to do with Christianity are Tigellinius, the villainous heavy, "the most cruel and unmerciful officer in Rome," and
Berenice, the dark, passionate woman, who loves Marcus and feels herself scorned, and is used by Tigellinius to pull him down.

spiritual yearnings in the night. Tigellinius comes for her decision: will she renounce Christ or die? She will die (IV, iii;
p. 22):

MERCIA. Farewell—Marcus.

MARCUS. (*Getting C*) No not farewell—Death
cannot part us—I too am ready. The· light hath
come—I know—I know—Thou hast shown me the
way . . . come my bride—

MERCIA. My bridegroom—

MARCUS. Thus hand in hand we go to our bridal
—Chrystos hath conquered—Come Mercia—come
my bride—come to the light beyond.

CURTAIN

Mercia and Lavinia as Christian Heroine are neatly contrasted in the scenes which establish their peculiar force.
Mercia, an apparition in the white robes of innocence, halts
the mob on her first appearance by her ethereal otherworldliness. In an equivalent early scene, Lavinia is accosted by
Lentulus, an epicene patrician, as she stands under guard:

LENTULUS. Do you turn the other cheek when
they kiss you, fascinating Christian?

LAVINIA. Dont be foolish (*To Metellus . . .*)
Please dont let your friend behave like a cad before the soldiers. How are they to respect and obey
patricians if they see them behaving like street
boys? (*Sharply to Lentulus*) Pull yourself together, man. Hold your head up. Keep the corners of
your mouth firm; and treat me respectfully. What
do you take me for?

LENTULUS. (*irresolutely*) Look here, you know:
I—you—I—

LAVINIA. Stuff! Go about your business. (*She
turns decisively away and sits down with her com-
rades, leaving him disconcerted*). (pp. 115-16)

Lavinia is forceful, practical, and very much of this world. She is one of Shaw's long line of visionary realists, like Caesar and Saint Joan. She chooses to die, not for Christianity, but "for something greater than dreams or stories. . . . for God" (p. 136), for "the coming of the God who is not yet" (p. 144).

Following his notions on extravagantly heretical groups, Shaw shows a Christianity which brings together those too good and those too bad for contemporary orthodox society. He has his Christians exhibit the widest variety of philosophic complexion, but their general temper is marked by cheer and vigor. The Centurion reports, "Theyre always laughing and joking something scandalous. Theyve no religion: thats how it is." They encourage each other, look after their Roman guards, and their characteristic hymn, which their guards have adopted unto themselves, is "Onward Christian Soldiers." In contrast, the Christian hymn which pervades *The Sign of the Cross* is "Oh Lead Us Home." The general tone of Christianity in Barrett's play is gloomy, exalted, death-devoted.

In *The Sign of the Cross*, and most Christian melodrama, the opposition between Christianity and paganism is presented as a conflict between a philosophy of self-denial and otherworldliness and a philosophy of sensual self-indulgence. When Marcus forcibly brings Mercia and his revellers together, the revellers sing a song of indulgence (III, iii; p. 27):

> Red wine to red lips—Hot breath to hot breath—
> Love's lips would waken me—E'en were I dead.
> *The Hymn of the Christians [imprisoned off stage]*
> *rises above the love song. The singers hesitate—break*
> *down and stop.*

The Christian hymn, as usual, is "Oh Lead Us Home." In the same philosophical vein, it doesn't count for Mercia that the rich Marcus is generous, because there is no self-denial in his generosity. Marcus finally declares "Thou taught me that

I never knew what shame meant until I knew thee. Never felt what sin was until I knew thy purity" (IV, iii; p. 18). Among Shaw's Christians only Ferrovius preaches this kind of self-abnegation. Significantly he is fearfully tormented by his inability to live according to his beliefs, and in the end reverts to a religion that suits his nature.

"Paganism," as Shaw presents it, is simply convenient, respectable orthodoxy, no different in Rome than in the British Empire. The Emperor is "the Defender of the Faith" (p. 110), a gentleman and a sporting enthusiast.[29] Burning "a morsel of incense" to the gods is a matter of social acquiescence, of submission to the status quo. The Captain urges, "you might at least do so as a matter of good taste, to avoid shocking the religious convictions of your fellow citizens" (p. 111). Megaera tells Androcles to "return to your duty, and come back to your home and your friends, and sacrifice to the gods as all respectable people do, instead of having us hunted out of house and home for being dirty disreputable blaspheming atheists" (pp. 104-5). In Shaw's play, the opposition of paganism and Christianity is presented as the eternal evolutionary opposition of orthodoxy and heterodoxy, institution and revolution, order and change.

In the final analysis, Shaw's treatment of Christian Melodrama is no different from his other adaptations of Melodrama to his own purposes. Shaw used Melodrama to present the Bunyanesque perils, conversions, instructive temptations, and Pilgrim's Progresses of the soul. Like Dick Dudgeon in *The Devil's Disciple*, Brassbound in *Captain Brassbound's Conversion*, Blanco in *Blanco Posnet*, and Barbara in *Major Barbara*, Lavinia and Ferrovius make a spiritual progress and discovery through trial and temptation. Like the Reverend

[29] Compare Barrett's Nero: "*He is fat, lame and half drunk. His manner nervous and shifty. He has th[e] aspect of a man who is constantly on the verge of delirium tremens. He is pompous and inflated, his eyes always shifting here and there as if expecting some terrible apparition or fearing assassination*" (III, ii; p. 13).

Anthony Anderson, Ferrovius discovers that his true faith lies in the sword. Lavinia anticipates by seeing him in the role of Bunyan's Valiant Man: "Something wilful in me wants to see you fight your way into heaven," she declares; "You will find your real faith in the hour of trial" (p. 133). The hour over, Ferrovius announces, "In my youth I worshipped Mars, the God of War. I turned from him to serve the Christian god; but today the Christian god forsook me; and Mars overcame me and took back his own. The Christian god is not yet. He will come when Mars and I are dust; but meanwhile I must serve the gods that are, not the God that will be" (p. 144).

Lavinia also discovers that what others "would have called my faith has been oozing away minute by minute whilst Ive been sitting here, with death coming nearer and nearer, with reality becoming realler and realler, with stories and dreams fading away into nothing." But underneath the stories she finds her true faith. She is ready to die, like Dick Dudgeon, "for nothing" (p. 136); for the (creative-evolutionary) God we shall know "When . . . we shall be gods ourselves" (p. 137); and in the end she lives to "strive for the coming of the God who is not yet" (p. 144).

Androcles was thus a blending, not only of Christmas Pantomime and parodied Christian Melodrama, but also, as Shaw ingenuously declared, of "the deepest realities of religion, the most unbearable of all subjects for the purely theatrical public." The play ends, however, with a final burst of pantomime. After Ferrovius has ransomed the faithful, by the sword this time rather than by the cross, Androcles has yet to be sent out to the lion. But Androcles and the lion are old friends, and together they tame the Emperor. The final note of the play is in the key that was to become increasingly important in Shaw's creation of a drama of ideas, the key of fable, the key of Extravaganza.

14

HISTORICAL DRAMA

". . . it is a received point among the poets that where history gives you a good heroic outline for a play, you may fill it up with a little love at your own discretion . . ."—PUFF in *The Critic*, Act II.

T H E History Play of the nineteenth century was characterized by three qualities: elaborate spectacle, romantic intrigue, and flamboyant histrionics. Over nearly half a century Shaw wrote four important plays in the genre: *The Man of Destiny, Caesar and Cleopatra, Saint Joan*, and *In Good King Charles's Golden Days*. The four plays are variously related to the nineteenth-century History Play in its three characteristic aspects. *The Man of Destiny*, for example, exploits two of these aspects, the predilection for romantic or (to use the more precise Shavian term) amoristic intrigue and the potential for histrionic display. *Caesar* exploits all three aspects. *Saint Joan* exploits significantly only the histrionic aspect, though it does so much more traditionally than either *Caesar* or *The Man of Destiny*. *Good King Charles* almost passes out of the range of the History Play, partly through its elaboration of what might be called Shaw's view of dramatic historiography. *Good King Charles* is a last essay in what was of constant concern in Shaw's attitude to the nineteenth-century History Play: the matter of historical truth.

A brief general glance at nineteenth-century Historical Drama makes it possible to discuss *The Man of Destiny, Caesar*, and *Saint Joan* in terms of their dramatic antecedents. The investigation of the three earlier plays then makes it possible to reconstruct Shaw's notion of historical truth and to consider the matter of *Good King Charles*; for the history-play antecedents of *Good King Charles* are not in the nineteenth century, but chiefly in the work of Shaw himself.

The Historical Drama of the nineteenth century was a genre posing some problems in definition. There never had been a distinct frontier between history and tragedy in English drama, and in the nineteenth century there was no distinct frontier between history and any other genre. Tom Taylor's *Historical Dramas*, for example, the only volume of plays he brought together in his lifetime (London, 1877), contains both *Plot and Passion*, a thrilling Melodrama with Napoleonic interest (1853), and *Arkwright's Wife, An Original Domestic Drama* (1873). But if the boundaries of Historical Drama were far from distinct, the terrain, nevertheless, had its characteristic features, spectacular, romantic, and histrionic.

As a vehicle for spectacle and costume, Historical Drama took much of its inspiration and information from James Robinson Planché, who worked directly with Charles Kemble and who created, with Kemble, Macready, and Charles Kean, the traditions of historical representation in the nineteenth century.[1] Originally the combination of pictorial splendor and historical "correctness" characteristic of the period was designed as an enhancement of legitimate drama. In an article entitled "Extravaganza and Spectacle," Planché defends himself against the charge of creating and abetting "a vicious taste for spectacle" by claiming that the result of his work for Charles Kemble was to make Shakespearean revival attractive and profitable, which it had not been before, and that in virtue of this fact the movement spread to Kemble's successors.[2] However, an earlier historian notes, with reference to the innovations on the legitimate stage, " 'Correctness of costume' was a phrase invented to excuse pageantry, as was 'accuracy of locality' for spectacle. 'Hamlet,' 'Lear,' 'Macbeth,'

---

[1] See Planché's *Recollections and Reflections* (London, 1872), I, 52-57; his *History of British Costume* (London, 1834); and his *Cyclopaedia of Costume or Dictionary of Dress* (London, 1876), 2 vols.

[2] *Temple Bar*, III (1861), 524-26.

'Coriolanus,' 'The Tempest,' 'Othello,' 'Henry the Fifth' were now 'revived.' "[3]

Planché's own *Charles the XII, an Historical Drama in Two Acts* (1828) is an attempt to apply directly the techniques used in the "historical illustration" of the histories and tragedies of Shakespeare and the legitimate drama. That the result shares the qualities of spectacular Melodrama is hardly surprising. The play presents a tale of traduced innocence (Major Vanberg) vindicated, pardoned, and rewarded; but it is primarily an opportunity for gorgeous costumery and spectacular effect (a cannonball blows up a set while the King stands cool and fixed; a set opens up to show the sea and a mighty fleet prepared). The provision of such opportunities remained a chief concern of Historical Drama for the rest of the century.

The characteristic nineteenth-century play with a claim to historical interest was a drama (costumed and spectacular) of "amoristic" intrigue. The influence of Scott (whose novels were much adapted for the stage) was toward driving the central and heroic figures of history out of the limelight, toward subordinating leading men and events to secondary romance. Unlike the early English history play, plays like Tom Taylor's *Lady Clancarty; or, Wedded and Wooed, A Tale of the Assassination Plot, 1696* (1874) made history a peg on which to hang minor romance, fictitious or genuine (see above, pp. 192-94). When Planché projected an opera with Mendelssohn on the siege of Calais by Edward III, he prepared a libretto featuring a heroic substitution for love, like that in *A Tale of Two Cities.* He wrote to Mendelssohn, "You seem to think that on the second pardon depends the whole opera—my notion was very different. I considered the opera depended upon the story of the two brothers; the historical portion being merely the *ground* upon which it is

[3] F. G. Tomlins, *A Brief View of the English Drama, from the Earliest Period to the Present Time* (London, 1840) , p. 79; cited in Nicoll, *A History of English Drama,* IV, 41.

worked. . . ."[4] Even plays where a notably loveless historical figure held the foreground necessarily provided a "love interest." For example, Bulwer-Lytton's *Richelieu* (1839), a favorite Barry Sullivan play, blends a struggle for power in the court of France with the romance of two non-historical characters. Richelieu is by far the most important personage in the play, but the young lovers are the focus of sympathetic interest. The villains are most villainous for their sexual interest in Julie de Mortemar, and Richelieu is most sympathetic when he works in the lovers' behalf. Boucicault's *Louis XI* (1855), another Historical Drama with a loveless leading part, similarly makes much of the love between Marie, daughter of Philip de Commines, and the banished, wronged, and vengeful Nemours.

Unlike *Clancarty*, *Louis XI* and *Richelieu* belonged to a group of plays whose chief business was to furnish a heroic part for a leading actor. Louis, for example, is a bravura role, combining the humours of Richard III with those of the dying Henry IV. Originally a Charles Kean part, it was revived by Irving for its virtuoso qualities.[5] Clinging to his crown on the edge of the grave, evilly disposed, and racked with guilt and the fear of death, Louis is a bundle of stunning contrasts. The part provides the chief interest in the play—an interest that is emphatically histrionic and sensational, not historic or even psychological. The historical setting is used, in a manner typical of the species, for its picturesqueness, its possibilities of romance and violence, and its suggestion to the audience that, however incoherent the character and events, "All Is True." Bulwer-Lytton's Richelieu is a similar

[4] Letter of 27 June 1839, in *Recollections and Reflections*, I, 305.
[5] "Originally," indeed, the play was adapted from another (in French) by Casimir Delavigne. Shaw knew the Boucicault version, and perhaps alludes to it in *Saint Joan*, with the same easy familiarity with which he alludes to Shakespeare in his Caesar play. The Dauphin in *Saint Joan* describes his son, "He that will be Louis the Eleventh," as "a horrid boy. He hates me. He hates everybody, selfish little beast!" (*Saint Joan*, p. 85).

role, providing splendid opportunities for acting. Like Louis XI, Richelieu is intended as a complex character, and, as with Louis, the complex characteristics fuse only under the pressure of magnificent acting and the imputed authority of history. Other plays in the same vein were W. G. Wills's *Charles I* (1872), written for Irving, and Tennyson's *Becket* (1893) "as Arranged for the Stage by Henry Irving and afterwards submitted to the Author."[6]

If the nineteenth-century History Play can be said to have had any philosophy at all, it was the theory of history implicit in *Becket*, and proclaimed in the very title of Scribe's *Le Verre d'Eau; ou, Les Effets et les Causes* (1840; adapted as *The Glass of Water* by W. E. Suter, 1863). *Becket* is particularly illuminating as an example of ambitious historical drama, since the issues suggested in Tennyson's play are very close to the historical issues expounded in *Saint Joan*. But the interest in *Becket* is almost entirely in persons and personal passions, and not at all in ideas or historical forces. In the scheme of the drama, love, jealousy, and friendship, and the misunderstandings between Henry and Thomas take precedence over the conflict between archbishop and king, church and crown. Quite unhistorically, the rivalry between Queen Eleanor and Fair Rosamund is used to provoke the catastrophe. In better days, King Henry had entrusted the protection of Rosamund to Becket. But when Becket spirits off Rosamund to a nunnery to save her from Queen Eleanor's knife, Eleanor makes it appear that the archbishop is presiding over the King's morals, and Henry speaks his fatal words about the pestilent priest. The intrigue over Fair Rosamund occupies the larger part of the play, and personal passions and a misunderstanding are treated as the hinges of history.

In *Le Verre d'Eau*, Scribe's influential play on the accession of Bolingbroke to power through Mistress Masham, Boling-

[6] Tennyson, *Works*, ed. Hallam, Lord Tennyson (London, 1909), IX, 455-526.

broke's philosophy of history is that little things (like a glass of water) are responsible for the greatest effects; and indeed, it is the littlest things, and the various passionate attractions, which govern the world of Scribe's play. Bolingbroke declares to his rapt student Abigail, later Mistress Masham:

> BOLINGBROKE. Il ne faut pas mépriser les petites choses, c'est par elles qu'on arrive aux grandes!... Vous croyez peut-être, comme tout le monde, que les catastrophes politiques, les révolutions, les chutes d'empire, viennent de causes graves, profondes, importantes... Erreur! Les États sont subjugués ou conduits par des héros, par des grands hommes; mais ces grands hommes sont menés eux-mêmes par leurs passions, leurs caprices, leurs vanités; c'est-à-dire par ce qu'il y a de plus petit et de plus misérable au monde. Vous ne savez pas qu'une fenêtre du château de Trianon, critiquée par Louis XIV et défendue par Louvois, a fait naître la guerre qui embrase l'Europe en ce moment! C'est à la vanité blessée d'un courtisan que le royaume a dû ses désastres; c'est à une cause plus futile encore qu'il devra peut-être son salut. Et sans allez plus loin... moi qui vous parle, moi Henri de Saint-Jean, qui jusqu'à vingt-six ans fus regardé comme un élégant, un étourdi, un homme incapable d'occupations sérieuses . . . savez-vous comment tout d'un coup je devins un homme d'État, comment j'arrivai à la chambre, aux affaires, au ministère? . . . je devins ministre parce que je savais danser la sarabande, et je perdis le pouvoir parce que j'étais enrhumé. . . . Le talent n'est pas d'aller sur les brisées de la Providence, et d'inventer des événements, mais d'en profiter. Plus ils sont futiles en apparence, plus, selon moi,

ils ont de portée... Les grands effets produits
par de petites causes... c'est mon système... j'y
ai confiance, et vous en verrez les preuves.[7]

In the play itself, the accent throughout is on intrigue and
accident and private passions. The destiny of the world is
altered because the Queen and the Duchess of Marlborough
have a weakness for the same witless guardsman, and arrange
a rendezvous for the same hour. Will and force of character
count for almost nothing at all.

NAPOLEON, CAESAR, AND SAINT JOAN

Romance, the exploitation of historical character for bravura roles, and even the spectacle characteristic of nineteenth-
century Historical Drama, all played a part in the creation
of Shaw's history plays. The first of them, *The Man of Destiny*, is closest to the Scribe-Sardou strain of historical romance,
with its diplomatic intrigues, contested papers, and amorous
concerns; and Shaw accordingly took care to subtitle his play,
"A Fictitious Paragraph of History." Shaw wrote it soon after

---

[7] *Théâtre de Eugène Scribe* (Paris, 1856), II, 121-22. "You shouldn't
despise the little things; it's through them that one achieves the great
things. . . . You think, perhaps, like everyone else, that political catastrophes, revolutions, the fall of empires, come from deep, weighty, important causes . . . Such a mistake! Nations are subdued or governed by
heroes, by great men; but these great men are themselves led by their
passions, their whims, their vanities; that is, by the most wretched and
trivial things in the world. I am sure you don't know that one window of
the Trianon, criticized by Louis XIV and defended by Louvois, started the
war that is raging through Europe at this moment! The wounded vanity
of a courtier has been responsible for the kingdom's disasters; an even
more trifling cause, perhaps, shall be responsible for its salvation. And
without looking any farther . . . I myself, I, Henry St. John, who up to
the age of twenty-six was looked upon as a fop, a fool, a man incapable
of serious pursuits . . . do you know how I suddenly became a statesman, how I got into parliament, into government affairs, into the ministry? I got to be minister because I knew how to dance the sarabande, and
I lost power because I was down with a cold. . . . The secret is not to try
to compete with Providence and manufacture events, but to profit from
events. The more trivial they appear, if you ask me, the more consequential
they are. Great effects from small causes . . . that's my system . . . I have
faith in it, and you shall see its results."

seeing Réjane in *Madame Sans-Gêne*, Sardou's Napoleon play, in which Napoleon "is nothing but the jealous husband of a thousand fashionable dramas, talking Buonapartiana" (*OTN*, III, 110). Shaw's play was deliberately remedial. It too is concerned with Napoleon's domestic character, but with a difference.[8]

The climax of *Madame Sans-Gêne* is a battle of wits in which an extraordinary woman attempts to save the credit of the Empress and the life of the latter's supposed lover. But in point of fact, Napoleon defeats Madame Sans-Gêne, and his tormenting jealousy is only assuaged by staging a test and securing a letter which prove that his wife is innocent after all. The action takes place during the height of Napoleon's power and presents a web of court intrigues, amoristic and political. (Madame Sans-Gêne successfully maneuvers to save her own marriage from Napoleon's divorcing hand, and Fouché uses the materials that fortune provides, à la Bolingbroke, to climb back into power.)

The intrigue in *The Man of Destiny* similarly centers on a letter, here compromising Napoleon's wife and the Director Barras. The letter, in a bundle of dispatches, is secured by a Strange Lady, acting for Mme. Bonaparte, through a trick involving sex-disguise; but the Strange Lady herself is captured by Napoleon, and the intrigue dissolves into a personal con-

[8] Mme. Réjane's company performed Sardou's play, in French, in July 1895. In his review, Shaw complained, "Napoleon is an inscrutable person, as becomes the Man of Destiny. . . . Surely the twenty minutes or so of amusement contained in the play might be purchased a little more cheaply than by the endurance of a huge mock historic melodrama which never for a moment produces the faintest conviction, and which involves the exhibition of elaborate Empire interiors requiring half an hour between the acts to set" (*OTN*, I, 177). On 1 November 1895, less than four months later, Shaw wrote to Ellen Terry: "To my great exasperation I hear that you are going to play Madame Sans Gêne. And I have just finished a beautiful little one act play for Napoleon and a strange lady . . . Besides, your place is not *after* Réjane. I was asked to do an English Madame Sans Gêne as an opera, for Florence St John. That was suitable enough: I said I'd do it if I had time, which I never had (time meaning will) "—*Ellen Terry and Bernard Shaw*, p. 16.

test over the letter with murderous stroke and counterstroke, numerous reversals, and a conclusion satisfactory to all. The character of Napoleon emerges as quite the opposite of "the jealous husband of a thousand fashionable dramas." Having secured the papers, and gathering from the Strange Lady that he is about to read of his own dishonor (with a duel, a public scandal, and a checked career in the offing), Napoleon is at his wit's end to get rid of these same papers, to pretend that they have never been recovered. He is quite ready to sacrifice the messenger from whom the dispatches were first stolen, and the Strange Lady must intrigue to save her initial victim, the messenger, in spite of himself. The damaging letter, which Napoleon reads on the sly, is eventually burned. Its effect on the destiny of the world is as if it had never existed.

Despite the elaborate and extremely "well-made" intrigue of *The Man of Destiny*, and despite its amoristic concerns, Shaw is most concerned to present a true and illuminating study of the nature of the future Emperor of Europe. Of the Emperor in *Madame Sans-Gêne*, Shaw wrote:

"Sardou's Napoleon is rather better than Madame Tussaud's, and that is all that can be said for it. It is easy to take any familiar stage figure, make him up as Napoleon, put into his mouth a few allusions to the time when he was a poor young artillery officer in Paris and to Friedland or Jena, place at his elbow a Sherlock Holmes called Fouché and so forth, just as in another dress, and with Friedland changed to Pharsalia, you would have a stage Julius Caesar; but if at the end of the play the personage so dressed up has felt nothing and seen nothing and done nothing that might not have been as appropriately felt, seen, and done by his valet, then the fact that the hero is called Emperor is no more important than the fact that the theatre, in nine cases out of ten, is called the Theatre Royal." (*OTN*, III, 110)

Shaw had a particular point, therefore, in taking the young

Napoleon of the Italian campaign and showing in this figure, without the stage accoutrements of Empire, the remarkable nature which was to create him Emperor. Shaw's Napoleon is one of Shaw's masterful realists, unhampered by idealism or altruism, by conscience or morality. He is simply and strongly ambitious, a talented actor, and extremely clear-seeing. In the economy of Shaw's playlet, the intrigue, for all its liveliness and importance, is subordinated to this revelation of character. The intrigue, in fact, is calculated to reveal the necessary superiority of a Man of Destiny to the very concerns which were the substance of the historical romance. Napoleon is a Man of Destiny because he is not simply a jealous husband in fancy dress; and the final inconsequence of the imbroglio over the letter is intended to suggest that Napoleon's rise to power would be a result, not of accident or of a web of passionate attractions, but of will.[9]

Along with its notable qualities as historical romance and historical analysis, *The Man of Destiny* also belongs to that most professional order of plays in which the author resorts to an extraordinary figure of history to provide an exceptional opportunity for acting. Napoleon, in keeping with his theatrical nature, has splendid speeches, sudden contrasts, and

[9] Another recent Napoleon play dealing with the Emperor's domestic difficulties was W. G. Wills's *A Royal Divorce* (1891). The Saturday Reviewer of the period reported: "Mr. W. G. Wills has shown himself an offender against historical accuracy before to-day, but never to the extent revealed in *A Royal Divorce*, at the New Olympic Theatre, wherein he revives Josephine to warn Napoleon on the eve of Waterloo of a conspiracy against him. Here, again, we are in the region of melodrama, and melodrama, moreover, arranged with a view to spectacular effect. . . . The keynote to the sentiment in the piece is the unfailing devotion of the unhappy lady to Napoleon, and his remorse and revived affection. . . . Mr. Murray Carson, excellent in make-up, reproduced many of the well-known external characteristics of Napoleon, such as the hands in the pockets, the quick, irritable walk, and the ever-present snuff-box, but failed to give the fiery impetuosity and stern will-power of the Child of Destiny" (*Saturday Review*, 72, 19 Sept. 1891, p. 334). Though Shaw's Man of Destiny was apparently tailored to the measure of Richard Mansfield, it was Murray Carson who first played the role, after Mansfield and Irving refused the play.

great bursts of rhetoric. He caps the play with a long speech on the English character in which *"his style is at first modelled on Talma's in Corneille's Cinna."* Shaw described *The Man of Destiny* as "hardly more than a bravura piece to display the virtuosity of the two principal performers" (*Plays Pleasant*, p. viii). Similarly, when Shaw wished to create a bravura part for Gertrude Kingston, he wrote the "historical" sketch *Great Catherine*. When he wished to create a heroic role for Forbes-Robertson "because he is the classic actor of our day and had a right to require such a service from me" (see above, p. 114), he wrote *Caesar and Cleopatra*.

In passing judgment on Historical Drama as represented by *Madame Sans-Gêne*, Shaw coupled a costume Napoleon with a stage Julius Caesar. Like *The Man of Destiny*, Shaw's *Caesar and Cleopatra* flies in the face of conventional historical romance. The very title of the piece invites comparison with Shakespeare's *Antony and Cleopatra* and excites expectation of a memorable romance between the aging conqueror and the fair young queen. In Shaw's prologue spoken by the hawk-headed Ra, the god asks, "Are ye impatient with me? Do ye crave for a story of an unchaste woman? Hath the name of Cleopatra tempted ye hither? Ye foolish ones; Cleopatra is as yet but a child that is whipped by her nurse." What he is about to show them, Ra adds, is something for the good of their souls (p. 89).

Caesar and Cleopatra is one of Shaw's "Three Plays for Puritans," three plays which flaunt the formula of "the romantic play: that is, the play in which love is carefully kept off the stage, whilst it is alleged as the motive of all the actions presented to the audience" (p. xvii). In the section of his preface called "Better than Shakespear?" Shaw writes, "The very name of Cleopatra suggests at once a tragedy of Circe, with the horrible difference that whereas the ancient myth rightly represents Circe as turning heroes into hogs, the modern romantic convention would represent her as turning hogs into heroes" (p. xxvii). Shaw's Caesar is not transfigured by a passion for Cleopatra, nor does sexual infatuation influence any of his actions or the future course of the world. Caesar is presented as a rare and complete being who accomplishes the reconquest and reordering of Egypt with a few thousand men, not through accident, but through will. (The accident which nearly upsets him—the killing of Pothinus— comes too late to affect Caesar's ordering of events.)

Caesar transforms Cleopatra from a child to a queen capable of holding her throne, teaches and forms her with care and kindness, but he does not love her—by virtue, it is implied, of his superiority. "Caesar loves no one," Cleopatra declares. "Who are those we love. Only those whom we do not hate: all people are strangers and enemies to us except those we love. But it is not so with Caesar. He has no hatred in him: he makes friends with everyone as he does with dogs and children" (p. 164). Though at one point Caesar admits to a particular blindness about women, Shaw couples his superiority to ordinary mortality with a superiority to the folly of the ordinary stage conqueror, romantic infatuation. In the interest of demonstrating Caesar's greatness, Shaw takes liberties with the chronicled probabilities of Caesar's sojourn in Egypt, and there is never the possibility of a Caesarion. The supreme irreverence toward the proprieties of the romantic history play is committed at the end of Shaw's play when Caesar asks, "And now, what else have I to do before I embark? . . . There is something I cannot remember: what can it be? Well, well: it must remain undone: we must not waste this favorable wind." However, as Caesar makes his final farewells and moves toward the gangway, Cleopatra appears:

> CLEOPATRA. Has Cleopatra no part in this leave-taking?
> CAESAR (*enlightened*) Ah, I knew there was some-

thing. (*To Rufio*) How could you let me forget
her, Rufio? (*Hastening to her*) Had I gone without
seeing you, I should never have forgiven myself.

(pp. 190-1)

Though aggressively heterodox toward certain conventions
of contemporary Historical Drama, toward other conventions Shaw was orthodoxy itself. *Caesar and Cleopatra* was his
first full-scale Historical Drama, and the elements of spectacle
and costume have a much greater part in the play than is
apparent merely in the reading. Though ready in 1899, *Caesar*
was not produced professionally until 1906 (in Berlin), owing
in large part to the huge cost of mounting.[10] Shaw wrote
to Siegfried Trebitsch in 1902 to urge a production in Vienna
"with Britannus changed into an echt Wiener bourgeois, and
a splendid *mise en scène*." In *Caesar*, he declared, "the staging
is just as much a part of the play as the dialogue."[11] Mention-
ing the play for the first time to Golding Bright, Shaw characterized it as "in five acts, containing eight scenes, & involving considerable variety and splendor of mounting."[12]

Actually the mounting of Caesar at the time of its copyright
performance involved nine scenes, eight changes, and eight
different sets. Act III, scene 1, the Quai before the Palace,
is repeated at the end, but with a practicable galley for the
final glorious exit of the conqueror (Caesar embarks, and
Cleopatra *"waves her handkerchief to Caesar; and the ship
begins to move,"* while the Roman soldiers cry "Hail,
Caesar!"). In the program he composed for the copyright performance (March 15, 1899), Shaw outlined the play as follows, in true spectacle-drama fashion:

[10] Shaw noted on a program of the copyright performance, sent to
Archibald Henderson and reproduced in *Man of the Century*, pp. 554-55,
"The production in London was first delayed by the difficulty of finding
about £6,000 to mount a play by an author so little believed in by theatrical speculators in the city."

[11] MS letters to Siegfried Trebitsch, 7 July 1902 and 16 August 1903.

[12] Letter of 15 Dec. 1898, *Advice to a Young Critic*, pp. 102-3.

ACT I.

Scene 1. The Courtyard of an Old Syrian Palace. Night.
  "   2. The Desert.   The Sphinx.
  "   3. The Throne Room in the Palace.

ACT II.

Alexandria. The Council Chamber of the Chancellors of the
King's Treasury.
The Burning of the Library.   The Capture of The Pharos.

ACT III.

Scene 1. The Quay of the East Harbor. The Carpet of
Apollodorus.
Scene 2. The Lighthouse.
(*Six months elapse between Acts III. and IV.*)

ACT IV.

Alexandria.   The Garden on the Palace Roof.
The Banquet.   The God's Answer.

ACT V.

The East Harbor.   Caesar's Farewell.[13]

It is significant that the first professional production (in Berlin) was by Max Reinhardt, whose name became a synonym for vastly elaborate spectacle.

Photographs of the first New York production (1906) show, not only the monumental sets, but also the stage crowds characteristic of historical spectacle.[14] Shaw took great trouble with these crowds, and in a letter written while rehearsing *Caesar* for America, he complains, "In the evenings I must prepare the stage business and write dozens of speeches, exclamations, whispers &c &c for the crowds (it is the only way of getting

[13] Reproduced in Henderson, *Man of the Century*, pp. 555-56. The one scene Shaw fails to mention appears in the "Day Bill" of the performance as "Act IV, Scene I. . . . Cleopatra's Boudoir" (Mander and Mitchenson, p. 65). The Prologue of the God Ra was written much later, as an alternative to the original Act I, scene 1.
[14] See Mander and Mitchenson, p. 67.

a natural effect); and in the mornings I must rehearse."[15] In two surviving pages of an undated typescript with his directions on the production of Act I, Shaw suggests the greatest possible splendor (and historicity) in the dress of even his soldiers, who compose a substantial portion of the stage crowds:

"The Roman soldiers should not, like modern armies, be dressed so that every man is, as to costume, a duplicate of every other. Caesar's soldiers were encouraged to decorate their weapons and armor as brilliantly as they could afford to. Consequently, though the shields, tunics, the coats of mail, the leather helmets, the greaves (one on the right knee only) and the baldrick are all *de rigeur*, they may be diversely colored and decorated."[16]

Since *Caesar and Cleopatra* is concerned with the public life of a man who wields both nations and men, crowds appear in five of the nine set scenes; and they are heard rioting offstage in a sixth.

How important Shaw considered the settings in the total effect of the play is suggested by the fact that Shaw sent drawings, "barbarous" but labored, when a production was contemplated in Germany, and insisted to his translator that "a great deal depends on them"; so much that he promised to engage an artist forthwith, "to make presentable pictures."[17]

[15] MS letter to Siegfried Trebitsch, 18 June 1906.
[16] "Notes to Act I." Typescript (carbon) with MS heading and beginning note in author's hand; unsigned and undated; 2 pp., numbered 27 and 28. Berg Collection, New York Public Library. In commencing his campaign to interest the Mansfields in *Caesar*, Shaw wrote to Mrs. Mansfield, "I had hoped to send you, by way of a New Year's call, a new play called 'Caesar and Cleopatra,' in which you are to be Cleopatra, sixteen years of age, with six changes of dress, each more stupendous than the last, whilst Richard, in a bald wig, rules the world as Julius Caesar" (Letter of 2 Jan. 1899, in Henderson, *Man of the Century*, p. 471).
[17] MS letter to Siegfried Trebitsch, 16 August 1903 (p. 3). The written evidence makes it possible to discount Sir Lewis Casson's testimony in "G.B.S. at Rehearsal," Mander and Mitchenson, p. 16: "In his whole his-

Caesar was presented to the world as a modern heroic part for a modern heroic actor. Costume and crowds, scenery and spectacle, were thoroughly in the line of the nineteenth-century treatment of history on the stage not only as an elementary part of audience appeal but as the adjuncts of a heroic atmosphere. However, whereas conventionally the heroes matched their tone to the visible grandeur, in Shaw's play Caesar is played off against this grandeur. He is first deflated during his apostrophe to the sphinx; he next stages his own anticlimactic reception by the Queen of Egypt. He preserves throughout the manner of a traveller; of a man who has come to look upon the splendors of Egypt with an explorer's curiosity and who does not quite belong to the world, Egyptian or Roman, of ordinary men. The result is that Caesar's heroic quality becomes an internal matter. His greatness is presented as something quite different from that of the ordinary con-

---

tory as a producer of his own or anyone else's plays, I never knew Shaw take any serious practical interest in anything beyond the casting and the acting. All the rest, including scenery, costumes, lighting and grouping, was of very minor importance, and personally, as a director, I sympathise with him." An example of Shaw's very practical interest in even the art of scene shifting is found in his typescript "Notes to Act I" of *Caesar*:

"In this act the scenes must be planned so as to enable the changes to be made without any interval, or at most very brief ones with tableau-curtains and continuous music. The sphinx and pyramid, with a back cloth representing the desert, can be ready behind the first scene. In the third, the desert cloth can be taken up; the wall of the square bay in which the throne stands can be shifted on in front of the Sphinx; the pyramid can be shifted off and the pillar wings on; and the throne and its platform, which should move on castors, can be pushed on. In this way the changes will be found quite practicable on old fashioned stages, where nothing but hand labor is available, and the Sphinx cannot be shifted.

"When elaborate hydraulic or electric machinery is available, the scenery can be improved accordingly; but the stage business should not be altered in such a way as to make the dialogue ineffective."

A note on music follows in which Shaw considers how the bucina and trumpet calls may be presented, and vents his customary spleen upon the cornet, forbidding its use on his stage. It is interesting that Shaw's sequence of scenes in the first act was clearly visualized in terms of the capabilities of the "old fashioned" stage, and was designed to provide spectacle without the long waits that it usually entailed.

quering hero, who acts and speaks up to the splendor of the setting. Caesar's greatness is established, not by the coloring lent to his actions by the magnificent setting, but by his superiority to the setting and by the independence of his actions and ideas.

Whereas Shaw called *Caesar and Cleopatra* both "An Historical Drama" and "A History," *Saint Joan* was from the beginning conceived as "A Chronicle Play." The difference is explained in an article written during the composition of *Saint Joan*, where Shaw observes that "The Cinema has restored to the stage the dramatic form used by Shakespear: the story told with utter disregard of the unity of place in a rapid succession of scenes"; he then declares "My next play will be a chronicle play which will be impracticable without a Shakespearean stage. . . . in writing it I shall ignore the limitations of the nineteenth century scenic stage as completely as Shakespear did."[18]

Nevertheless, *Saint Joan* is in the plainest way a direct-line descendant of a characteristic species of the nineteenth-century historical drama with which Shaw was entirely familiar: the heroic history play written for a woman star. It was, significantly, after seeing Sybil Thorndike in *The Cenci* that Shaw fixed upon the actress who would create the leading role in England and wrote his play.[19] *Saint Joan* was clearly designed to provide for the heroic actress what *Caesar and Cleopatra* provides for the heroic actor: a modern heroic starring part; and, accordingly, it was conceived in terms of the plays which Madame Ristori brought to Dublin, since it

[18] *Shaw on Theatre*, pp. 179-80. Though written in 1923, the article was not printed until 14 Nov. 1926 in the *New York Herald Tribune*.

[19] See George W. Bishop, *My Betters* (London, 1957), p. 127, and Hesketh Pearson, *Bernard Shaw, His Life and Personality*, p. 377. Pearson quotes Sybil Thorndike as having said to him, "*The Cenci* . . . got me the greatest part of my career. It was after the trial scene, I think, that Mr. Shaw said he had found the actress for Joan."

was Madame Ristori, Shaw declared, who completed his education in respect of "how far the grand style in acting can be carried by women."[20]

Women stars touring the provinces with four or five roles and relying on the support of the stock companies were frequent visitors when Shaw was in Dublin; and among the stars who came were Mlle. Beatrice, Kate Bateman, Ada Cavendish, Adelaide Neilson, and Adelaide Ristori. If her strengths lay in the direction of heroic tragedy, a female star required a body of plays equivalent to the repertory of "legitimate" male stars like Barry Sullivan. She needed dominant feminine roles equal to the great masculine roles of Shakespeare supplemented by Edward Moore, Bulwer-Lytton, and Sheridan Knowles, which formed the male tragedian's stock in trade. Among the attempts to form something like such a repertory were the plays with which Madame Ristori so impressed Shaw in Dublin: Schiller's *Maria Stuart*, Giacometti's *Marie Antoinette* and *Elizabeth, Queen of England*, and Legouvé's *Medea*. Other woman stars of heroic bent also appeared in these plays, variously adapted according to the language of the performer. Three of the four were history plays. Two of them, *Maria Stuart* and *Marie Antoinette*, culminate in martyrdom.[21]

Of the four plays, *Marie Antoinette* is superficially most

[20] *Ellen Terry and Bernard Shaw*, p. xix.

[21] It should be noted that there were other repertory traditions available to Shaw. In the seventies, leading actresses brought to Dublin dramas and melodramas with dominant women's parts like Daly's *Leah the Forsaken* (1863), Tom Taylor's *Mary Warner* (1869), Wilkie Collins' *New Magdalen* (1873). Later there were the "splendid women's parts pouring from the Ibsen volcano and minor craters" (*OTN*, I, 17), which Shaw constantly urged upon Ellen Terry, Ada Rehan, and other actresses whose powers he felt were being wasted. Sarah Bernhardt toured with the woman-plays specially provided by Sardou, to which Shaw gave the elastic name, "La Toscadora" (*OTN*, I, 133); and Duse brought a repertory of Dumas *fils*, Sudermann, and Ibsen. Nevertheless, as a play written for a woman star, *Saint Joan* is a direct continuation of the line of the most "legitimate" women-plays of the nineteenth century, historical, tragic, and rhetorical, elevated in diction and sentiment.

like *Saint Joan*. It is highly operatic, highly rhetorical, and structurally a historical pageant showing, like *Saint Joan*, the highlights and crises on the road to martyrdom. The prologue presents the Queen on the eve of performing Beaumarchais at the Petit Trianon despite warnings about the possible revolutionary consequences. Then follows, episodically, the progression of her vicissitudes from 1791 to 1793: the execution of the King, separation from her children, and finally her own beheading (Act V), in which she is first given over to the executioner who ties her hands and cuts her hair and then led off stage to the sound of funeral drums. Then:

> SCENE SECOND. *The Guillotine and place of execution. Grand Tableau of the execution of* MARIE ANTOINETTE.

A direct link between the nineteenth-century woman's heroic-historical pageant play, as represented by *Marie Antoinette*, and *Saint Joan* was Tom Taylor's *Jeanne Darc (Called the Maid); a Chronicle Play, in Five Acts* (1871).[22] Structurally the play is quite similar to *Saint Joan*, though Taylor's La Hire is magnified as much as possible to make a romantic, if subsidiary, male part. Like Shaw's Scene I, Taylor's Act I, "The Maid Mystic," concerns the first step, from the village to the court. On coming to her village, La Hire (and through him de Baudricourt) is sufficiently convinced of Jeanne's mission to help her get to the Dauphin. Act II, The Winning at Court, corresponds to Shaw's Scene II. La Trémouille, as in *Saint Joan*, is almost a villain and wishes to fight La Hire. Jeanne is given her chance through the aid of the Queen and, as in *Saint Joan*, picks out the King-to-be from the crowd. In Taylor's play, the act ends

[22] In Taylor's *Historical Dramas* (London, 1877). A different version is printed in *Sergel's Acting Drama*, in prose rather than verse. Presumably Taylor knew Schiller's *Jungfrau von Orleans*, but his play does not depend upon it. Earlier *Joans* on the English stage included a notable production by Macready in 1837.

as the Maid cries: "Who follows me to rescue Orleans and ransom France?"

> LA HIRE. Sang Diou! [*sic*] I do for one!
> (*The crowd draw their swords and press forward with a general shout*). And I!

In Shaw's play, Joan draws her sword and shouts, "Who is for God and His Maid? Who is for Orleans with me?"

> LA HIRE (*carried away, drawing also*) For God and His Maid! To Orleans!
> ALL THE KNIGHTS (*following his lead with enthusiasm*) To Orleans!

—whereupon the actors form an old-fashioned curtain tableau: "*Joan, radiant, falls on her knees in thanksgiving to God. They all kneel, except the Archbishop, who gives his benediction with a sign, and La Tremouille, who collapses, cursing.*"

Act III of *Jeanne Darc*, "The Maid Martial," presents the raising of the siege at Orleans and corresponds to Shaw's Scene III, the change in the wind before Orleans. The sum of the action Taylor presents is narrated in Shaw's Scene IV, the "concerted" scene between Warwick, Cauchon, and de Stogumber (see above, pp. 51-2) in which Shaw's chronicle play becomes a drama of ideas. Significantly, it is the one scene (aside from the epilogue) which has no equivalent in Taylor's orthodox five-act movement.

Taylor's Act IV, "The Maid Manifest," presents the coronation at Rheims, Jeanne's decision to go home thereafter, and her change of mind. Shaw's Scene V, in the Cathedral at Rheims, begins just after the ceremony and presents precisely the same events. In Taylor's play, as in *Saint Joan*, the courtiers are glad to see Jeanne return to the farm for various uncharitable reasons. They all speak out formally in turn, just like the General, King, and Archbishop in *Saint Joan*; though Shaw's figures speak, not merely personally, but from their various institutional points of view. In Taylor's play, the military figure, La Hire, remains faithful, exhorts Jeanne to go on to Paris, and arouses the voices.

La Hire is also romantically introduced into Taylor's Act V (the trial and execution of Jeanne), where he is present in disguise. The proceedings are more or less the same as in Shaw's corresponding Scene VI, but the trial is presented as dreadfully prejudiced. In Taylor's play, Jeanne recants at the sight of the rack, for fear of torture and burning, and then, her voices silent, rejects La Hire's available rescue and repudiates her recantation. As in Shaw's play, there is a solemn excommunication, but, unlike Joan, Jeanne is visibly burned for the grand finale.

That Shaw certainly knew Taylor's play and in all likelihood saw it performed in Dublin is by no means overwhelmingly important.[23] The close resemblance between the two plays is attributable to the marshalling, by two competent playwrights, of nearly identical material into an identical form. Shaw demonstrably relied on a version of Quicherat's publication, beginning in 1841, of the documents and reports of Joan's trial and rehabilitation—as did Tom Taylor (see his introduction in *Historical Dramas*). Shaw later wrote of Joan's trial that it was "a drama ready made, only needing to be brought within theatrical limits of time and space to be a thrilling play" (*On the Rocks*, p. 175). His chronicle play belonged to a type he described as "all big scene, with climaxes";[24] and the big scenes and their climaxes would have

---

[23] Shaw mentions Taylor's play in his retrospective preface to *Ellen Terry and Bernard Shaw*. Writing about the demands placed upon the old stock-company actors, Shaw notes, "At my first visit to the theatre I saw on the same evening Tom Taylor's three-act drama Plot and Passion followed by a complete Christmas pantomime, with a couple of farces as *hors d'oeuvre*. Tom Taylor's Joan of Arc had Massinger's New Way to Pay Old Debts as a curtain raiser. Under such circumstances serious character study was impossible" (p. xvi).

[24] Henderson, "Shaw Self-Revealed," p. 439.

been equally apparent to the two playwrights working in the same tradition, bent on creating a heroic-historic drama with a bravura leading role.

"TRUE HISTORY" AND *GOOD KING CHARLES*

Yet, for all the evident links between his histories and the history-play tradition of the nineteenth century, Shaw repudiated these traditions and claimed no later forerunners in the genre than Shakespeare. He equated the nineteenth-century history play with historical romance and tended to ignore even the heroic-historical strains on the severing issue of historical truth. In introducing *Good King Charles* to the Malvern Festival of 1939, Shaw declared, "The 'histories' of Shakespear are chronicles dramatized; and my own chief historical plays, Caesar and Cleopatra and St Joan, are fully documented chronicle plays of this type. Familiarity with them would get a student safely through examination papers on their periods. . . . A much commoner theatrical product is the historical romance, mostly fiction with historical names attached to the stock characters of the stage" (*Good King Charles*, p. 153). Shaw sometimes undervalued his own *Man of Destiny* and ostentatiously labelled it "A Fictitious Page of History" because the fiction seemed to overweigh the truth. And when an interviewer innocently asked, "Should a dramatist who is writing an historical play be allowed to clothe his characters in garbs of romance," Shaw replied:

"If the characters are clothed in the garb of romance, as you so romantically put it, they are not historical. No historical character is worth dramatizing at all unless the truth about him or her is far more interesting than any romancing.

"A good play about Rip Van Winkle is not spoiled by calling it Rip Parnell; but it does not thereby become an historical play.

"Shakespeare always stuck close to the chronicles in his

histories. And they survive, whilst hundreds of pseudo-historical plays have perished."[25]

It is true that Shaw's histories often lie as close to their sources as Shakespeare's description of Cleopatra in her barge. Shaw wrote of his *Caesar* in 1918, "It is what Shakespeare called a history: that is, a chronicle play; and I took the chronicle without alteration from Mommsen. . . . I stuck nearly as closely to him as Shakespeare did to Plutarch or Holinshed." But Shaw also remarks, "I read a lot of other stuff, from Plutarch, who hated Caesar, to Warde-Fowler; but I found that Mommsen had conceived Caesar as I wished to present him, and that he told the story of the visit to Egypt like a man who believed in it, which many historians dont."[26]

"Historical truth" then was not for Shaw simply a matter of fact, but a matter of interpretation; and his quarrel with the nineteenth-century History Play was not simply with its romantic fictions but also with its documented facts, romantically or trivially interpreted. Historicity for its own sake was of no more value to Shaw in a History Play than verisimilitude for its own sake in drawing-room comedy. Therefore, after announcing, on the first program of *Caesar and Cleopatra*, that "The Play follows history as closely as stage exigencies permit," and appending a great list of authorities, Shaw adds, "Many of these authorities have consulted their imaginations, more or less. The author has done the same."[27] More significantly, discoursing on the composition of various sorts of plays, Shaw told Archibald Henderson, "Then there is the chronicle play, in which you arrange history for the stage. The value of the result depends on your grasp of historical issues—whether your history is big history or Little

[25] "The Theatre To-day and Yesterday According to Bernard Shaw in answer to questions asked by Roy Nash," *Manchester Evening News*, Dec. 6, 1938.
[26] Letter to Hesketh Pearson in *Bernard Shaw*, p. 212.
[27] Reproduced in Henderson, *Man of the Century*, p. 555.

Arthur's history."[28] In the preface to *Saint Joan*, Shaw flatly declares that "my drama of Saint Joan's career, though it may give the essential truth of it, gives an inexact picture of some accidental facts." He derides the "old Jeanne d'Arc melodramas," which, "reducing everything to a conflict of villain and hero, or in Joan's case villain and heroine, not only miss the point entirely, but falsify the characters, making Cauchon a scoundrel, Joan a prima donna, and Dunois a lover." But Shaw admits that he himself, as "the writer of high tragedy and comedy, aiming at the innermost attainable truth, must needs flatter Cauchon nearly as much as the melodramatist vilifies him" (*St. Joan*, p. 50).

What, then, is the nature of this "essential truth," this "innermost attainable truth," which makes the difference between big history and Little Arthur's history? There are two aspects of Shaw's demand for essential truth which pervade the very fabric of his plays and provide glaring contrasts with the traditions of the nineteenth century. One of these is Shaw's concern to dramatize the historical issues rather than the private passions of a particular historical moment. The other is his desire to give to the past the immediacy and familiarity of the present. Though seemingly opposed, these aims are genuinely complementary, and Shaw suggests as much when he writes, in the preface to *Saint Joan*:

"To see her in her proper perspective you must understand Christendom and the Catholic Church, the Holy Roman Empire and the Feudal System, as they existed and were understood in the Middle Ages. If you confuse the Middle Ages with the Dark Ages, and are in the habit of ridiculing your aunt for wearing "medieval clothes," meaning those in vogue in the eighteen-nineties, and are quite convinced that the world has progressed enormously, both morally and mechanically, since Joan's time, then you will never understand why

[28] Henderson, "Shaw Self-Revealed," p. 438.

Joan was burnt, much less feel that you might have voted for burning her yourself if you had been a member of the court that tried her; and until you feel that you know nothing essential about her." (p. 27)

The heroic-historical plays of the nineteenth century and earlier were not concerned to give immediacy and familiarity to the past, but to create a remote and splendid world, shining by contrast with the present, and evoked by every scene and costume, every syllable and sentiment of the highly artificial, highly impassioned language spoken on the stage. Shaw, by contrast, goes out of his way to provide reminders of contemporaneity through jibes, seeming anachronisms, colloquial diction, and prosaic behavior. When the crowd cries "Egypt for the Egyptians," when Apollodorus declares, "My motto is Art for Art's sake," when Ftatateeta complains to Cleopatra, "You want to be what these Romans call a New Woman," when Caesar deplores such superstitions as table-rapping "in this year 707 of the Republic," when Apollodorus reports that Caesar "was settling the Jewish question when I left," the audience is being deliberately jarred out of the "illusion," of a complete, integral, and separate stage world by the seeming topicality and modernity of the allusions. The fact that Caesar, for example, *did* "settle" the "Jewish question" while in Alexandria simply reinforces Shaw's point: the relevance and immediacy to the present of his dramatized transactions from the past. Problems of right rule and fitness to rule, of realism and idealism, and, most important, of the ethics of judgment and vengeance (the particular theme of the entire volume of *Three Plays for Puritans*) are meant to be grasped by the audience in the present tense as well as in the past.

Shaw also declared he had returned to the methods of Shakespeare because both exploit the contemporary vernacular in their heroic history plays rather than confine knights and Romans to an elevated, poetic-academic language, without

—·[373]·—

lapse and without salt.[29] But Shaw does not actually ignore the conventions of language as they existed in the later heroic-historical drama. The first words of the original opening of *Caesar and Cleopatra* declare Shaw's method through the play: he will use the conventions of elevated diction and modern idiom together, like his apparent anachronisms, to wittily force a junction between past and present. The soldiers before the palace are dicing:

> BELZANOR. By Apis, Persian, thy gods are good to thee.
>
> THE PERSIAN. Try yet again, O captain. Double or quits! (p. 91)

A little later, Belzanor demurs from selling Cleopatra, a descendant of the Nile, to the invaders:

> ... the lands of our fathers will grow no grain if the Nile rises not to water them. Without our father's gifts we should live the lives of dogs.
>
> PERSIAN. It is true: the Queen's guard cannot live on its pay. (p. 96)

Shaw also makes use of the conventions of "historical" speech for purposeful contrast between Romans and Egyptians. The ordinary speech level of the Romans is much more colloquial and "modern" than that of the Egyptians. It is significant that both of Shaw's vastly different prologues to *Caesar* (that of the Egyptian soldiers and that of the Egyptian god Ra) use the same mock heroic-historical diction, so that Caesar's rhetoric in the formal address to the sphinx which opens Act I shows by contrast modern and Roman.

For Shaw, the "essential truth" of any historical conflict lay in the ideas (and the institutions insofar as they embodied the ideas) at stake in the conflict. Consequently, Shaw's history-makers are the men and women who embody passionate ideas,

[29] See Shaw's note to *Caesar*, "Apparent Anachronisms," p. 195.

—·[374]·—

dramatically articulating and expounding themselves. He declares in his preface to *Saint Joan* that, though the extant accounts give warrant to neither the intelligence nor the freedom from petty passions with which he has endowed his Archbishop and his Inquisitor,

". . . it is the business of the stage to make its figures more intelligible to themselves than they would be in real life; for by no other means can they be made intelligible to the audience. And in this case Cauchon and Lemaître have to make intelligible not only themselves but the Church and the Inquisition, just as Warwick has to make the feudal system intelligible, the three between them having thus to make a twentieth-century audience conscious of an epoch fundamentally different from its own." (p. 51)

Shaw as historian belonged very much to the idealist schools of the nineteenth century; for he presented ideas, embodied in men, as the realities of history, and will, not accident, as its driving energy.

But *Saint Joan* no more than *Caesar* allows of the pastness of the past, for all Shaw's concern to dramatize the historical issues of the age. The irruptions of Protestantism against the Church, Nationalism against the feudal system, which culminate in the burning of Joan, have another dimension: the everlasting conflict of orthodoxy and heterodoxy; a fact, to Shaw, not merely of history but of the historical process, of enormous present concern, and the subject in a sense of at least half his plays. He wants the audience to feel more than that they too as members of the court that tried her might have burned Joan; he wants them to realize they are probably burning her still.[30]

[30] Shaw's epilogue, where Joan offers to come back to the consternation of all those who have killed and canonized her, is designed to underline the timeless aspect of the chronicle. Like Caesar and Joan, however, Shaw

In his last history play, *In Good King Charles's Golden Days*, Shaw carries his principles and practice to a logical culmination by writing, not a fictitious history, but *A True History that Never Happened.* To present his truths, Shaw invents a collision between Newton, Godfrey Kneller, King Charles II, and George Fox; between the scientist and the artist, the worldly governor and the unworldly saint. They are intended to represent and debate the four highest activities and modes of thought given to mankind, and external veracity is altogether abandoned for the sake of essential truth. For example, Newton, devoted to a rectilinear universe, is aware of something "amiss with the perihelion of mercury" and is terribly shaken by a glimpse of Einsteinian curvature. Kneller is endowed with Hogarth's ideas—"the line of beauty is a curve"—and a generalized artistic temperament. Fox visits Newton because his friends in the Royal Society "tell me things my mind cannot reconcile with the word of God." Nevertheless, Shaw himself draws the contrast between his true history and the many historical romances which "have introduced their heroines as Nell Gwynn, and Nell's principal lover as Charles II. . . . Now anyone who considers a hundred and fiftieth edition of Sweet Nell of Old Drury more attractive than Isaac Newton had better avoid my plays: they are not meant for such" (pp. 153-54).[31]

---

permitted no divorce between practical considerations and occult motives. When Archibald Henderson "frankly deplored the Epilogue, as a Shavian gloss upon the play, which, for all its beauty and reverence, shattered the historical illusion . . ." Shaw replied, "You're quite wrong there, Henderson. The Epilogue is indispensable as brief reflection will show you. The Epilogue will never be omitted as long as actresses are actresses. *Saint Joan* will always be a star play for a big actress. Catch her cutting the Epilogue and letting Stogumber steal the end of the play from her!" (Henderson, *Man of the Century*, p. 600).

[31] Some of the historical romances Shaw has in mind were *The King's Rival* by Tom Taylor and Charles Reade (1854), *Nell Gwynne* by W. G. Wills (1878), and the said *Sweet Nell of Old Drury* by P. Kester (1900). There is record of at least nine different plays using the actress's name in the title. Joseph Knight wrote of Wills's *Nell Gwynne* (*Theatrical*

It is true that, though Newton is "a stage astronomer: that is, an astronomer not for an age but for all time," Shaw is anxious to present him in his personal idiosyncrasies, "and I have chapter and verse for all his contradictions" (Preface, p. 155). Similarly, Shaw is anxious to do some historical justice to Charles, to present what he felt to be essential truth about the man, his politics, and his domesticity. It is true that there is an attempt to evoke, abstract, and chronicle the age through a sizable mass of detail from Little Arthur's history, including bits from the contemporary stage, allusions to Jeffries and Old Noll, representatives of current points of view and ways of life, boudoir gossip and personalities, anticipations of Dryden's "Absalom" and Swift's *Tale of a Tub*, advance sketches of the rise of the Churchills and the Glorious Revolution. But these elements of true history are less comfortable here than in the earlier histories. However abundant, they are peripheral to the fundamental organization of the play. *Good King Charles* is fundamentally an allegorical fable —and therefore not only unhistorical, but even extratemporal— of the meeting of four universal temperaments, four universal modes of thought.

In point of fact, though *Good King Charles* is still related to Historical Romance, in the realm of Shaw's own developed genres it is more Political Extravaganza than History Play. The resemblance of the discourses on government and of

---

Notes, p. 221), "His means are commonplace enough, turning, as in the early comedy of Scribe, upon people putting letters into wrong envelopes, and the like." The best of the group was unquestionably *The King's Rival*, a fine drama featuring Charles, Nell, and Samuel Pepys. The romantic hero is the young Duke of Richmond. The heroine, Frances Stewart, is loved and pursued by King Charles. The language and atmosphere convey a genuine sense of the period, and Shaw perhaps alludes to the play when he has Charles declare to Queen Catherine that he was only once really unfaithful to her, "with the woman whose image as Britannia is on every British penny, and will perhaps stay there to all eternity. And on my honor nothing came of that: I never touched her. . . . I was furious when she ran away from me and married Richmond" (p. 227).

Charles's domestic relations to portions of *The Apple Cart* is not simply the effect of accident and old age but of genre similarity. Both plays show a king keeping his place by his wits. Both plays characteristically combine an interest in a king's amorous and political affairs, and both show a king with a libertine reputation faithful, in his own fashion, to his wife. Both plays are concerned with the mob and its dubious leaders and the government and its true proprietors, with questions of power and rule. Like Boanerges in *The Apple Cart*, Titus Oates is a modern demagogue, and the Popish Plot in *Good King Charles* evokes the burning of the Reichstag.

The tendency of Shaw's histories toward Extravaganza was early observed by critics of *Caesar*, much to Shaw's annoyance, for Extravaganza then implied an unredeemed frivolity. Long before its production, Archer wrote to Gilbert Murray about the script of *Caesar*, "I think Shaw has invented a new genre in this sort of historic extravaganza, though fortunately no one but he is likely to practise it. . . ."[32] When Forbes-Robertson was trying out *Caesar* in the provinces, Shaw wrote to him (1 Nov. 1907), "I have no doubt that your Caesar will be a stroke of work of the kind that this generation of Londoners has seen nothing of. Indeed the whole difficulty is that the grand school has gone under so completely that the public has got rusty in its perception of it; and Caesar will begin by puzzling them. But after a little that will wear off. . . ." After the London opening, however, Shaw wrote to Forbes-Robertson (31 Jan. 1908), "The Press, headed by Walkley, said of *Caesar* exactly what they said of *Arms and the Man* in 1894—Offenbach and Meilhac and Halévy—opera bouffe."[33]

---

[32] Letter of 2 Aug. 1899, Charles Archer, *William Archer, Life, Work, Friendships*, p. 246. In *The Old Drama and the New*, Archer describes *Caesar* as "the most hopeless nondescript in literature—a thing far too serious to be called an extravaganza, and far too nonsensical to be called a serious play" (p. 350).

[33] Hesketh Pearson, *Bernard Shaw*, pp. 279-80, 281. In his review of

The critics called *Caesar* Opera-Bouffe and Extravaganza for reasons which give no clue to Shaw's later use of the form. The Extravaganza was rooted in burlesque, that is, in the light and irreverent treatment of a heroic subject. Since *Caesar* was clearly a rebuke to certain heroic-historic conventions and was highly amusing, often at the hero's expense, it was observed to be nearly related to pieces like Offenbach's *La Belle Hélène*. Charles II and his times, on the other hand, were regarded as anything but heroic, and in 1939 the Burlesque-Extravaganza of the nineteenth century had long been out of vogue; therefore *Good King Charles* was spared the association. But *Good King Charles* was a culmination of Shaw's use of History Play forms not only as an abstraction of historical truth from historical event in a *True History that Never Happened* but as a true Shavian Extravaganza; for the overall thrust of Shaw's intellectual drama through his career was toward Extravaganza as a medium for the drama of ideas.

Three Plays for Puritans (1901), Max Beerbohm called Caesar "extravagant historical comedy" (*Around Theatres*, I, 151).

15

EXTRAVAGANZA

P L A C E D in the perspective of his entire dramatic career, Shaw's turn to Extravaganza was the last stage of his liberation from the literal realism which had confused the issue of Ibsenism at the end of the nineteenth century. Shaw, who had seen through the confusion more readily than most of the prophets and persecutors of the new drama, did not altogether escape the initial influence of realistic doctrine. Consequently, one can observe a clear movement from the early Unpleasant Plays, with their contemporary middle-class settings, social concerns, and journalistic associations, to the late Extravaganzas, with their remote and fanciful settings, universal concerns, and associations with fairy tale, fable, and parable. From the vantage point of the late plays, it is possible to trace the rising current of Extravaganza in such phenomena as the historical irreverence of *Caesar*, and the pantomime absurdities of *Androcles*. It is also possible to trace the progressive rise of a fantastic extravagance in atmosphere, and to describe the Extravaganza as the final formal embodiment of the atmosphere of the Discussion Plays. It is certainly true that the first play in which Extravaganza serves as a genre foundation is *Back to Methuselah* (1918-20), the successor to *Heartbreak House*. Thereafter, Extravaganza becomes the dominant though by no means exclusive mode in Shaw's play-making until his death. It is the mode of *The Apple Cart, A Political Extravaganza* (1929); *Too True to Be Good, A Political Extravaganza* (1931); *On the Rocks, A Political Comedy* (1933); *The Simpleton of the Unexpected Isles, A Vision of Judgment* (1934); *Geneva, Another Political Extravaganza* (1938-39); and *Farfetched Fables* (1948). In these plays, fantasy is frankly embraced, not only for event and setting but often for the kind of irrational proposition rationally pursued that both Aristophanes and Gilbert used as fundamental comedic ideas. For example, in *Back to Methuselah* we are asked to suppose that the human race can regulate its life span at will; in *Geneva* that the great dictators can be summoned before the International Court like ordinary disturbers of the peace. Using such dramatic propositions to generate a play, Shaw came closest to creating a fully incarnated philosophical drama, and left farthest behind the devotion to surface naturalism of the end-of-the-nineteenth-century critical advance-guard.

Shaw's early experience of Burlesque-Extravaganza did not at first dispose him to accept it as a proper vehicle for his "drama of unsettled ideals."[1] The standard of frivolity identified with the genre (perhaps the recollection of Opera-Bouffe choruses), the disappointed idealism behind Gilbert's topsy-turvydoms, and the initial attractions of the party of literary realism led him to repudiate with energy the term "extravaganza" when it was applied to his earliest attempt to discredit the conventions of romantic heroism.

In 1894 there was a heated controversy, soon buried, over the character of *Arms and the Man*. The reaction of the critics was summarized by A. B. Walkley: "But after laughing some of us began to think, and many of us, I fear, to think wrong. This fun of Mr. Shaw's is all very well—so runs the general criticism—only it is not Mr. Shaw's. It was invented by the author of *The Palace of Truth* and *Engaged*. It is merely secondhand Gilbertism."[2] The worst offender, in Shaw's view,

---

[1] In Dublin, Shaw had had opportunity to see a considerable amount of Burlesque, Extravaganza, and Opera-Bouffe, by Offenbach, F. C. Burnand, Gilbert, H. J. Byron, Planché, Robert Reece, John Brougham, Watts Phillips, Alexandre Lecocq, and others. He notes in "What George Bernard Shaw Looks Forward To," *Bristol Evening Post*, 3 Dec. 1946, p. 2, "I made my first acquaintance with Gilbert and Sullivan at the Gaiety in 'Trial by Jury'; and remember very well how astonishingly 'churchy' Sullivan's music sounded after Offenbach."

[2] "Arms and the Man," *The Speaker*, IX (28 April 1894), 471.

was William Archer who, as chief propagandist for Ibsen, should have known better; and much of Shaw's counterblast is directed at him. In the course of his friendly review, Archer uses the word "extravaganza" half a dozen times. He instructs the reader that though *Arms and the Man* is as funny as any Farce—"we laughed at it wildly, hysterically; and I exhort the reader to go and do likewise"—yet, "he must not expect a humdrum, rational, steady-going farce, like *Charley's Aunt*, bearing a well-understood conventional relation to real life. Let him rather look for a fantastic, psychological extravaganza, in which drama, farce, and Gilbertian irony keep flashing past the bewildered eye. . . ." The second and third acts, Archer declares, are "bright, clever, superficially cynical extravaganza." The setting in a real Bulgaria during the recent Balkan war instead of in "Grünewald and Gerolstein" (the realm of Offenbach's *Grande Duchesse*) is part of the immense joke. "If one could think that Mr Shaw had consciously and deliberately invented a new species of prose extravaganza, one could unreservedly applaud the invention . . . But I more than suspect that he conceives himself to have written a serious comedy, a reproduction of life as it really is. . . ."[3]

Shaw responded to this criticism with "A Dramatic Realist to his Critics," a documentary justification of the apparent absurdities of his play. "To a man who derives all his knowledge of life from witnessing plays," he notes scornfully, "nothing appears more unreal than objective life. A dramatic critic is generally such a man; and the more exactly I reproduce objective life for him on the stage, the more certain he is to call my play an extravaganza."[4] Later, on request, Shaw furnished a preface to Archer's *Theatrical 'World' of 1894* in which he repudiates his "imaginary success as a conventionally cynical and paradoxical castigator of 'the seamy side of human

[3] Reprinted in William Archer, *The Theatrical 'World' of 1894*, pp. 110-11, 117.

[4] *The New Review*, 11 (1894), p. 56.

nature' " (an allusion to Gilbert), and deplores the vogue of his plays as "a novel sort of extravaganza" (pp. xxvi-xxvii).

Thirty-five years after he had so disdainfully thrown "Extravaganza" back at the heads of the critics, Shaw declared in an interview (following the Birmingham Festival opening of *The Apple Cart*), "Critics rely very much on labels . . . The full title should have read: *The Apple Cart—A Political Extravaganza in Two Acts and an Interlude*. The word 'extravaganza' would have helped them . . ."[5] His play, he adds, is intended as a salutary lesson, and it is evident that he no longer associates Extravaganza with pointless fun and soured idealism. In the interval between the *Arms and the Man* controversy and the *Apple Cart* interview, Shaw had taken to using the drama as "a means of foreseeing and being prepared for realities as yet unexperienced, and of testing the feasibility and desirability of serious Utopias" (Shaw's definition of the "realistic imagination," *Misalliance*, p. 103). He had turned from discrediting fixed idealisms by a standard of actuality to commenting upon actualities through a medium of fantasy.

ROOTS AND FOUNDATIONS

There was both a formal and a pragmatic aspect to Shaw's eventual open appropriation of the name and the conventions of Extravaganza. Plays like *The Apple Cart* and *The Simpleton* were formally Extravaganzas in their use of an imaginary world to comment on the actual. They were pragmatically Extravaganzas in adopting a number of the genre's conventional characters and devices, and in embodying, however incongruously, a political and philosophical substance. The qualities of nineteenth-century Extravaganza which were the fountainhead of its usefulness to Shaw were not necessarily those qualities most important in its popular life on the stage; but none of them were negligible.

[5] George W. Bishop, *Barry Jackson and the London Theatre* (London, 1933), p. 117.

Extravaganza, a dominant form peculiar to the nineteenth-century theater, grew out of the Burlesque tradition. The first to distinguish between the various developments in the tradition was James Robinson Planché, who applied and popularized the term "Extravaganza" to separate "the whimsical treatment of a poetical subject from the broad caricature of a tragedy or a serious opera, which was correctly termed a 'Burlesque.' "[6] Like any living form, however, Extravaganza was difficult to keep within the bounds of a definition, and contemporary writers found it convenient to ignore fine differences between Burlesque and Extravaganza, and used the terms interchangeably. There were in fact three terms relevant to Shaw's later work frequently conjoined in the nineteenth century: Burlesque, Extravaganza, and Opera Bouffe. Properly speaking, these were three different, but never clearly distinguished, varieties of a general theatrical mode. Coincidentally there are three names of particular importance in the nineteenth-century history of Burlesque-Extravaganza on the English stage: James Robinson Planché, Jacques Offenbach, and W. S. Gilbert.[7]

[6] J. R. Planché, *Extravaganzas* (London, 1879), II, 66; quoted in Rowell, *The Victorian Theatre* (London, 1956), p. 70.

[7] The Burlesque-Extravaganza owed much of its development and popularity on the nineteenth-century English stage to the patent conditions at the beginning of the century, when, during most of the year, the spoken drama was the preserved domain of two theaters, Drury Lane and Covent Garden. Technically, Burlesque and Extravaganza were forms of the "Burletta"; that is, they were quasi-musical pieces in less than five acts which could be performed in theaters without patent privileges. Before Gilbert, the musical portions of English Burlesque-Extravaganza were generally not original, but rather, new and amusing words were set to familiar and popular songs as in the eighteenth-century ballad-opera. Thus, in Planché's *The White Cat* (1842), Prince Paragon, having been sent to find a dog small enough to fit through a thumb ring, sings Gilbert-like verses to "Oh, Ruddier than the Cherry":

> "From Perth to Pondicherry,
> From Bow to Bedfordbury,
> No dog so small,
> Exists at all,
> Of that I'm certain—very!" etc.

The characteristic attributes of Burlesque-Opera Bouffe-Extravaganza were music; feminine display; topical allusion; humor of the irreverent, the absurd, and the risqué; and an interpenetration of the fanciful and the familiar. However, there were occasional plays without music which otherwise reflected the tone and conventions of extravaganza; and Gilbert threw over the previously indispensable women in tights and eliminated the sexually risqué, so that in 1886 William Archer could trumpet the "decline of opera-bouffe and burlesque" and the simultaneous "victory of Gilbertian extravaganza over opera-bouffe as adapted for the London market," which for Archer was "the victory of literary and musical grace and humour over rampant vulgarity and meretricious jingle."[8] Nevertheless, the common compositional principle persisted through change, and held together the whole diversified mode of Burlesque, Opera Bouffe, Extravaganza. Gilbert's productions, like Offenbach's and Planché's, depend upon an interpenetration of the fanciful and familiar, of remote and contemporary worlds.

In traditional Burlesque, which descended from the eighteenth century, the interpenetration of cockney and classical, of actual and ideal, was a means of perpetrating the deflating caricature of an elevated genre, or of a subject with heroic, operatic, or legendary claims. Planché distinguishes his departure from tradition as the "whimsical treatment of a poetical subject" rather than its broad caricature; but in the first of his "long line of extravaganzas which for nearly thirty years have been, without a single exception, honoured by the approbation of the public," Planché provided a classical subject, treated with wild indignity, in a classical *mise en scène*, treated with perfect sobriety. He himself credits much of the success of the piece, *Olympic Revels; or, Prometheus and Pandora* (1831), to the impact upon each other of the decorous classical costumes and the absurd cockney doggerel,

---

[8] "Are We Advancing?" in *About the Theatre* (London, 1886), pp. 20-21.

and he clung to the principle in adapting the form to a rich new vein of material: "To the classical extravaganzas succeeded those founded on the fairy tales of Perrault, Madame D'Aulnoy, and their imitators," where still he proceeded on a plan of "rigidly adhering to truth and picture in costume and scenery (now medieval), while the dialogue was of course a tissue of anachronisms and absurdities."[9]

Anachronism, the deliberate yoking of worlds separate in time and thought, was considered a hallmark of Burlesque-Extravaganza. Therefore, when Shaw's *Caesar and Cleopatra* first affronted the critics, they found a critical key in the tradition of such plays as Planché's *The Golden Fleece; or, Jason in Colchis and Medea in Corinth: A Classical Extravaganza in Two Parts* (1845) and Offenbach's later (1867) and enormously popular *La Belle Hélène, Opera Bouffe en Trois Actes*. Shaw's common-sense air toward Caesar and Cleopatra seemed very like that of Henri Meilhac and Ludovic Halévy, Offenbach's librettists, toward the classical-heroic Paris and Helen. In *La Belle Hélène*, the authors treat their personages as Parisian boulevardiers. They show, in effect, what it is to look at heroic myth from a practical shopkeeping point of view. Calchas, the high priest, is businesslike about monthly figures on offerings, and Paris and Helen flirt. If Shaw introduces a steam engine into the lighthouse at Alexandria and gives his native Englishman a taste for respectable blue, Meilhac and Halévy set their third act at a contemporary seaside resort, and make their Heroic Games contests in charades, pun-making, and *bouts-rimés* (the charade is "locomotive"). Calchas puns on the language of Argos and *argot*, and Helen hypocritically sighs that the hand of fatality is always upon her, and wishes she had been born "*une bourgeoise paisible, la femme d'un brave negociant de Mitylène.*" As in *Caesar*, the yoking of worlds usually kept separate in the mind illuminates the contemporary world more than the remote.

[9] "Extravaganza and Spectacle," *Temple Bar*, III (1861), 528-29.

In the interpenetration of worlds in Burlesque-Extravaganza, the remote world was not necessarily heroic or historic;
it could also be magical or visionary, theatrical or utopian,
a fairyland, a stage-world, or a mythical South Sea kingdom.
The proximate world, however, had to be the contemporary
world, the area of ordinary living and of topical allusion.
Potentially the Burlesque-Extravaganza was double-edged,
for if (as in most Burlesque) the contemporary world could
serve as a devastating comment on an ideal world, in the
hands of a Fielding or an Aristophanes the roles were easily
reversed. Actually, the antecedents of nineteenth-century Burlesque-Extravaganza, historic and theoretic, supported the reversal. Planché declared that his first burlesque, *Amoroso,
King of Little Britain* (1818) was a direct imitation of W.
Barnes Rhodes's *Bombastes Furioso* (1810). *Bombastes Furioso, A Burlesque Tragic Opera, in One Act* (still alive in
Dublin during Shaw's boyhood) is a mixture of burlesque-
heroic verse and song which stems in turn from the line of
eighteenth-century Burlesque whose greatest practitioners
were Fielding and Gay.[10] And if these two are to be counted
among the progenitors of nineteenth-century Extravaganza,
so also is Aristophanes. "My ambition," wrote Planché in
retrospect, "was to lay the foundation for an Aristophanic
drama . . . As an experiment, I ventured to adapt one of the
Athenian satirist's own extravaganzas, *The Birds* . . . It was a
succès d'estime, not *d'argent*." To Planché's mind, Gilbert
was the new Aristophanes as well as his own successor.[11]

From the impulse in the tradition toward a reflex criticism

[10] See *ibid.*, pp. 524, 527. Shaw often endows characters with a penchant
for absurd heroics, but his only use of the *Tom Thumb-Bombastes* strain
for the tone of an entire play is in *The Admirable Bashville; or, Con-
stancy Unrewarded* (a blank-verse burlesque of his own novel, *Cashel
Byron's Profession*), which Shaw himself put in a class with "Carey's
Chrononhotonthologos, Fielding's Tom Thumb, and even Bombastes Furioso" (*Translations and Tomfooleries*, p. 89).

[11] "Extravaganza and Spectacle," p. 531. See also Planché's *Recollections and Reflections* (London, 1872), II, 79-82.

upon the contemporary world derived the possibilities which made nineteenth-century Burlesque-Extravaganza useful to Shaw: the possibilities of Political and Philosophical Extravaganza. The deflation of pretentious literary and theatrical forms, ideal worlds, and sentimental conventions, which was traditionally the chief business of Burlesque, was not important to Shaw, for he had already done this business in his own way (the way of *Arms and the Man* and *Mrs. Warren's Profession*). It was the other edge of the blade which Shaw found useful. His own Extravaganzas do not comment upon an imaginary world by means of the real and commonplace; they comment upon the real and commonplace world by means of the imaginary.

POLITICAL EXTRAVAGANZA

Topical political satire had been among the principal attractions in the Extravaganzas of Aristophanes and the Burlesques of Gay and Fielding; and though the English stage of the nineteenth century dwelt under a censorship originated by a government that had suffered too much Fielding, the topical and scandalous propensities of Burlesque-Extravaganza led it back into the paths of wickedness. Where the authority of government threatens, the political can be as risqué as the sexual. In the nineteenth-century theater (which is generally presumed to have been innocent of politics), the normal vehicle for topical political satire was the Burlesque-Extravaganza.

Since all plays were read before licensing, most topical political comment took the form of "hits," injected for performance by author or actors and made through incongruous aside or even through make-up. A representative entertainment of this class is Charles Millward's *Blue Beard* (Birmingham, 1869), in which there are many such "hits," wholly incongruous and utterly unconnected with the fable, ranging from general comments on elections and election bills to specific digs at Robert Lowe, Chancellor of the Exchequer, and his scheme of anticipatory taxation.[12] In an article on the coming of Burlesque to Boston, William Dean Howells notes that the English pieces brought by the touring London troupes had been equipped with "some political allusions which were supposed to be effective with us," but which were received with apathy. "It was conceivable," he adds, "from a certain air with which the actors delivered these, that they were in the habit of stirring London audiences greatly with like strokes of satire; but except where Rebecca offered a bottle of Medford rum to Cedric the Saxon, who appeared in the figure of ex-President Johnson, they had no effect upon us."[13] Planché writes in his *Recollections* (linking the political and sexual risqué quite as a matter of course):

"Any profane expression or indecent situation, any coarse allusion or personal insult to those in authority over us, may be, and *has been*, foisted into a burlesque or a pantomime after its performance has been sanctioned by the licenser; and, in the recent instance of the Christmas harlequinades [1871], it is well known that the examiner's directions to omit the common-place jokes upon certain members of the Cabinet, while they gave rise to considerable acrimonious correspondence in the daily journals . . . were never paid the slightest attention to, but continued to be uttered and to

[12] Charles Millward, *The Grand Comic Christmas Pantomime Entitled Blue Beard*, Birmingham: Printed at the Theatre Royal Printing Works (1869). The amount of topical political allusion in the text of *Blue Beard* is unusual, but it can be explained by the printing of this particular playbook for an original production in Birmingham, where the Lord Chamberlain's disapproval was of less account. It is unlikely that "hits" invented during production would make their way into the texts. *Blue Beard*, it should be noted, is a Christmas Pantomime; but it is also an Extravaganza. At this period the difference between the two was often the mere addition, in Pantomime, of a truncated harlequinade. At the end of his apologia, "Extravaganza and Spectacle," Planché complains that recently "Extravaganza has been patched on to Pantomime, to the serious injury of both" (p. 532).

[13] W. D. Howells, "The New Taste in Theatricals," *Atlantic*, 23 (1869), 641.

excite the roars and plaudits of the galleries to the last night of representation."[14]

A far more integral and organic form of Political Extravaganza seems to date from an event in the late sixties, the arrival of the Offenbach, Meilhac, and Halévy *La Grande Duchesse de Gérolstein*, an Opera Bouffe of enormous popularity and great germinal power in the English theater.[15] The contemporary political reference of *La Grande Duchesse* was structural rather than decorative, built into the fable and character. The work was presented in Paris in the midst of the debate on the reorganization and expansion of the armed forces; when the Mexican adventure, the latest in a costly series, was just drawing to a close, and war with Prussia over the Grand Duchy of Luxemburg seemed imminent; when France was apparently the leading military power in Europe, and Napoleon III was attempting to consolidate his power by invoking the glories of the First Empire. The opera was an irresistible satire of war and militarism. The leading satirical

[14] *Recollections and Reflections*, II, 109-10.
[15] In 1893 Shaw could write, *à propos* of comic opera in general, "The effect on the public of the long degeneration from La Grande Duchesse, with its witty book and effervescent score, down to the last dregs of that school . . . seems now to be nearly complete," though he adds, "Managers are still trying to pick profits out of the dregs of the Offenbach movement" (*Music in London*, III, 34, 35). *La Grande Duchesse* had a considerable vogue in Dublin when brought by an English touring company (and billed as "Offenbach's celebrated Operatic Extravaganza," *D.E.M.*, 11 May 1869), and it was one of the three pieces brought by Mlle. Schneider (the original Duchess) and her Parisian company less than a year later. After the opening of the Gaiety in 1871, Offenbach, in English and French, was apparently among the most popular theatrical fare in Dublin, measured by the number of companies and the quantity of performance. This was the period Shaw writes of as "the days when La Grande Duchesse was shuddered at as something frightfully wicked, when improper stories about Schneider formed the staple of polite conversation, and young persons were withheld from the interpolated *can-can* in the second act as from a spectacle that must deprave them for ever." Then, Shaw adds, "the many-headed received a rapturous impression of opera bouffe as a delightful and complete initiation into life—the very next thing, in fact, to a visit to the Paris of Napoleon III . . ." (*Music in London*, III, 34).

figure is General Boum, who periodically has to be forcibly restrained from hurling himself on the enemy, and who takes his snuff by firing off a double-barrelled pistol and breathing in its fumes. The war is frankly a distraction for the Grand Duchess, contrived by her minister Puck in order (like the Emperor) to stay in power. The victory is won humanely by Private Fritz, the irrepressible, bad soldier, who talks to the choleric General commonsensibly, scandalizing military propriety and outraging military ideals. Having been promoted to General himself by the amorous interest of the Duchess, he allows his liquor supplies to fall into the hands of the enemy on the night before battle. The combination of political satire and the domestic and amorous interests of the ruler of a mythical kingdom is typical among extravaganzas with an integral political bent. The same combination may be seen in *The Apple Cart*.

W. S. Gilbert, as Shaw points out, worked at translating Offenbach (*Les Brigands*); and there is a current of political satire in Gilbert stronger than the present general conception of his Extravaganzas would allow for. His critical tendency is always toward political and philosophical generality, but he sometimes slips into satire of specific political figures and institutions. A notorious example is the caricature of W. H. Smith, Disraeli's First Lord of the Admiralty, as Sir Joseph Porter in *Pinafore* (1878).[16] Almost forgotten, however, is "F. Tomline" (W. S. Gilbert) and Gilbert Arthur à Beckett's very successful *The Happy Land: A Burlesque Version of "The Wicked World"* (also by W. S. Gilbert; both 1873), in which the authors brought three leaders of the current government on stage and, in consequence, earned the disapproval

[16] Gilbert was careful to assure Sullivan in advance that any resemblance to W. H. Smith would be counteracted by "the fact that the First Lord in the opera is a *Radical* of the most pronounced type." Nevertheless, the real First Lord was soon known as "Pinafore Smith" (see Pearson, *Gilbert: His Life and Strife*, p. 95).

of the official censorship. A prefatory note to the quickly produced published version (London, 1873), reads:

> *This book contains the* EXACT TEXT *of the piece as played on the occasion of the Lord Chamberlain's official visit to the Court Theatre, on the 6th March, 1873* [three days after opening]. *Those who will take the trouble to compare the original text with the expurgated version, as played nightly at the Court Theatre, will be in a position to appreciate the value of the Lord Chamberlain's alterations.*
>
> THE AUTHORS

In Gilbert's political satire, the genre principle of an interpenetration of the ordinary world and an imaginative otherworld becomes the principle of the action itself. From Planché's fairy-tale kings and kingdoms, Gilbert shaped a series of naïve Utopias into which he introduces shattering doses of contemporary civilization. In *The Happy Land*, which is Fairyland, the female fairies induce their scapegrace brothers (who take trips to earth for dissipation) to send up three earthlings in their places. The three, who come singing "We are three statesmen old and tried," are Mr. G. (Gladstone), the leader, pompous and given to oratory; Mr. L. (Robert Lowe, Chancellor of the Exchequer, 1868-1873), obsessed with facts, figures, and political economy; Mr. A. (A. S. Ayrton, Commissioner of Public Works, 1869-1873), tasteless in art and fond of rows. The statesmen show the fairies how to set up a popular government along English cabinet-parliamentary lines. This brings chaos and revolt to Fairyland.[17]

---

[17] Specifically, the pinch-penny economy and the timid foreign policy of the ministry are derided: "Isn't political economy the same thing as social economy? . . . Quite the reverse. Social economy means spending a penny to save a pound. Political economy is spending a pound to save a penny" (p. 10). "Arbitration, my dear, is that conscious power which enables the strong man to take to his heels in the face of danger" (p. 15). In 1871 Gladstone's ministry had acquiesced to the Russian denunciation of part of the treaty which had ended the Crimean War, and

The great popularity of *The Happy Land* brought imitators of various kinds. A few months after *The Happy Land*, Robert Reece produced a burlesque of Bulwer-Lytton's *Richelieu* (as acted by Irving) called *Richelieu Re-dressed*, in which, according to the *Daily Telegraph*, itself one of the victims of the piece, the author twisted the story "that it may at once serve as an operatic extravaganza and a political pasquinade" (29 Oct. 1873). The Cardinal was presented as a happy combination of the mannerisms of Irving and the appearance of Gladstone. The *Times* reported, with a glance at Aristophanes,

"Considered merely as a 'parody' on a deservedly popular play, *Richelieu Redressed* is exceedingly droll, but it is not in this character that it will reach the notoriety which it probably will attain, unless it is stopped short in its career by some pressure from without. It is the 'Knight side' of the piece, rather than the 'Frog side,' which evokes the shouts of the audience. All can see that Richelieu, whose apology for a Cardinal's robe barely conceals the attire of a modern 'Right Honourable,' is not meant for Richelieu at all; that the anxiety which he displays as to the result of certain elections has little to do with any conspiracy of the 17th century; and that when, after attempting to lift an unwieldy sword inscribed 'public approbation,' he lets it drop, but consoles himself by remarking that he has still a 'Birmingham blade which is *bright*,' the last word in this proposition is not [to] be re-

---

to the German annexation of Alsace-Lorraine. A friendly historian notes, "These transactions . . . left an uneasy sense that Gladstone was not vigorous enough in foreign affairs. The *Alabama* claims award of the following year increased this impression at the time, although posterity feels gratitude to the statesmen who avoided war with America. There was perhaps more substance for the suspicion that Gladstone's instinct for economy in taxation inclined him to shorten supplies for army and navy; at least it caused differences with some of his own colleagues, as well as furnishing Opposition with a text" (G. M. Trevelyan, *British History in the Nineteenth Century and After* [London, 1927], p. 364).

garded as an adjective. If any difficulty remains on the subject it is completely removed by the 'make-up' of Mr. E. Righton, who never so thoroughly identified himself with a character as he does with this 'Right Honourable' Lord Cardinal." (*Times*, 29 Oct. 1873, p. 8)

The *Daily News* mentions *The Happy Land* as the obvious inspiration and gives an account of Reece's play as a triumph of pertinent impertinence:

"The spectacle of the Prime Minister taking the audience into his confidence, indulging in outspoken reflections on his policy, and evolving the schemes he has in view for retaining power at any price, is eminently ludicrous; but when he bursts forth into song and ends with a break-down the amusement of the audience knows no bounds. The Duke of Orleans—Richelieu's enemy—turns out to be none other than Mr. Disraeli; while three Secretaries of State judiciously keep their faces hidden behind black hats 'for fear of the licensor.' It is, however, conveyed to the audience by unmistakable signs that they are intended to present Lord Granville, Mr. Lowe, and Mr. Cardwell. All sorts o[f] topics are touched upon in the burlesque, including the Ashantee War and the Tichborne case, but the greatest capital is made out of the recent elections, and the famous letter commencing 'My dear Grey' is utilized with good effect. . . . The burlesque was received most enthusiastically, and it only requires an edict from the Lord Chamberlain to render it one of the successes of the season." (*Daily News*, 28 Oct. 1873)

Like *The Happy Land*, Reece's Burlesque was extremely successful, though it lacked the assistance of the Lord Chamberlain. Like *The Happy Land* it was brought to Dublin and presented with much éclat during a two-week visit of Sefton's Comedy Company as *Richelieu Re-dressed; or, The Last of Mr. G—* (*D.E.M.*, 22 June 1874).

A morphological link between Gilbert and Shaw was another Extravaganza of 1873, written under the spell of recent success by Gilbert's collaborator, Gilbert Arthur à Beckett. In à Beckett's *Last of the Legends; or, The Baron, the Bride, and the Battery*, a medieval baronial clan wakes in the ruins of its castle in the year 2073, having slept for a thousand years as the result of a rash vow. They are visited by Smith, an English Duke of the future, who is eventually obliged to marry into the family to relieve them of their curse. The future, as Smith presents it, comments on the present (1873) by extrapolation and contrast. Smith dines on "food globules" only. He reveals that having done away with doctors and lawyers the men of the future are never ill and never quarrel. England is periodically invaded—"Last year we had the Figi [*sic*] Islanders"—but nobody minds. "Its good for trade, and introduces foreign capital." Burlesque is extinct, and coal is so rare and precious that it is set with diamonds and worn in rings. (An acute coal famine in the Lancashire coal fields occurred in 1873, and the colliery price had risen in a few years from 4s./ton to over 20s.)

Smith has a mesmeric apparatus that "sends anyone into a clairvoyant state instantly." He uses it to transport the entire medieval clan back two centuries to 1873: a year in which Gladstone attempted to bolster his weakening ministry by making shifts in the Cabinet, he himself taking on the duties of the Exchequer in place of the unpopular Lowe; a year in which the grand sensation was the two-week visit of the Shah of Persia; in which a series of spectacular railway disasters had called attention to an accident rate discussed in Parliament as "a national scandal"; in which an outbreak of typhoid in London had been traced to the milk; in which public-house customers were still smarting under a recent temperance victory, shortening hours particularly on Sunday. "Now," says Smith, "what do you all see? (*tremolo in orchestra*)."

KARL. (*clairvoyant business*) A ministerial move, yet no new faces,

SMITH. The British Government exchanging places!

ERLIN[DA]. The world gone mad to see a blazing star!

A locomotive jewel shop—

SMITH.   The Shah!

SIR H[UBERT]. Three hundred people—seeking mere diversion,

Upset and smashed—

SMITH.   A Railway Excursion!

LADY B[ERTHA]. Poor little pigeons shot, as each one passes!

SMITH. The sport, *de rigueur*, of the upper classes!

SELTZ[ERWASSER]. Fat, gravy, joint—all come to grief!

A terrifying dish! (*shudders*)

SMITH.   Australian Beef!

WIL[HELM]. Poison!—for rich and poor—for serge and silk!

And no inspector stops it!

SMITH.   London Milk! . . .

FRITZ. The bigots rob the poor man of his one day.

SMITH. Wicked museums locked up tight on Sunday!

SELTZ[ERWASSER]. A British tax-payer keeps up his pecker!

SMITH. *That's* plain enough! A change of the Exchequer!

                    (*French A. E.*, p. 11)

Four of Shaw's Extravaganzas (six if we count the last three parts of *Methuselah* separately) are set at least partly in the appreciable future. In these plays, a world of the future func-

—·[396]·—

tions as the Extravaganza Otherworld and, through extrapolation, contrast, and extra-temporal tourism, it serves to illuminate the present moment. Nearly all these elements in Shaw's
use of a future Otherworld are present in à Beckett's *Last of
the Legends.*

Gilbert used the Otherworld formula of *The Happy Land*
for a more generalized satire of political institutions in a
number of his later Extravaganzas: in *Iolanthe; or, The Peer
and the Peri* (1882), for example, and *The Gondoliers; or,
The King of Barataria* (1889). The most thoroughly political
of these later pieces was Gilbert's *Utopia, Limited; or, The
Flowers of Progress* (1893), a straightforward reworking of
The Happy Land in political themes and their dramatic
embodiment. In *Utopia, Limited,* Fairyland is replaced with
a mythical South Sea kingdom of Anglophiles. The Utopians
go so far as to import a number of English types, representative of what made England great, to remodel their country
along English lines. These "Flowers of Progress" include a
County Councillor, a company promoter, a Q.C., a Lord
Chamberlain, a naval captain, a captain in the Horseguards.
The original Utopian government was a monarchy under
King Paramount the First, a despot liable to be blown up
at any moment for any lapse from political or social propriety. The Utopian Vice-Chamberlain explains: "After
many unhappy experiments in the direction of an ideal
Republic, it was found that what may be described as a
Despotism tempered by Dynamite provides, on the whole, the
most satisfactory description of ruler—an autocrat who dares
not abuse his autocratic power."[18] The reform proposed by
the representatives of English greatness is a state in which
everyone becomes a Limited Liability Association.

> KING . . . And do I understand you that Great
> Britain

[18] *Utopia, Limited,* in *Plays & Poems of W. S. Gilbert* (New York, 1932),
p. 587.

Upon this Joint Stock principle is governed?
MR. GOLD[BURY]. We haven't come to that,
exactly—but
We're tending rapidly in that direction.
The date's not distant. (p. 622)

The reform of Utopia proceeds with such vigor that soon, as the King tells the Flowers of Progress, poverty is obsolete and hunger is abolished ("We are going to abolish it in England"), the peerage is remodelled on an intellectual basis ("We are going to remodel it in England"), and, in short, "this happy country has been Anglicized completely" (pp. 629f.). Eventually, however, the perfection of Utopia leads to revolution. The reconstructed Army and Navy have been made so invincible that war is impossible; the sanitary code has been made so drastic that "all the doctors dwindle, starve, and die!" The remodelled laws "Have quite extinguished crime and litigation:/ The lawyers starve, and all the jails are let/ As model lodgings for the working-classes!" It is then that the English-educated Princess remembers "the most essential element of all!"

> Government by Party! Introduce that great and glorious element—at once the bulwark and foundation of England's greatness—and all will be well! No political measures will endure, because one Party will assuredly undo all that the other Party has done; and while grouse is to be shot, and foxes worried to death, the legislative action of the country will be at a standstill. Then there will be sickness in plenty, endless lawsuits, crowded jails, interminable confusion in the Army and Navy, and, in short, general and unexampled prosperity! (p. 645)

There is a great difference between the casual topical references of Millward's *Blue Beard* and the essential political texture of Gilbert's *Utopia, Limited*; nevertheless, they are opposite ends of a wide range embodying one of the important elements of the Burlesque-Extravaganza tradition. On this range, however, *Utopia, Limited* is neither more nor less Political Extravaganza than *Geneva* or *Too True to Be Good*. In choosing Extravaganza as the proper vehicle for his political comment, both topical and general, Shaw was following in the beaten paths of the nineteenth-century drama.

The Apple Cart, A Political Extravaganza (1929) was the first of Shaw's plays to adopt the name. Of all Shaw's Extravaganzas it is the most conservative in relation to its generic roots (the Offenbach strain of Opera Bouffe-Extravaganza), and consequently Shaw felt it was the most liable to debasement to a common denominator. He objected bitterly to Max Reinhardt's treatment of *The Apple Cart* as vulgarized Offenbach, to his excision of everything delicate and Mozartian, such as the "overture," in order to begin with "a vulgarized Boanerges waiting for a vieux marcheur king, a male Duchess of Gerolstein" (see above, p. 55). *The Apple Cart* was not simply Opera Bouffe and Extravaganza; it was Political Extravaganza. For Shaw, this meant that it had a most serious dimension, an over-all reference to the immediate political reality which was the most desperate subject of the age. The Otherworld of *The Apple Cart* is an extrapolation of this reality. The play, he wrote, "is intended as a salutary lesson, as I feel it is a state of things into which we could drift."[19] But the ultimate seriousness of the play, Shaw found, could be easily evaded by judicious cutting, whereas the conspicuous traits of Extravaganza were fatally ingrained.

The Apple Cart is set in a mythical realm, an England of the future (there is an early reference to the death of one character's father in 1962); almost all the characters bear classical or mythological names (e.g. Pamphilius, Sempronius,

[19] Bishop, *Barry Jackson and the London Theatre*, p. 118.

Balbus, Crassus, Boanerges, Lysistrata, Proteus); there is a plot in which a legitimate king out-maneuvers his democratic cabinet in a contest for power; a lady cabinet minister, whose parliamentary security is based on her talent for mimicry and singing comic songs, appears in an elaborately buttoned, braided and epauleted court uniform. The play presents both the King's politics and his amours, not even troubling to put them into a plot relationship. All these, and particularly the last, were the hallmarks of Opera Bouffe and Extravaganza, in which rulers of mythical kingdoms were always beset by conspiracies and tangled in complicated and often improper affairs. Offenbach's *La Grande Duchesse*, where conspiracies of the ministry alternate with those of the bedchamber, was the universal model and prime example; but a work with closer thematic resemblances to *The Apple Cart* was James Albery's Extravaganza-based fairy play, *Oriana, A Romantic Legend* (1873), in which King Raymond is much given to amorous adventure and to neglecting his queen, Oriana, along with his political affairs. Consequently a popular demagogue, a peasant named Oxeye, seeks power and foments a revolution. Eventually, Oriana herself quells Oxeye's revolution with the help of the disguised King Raymond. Legitimacy triumphs, politically and domestically; the demagogue is vanquished and the royal couple are reunited.

There is a similar conjunction of the domestic and the political, and a similar opposition of a prince and a demagogue, in Sardou's *Rabagas* (1873), adapted by Stephen Fiske as *Robert Rabagas* and billed as a "Political Satire" when brought by Wyndham's company to the Gaiety Theatre, Dublin, in 1874 (*D.E.M.*, 16 Oct. 1874). Strictly speaking, *Rabagas* was not an Extravaganza. However, like some of Gilbert's earlier work, and like Shaw's own Political Extravaganzas, it is an adaptation of the form to the theater of prose. *Rabagas*, like the conventional Opera Bouffe, is set in a fanciful European principality, in this case, however, called Monaco. As in

The Apple Cart, a power struggle is in progress between the Prince and a clever and unscrupulous lawyer and demagogue, Robert Rabagas, the head of an unofficial revolutionary cabinet. The Prince is aided by Mrs. Blount, an American adventuress of sorts and the center of amorous interest. On the eve of insurrection, the Prince and Mrs. Blount convince the demagogue that he is a natural aristocrat who must, after all, become the Prince's minister. Rabagas is outmaneuvered, and his promotion is his downfall. The topicality of *Rabagas* was in its reflection on Léon Gambetta, the French republican statesman, and the period of political turmoil which followed the Franco-Prussian war; but it also presents, like *The Apple Cart*, wider issues of demagoguery and aristocracy.

The resemblance of *The Apple Cart* to *Oriana* and *Rabagas* is largely a matter of similar generic materials in similar proportions. The power struggle in *The Apple Cart* lies between a democratic cabinet, under the leadership of Joseph Proteus, and a restive English monarch, King Magnus. In the struggle, Proteus attempts to silence Magnus forever, to make him a "dumb king," by threatening to go to the country on the issue of parliamentary supremacy. (The crisis has been provoked by King Magnus's evident disposition to revive the royal veto.) The King, who knows that much of his popularity depends upon his reputation as a libertine, has an Orinthia, an orchid among women, to complement his garden-variety wife. Between his apparent cornering by Proteus in the First Act and his triumphant escape to pursue his own way in the last, the King visits Orinthia in her palace apartments, soothes her, makes love to her, wrestles with her, and eludes her designs to become queen in his wife's place. He then returns to defeat Proteus by threatening to abdicate, to run for Parliament as a commoner, and to form his own party. As in *Oriana*, (though the terms are altered), Legitimacy triumphs politically and domestically.

The true political dimension of *The Apple Cart* is its philosophical concern with right rule and the practical workings of democracy in an industrial civilization like England. Shaw's Otherworld method is to carry to their logical extremes tendencies already present in the political life of England, and to embody them in an England of the future. He shows an England of the future devoted to luxury industries, caught between Washington and Moscow, in which only seven percent of the electorate vote. Politics, "once the centre of attraction for ability, public spirit, and ambition," is no longer a vocation for the best men or for a trained ruling class. The seats of power and attraction in the country are now the great corporations, of which the greatest, "Breakages, Limited" is an ultimate projection of the vested interest of private industry (in an affluent society) in shoddiness and waste and in the deterioration and replacement of goods. Through control of the press, Breakages controls the democracy and its elected government. It is well represented even in the cabinet with which King Magnus contends, though that cabinet also contains recognizable caricatures of the Labour party leaders of 1929.

The central political concern of *The Apple Cart*, the problem of right rule in a modern industrial democracy, was a topical concern in a year that the Labour party took power. The contest between Magnus and Proteus gives analogical form to that concern, since they are overtly symbolic personages. Proteus, the shape-changer, is the people's ideal executive instrument. King Magnus (Magnyfycence) is his opposite, their protection against even themselves. But the conflict, Shaw wrote, "is not really between royalty and democracy. It is between both and plutocracy, which, having destroyed the royal power by frank force under democratic pretexts, has bought and swallowed democracy" (*Apple Cart*, Preface, p. 170).

Proteus, the supremely flexible democratic executive, and Magnus, the undemocratic guardian of extra-temporal values, do not complete the alternatives of modern government. There is new force in the cabinet, comic for the moment because inexperienced; a bullish strong-man, a roarer like Albery's Oxeye, and a different sort of demagogue from Joseph Proteus. Boanerges, the new trade-union member and President of the Board of Trade, has the makings of a dictator. He comes to his first meeting with the King dressed in a proletarian blouse and cap. Democracy, he has discovered, is largely a matter of telling the people what to do. He is temporarily managed by the King, but is ultimately made dangerous by being both flattered by the King and his ladies (like Rabagas) and by being educated. "The King sees at once that Boanerges . . . is of the governing class. The revelation that comes to Boanerges is that the King is also a member of the governing class."[20] In the succeeding Political Extravaganzas, the Strong Man generated out of the weakness of democracy was to be a constant and disturbing concern.

The Extravaganzas which succeeded *The Apple Cart* serve as an almost continuous political chronicle of the time, though in the end events came too rapidly for the leisurely making of fables. *Too True to Be Good, A Political Extravaganza* (1931), presented the effects of the war and peace, not on the generations that made it (*Heartbreak House*), but on those which were themselves formed by it. *On the Rocks, A Political Comedy* (1933), presents the disaster of depression. *The Simpleton of the Unexpected Isles, A Vision of Judgment* (1934), projects the Russian revolution coming home to England as an allegorical Day of Judgment (nationally administered). *Geneva, Another Political Extravaganza* (1938-1939) presents the turn toward dictatorships, the beginnings of modern internationalism, and the forces that led to the Second World War. All are concerned with political institutions, and each is a fusion of topicality and fantasy.

[20] *Ibid.* (quoting Shaw).

In the course of composing *Too True to Be Good*, Shaw wrote that the play dealt with "the break-up of European morals by the war."[21] Before this contemporary concern can emerge, however, the key of fantasy has been established, for the curtain rises on one of the principals lying ill with the German measles while *"Near her, in the easy chair, sits a Monster. In shape and size it resembles a human being; but in substance it seems to be made of a luminous jelly with a visible skeleton of short black rods. It droops forward in the chair with its head in its hands, and seems in the last degree wretched"* (p. 28). The Monster is a poor sick bacillus, infected by the patient's disorder and unjustly blamed for it, who engages a visiting doctor in a professional discussion.

The patient kidnaps herself by running off with a burglar and his mistress-accomplice to that favored locale of Extravaganza, a nameless tropical country where everyone finds himself out. There, in an allegorical setting, Aubrey the Burglar, a clergyman as well as a thief, meets his father, a relic of nineteenth-century secular rationalism who has been shaken by relativity, the principle of indeterminism, and the war. Though he has lost his own faith, the Elder cannot forgive either his son's ordination or his dishonesty.

> A U B R E Y . Why do you make such a fuss about nothing?
>
> T H E   E L D E R . Do you call the theft of a pearl necklace nothing?
>
> A U B R E Y . Less than nothing, compared to the things I have done with your approval. I was hardly more than a boy when I first dropped a bomb on a sleeping village. (p. 88)

Shaw uses the fantastic machinery of his play to project, topically enough, the contemporary spiritual restlessness which accompanied the negative freedom from illusions and re-

---

[21] MS postcard to Siegfried Trebitsch, 15 June 1931.

straints. However, *Too True to Be Good* also embodies a simpler political theme. Shaw explains in his preface that the great popular support of capitalism and the real opposition to socialism are founded in the tantalizing possibility of becoming enormously rich. "My play is a story of three reckless young people who come into possession of, for the moment, unlimited riches, and set out to have a thoroughly good time with all the modern machinery of pleasure to aid them. The result is that they get nothing for their money but a multitude of worries and a maddening dissatisfaction" (*Too True*, p. 3). The play is a parable designed to show not only that the old certainties are bankrupt but that, in the current state of things, limitless wealth combined with limitless freedom, the Grand Prize of Capitalism, is not worth the bother.

With the deepening depression and the continental collapse of democratic capitalism, Shaw's political fables became increasingly immediate in their topical reference. *On the Rocks*, Shaw's play on the depression, was subtitled *A Political Fantasy in Two Acts* in the "First Rough Proof" and *A Compendium of Contemporary Politics* in the "First Revise after Rehearsal." Both descriptions suit the play, though it was finally called *A Political Comedy*, perhaps in order to weight the balance neither toward fantasy nor topicality.

The fantasy of *On the Rocks* lies in the central sequence of events and its generating comedic idea. (The setting, in contrast, is as immediately contemporary as possible.) The play is meant to project, not what is happening, but what might happen in the contemporary crisis if, wonderfully, a Prime Minister of England were brought up to date and seriously began to think.

The central figure of the play is Arthur Chavender, Liberal Prime Minister and figurehead of a national-emergency Coalition Cabinet. He begins genial, buoyant, and in a state of high nervous frenzy because the unemployed are in the streets

and England is in an economic collapse. His incompetence to
deal with the crisis is reflected in an abundance of activity
which accomplishes nothing. He is one of Shaw's line of
democratic statesmen in Extravaganza to which Burge, Lubin,
Burge-Lubin, and Bolge-Bluebin of *Methuselah*, and Joseph
Proteus of *The Apple Cart* belong. "You dont govern the
country, Arthur," his wife tells him, "The country isnt governed: it just slummocks along anyhow." And he replies, "I
have to govern within democratic limits. I cannot go faster
than our voters will let me" (p. 199).

In the course of the play, Chavender is mysteriously transformed from Proteus to King Magnus, and the action then
follows the pattern of political extravaganza as laid down in
The Apple Cart. In both plays, one man in an ambiguous
position of leadership maneuvers against a cabinet group.
Chavender presents a radical program of nationalization and
economic reorganization to meet the crisis, and he is challenged by the head of conservative and parliamentary power
in his coalition cabinet, Sir Dexter Rightside. In Shaw's 1929
fable on England's prosperity, King Magnus was more or less
victorious; but in the 1933 fable on her adversity, Chavender
is flatly defeated. The only alternative in this period of tot-
tering democratic institutions seems to be dictatorship, though
Chavender declares, "I'm not the man for the job . . . And
I shall hate the man who will carry it through for his cruelty
and the desolation he will bring on us and our like" (p. 273).
The play ends to the sound of breaking glass, the percussion
of police clubs, and the singing of "England, Arise!" The
fantasy of the Minister who is redeemed and made whole,
which grew out of England's political and economic actuality,
returns to it in the end. Nothing has happened; and the failure
of Chavender even when transformed is Shaw's parable, his
unhappy demonstration, of the failure of parliamentary democracy.

The representation of recognizable and controversial public figures was a sensational effect of political extravaganza notably employed in *The Happy Land* and *Richelieu Re-dressed.* The use of living models for characters was common in Shaw's dramaturgy; but the use of public figures in their public functions is a particular mark of his Extravaganza. In *The Apple Cart*, Proteus is recognizably Ramsay MacDonald and Boanerges is recognizably John Burns. In *Back to Methuselah*, Lubin and Joyce Burge are sketches of Asquith and Lloyd George. And in *Geneva, Another Political Extravaganza*, a number of the chief personages are caricatures of the most notable international political figures of the time. Hitler appears as "Ernest Battler," in the dazzling costume and winged helmet of an operatic Siegfried. Mussolini appears as "Bardo Bombardone," in drapery and laurel crown. Austen (not Neville) Chamberlain appears as "Sir Orpheus Midlander" in court costume and monocle. Franco appears as "General Flanco de Fortinbras" in resplendent military uniform.[22] In addition, Shaw takes care to include representatives of every moving force he can perceive in international affairs, including a Russian Commissar, a Spirit of Geneva, and a Spirit of Camberwell. The Spirit of Geneva is embodied in the Secretary of the League, a sketch from life of Sir Eric Drummond, the permanent British Secretary General. The Spirit of Camberwell is embodied in its daughter, Miss Begonia Brown, a thorough English patriot, whose parochialism is so refined as to make her despise Peckham, "another part of London, adjacent to Camberwell and equally and entirely indistinguishable from it" (p. 97).

The central fantasy, the comedic idea, in *Geneva* is an application of English common law to international affairs. A neglected section of the League of Nations, the Committee

---

[22] See Rattray, *Bernard Shaw: A Chronicle*, p. 260. Shaw sketches Sir Eric Drummond and Sir Austen Chamberlain in "The League of Nations" (1929), in *What I Really Wrote About the War*, pp. 400-403.

for Intellectual Co-operation, calls upon the International Court at The Hague to issue warrants against governments. "The stupendous and colossal joke of the present proceedings is that this court has summoned all the dictators to appear before it and answer charges brought against them by the Toms, Dicks, Harriets, Susans and Elizas of all nations" (p. 88). The dictators answer the summons because "Where the spotlight is, there will the despots be gathered" (p. 86). The trial, or rather, the apology of the dictators is directed by the playwright at an audience prepossessed with liberalism and Parliamentary democracy. But the dictators are also exposed in their narrowness, claptrap, and delusions. The Judge declares to all sides, "I give you up as hopeless. Man is a failure as a political animal. The creative forces which produce him must produce something better" (p. 122). And this judgment is followed by the apparent end of the world. First it is announced that Battler's troops have invaded Ruritania (Poland); then, "that the orbit of the earth is jumping to its next quantum. . . . Humanity is doomed." With this real and this false apocalypse, the comedy is brought to an end.

Geneva exists in several versions, for after its festival production in August 1938, it required revision for its London opening in November, and further revision (including a whole new act) during its subsequent tour of America (1939-1940) to take account of the beginning of the Second World War. In a program note to the London opening, after relating the original suggestion for the play, Shaw declared, "That was how the play began. How it will finish—for in the theatre it only stops: it does not finish—nobody knows."

Ultimately *Geneva* suffered for its immediate topicality. But despite the looseness and inconclusiveness, it manages, by way of "Fantasy" and "Fancied . . . History," to present Nationalism and Internationalism in the contemporary world, current democracy and current dictatorship, the actualities of British foreign policy, and the leading political personages of the day. It is with an eye to the dramatic kinship of his Political Extravaganzas that Shaw cites in his preface, as evidence of "no change in the natural political capacity of the human species," the comedies of Aristophanes (p. 14).

PHILOSOPHICAL EXTRAVAGANZA

Shaw's Extravaganzas were of two kinds, philosophic (or religious) and political. The two are not really separable, however, since the central dogma of Shaw's religious philosophy was creative evolution, and the political crisis of the age, he held, was a biological crisis if rightly understood. Mankind, the most advanced organ of the Life Force in its evolution from blind will to self-understanding, was faced with the problem of social complexity, the problem of organizing and administrating civilization. The World War and its immediate aftermath, Shaw declared, had confirmed a growing doubt "whether the human animal, as he exists at present, is capable of solving the social problems raised by his own aggregation, or, as he calls it, his civilization" (*Methuselah*, p. x). If mankind can meet the crisis, it will have taken a further step in creative evolution; if not, "we shall go the way of the mastadon and the megatherium and all the other scrapped experiments" (*Methuselah*, p. 80).

Prosaically as an artist and thinker, poetically as the embodied projective imagination of the Life Force, Shaw found it clearly in his province to expound the crisis and point out means of overcoming it. To this end he invented his series of parables set in fanciful Otherworlds, into which the implicit tendencies and obscured issues of the critical times were projected and (as is the habit where extrapolation and parable are applied to current crises) wrought up to apocalyptic ultimates. Some of these parables were more topical, narrower in their focus, more "political," others more general, more directly concerned with evolutionary fundamentals, more "philosophical." In the latter class are *Back to Methuse-lah* and *The Simpleton of the Unexpected Isles.*

The only writer who can be credited with giving Ex-travaganza a philosophical turn on the nineteenth-century English stage is W. S. Gilbert. His philosophy, as Shaw fre-quently pointed out, was not very profound, but it had "an intellectual foundation—with a certain criticism of life in it" (*Music in London*, II, 75). The plays where Gilbert's phi-losophizing bent was most in evidence belong to the period before he made his vast success with *Pinafore* (1878), and after he had established himself as a dramatist with a series of conventional Burlesques on serious operas such as *Dulca-mara; or, The Little Duck and the Great Quack* (1866; on *L'Elisir d'Amore*); and *The Merry Zingara; or, The Tipsy Gipsy and the Pipsy Wipsy* (1868; on *The Bohemian Girl*). In the period between these earlier Burlesques and the Savoy Extravaganzas, Gilbert produced a series of blank-verse come-dies, such as *The Palace of Truth* (1870), *Pygmalion and Galatea* (1871), and *The Wicked World* (1873), that he evi-dently considered the best work of his life.[23] They are plays without music, but they draw upon the literary conventions of musical Extravaganza, and they feed the musical Extrava-ganza Gilbert later produced with Sullivan. (One of Gilbert's last efforts was to make *The Wicked World* into a "Fairy Opera," *Fallen Fairies* [1909], set to music by Edward Ger-man.) They are all, in effect, wholly spoken Extravaganzas (anticipating Shaw), fantasies designed to convey generalized views on human nature and the conditions of human ex-istence.

Gilbert's reflections on life as it is were given value through his inventions of life as it is not. In *The Palace of Truth* he creates an enchanted ground where all who enter must, with-out realizing it, tell what they know, think, and are, while they move and grimace in tune to masks and poses they no

[23] See Pearson, *Gilbert: His Life and Strife*, pp. 246-47.

longer are able to maintain. In *Topsy-Turvydom* (1874) he invents a country of reversal where men act like women and women like men, where people are born old and wise and grow young and ignorant, where beauty is shunned and ugliness prized, and where, in fact, all values seem to be inverted. In *The Wicked World, An Original Fairy Comedy* he invents a paradise where love has never been known and then shows the results of its introduction. In *Pygmalion and Galatea* he postulates an instance of humanity, Galatea, who has arrived at maturity without having gone through a course of hardening and spoiling by life. All these plays draw much of their tone and atmosphere from Planché's Fairy Extravaganzas, refashioned to suit Gilbert's philosophical purposes.

With his fairy worlds as a vehicle, Gilbert contrives a commentary on life that is mournfully critical. For example, in *The Wicked World* the fairies have heard of Earth as a sinful, dreadful place made bearable by love; and it appears to them, in their already blessed state, that love would be a crowning blessing. Three mortal men are therefore introduced, and with them the unknown feeling. But immediately the fairies lose their innocence and their happiness, and all the earthly sins and crimes are bred among them by this single passion. Ultimately they learn to reject love with horror. In *Pygmalion and Galatea*, the statue who comes to life as a woman with her mind and feelings complete sees the world, responds to it, and judges it with an unclouded vision and an unarmored sensitivity which make her both vulnerable and superior. In the end she resumes her pedestal and turns to stone, heartbroken and at last capable of irony:

> Farewell, Pygmalion—I am not fit
> To live upon this world—this worthy world.

Admittedly, Gilbert's philosophizing on the shortcomings of the real world as measured against an ideal virtue, truth, and harmony, had little to give to the current of Shaw's own speculation. Nevertheless, it is a matter of some importance for Shaw's development that, alone of the playwrights of the nineteenth century, Gilbert used the *donnée* of Extravaganza, the fantastic Otherworld, to comment on life in general; that even before Gilbert began the labor of making Burlesque-Extravaganza respectable, he had formed from its apparently unpromising materials a most effective instrument for what Shaw came to consider the first duty of the dramatist: to "interpret the passing show by parables."

Back to Methuselah, the first of Shaw's Philosophical Extravaganzas, is conceived as a cycle of five plays presenting a complete synopsis—historical, political, scientific, and religious—of Shaw's vision of life in general. It is a re-creation of scriptural material in part and of the cosmic drama as a whole, and as such it is related to the medieval scriptural cycles, to Wagner's cyclical music-drama and to Ibsen's philosophical poetic drama.[24] But *Back to Methuselah* is also a

[24] An early subtitle for *Methuselah* was "A Play Cycle." (See Mander and Mitchenson, p. 184). In the preface, it is advertised as "The Religious Art of the Twentieth Century"; "Creative Evolution is already a religion . . . But it cannot become a popular religion until it has its legends, its parables, its miracles" (*Methuselah*, p. lxxvii). Shaw described *Methuselah*, during the writing, as "a huge tetralogy (like Wagner's Ring)"; see above, p. 60 and note. In his preface, Shaw notes the "poetic aspiration" after Creative Evolution in Ibsen's *Emperor and Galilean*, as well as its concern with cosmic history; but Ibsen "left that vision of the future which his Roman seer calls 'the third Empire' behind him as a Utopian dream when he settled down to his serious grapple with realities in those plays of modern life with which he overcame Europe . . ." (*Methuselah*, p. lxxxiii). Shaw's Cain, and his entire development of the relationship of death to life which is a leading motif of *Back to Methuselah*, is prefigured in his analysis of Ibsen's Cain in *Emperor and Galilean*: "Cain, who slew because he willed, willed because he must, and must have willed to slay because he was himself, comes upon the stage to claim that murder is fertile, and death the ground of life, though, not having read Weismann on death as a method of evolution, he cannot say what is the ground of death" (*Quintessence of Ibsenism*, in *Major Critical Essays*, p. 50).

compendium of the dramaturgy which was to dominate Shaw's last period; that is, of the methods and resources of Extravaganza.

As the successor to *Heartbreak House, Methuselah* makes plain the transition from Discussion Play to Extravaganza. If *Heartbreak House* was a complex discussion with a parable ending, *Methuselah* is a complex parable with a discussion core. "The Gospel of the Brothers Barnabas," the second play of the cycle and the only one set in the present day, is a discursive exposition with a country-house setting of the biological, political, and metaphysical themes embodied as fantasy in the rest of the cycle.

The discourse by the Brothers, significantly a biologist and a theologian, provides the creative evolutionary rationale of the cycle, the ground of the "religion that has its intellectual roots in philosophy and science just as medieval Christianity had its intellectual roots in Aristotle" (p. 79). The discourse expounds the significance of "In the Beginning: B.C. 4004 (In the Garden of Eden)," which is the first part of the cycle and Shaw's Genesis; and it rationalizes the millennial advance toward the Kingdom of God in the last three parts of the cycle, Shaw's Revelation. The Barnabas commentary on *Genesis* ("the most scientific document we possess"), like the Christian commentaries on the Old Testament, interprets the old truth according to the new light (pp. 73-77). The Barnabas rationalization of Shaw's Revelation makes plain the bearing of the succeeding Otherworlds on the contemporary world and the connection between the biological and the political-social crises of the current age. Man lives too short a time, the Brothers declare, to be either mature or responsible. An adolescence of one hundred years or so would give him maturity; the prospect of three hundred years to live would give him responsibility.

The Gospel of the Brothers Barnabas is expounded to "Lubin" and "Joyce Burge," caricatures of the Liberal party

—·[413]·—

statesmen who in actual life had just led the country into and through the World War and the Peace. The introduction of contemporary political figures helps establish the relevance of the surrounding fantasy to the contemporary world. At the same time it puts a seal upon the transition from Discussion Play to Extravaganza.

Each of the remaining four sections of *Methuselah* embodies a different form of the fantastic Otherworld characteristic of nineteenth-century Extravaganza. Superficially, the Otherworld of "In the Beginning," the Garden of Eden, is parodied myth, an irreverent treatment of familiar mythic and heroic material in which Adam and Eve carry on like commonplace husband and wife. The Otherworld of "The Thing Happens," "*The official parlor of the President of the British Islands*" in the year 2170, evokes the imaginary kingdoms of Opera Bouffe and Political Extravaganza, in which the action is compounded out of the amorous concerns and the political affairs of the rulers of the land. It also suggests Gilbert's limited Utopias, with their earnestly mad institutions. Like Gilbert's Utopians, "the English people have become a Joint Stock Company admitting Asiatics and Africans as shareholders" (p. 120). England is managed by specially trained and imported Chinese and negro civil servants, an arrangement which "ends in the public services being so good that the Government has nothing to do but think." Parliament is now composed chiefly of harmless lunatics; but "the English people always did elect parliaments of lunatics. What does it matter if your permanent officials are honest and competent?" (p. 93).

The Otherworld of Part Four of *Methuselah*, "Tragedy of an Elderly Gentleman," is even more Gilbertian. The British Isles have become the Fortunate Islands once more, and the inhabitants, like the elect of *The Happy Land* and *The Wicked World*, are an exclusive species free from the frailties and distresses of common mortality. The Otherworld of Part Five, "As Far As Thought Can Reach," suggests both this Gilbertian fairy world and the world of Classical Extravaganza as handled by Planché (e.g. in *Olympic Revels*) and Gilbert (e.g. in *Thespis; Pygmalion; Happy Arcadia*). The scene is an Arcadian landscape, literally the Golden Age returned. There is "*A sunlit glade . . . the steps and columned porch of a dainty little classic temple . . . wooded heights . . . a grove . . . an altar*" and the curved benches of a theater, on a "*Summer afternoon in the year 31,920 A.D.*" A dance of youths and maidens is in progress to the music of a flute-player. "*Their dress, like the architecture of the theatre and the design of the altar and curved seats, resembles Grecian of the fourth century B.C., freely handled*" (p. 199).

The fantastic Otherworlds of *Back to Methuselah* are brought to bear on the contemporary world by a variety of means, from anachronism to extrapolation. Without a perceptible blush, Cain in "In the Beginning" speaks of his brother as "a true Progressive" for having abandoned vegetarianism, talks in the clichés of contemporary military and amoristic romance, and even quotes Tennyson: "My strength is as the strength of ten because my heart is pure" (p. 27). Cain is a modern romantic idealist; and Shaw combines his traditional associations with the more recent clichés to say something damaging about the "cinema-fed romanticism" which, in his view, made possible the First World War. Extrapolation occurs in "The Thing Happens," where governmental institutions are a satirical projection of contemporary tendencies on an unchanging ground of the "immaturity" of the English and their inability to govern themselves.

But perhaps the chief device for bringing about a significant interpenetration of worlds is that of the visitor from the immediate to the remote. The Otherworld visitor—a staple of Utopian fiction—was also a fundamental mechanism of many Gilbertian fantasies (*The Happy Land, The Wicked World, Pygmalion and Galatea, Utopia, Limited*). The parlor maid and the rector of Shaw's "Brothers Barnabas" become the voyagers to the Otherworld of "The Thing Happens." When found out, they give a plain account of the fear, drudgery, and alcoholic consolations of life in our dark ages which horrifies the imperfect Utopians with their highly socialized and equitably organized society. But the visitors are in a sense travellers from the future as well as from the past. They serve not only to yank contemporary England into the neighborhood of Utopia but also to expose that side of Utopia which is a satirical projection of contemporary England. They represent a new species, at once the remedy and the foil for the childishness of the chosen leadership and the narrowness of the bureaucratic mind. Through them the characteristic "interpenetration of worlds" is doubly achieved.

In Part Four, the "Tragedy of an Elderly Gentleman," the interpenetration is achieved by the visit of short-lived rulers from Baghdad, capital of the British Empire, and from a rival Napoleonic empire, to the island kingdom of the long-lived. The dress of the visitors in the year 3000 is *suitable for public official ceremonies in western capitals at the XVIII-XIX fin de siècle,"* and their speech and habits of mind are coeval; for while the long-lived were establishing themselves in England and Ireland, the rest of the world went through cycles of civilization, war, and barbarism, in which the incapacity of the short-lived to organize the civilizations they achieve leads to their inevitable collapse. "You will then begin all over again as half-starved ignorant savages, and fight with boomerangs and poisoned arrows until you work up to the poison gases and high explosives once more, with the same result" (p. 178). The immediate effect of this cycle is to cut across evolutionary time, to place under the criticism of the Fortunate Islanders representatives of a civilization more or less in the same state of crisis as Shaw's own, with the same institutions, the same social and economic attitudes, and the same failures in government.

In "As Far as Thought Can Reach," the two central events

of the play, the birth of an Arcadian and the unveiling of the "dolls," are also designed to bring contemporary values and attitudes into the critical orbit of Shaw's remote world. In the event of the "dolls," where Shaw's intentions are plainer, Pygmalion, a brilliant scientist, has combined his skill with that of Martellus, a great sculptor, to create, like God, a human couple who walk, dance, love, preach, and eventually kill. But Pygmalion's creatures are "prehistoric"; that is, they are lower than Pygmalion on an evolutionary scale. They are, in fact, the representatives of contemporary man in Shaw's evolutionary Otherworld, and an abstract of our own millennia. The masculine figure announces himself: "My name is Ozymandias, king of kings." His consort is "Cleopatra-Semiramis." They are romantics, idealists, and determinists, like Cain, who raise their illusions about themselves into a religious orthodoxy. Their speech is a burlesque rhetorical bombast. To Martellus they are clearly not alive; they are simply elaborate automata. The male figure is asked what he thinks of what he sees around him:

> THE MALE FIGURE. I have not seen a newspaper today.
> THE FEMALE FIGURE. How can you expect my husband to know what to think of you if you give him his breakfast without his paper?
> MARTELLUS. You see. He is a mere automaton.
> (p. 229)

After they have displayed their capacity for lying, killing, and wishing evil ("Do you blame us for our human nature?"), they die a stage death to the sound of music ("Illusions, farewell: we are going to our thrones"). And Strephon cries to an Ancient, "For heaven's sake dont tell us that the earth was once inhabited by Ozymandiases and Cleopatras. Life is hard enough for us as it is" (p. 238).

The other central event of the play, the birth of Amaryllis, called the Newly Born, is the focus of an interpenetration of worlds achieved very much on the biological principle suggested by Conrad Barnabas as the dull scientific foundation of *Genesis*: ontogeny recapitulates phylogeny. The life of the Arcadians, like that of the blastoderm, recapitulates the history of the race. In the new Arcadia, the inhabitants are born from an egg at an apparent age of about eighteen. In the egg they are several sorts of animal and primitive human being; but then, for four years, they live the lives of nymphs and shepherds such as never were, passing their time in the love of art, beauty, and each other. At the end of their fourth year, these toys cease to satisfy them. They lose their beauty and their sociability, they put aside childish things, and they devote themselves to the ecstasies of thought. They become Ancients, again as immortal as Adam before he invented death.

Throughout the play the "children" echo conventions of *our* theater and *our* world, particularly those concerning love and art, not only for the joke but to show them as strictly the formations of adolescence—the adolescence of the race. Chloe tells Strephon, a two-year old who is heartbroken over the changes in his four-year old mistress, "You must recognize facts and face them. It is no use running after a woman twice your age" (p. 206). Ecrasia, an aesthete, the arbiter of beauty and cultivated pleasure, declares "if the ancients had thoroughly grasped the theory of fine art they would understand that the difference between a beautiful nose and an ugly one is of supreme importance: that it is indeed the only thing that matters" (p. 242). The Newly Born comes trailing clouds of "archaic" sensibility and sheds them visibly from moment to moment. She falls in love immediately but ceases to be jealous after twenty minutes. She uses the word "murder," and a She-Ancient declares, "That is one of the funny words the newly born bring with them out of the past. You will forget it tomorrow" (p. 211).

—·[418]·—

There are numerous resemblances in method and detail between Gilbert's Mythological Comedy *Pygmalion and Galatea* and *Back to Methuselah*; in particular, Gilbert's fundamental conception of the statue-become-a-woman is very like that of the Newly Born. Both figures function dramatically as an advanced consciousness come into the world in a wholly virgin state—as a young woman born fully grown and articulate, but with innocent eyes and naïve modes of expression. The difference is that Galatea's direct responses and naïve simplicity are the measure of her superiority to the world and the standpoint from which it is judged, whereas the direct responses and naïve crudities of the Newly Born are the measure of her immaturity.

In *Methuselah*, Adam discovers death when he finds a fawn with a broken neck. In Gilbert's *Pygmalion*, Galatea discovers death when Leucippus brings in a fawn he has casually slain. In *Methuselah*, the Newly Born is distressed at the coming of darkness and at discovering "there is something the matter with me. I want to lie down. I cannot keep my eyes open." In *Pygmalion*, Galatea is afraid that the light is gone forever and, as she grows sleepy, that she is turning back to marble. Both Gilbert and Shaw exploit the Pygmalion legend directly to declare themselves on the relation of art and life.

Gilbert's Pygmalion wishes life for his work, not because he has foolishly fallen in love with its beauty, but from artistic ambition and disappointed idealism. He says, comparing himself to the gods,

> *I* am no bungler—all the men *I* make
> Are straight limbed fellows, each magnificent
> In the perfection of his manly grace:
> I make no crook-backs—all *my* men are gods,
> My women goddesses—in outward form.
> But there's my tether—I can go so far,

And go no farther—at that point I stop,
To curse the bonds that hold me sternly back.

(French A. E., p. 11)

Martellus, the artist half of Shaw's Pygmalion, has outgrown his Gilbertian counterpart's romantic idealism; but he too, as he approaches adulthood, can be satisfied with creating nothing less than life itself. The evolution of art, as he has recapitulated it in his own life, is from the representation of external beauty to the representation of thought; it is an attempt "to get nearer and nearer to truth and reality, discarding the fleeting fleshly lure, and making images of the mind that fascinates to the end. But how can so noble an inspiration be satisfied with any image, even an image of the truth? In the end . . . art is false and life alone is true" (p. 219). Though Gilbert's and Shaw's conclusions on the issue they both raise are diametrically opposed, the devices Gilbert employed to develop his conclusions may be found scattered broadside through the whole of *Methuselah*.

Gilbert provided Galatea, for an approach to the world around her, with a charming and amusingly incredible trick of speech. Able to speak fluently, and with a firm grasp of the most complicated abstract and moral categories, Galatea is nevertheless ignorant of some of the simplest words and concepts. When she is told that she is a woman, she asks Pygmalion if he is one too. She mistakes the meaning of "soldier," but learning it, she is capable of an extremely complex verbal and moral response:

GAL.   Leucippus! Who is he?
PYG. A valiant soldier.
GAL.   What is that?
PYG.   A man
     Who's hired to kill his country's enemies.
GAL. (*horrified.*) A paid assassin! (pp. 20-21)

Shaw exploits this device in "As Far as Thought Can Reach"

—·[420]·—

as part of a continuous playing upon language as the vehicle of thought, one of the cycle's recurrent motifs. The Newly Born arrives knowing the word "murder," but having to ask "What is a tail?"

THE HE-ANCIENT. A habit of which your ancestors managed to cure themselves. (p. 247)

She is told that she is falling asleep and that the light will come back tomorrow.

THE NEWLY BORN. What is tomorrow?
ACIS. The day that never comes. (p. 250)

Gilbert's device, used incidentally in "As Far as Thought Can Reach," plays a vital part in "In the Beginning" in a greatly elaborated form. Much of the dialogue is devoted to the efforts of the "newly born" Adam and Eve to find words for concepts and concepts for words. For example, Adam declares that he will clear the nettles away tomorrow, and the Serpent laughs:

THE SERPENT. Adam has invented something new. He has invented tomorrow. You will invent things every day now that the burden of immortality is lifted from you.
EVE. Immortality? What is that?
THE SERPENT. My new word for having to live for ever.
EVE. The serpent has made a beautiful word for being. Living.
ADAM. Make me a beautiful word for doing things tomorrow; for that surely is a great and blessed invention.
THE SERPENT. Procrastination.
EVE. That is a sweet word. I wish I had a serpent's tongue.

Adam suddenly takes fright: "There is a terrible danger in this procrastination."

> EVE. What danger?
> ADAM. If I put off death until tomorrow, I shall never die. There is no such day as tomorrow. . . .
> (pp. 13, 14)

The echo of Adam's "tomorrow" by Acis in "As Far as Thought Can Reach" suggests how the whole of the cycle is elaborately bound together. There are constantly recurring and developing themes, as there are constantly recurring character types. Death, the word which Adam invents when he finds the fawn with the broken neck, and the thing he invents as his refuge from immortality, is carried on as a motif in the person and speeches of Cain, in the allusions to the World War in "The Brothers Barnabas," in Cain Adamson Charles Napoleon, in the Dolls and the slaying of Pygmalion, and in the final aspiration of the "immortal" Ancients (who still remain subject to fatal accident) to be delivered "from the body of this death" (p. 248). There are similar linking motifs of sex, art, and language.

But *Back to Methuselah* is also bound together by its common focus. The cycle is a synopsis, in parable and fantasy, in a series of Otherworlds, of a unified philosophic vision of the world. And the various parables, each of the successive fantastic worlds, and the fable as a whole, are all brought to bear upon the contemporary world, indeed upon the topical world, and on what Shaw had the acuteness to name as the urgent crisis of the age and of the civilization.[25]

---

[25] *Farfetched Fables* (1948), the last of Shaw's Extravaganzas, is a short variation in six fables on the themes of *Back to Methuselah*. It starts in the post-atomic present, and projects the evolutionary future, carrying matters beyond the Elders of *Methuselah*, to a state of disembodied thought. It has never been commercially produced, and is interesting chiefly in relation to the early cycle.

The Simpleton of the Unexpected Isles, A Vision of Judgment (1933) was a return to the vein of Philosophical Extravaganza, though the political and philosophical are again inextricable. Shaw wrote, soon after its composition, "My bolt is shot as far as any definite target is concerned and now, as my playwright faculty still goes on with the impetus of 30 years vital activity, I shoot into the air more and more extravagantly without any premeditation whatever—*advienne que pourra*. The first of these two plays [*The Simpleton* and *The Millionairess*], which were written mostly in the tropics, is openly oriental, hieratic and insane."[26]

The play begins with a prologue in a tropical port of the British Empire in more or less present time and moves about twenty years into the future to "The Unexpected Isles," a British Crown Colony somewhere in the East, which appeared one day out of the sea. Shaw declared, "I could not have written it exactly as it is if I had not been in India and the Far East, though almost all my life as a playwright I have hankered after a dramatization of the Last Judgment."[27] Be that as it may, Oriental Extravaganza had been a flourishing mode in Burlesque-Extravaganza of the nineteenth century, as for example in Robert Reece's *Brown and the Brahmins; or, Captain Pop and the Princess Pretty-Eyes, An Oriental Burlesque* (1869); in Offenbach's *Ching-Chow-Hi; or, A Cracked Piece of China* (1865); in Gilbert's *The Mikado; or, The Town of Titipu* (1885); in George Dance and Edward Solomon's *The Nautch Girl; or, The Rajah of Chutneypore* (1891, reviewed in *Music in London*, I, 228-30); and in the countless extravaganzas and pantomimes based on the Arabian Nights.

The remote island setting of *The Simpleton* and the title

[26] Letter to Nora Ervine, 12 May 1934, in St. John Ervine, *Bernard Shaw*, p. 555. Shaw wrote, of the same two plays, to Siegfried Trebitsch, "One is an ultra-fantastic oriental modern (or futurist) play, the other a contemporary comedy. No plots, and contents indescribable" (MS postcard, 26 June 1934).

[27] Hesketh Pearson, *G.B.S.; A Postscript* (New York, 1950), p. 62.

itself were also reminiscent of nineteenth-century Extravaganza. For example, among the pieces Shaw might have seen in Dublin were Charles Horsman's *Charmian and Badoura; or, The King of the Conjugal Isles* (Gaiety, Dublin, 7 July 1873) and Reece and Lecocq's *The Isle of Bachelors* (Gaiety, Dublin, 6 March 1875; based on Lecocq's *Les Cent Vierges*). An anonymous Burlesque at the Queen's, Dublin, was called *Corin; or, The King of the Peaceful Isles* (1871). Planché wrote extravaganzas called *The Island of Jewels* (1849); *The Invisible Prince; or, The Island of Tranquil Delights* (1846); *Telemachus; or, The Island of Calypso* (1834). Albery's *Oriana* is set "Near the Happy Isles," seen in the painted distance, in "Days gone by"; and a number of Gilbert's extravaganzas (e.g. *The Gondoliers; Utopia, Limited*) are set, at least in part, on a generic South Sea island. The fanciful island was useful in Extravaganza for providing a circumscribed wonderland set off by distance and difficulty, though often, as in *Oriana* and *The Simpleton*, it was also set off by time.

The contained Otherworld of the Unexpected Isles is brought to bear on the actual world across both time and distance. The meeting of worlds in spite of distance is indeed the prime concern of the play, in a fusion of genre-technique and subject matter. For *The Simpleton* is in great part a parable on empire, on the reciprocal impact of East and West, contrasting its best hopes with its actual offspring. The island Otherworld is the laboratory of an experiment in which Prola and Pra, an oriental priestess and priest, form a mixed family with four occidentals "to try out the result of a biological blend of the flesh and spirit of the west with the flesh and spirit of the east" (p. 43). The result of initial contact is the illumination of one culture by the other; but the final result of the mingling is sterile and disappointing.

The geographical distance between everyday England and the Unexpected Isles is also bridged by the device of the Otherworld traveller. The Simpleton is a quintessential English curate, a paragon of innocent respectability, who has been suddenly set down in the Unexpected Isles to his utter confusion. Into a tropical climate of moral, social, and religious exoticism, he brings not only the parochial convictions of the Church of England but England itself: "England that is me: I that am England! Damn and blast all these tropical paradises" (p. 49). However, despite his sincere horror and his righteous indignation, the Simpleton, like the nation he represents, is mightily attracted to Love, Pride, Heroism, and Empire, and cannot help himself from marrying into the polygamous and polyandrous family.

The Simpleton is a traveller across a distance in space (which turns out to be a moral and spiritual distance as well). Distance in time, the other condition of the island Otherworld, is bridged by making the future world of *The Simpleton* an extrapolation, a projection of the British Empire to the time of its disruption by parochialism—by a conflict on differences in conventional social and religious morality. England withdraws from the Empire, declares for a "right little, tight little island," and the Irish Free State prepares to "lead the attack on treason and disruption" (p. 59).

Immediately thereafter, the Last Judgment begins. Shaw's Vision of Judgment also bridges temporal distance, less as an extrapolation of present tendencies than as a fanciful recreation of the revolutionary present in the visionary future. It is his translation into universal fable of the systematic and continuous valuation of social utility which, he declared, had already eliminated whole classes in the Soviet Union. Judgment is presented as coming to the nations individually, like revolutions, and in his preface, Shaw equates the work of the Angels with the work of the Tcheka, "carrying out the executive work of a constitution which had abolished the lady and gentleman."

"Simple enough; and yet so hard to get into our genteel heads that in making a play about it I have had to detach it altogether from the great Russian change, or any of the actual political changes which threaten to raise it in the National-Socialist and Fascist countries, and to go back to the old vision of a day of reckoning by divine justice for all mankind." (*Simpleton*, pp. 13-14)

Judgment is announced, in Shaw's fantasy, by another kind of Otherworld visitor: a genuinely winged and volant, though unheroic, angel. Judgment is rendered, in Shaw's fantasy, in terms of the society and politics of present-day England, and is thus brought satirically home.

The imperial and apocalyptic-revolutionary aspects of *The Simpleton* are united under the final, inclusive, philosophic aspect of Shaw's vital reality. The experiment on the Unexpected Isles has been an effort of Pra and Prola, Priest and Priestess of the Life Force, to create a Utopia, and the theme of Utopia, implicit in all of Shaw's Extravaganza, is here an explicit theme throughout. Pra declares, "Our dream of founding a millennial world culture: the dream which united Prola and Pra as you first knew them, and then united us all six, has ended in a single little household with four children, wonderful and beautiful, but sterile" (p. 53). "We mustnt pretend to be omniscient," the inspired Simpleton says; "We must have an ideal of a beautiful and good world. We must believe that to establish that beautiful and good world on earth is the best thing we can do, and the only sort of religion and politics that is worth bothering about" (p. 62). Prola and Pra turn out to be the two aspects of the Life Force first projected in *Man and Superman*; and if their modern-world offspring, Love, Pride, Heroism, and Empire, are unsuccessful experiments, Prola and Pra are prepared to try again. The priestess declares:

> There are still a million lives beyond all the
> Utopias and Millenniums and the rest of the jig-
> saw puzzles: I am a woman and I know it. Let men
> despair and become cynics and pessimists because
> in the Unexpected Isles all their little plans fail:
> women will never let go their hold on life. We
> are not here to fulfil prophecies and fit ourselves
> into puzzles, but to wrestle with life as it comes.
> And it never comes as we expect it to come. . . .
> PRA. There is no country of the Expected. The
> Unexpected Isles are the whole world. (p. 80)

The failed imperial dream of a millennial culture and the
still promising socialist dream of a millennial society are neither of them allowed finality in the unifying creative-evolutionary gloss which ends the fable. Though Shaw turned to Extravaganza as a form in which he could project Utopias for the
criticism of contemporary life, in the end he holds up Life,
in some sense of uncertainty and unlimited possibility, as the
measure and criticism of all Utopias.

As a group, Shaw's Extravaganzas are unquestionably the
most under-appreciated of his plays. Just as the best of the
Discussions are thought to be, from a theatrical point of view,
static, argumentative, and dialectically over-refined, while in
fact they are full of farcical activity, vigorous character, and
broad theatricalism, so the Extravaganzas are thought to be
theatrically crude, allegorically dull, and relatively empty,
while in fact they are inventive, exciting, and as full of meat
as an egg. Of course not all the Extravaganzas are equally
good; *Geneva* is inferior to *On the Rocks* as *On the Rocks*
is inferior to *Too True to be Good* and *The Simpleton*. But
as a group, headed by *Back to Methuselah*, they are among
Shaw's most noteworthy and least noted achievements for the
modern theater. They are the most advanced of Shaw's plays

in their invention and exploitation of non-Euclidean worlds for philosophic and parabolic purposes, in their thematic structures and use of structural analogue, in their use of open allegory and frankly symbolic action and setting. The disregard of realistic canons in these cerebral fantasies can be deplored as evidence of Shaw's declining abilities only from the standpoint of doctrinaire dramatic naturalism. Otherwise it must be seen as Shaw's enrichment of a theater rather too limited by naturalistic predilections. It is matter for sermonizing, however, that the plays and the techniques which bring Shaw into the company of the most interesting, as well as the most extravagant and uncompromisingly intellectual advance-guard playwrights of the mid-twentieth century should, in his case, so clearly descend from the nineteenth-century Burlesque-Extravaganza; for through a good part of the nineteenth century, when the intellectual and dramatic pretensions of the theatrical advance-guard centered on realism, Burlesque-Extravaganza was considered the most frivolous and mindless of forms. Shaw capped his heterodox career, having always made the greatest intellectual claims for the drama, by making nineteenth-century Extravaganza the vehicle for his drama of ideas.

IV

CONCLUSION

16

RHETORICAL DRAMA AND THE DRAMA OF IDEAS

N O aspect of Shaw's accomplishment in the modern theater was more important than his creation of a modern rhetorical drama, a rhetorical drama of impassioned ideas; and it is surely no disparagement to point out that he created it from the refractory materials and traditions that came to his hand. The rhetorical drama of the eighteenth and nineteenth centuries was a drama of passions and sentiments, not ideas. It used language, like action, for the externalization of emotion —and its conventions granted emotion a complete expressibility. The actor's part was conceived as a succession of states of feeling, and he acted Joy, Grief, Fear, Anger, Pity, Scorn, Hatred, Jealousy, Wonder, and Love, uttering all the while the mighty language commensurate with his emotion. Acting handbooks systematized the passions and described how each was to be mimed. Aaron Hill, for example, the author of one important handbook, sketched the bounds and divisions of his subject by announcing, "there are only ten dramatic passions;—that is, passions, which can be distinguished by their outward marks, in action; all others being relative to, and but varied degrees of, the foregoing."[1] Hill conceived of the actor as an instrument to be tuned successively to whichever of the passions was implicit in his lines. All the passions were to be

[1] Aaron Hill, *An Essay on the Art of Acting*, in *The Works of the Late Aaron Hill, Esq.* (London, 1753), IV, 357. According to A. S. Downer, "Players and Painted Stage: 19th Century Acting," *PMLA*, 81 (1946), p. 575, the sources for all the important handbooks of the nineteenth century were Hill's *Essay*; Henry Siddons' *Practical Illustrations of Rhetorical Gesture and Action, Adapted to the English Drama. . . . Embellished with numerous engravings, Expressive of the various passions* (London, 1807); and Leman Thomas Rede's *Road to the Stage* (London, 1827).

expressed visibly by a combination of facial mask and bodily tension, and the changes of passion were defined points, or "rests," where the actor altered his tuning.[2]

The drama of passions verbally expressed that was served by this theory of acting was partly Elizabethan and Jacobean (and therefore not wholly appropriate) and partly contemporary. In Shaw's time, most of the extant eighteenth-century plays of the passions were plays with virtuoso roles for starring actors (e.g. Barry Sullivan's favorite, *The Gamester; A Tragedy in Five Acts* [1753] by Edward Moore). But nineteenth-century serious playwrights kept up the tradition with attempts at five-act blank-verse legitimacy which included the Reverend Henry Milman's *Fazio; A Tragedy in Five Acts* (1816), the much esteemed tragedies of James Sheridan Knowles, and the theatrically less esteemed efforts of the notable Romantic and Victorian poets.[3] In this tradition of Shake-

[2] Hill, *Essay on the Art of Acting*, pp. 358, 367-68. Hill wishes the actor to "conceive a strong idea of the passion" in his own imagination, but he offers his formula of muscular tension plus facial expression for the tuning (for example: Hatred is expressed "by muscles intense—and aversion in the eye"; Wonder "by muscles intense—and an awful alarm in the eye"; Love, "by muscles intense,—and a respectful attachment in the eye"; Scorn, "by muscles languid and neglected—with a smile in the eye, to express the *light*, or a frown in the eye, for the *serious* species" [p. 401]. "For these are nature's own marks, and impressions, on the body, in cases where the passion is produced by involuntary emotions.—And when natural impressions are imitated, exactly, by art, the effect of such art must seem natural" [p. 361]). Implicit in Hill's muscular arrangements are the standardized bodily attitudes illustrated by the engravings in Siddons' *Practical Illustrations of Rhetorical Gesture and Action*. Siddons refines on the concepts in Hill's *Essay* without really departing from them. He illustrates emotions with both bodily attitudes and expressive gesture, and notes, "The reflections and reasonings, which are admitted on the theatre, are always divided in two parts,—the sentiments of the heart, and the passions. It is from these that *gesture* receives its more particular modifications, the determinate degree of warmth, the transition or the repose more or less marked, &c." (p. 58).

[3] See Introduction above, p. 3. For Shaw on the "artificial high horses" of the nineteenth century, see above, pp. 83-4. As late as 1887, Boucicault ventured a definition of comedy and tragedy as follows: "Comedy aspires to portray by imitation the *weaknesses* to which human beings are subject . . . Tragedy aspires to portray the *passions* to which strong natures

speare passed through eighteenth-century dramaturgy and psychology, Joanna Baillie produced her three volumes actually called *Plays on the Passions* (1798, 1802, 1812). But much more important in the nineteenth century than the attempts at elevated legitimacy, dramatic speech as the rhetoric of the passions flowed into the most popular channels of the contemporary theater: into opera, "drama," and Melodrama. And it remained the tradition of great acting, and the tradition of the Shakespearean stage.[4]

William Archer, life-long champion of "natural" modes and more or less Shaw's contemporary, pictures the rhetorical convention in terms which help explain Shaw's appreciation and his desire to bring it alive in his own work. Archer recalled in 1923 Edwin Booth playing in a scene from Bulwer-Lytton's *Richelieu*: "Edwin Booth's rendering of this passage was one of the few performances I can recall which enabled me to realise the *kind* of effect which the great actors and actresses of the great age of rhetorical acting used to produce. It was thrilling, startling, electrifying, beyond anything dreamt of on our humdrum realistic stage. It was not imitation—it was passion incarnate."[5] Of course there were great differences between actors, and between generations of actors, all of whom declaimed the rhetoric of the passions. Boucicault noted, for

---

are subject, and a resistance to their influence." (In *The Art of Acting; A Discussion by Constant Coquelin, Henry Irving and Dion Boucicault*, in *Papers on Acting*, 5th Ser., II, New York, 1926, p. 55.)

[4] For Shaw's analysis of opera as supreme drama of the passions, see above, pp. 40-4. For the rhetorical qualities of Melodrama, see above, p. 83. When speaking generally, Shaw was more apt to acknowledge the operatic strain in his work than the melodramatic. Thus, he writes of himself: "Handel's and Mozart's symmetry of design formed his classical taste; and from Rossini and Verdi as well as from Shakespeare he acquired the grandiose and declamatory elements hidden beneath his superficially colloquial and 'natural' dialogue." (From a running commentary on William Irvine's *Universe of G. B. S.* [New York, 1949], p. 13.)

[5] *The Old Drama and the New*, p. 250. Cf. Shaw's descriptions of Sullivan's energy in action and Salvini's volcanic power in repose, and his instructions to Irene Vanbrugh and Mrs. Patrick Campbell, pp. 103-04, 106-07 above.

example, in 1882, that "Before this century the great French tragedians before Talma and the great English tragedians before Kean used their treble voice—the teapot style. They did it as if they played on the flute. Then came the period when the tragedian played his part on the double bass *so*. . . . There was no reason for it. Now we perform that part in the present age in what is called the medium voice." The idea, he notes, "is that the tragedian never has to use his own voice," because tragedy is "transcendental drama." "The transcendental drama assumes that the dialogs are uttered by beings larger than life, who express ideas that no human being could pour out."[6] Similarly there were fashions which successively elevated superhuman dignity and superhuman energy as the touchstone of acting in the rhetorical mode; but the standard of utterance "by beings larger than life, who express ideas that no human being could pour out" remained constant.

The tendency of Shaw's playwriting was not toward "passion incarnate," but toward a drama of incarnate ideas. Nevertheless, he also needed a verbal medium, a theatrical convention which would express ideas that no human being could pour out, and express them in a manner thrilling, startling, and electrifying; and for this he bypassed contemporary modes of both fashionable and avant-garde playwriting and drew upon the obsolete rhetorical drama of the passions. To convert the medium to his own purposes—a formidable task on the face of it—Shaw simply made ideas into passions of the mind.

By treating ideas as passions, Shaw was able to fuse the new and the old into something theatrically viable, and to secure to this medium for ideas both the superabundant energy of the rhetorical convention and its superhuman expressiveness. When his plays were criticized for cold rationality and the lack of human passion, Shaw replied,

[6] Dion Boucicault, *The Art of Acting*, in *Papers on Acting*, 5th Ser., Vol. I (New York, 1926), pp. 28-29.

". . . not for a moment will you find in my plays any assumption that reason is more than an instrument. What you will find, however, is the belief that intellect is essentially a passion, and that the search for enlightenment of any sort is far more interesting and enduring than, say, the sexual pursuit of a woman by a man, which was the only interest the plays of my early days regarded as proper to the theatre: a play without it was 'not a play.'

"Neither have I ever been what you call a representationist or realist. I was always in the classic tradition, recognizing that stage characters must be endowed by the author with a conscious self-knowledge and power of expression, and, as you observe with genuine penetration, a freedom from inhibitions, which in real life would make them monsters of genius. It is the power to do this that differentiates me (or Shakespeare) from a gramophone and a camera."[7]

Critics other than Shaw, especially those devoted to naturalistic illusion in the theater, have noticed that Shaw's characters have superhuman powers of expression. Other observers have noticed that they have superhuman energy as well. For example, W. H. Auden writes: "His plays are a joy to watch, not because they purport to be concerned with serious problems, but because they are such wonderful displays of conspicuous waste, because the energy shown by any of his characters is so wildly in excess of what their situation practically requires that if it were to be devoted to anything 'worthwhile,' they would wreck the world in five minutes."[8] Both qualities, energy and expressiveness, were fundamental to Shaw's drama of passionate ideas. Both stem from the rhetorical drama of the passions as it flourished in performance into the nineteenth century.

[7] "Mr. Shaw on Mr. Shaw," *N. Y. Times*, 12 June 1927, Sec. VII, p. 1.

[8] "The Fabian Figaro," in *George Bernard Shaw, A Critical Survey*, ed. Louis Kronenberger (New York, 1953), p. 156.

One student of Shaw's rhetorical drama points out that Shaw knew nothing of formal rhetoric and associated the word with stagey, empty, old-fashioned verbiage.[9] It is true that Shaw sometimes used the word in its modern pejorative sense, and it is equally true that the workings of the rhetorical dramatic tradition in the linguistic fabric of Shaw's plays are hard to find by formal rhetorical analysis. Indeed, rendering the tradition fit for modern service required a surface of "superficially colloquial and 'natural' dialogue" (see note 4). The elevated rhetorical tradition manifests itself in three characteristics of Shaw's plays: a verbal mesh of "ceaseless point-making" as Shaw called it, supporting and binding together a discourse full of argument, contradiction, and surprise; punctuating shifts into more formal and overtly poetic styles; and "set-piece" declamations marking climaxes of event or argument.

The energy and continuity of almost any scrap of dialogue from a Shaw play comes not so much from sparkling wit as from the first of these characteristics, the mesh of ceaseless point-making. Inconsistent renderings of similar words and related phrases in Siegfried Trebitsch's translation of *The Devil's Disciple* provoked Shaw to declare, "I know ten times as much about all those *dramatis personae* as you do, or as you ever will. . . . I remember every word they say, and keep alluding to these sayings pages after you have forgotten them. My stage effects are based on that."[10] In a later letter to Trebitsch, Shaw notes, "My method of getting a play across the footlights is like a revolver shooting: every line has a bullet in it and comes with an explosion."[11]

[9] Robert Lee Scott, *Bernard Shaw's Rhetorical Drama: A Study of Rhetoric and Poetic in Selected Plays*, Ph.D. thesis, U. of Illinois, 1955 (University Microfilms), pp. 1ff. Mr. Scott equates the "rhetorical tendency" of Shaw's plays with their persuasive purpose. He examines the plays as persuasive instruments, but suggests how such devices as exemplary characters have a dramatic, or poetic, function as well.

[10] MS letter to Trebitsch, 10 Dec. 1902.

[11] Typescript letter to Trebitsch, 17 June 1922.

His own method, Shaw felt, was also the method of Shakespeare. In a general review and critique of Beerbohm Tree's Shakespearean productions, Shaw observed that, despite the universal and long-continued treatment of Shakespeare as an august convention, "there has always been between the author and actor a genuine bond of stage method, of rhetoric, of insistence on exceptionally concentrated personal force and skill in execution, of hammering the play in by ceaseless point-making." Shaw praises Louis Calvert, an actor for whom Elizabethan language was still alive, for the "perfect intelligence, that finds the nail in every phrase and hits it on the head unerringly."[12] He had similar praise for Forbes-Robertson, whom he pronounced the true classical heroic actor brought up to date. It was precisely Shakespeare's bond with the actor that Shaw coveted for himself. In a relationship like that between composer and performer, he sought to provide a text that insisted on concentrated force and skill. He required of the actor-interpreter a rhetorical virtuosity which would drive home the nail he had planted in every phrase.

A second evidence of the rhetorical tradition in the linguistic fabric of Shaw's plays is his use of a favorite device of the Elizabethans: the deliberate shift to a more heightened, formal rhetoric to achieve heightened intensity. In Shaw's early plays a suddenly heightened manner of speaking was usually evidence of a pose, romantic, heroic, or idealistic (for example, Napoleon's posturing in *The Man of Destiny*). But in later plays, a sudden shift to patterned, semi-poetic, ritualistic speech regularly indicates a passionate intensity of perception or revelation which transcends the ordinary levels of the play. So, for example, the persons in *Heartbreak House* suddenly rise out of themselves, or rather speak from their innermost selves, as the first act closes in darkness:

CAPTAIN SHOTOVER (*raising a strange wail in the darkness*) What a house! What a daughter!

[12] "The Dying Tongue of Great Elizabeth," *The Saturday Review*, 99 (Feb. 1905), pp. 169, 170.

MRS HUSHABYE (*raving*) What a father!

HECTOR (*following suit*) What a husband!

CAPTAIN SHOTOVER. Is there no thunder in heaven?

HECTOR. Is there no beauty, no bravery, on earth?

MRS HUSHABYE. What do men want? They have their food, their firesides, their clothes mended, and our love at the end of the day. Why are they not satisfied? Why do they envy us the pain with which we bring them into the world, and make strange dangers and torments for themselves to be even with us?

CAPTAIN SHOTOVER (*weirdly chanting*)
I built a house for my daughters, and opened the doors thereof,
That men might come for their choosing, and their betters spring from their love;
But one of them married a numbskull;

HECTOR (*taking up the rhythm*) The other a liar wed

MRS HUSHABYE (*completing the stanza*)
And now must she lie beside him, even as she made her bed. (*H. House*, pp. 78-79)

At the end of *Back to Methuselah*, there is a similar scene where Adam, Eve, Cain, the Serpent, and Lilith come to look at "what has come of it," to speak, pass judgment, and vanish one by one. Similarly, in the Epilogue to *Saint Joan*, Cauchon, Dunois, the Archbishop, Warwick, De Stogumber, the Inquisitor, the soldier who gave Joan a cross, the Executioner, and King Charles kneel successively and chant Joan's praises. ("The girls in the field praise thee; for thou hast raised their eyes; and they see that there is nothing between them and heaven. . . . The dying soldiers praise thee, because thou

—·[438]·—

art a shield of glory between them and the judgment," etc.) When Joan threatens to return, they fall back into prose and, repeating the pattern, successively withdraw (pp. 161-63).

The set speech, the third "rhetorical" characteristic of Shaw's playwriting, was a normal feature in older rhetorical drama, in which it came like an aria or a virtuoso cadenza. It underwent an evolution in Shaw's dramaturgy similar to that of the style shift. Shaw always took care to provide what the old actor in Pinero's *Trelawny of the "Wells"* called "a real *speech*; [some]thing to dig your teeth into"; but in his earliest plays the set speeches were carefully imbedded and naturalized, so that, for example, Mrs. Warren's magnificent apology is broken and seemingly guided by the punctuating comments and questions of her daughter. In contrast, the splendid, unbroken, five-minute speeches of the Inquisitor in *Saint Joan* and of King Magnus in *The Apple Cart* are frankly orations (King Magnus, addressing his cabinet, is even politely applauded), and the preacher-burglar of *Too True to be Good* closes that play with a sermon. Between the extremes are such evident occasions for rhetorical virtuosity as Candida's explanation of her decision in *Candida*, the Prologue of the God Ra and Caesar's address to the sphinx in *Caesar and Cleopatra*, Undershaft's apologia in *Major Barbara*, Dubedat's death speech in *The Doctor's Dilemma*, Lina Sczcepanowska's rejection of bourgeois domesticity at the end of *Misalliance*, and Napoleon's discourse on the English in *The Man of Destiny*. Since Napoleon is given a histrionic temperament, his auditor sits down and *"composes herself to listen to him"* whereupon *"Secure of his audience, he at once nerves himself for a performance. He considers a little before he begins; so as to fix her attention by a moment of suspense. His style is at first modelled on Talma's in Corneille's Cinna; but it is somewhat lost in the darkness, and Talma presently gives way to Napoleon, the voice coming through the gloom with startling intensity."* At the end of the speech, Shaw exploits a sudden shift in style. Asked for the application of his generalities on the English character, Napoleon explains himself, *"dropping his rhetorical style"* (pp. 186-87). Similarly, Mrs. George's trance in *Getting Married*, where she speaks not in her own person, but as Woman, is an obvious link between the resource of the style shift and that of the virtuoso set speech, both marks of the rhetorical convention on the verbal medium of Shaw's plays.

The intellectual substance of Shaw's rhetorical drama of ideas—its reason for being—was expressed in an impassioned interplay of variously representative persons. The complement of the virtuoso aria was the multi-voiced "concerted scene," such as the quartet in *Rigoletto* "with its four people expressing different emotions simultaneously" (*London Music*, p. 393), or the trio in *Saint Joan* (Scene IV), with its three people expressing different passionate ideas, and concerting them into a harmony against Joan (see above, pp. 51-2). However, the frankness of Shaw's use of the Bishop, the Earl, and the Chaplain as spokesmen for Catholicism, feudalism, and English parochialism should not distract from the immense variety in Shaw's invention of the persons of his drama of ideas; for it is not quite true that "Just as Victor Hugo gives a passion apiece to each of his characters and lets them fight it out, so Shaw gives a philosophy apiece to each of his characters and lets them argue it out."[13] There is considerable difference between a symbolic figure like the compulsive preacher without a doctrine who preaches the sermon at the end of *Too True to Be Good*, a personification like the sinister Lucius Septimus who appears each time the vengeance theme is touched in *Caesar and Cleopatra*, and a representative figure like Mrs. Warren or John Tarleton.

Though any simple critical formula of personification and debate for Shaw's drama of ideas is bound to fail in applica-

[13] Archibald Henderson, *Shaw, Life and Works*, p. 437.

tion, there are certain kinds of "idea" figures which appear again and again, and it is possible to summarize Shaw's practice by ignoring the extraordinary individuation of his persons. There are first of all, especially in the early plays, grouped personifications of the basic attitudes in Shaw's social psychology: realism (practical and visionary), idealism, and philistinism. Second, there are the personifications of particular ideals: as gentlemanliness, romantic love, revenge, and heroism. Then there are representatives of particular groups, classes, and institutions: as aristocracy and plutocracy; church, state, and feudality; the English and the Irish; spinsters and prostitutes. And finally, there are personifications of evolutionary forces, social and biological: as heterodoxy and orthodoxy, creativity and fecundity. An expressive and impassioned interplay of these many sorts of personages produced the drama of ideas.

In the course of Shaw's critical and playwriting career, there was a shift in his view of the direct appeal of things intellectual. This shift is paralleled in turn by the development of his drama of ideas through its three major stages. In his early criticism, Shaw was quite firmly convinced that "It is feeling that sets a man thinking, and not thought that sets him feeling."

"The secret of the absurd failure of our universities and academic institutions in general to produce any real change in the students who are constantly passing through them is that their method is invariably to attempt to lead their pupils to feeling by way of thought. . . . Which is the greater educator, pray—your tutor, when he coaches you for the Ireland scholarship or Miss Janet Achurch, when she plays Nora for you? You cannot witness *A Doll's House* without *feeling*, and, as an inevitable consequence, thinking . . ."[14]

[14] "The Religion of the Pianoforte," *Fortnightly Review*, 61 (1894), 262-64.

In *Our Theatres in the Nineties*, Shaw campaigned to show that "in these plays which depend wholly on poignant intensity of expression for the simple emotions the sceptre has passed to the operatic artist"; but he advocated in their place "the drama in which emotion exists only to make thought live and move us" (*OTN*, I, 138; 1 June 1895). In criticizing A. W. Gattie's *The Honorable Member* (1896), Shaw declares "people's ideas, however useful they may be for embroidery, especially in passages of comedy, are not the true stuff of drama, which is always the naïve feeling underlying the ideas" (*OTN*, II, 192). But by the end of his work as a practical theater critic, Shaw was already making the extensions of theory which are carried out in the "Don Juan in Hell" episode of *Man and Superman* and in the mode of the Discussion Play. It is significantly in connection with Forbes-Robertson's notable Hamlet that Shaw first gives evidence of the new approach. He writes of Hamlet,

"He is none of your logicians who reason their way through the world because they cannot feel their way through it: his intellect is the organ of his passion: his eternal self-criticism is as alive and thrilling as it can possibly be. The great soliloquy—no: I do NOT mean 'To be or not to be': I mean the dramatic one, 'O what a rogue and peasant slave am I!'—is as passionate in its scorn of brute passion as the most bull-necked affirmation or sentimental dilution of it could be." (*OTN*, III, 203; 2 Oct. 1897)

The notion of passionate intellect and intellectual passion as self-sufficient and engrossing entities grew in Shaw thinking and in his dramatic practice. The envisaged heaven of *Man and Superman*, the evolutionary future of *Back to Methuselah* reflect his cancellation of the oppositeness of supposedly hot passion and supposedly cold thought. Like some of the saints, Shaw eventually found that the only fit comparison for the ecstasies of contemplation were those of love. In 1926, he declared: "intellect is a passion capable of giving a more lasting enjoyment than any other passion. . . . Intellect has ecstasies which will finally supersede the orgasms of physical passion as the climaxes of human happiness."[15] From *Methuselah* on, Shaw never dropped this theme. In *Far-fetched Fables* (1948), almost Shaw's last play, a woman of the future lecturing on primitive man declares, "To initiate births they had to practise personal contacts which I would rather not describe. Strangest of all, they seem to have experienced in such contacts the ecstasies which are normal with us in our pursuit of knowledge and power, and culminate in our explorations and discoveries" (p. 119). In *Buoyant Billions* (1947), the last significant word in the play declares, "Mathematical passion alone has no reaction: our pleasure in it promises a development in which life will be an intellectual ecstasy surpassing the ecstasies of saints" (p. 60).

The three major crystallizations of Shaw's drama of ideas follow the developments in Shaw's view of passion and intellect. Melodrama, Discussion, and Extravaganza are respectively emotional, discursive, and symbolic-analogic modes of the drama of ideas. Shaw found the melodramatic mode useful for the thrills and perils which could be relied upon to engage the interests and emotions of the audience. He also found in Melodrama a potential of Bunyanesque allegory, so that in *The Devil's Disciple* the conventional ideals of religiosity, romance, and gentlemanliness are personified, as snares to truth and virtue, in Mrs. Dudgeon, Judith, and General Burgoyne. But Shaw felt it a prime necessity to engage the audience emotionally in, for example, the anxiety and suspense of the hero's mounting the platform to be hanged (see above, pp. 202-03). In Melodrama, the naïve feeling is the source of dramatic interest and intellectual engagement; "feeling sets a man

---

[15] Henderson, "Shaw Self-Revealed," *Fortnightly Review*, 125 (1926), 436.

thinking"; and in *The Devil's Disciple*, Shaw exploits the conventional sympathy for the good-bad hero to undercut the personified conventional ideals.

The development of Shaw's trust in the impassioned activity of intellect as a source in itself of dramatic interest coincided with his development of the discursive mode. The able critic A. B. Walkley noted the change in a review of *The Doctor's Dilemma* (Court, Nov. 1906): "This foible of discursiveness has been steadily gaining on him. *John Bull* was more discursive than *Man and Superman*. *Major Barbara* was more discursive than *John Bull*. *The Doctor's Dilemma* is more discursive than *Major Barbara*. Needless to point out that this discursiveness is not a new method, but a 'throwing back' to a very old method. It was, for instance, the method of Shakespeare."[16]

Earlier, Walkley devoted a brilliant review of *Man and Superman* to exposing "the masked interdependence of the action-plot and idea-plot and the curious way in which the one is warped and maimed in being made to serve as the vehicle for the other." Walkley's criticism is not directed at the existence of an "idea-plot," but at the "parasitic nature of the action-plot," which is "well-nigh meaningless without the key of the idea-plot." "If Mr. Shaw's play were a real play there would be no need to explain the action-plot by laborious reference to the idea-plot. The one would be the natural garment of the other; or rather the one would be the flesh of which the other was the bones."[17]

Man and Superman was a half-way house between the emo-

---

[16] *Drama and Life* (London, 1907) , p. 239. In an earlier review of the Court Theatre *Major Barbara*, Walkley is led by opportunity into a less perceptive and more exasperated comment: "In perfect innocence Mr. Shaw puts his apology into the mouth of one of the people in *Major Barbara*. 'Andrew, this is not the place for making speeches'; and Andrew replies, 'I know no other way of expressing myself.' Exactly! Here is a dramatist who knows no other way of expressing himself in drama than the essentially undramatic way of speech-making" (p. 233).

[17] *Ibid.*, pp. 226, 230.

tion-based drama of ideas and the discursive drama of ideas. If Shaw wished to reply to Walkley's critique (and there is some evidence of such a wish: see above, pp. 290-91), he replied by perversely dispensing altogether with the action-plot, so that it could no longer pretend to compete with the idea-plot. The matters of intellectual concern were now plainly talked about, the development of the argument was the development of the drama, and the action illustrated the discourse. In the Melodramas, action-plot and idea-plot were equally important, but the emotional fabric of the action-plot was treated as the source of dramatic interest; in the succeeding Discussion Plays, action-plot was completely subordinated to idea-plot, and the flow and progress of the dialectic was treated as the source of dramatic interest; in the Extravaganzas, the action-plot *was* the idea-plot, and the spectacle of the ideas working themselves out in action was the source of dramatic interest.

The preface to *Back to Methuselah* flatly announces that "art has never been great when it was not providing an iconography for a live religion" (p. lxxviii). Legend, parable, and drama "are the natural vehicles of dogma," though by no means to be mistaken for it. *Back to Methuselah* was Shaw's attempt to give flesh to the Logos of a new religion, and the Extravaganza which succeeded the Discussion Play was an attempt to directly embody speculative and critical notions in the situations and events of a play. The result was apparent fantasy. The mind expressing itself in comprehensive dramatic images produced a drama that was also fable and parable, and, in some cases (notably *Back to Methuselah* and *The Simpleton of the Unexpected Isles*), Shaw's equivalent of his description of Wagner's *Ring*. "The philosophic part," he wrote, "is a dramatic symbol of the world as Wagner observed it."[18] Not all the Extravaganzas have the universal scope of *Methuselah* or *The Simpleton*; but the action, even of those of

[18] *The Perfect Wagnerite*, p. 218.

narrow scope, is in the concrete dramatic image of the thought. In the drama of ideas, as in the long line of Shaw's imaginative realists, the union of passion and intellect culminates in something one has to call vision. In Shaw's Extravaganzas, as in the contemplations of his Saint Joan, present thoughts are clothed in such concreteness that they speak and act before the senses in parables of futurity.

The "significant action," in a dramatic sense, of Shaw's playwriting career can be given brief statement: he converted a rhetorical drama of the passions into a rhetorical drama of impassioned ideas, using as his vehicle the most popular and "theatrical" modes of the nineteenth-century theater. Such a synopsis leaves much to be inferred. But Shaw's exploitation of stock-company stereotypes; his deliberate attempts to embarrass, if not destroy, certain romantic conventions and genres; his exploitation of the rhetorical aspects of opera and music; his campaigns as a critic for and against certain kinds of drama and acting; even his use of "comedic paradox," and of the wit and irony, the flirtation with logic and illogic, which are the weapons of intellect however impassioned, are all implicit in the central, governing action of Shaw's playwriting career. There remains much, of course, that a single statement does not account for. For example, the great variations in the form of Shaw's drama of ideas are partly the consequence of his developing notions of the inherent interest of passionate thought and partly the consequence of the difference between Shaw preaching an attitude of moral and political realism and Shaw preaching a religion of creative evolution—between Shaw attacking the illusions and orthodoxies of the past and Shaw giving shape to the myths and orthodoxies of the future. It is a compliment to the variety and pliability of the nineteenth-century popular theater that it was able to keep pace with the changes and furnish so much that was essential to the three basic modes.

In a study of Shaw's relations with the nineteenth-century theater, it becomes notably apparent that stage conventions, critical debates, and indeed whole genres which went into the shaping and the substance of Shaw's drama of ideas have altogether dropped out of view without damaging his vitality. Revivals of Shaw are frequent, and they are not yet made in an antiquarian spirit. However, where a theater is literarily self-conscious, plays survive their initial productions by virtue of qualities which, after they charm in the theater, can capture an audience outside it. Consequently, however much Shaw was indebted to the dead conventions and genres, they are much more indebted to him. The nineteenth-century theater had a most awesome vitality which rose from other than literary greatness. Therefore, in its proper self, it was a perishable theater, and its literary remains, which were then most warm, are now most cold. Nevertheless, Shaw brought it into our time in his own plays, in a form not only literary, but theatrically viable and theatrically fertile. He saves the uses and the energies of the mortal nineteenth-century popular theater for a future classical repertory and for the living tradition.

BIBLIOGRAPHY

BIBLIOGRAPHY

À Beckett, Gilbert Abbot, *The Quizziology of the British Drama*, London, 1846.

Albery, James, *The Dramatic Works of James Albery*, ed. Wyndham Albery, 2 vols., London, 1939.

Archer, Charles, *William Archer, Life, Work and Friendships*, London, 1931.

Archer, William, *About the Theatre; Essays and Studies*, London, 1886.

———— *English Dramatists of To-Day*, London, 1882.

———— *The Old Drama and the New; An Essay in Re-Valuation*, Boston, 1923.

———— *The Theatrical 'World' of 1893-1897*, 5 vols., London, [1894-] 1898.

Auden, Wystan Hugh, "The Fabian Figaro," in *George Bernard Shaw: A Critical Survey*, ed. Louis Kronenberger, New York, 1953, pp. 153-57.

Barrymore, John, *Confessions of an Actor*, Indianapolis, 1926.

Beerbohm, Max, *Around Theatres*, 2 vols., New York, 1930.

Belasco, David, *Six Plays*, Boston, 1929.

Belmont, Eleanor Robson, *The Fabric of Memory*, New York, 1957.

Bentley, Eric, *Bernard Shaw, 1856-1950*, Amended Edition, New York, 1957.

———— ed., *Let's Get a Divorce! and Other Plays*, New York, 1958.

———— *The Playwright as Thinker; A Study of Drama in Modern Times*, New York, 1946.

"The Bible and the Stage," *Spectator*, 70 (4 Feb. 1893), 155-56.

Bishop, George W., *Barry Jackson and the London Theatre*, London, 1933.

———— *My Betters*, London, 1957.

Boucicault, Dion, *The Art of Acting*, Dramatic Museum of Columbia University *Papers on Acting*, Fifth Series, Vol. I, New York, 1926.

———— "The Art of Dramatic Composition," *North American Review*, 126 (1878), 40-52.

———— "The Decline of the Drama," *North American Review*, 125 (1877), 235-45.

———— *Forbidden Fruit & Other Plays*, ed. Allardyce Nicoll and F. Theodore Clark, in *America's Lost Plays*, Vol. I, Princeton, 1940.

Bullough, Geoffrey, "Literary Relations of Shaw's Mrs Warren," *Philological Quarterly*, 41 (January, 1962), 339-58.

Bulwer-Lytton, Edward George, Baron Lytton, *The Dramatic Works of the Right Hon. Lord Lytton*, London, 1873.

Campbell, Bartley, *The White Slave and Other Plays*, ed. Napier Wilt, in America's Lost Plays, Vol. XIX, Princeton, 1941.

Chancellor, E. Beresford, *The Pleasure Haunts of London*, London, Boston, and New York, 1925.

Clinton-Baddeley, V. C., *All Right on the Night*, London, 1954.

———— *The Burlesque Tradition in the English Theatre After 1660*, London, 1952.

Coquelin, Constant, *Art and the Actor*, Dramatic Museum of Columbia University *Papers on Acting*, Second Series, Vol. II, New York, 1915.

———— et al., *The Art of Acting; A Discussion by Constant Coquelin, Henry Irving, and Dion Boucicault*, Dramatic Museum of Columbia University *Papers on Acting*, Fifth Series, Vol. II, New York, 1926.

Craig, Edward Gordon, *Henry Irving*, New York, 1930.

Daily News (London), 28 October, 1873.

Daily Telegraph (London), 29 October, 1873.

Davey, R., "Heartsease," *The Theatre; A Monthly Review of the Drama, Music, and the Fine Arts*, N.S., I (June 1880), 359-63.

Dickens, Charles, *Vincent Crummles: His Theatre and His Times*, arranged by F. J. Harvey Darton, London, 1926.

Dictionary of National Biography, ed. Sir Leslie Stephen and Sir Sidney Lee, London, 1921-1922.

Disher, Maurice Willson, *Melodrama; Plots that Thrilled*, London, 1954.

Downer, Alan S., "Harley Granville-Barker," *Sewanee Review*, 55 (1947), 627-45.

———— "Players and Painted Stage; Nineteenth Century Acting," *PMLA*, 61 (1946), 522-76.

Dublin Evening Mail, 1864-1876.

Duggan, G. C., *The Stage Irishman: A History of the Irish Play and Stage Characters from the Earliest Times*, Dublin, 1937.

Dukes, Ashley, "A Doll's House and the Open Door, With Two Letters from George Bernard Shaw," *Theatre Arts Monthly*, 12 (January 1928), 21-38.

Dumas, Alexandre (*fils*), et al., "The Bible on the Stage," *The New Review*, VIII (February 1893), 183-89.

Elgar, Sir Edward, *Letters of Edward Elgar and Other Writings*, ed. Percy M. Young, London, 1956.

[Eldredge, H. J.] (Reginald Clarence, pseud.), *"The Stage" Cyclopaedia; A Bibliography of Plays*, London, 1909.

Enciclopedia dello Spettacolo, 8 vols. to date, Rome, 1954-1961.

Enthoven Theatre Collection, Unidentified review of Bronson Howard and Frank Marshall's *Brighton*, dated 24 January 1880.

Erle, Thomas W., *Letters From a Theatrical Scene-Painter; Being Sketches of the Minor Theatres of London as They Were Twenty Years Ago*, London, 1880.

Ervine, St. John, *Bernard Shaw; His Life, Work and Friends*, London, 1956.

Fergusson, Francis, *The Idea of a Theater*, New York [1956].

Film Index: A Bibliography, ed. Harold Leonard, New York, 1941.

Filon, Augustin, *The English Stage*, London, 1897.

Fitz-Gerald, S. J. Adair, *Dickens and the Drama*, London, 1910.

Forbes-Robertson, Sir Johnston, *A Player Under Three Reigns*, Boston, 1925.

Gaiety Theatre, Dublin, *Souvenir of the Twenty-Fifth Anniversary of the Opening of the Gaiety Theatre 27th November, 1871*, Dublin, 1896.

Gilbert, Sir William Schwenck, *Original Plays by W. S. Gilbert*, London, 1876.

———— *Plays & Poems of W. S. Gilbert*, New York, 1932.

———— *A Stage Play*, Dramatic Museum of Columbia University Papers on Playmaking, Third Series, Vol. III, New York, 1916.

Granville-Barker, Harley, "Exit Planché—Enter Gilbert," *The Eighteen-Sixties; Essays by Fellows of the Royal Society of Literature*, ed. John Drinkwater, Cambridge, 1932.

[Grein, Alice Augusta] (Michael Orme, pseud.), *J. T. Grein: The Story of a Pioneer 1862-1935 . . . Foreword Written by Conal O'Riordan and Censored and Revised by George Bernard Shaw*, London, 1936.

Grein, J. T., *The New World of the Theatre, 1923-1924*, London, 1924.

———— *The World of the Theatre; Impressions and Memoirs, March 1920-1921*, London, 1921.

Grove's Dictionary of Music and Musicians, ed. Eric Blom, 5th ed., London, 1954.

Halline, Allan G., ed., *American Plays*, New York, 1935.

Hazlitt, William, *Hazlitt on Theatre*, ed. William Archer and Robert Lowe, New York, 1957.

——— *The Complete Works*, ed. P. P. Howe, 21 vols., London, 1930-1934.

Henderson, Archibald, *Bernard Shaw; Playboy and Prophet*, New York, 1932.

——— *George Bernard Shaw; His Life and Works*, London, 1911.

——— *George Bernard Shaw: Man of the Century*, New York, 1956.

——— "George Bernard Shaw Self-Revealed," *Fortnightly Review*, 125 (1926), 433-42, 610-18.

——— *Table-Talk of G.B.S.*, London, 1925.

Hill, Aaron, *An Essay on the Art of Acting*, in *The Works of the Late Aaron Hill, Esq.*, London, 1753, Vol. IV.

Howard, Bronson, *The Autobiography of a Play*, Dramatic Museum of Columbia University *Papers on Play-Making*, First Series, Vol. II, New York, 1914.

——— *The Banker's Daughter and Other Plays*, ed. Allan G. Halline, in America's Lost Plays, Vol. X, Princeton, 1941.

Howells, William Dean, "The New Taste in Theatricals," *Atlantic Monthly*, 23 (May 1869), 635-44.

Huneker, James, "The Quintessence of Shaw," in *George Bernard Shaw: A Critical Survey*, ed. Louis Kronenberger, New York, 1953, pp. 7-25.

Illustrated London News, 87 (19 September 1885) and 125 (19 November 1904).

Illustrated Sporting and Dramatic News, III (18 September 1875) and VII (7 April 1877).

Irvine, William, *The Universe of G.B.S.*, New York, 1949.

James, Henry, *The Scenic Art; Notes on Acting & the Drama: 1872-1901*, ed. Allan Wade, New York, 1957.

Jefferson, Joseph, *The Autobiography of Joseph Jefferson*, New York, 1890.

Jones, Doris Arthur, *Taking the Curtain Call; The Life and Letters of Henry Arthur Jones*, New York, 1930.

Jones, Henry Arthur, *Representative Plays by Henry Arthur Jones*, ed. Clayton Hamilton, 4 vols., Boston, 1925.

Kavanagh, Peter, *The Irish Theatre; Being a History of the Drama in Ireland from the Earliest Period up to the Present Day*, Tralee, 1946.

Knight, Joseph, *Theatrical Notes*, London, 1893.

Knowles, James Sheridan, *The Dramatic Works*, 3 vols., London, 1841.

Lawrence, W. J., "Madame Céleste," *The Gentleman's Magazine*, 265 (October 1888), 391-410.

Levey, R. M., and O'Rorke, J., *Annals of the Theatre Royal, Dublin, From its Opening in 1821 to its Destruction by Fire, Feb. 1880*, Dublin, 1880.

Lewes, George Henry, *On Actors and the Art of Acting*, London, 1875.

Loraine, Winifred, *Head Wind; The Story of Robert Loraine*, New York, 1939.

Lowenstein, F. E., *The Rehearsal Copies of Bernard Shaw's Plays; A Bibliographical Study*, London, 1950.

MacCarthy, Sir Desmond, *The Court Theatre, 1904-1907; A Commentary and Criticism*, London, 1907.

———— *Shaw*, London, 1951.

McCarthy, Lillah, *Myself and My Friends . . . With an Aside by Bernard Shaw*, London, 1934.

Malvern Festival [Illustrated Souvenir] 1929-1939, 1949.

Mander, Raymond, and Mitchenson, Joe, *Theatrical Companion to Shaw; A Pictorial Record of the First Performances of the Plays of George Bernard Shaw*, London, 1954.

Meilhac, Henri, and Halévy, Ludovic, *Théâtre*, 8 vols., Paris, 1900-1902.

Mommsen, Theodor, *The History of Rome*, tr. William Purdie Dickson, New ed. rev., 5 vols., New York, 1900.

Morley, Henry, *The Journal of a London Playgoer, From 1851 to 1866*, London, 1866.

Nicoll, Allardyce, *A History of English Drama, 1660-1900*, 6 vols., Cambridge, 1952-1959.

Niklaus, Thelma, *Harlequin Phoenix; or, The Rise and Fall of a Bergamask Rogue*, London, 1956.

O'Neill, Michael J., "Some Shavian Links with Dublin as Recorded in the Holloway Diaries," *Shaw Review*, II (May 1959), 2-7.

Oxford Companion to the Theatre, ed. Phyllis Hartnoll, 2nd ed., London and New York, 1957.

Page, Will A., *Behind the Curtains of the Broadway Beauty Trust, Including Several Letters by Bernard Shaw*, New York, 1926.

Pearson, Hesketh, *Bernard Shaw; His Life and Personality*, London, 1942.

———— *G.B.S.; A Postscript*, New York, 1950.

Pearson, Hesketh, *Gilbert; His Life and Strife*, London, 1957.

Pemberton, T. Edgar, *Sir Charles Wyndham, A Biography*, London, 1904.

Pinero, Arthur Wing, *Robert Louis Stevenson as a Dramatist*, Dramatic Museum of Columbia University *Papers on Play-Making*, First Series, Vol. IV, New York, 1914.

———— *The Social Plays of Arthur Wing Pinero*, ed. Clayton Hamilton, 4 vols., New York, 1917-1922.

Planché, James Robinson, *A Cyclopaedia of Costume, or Dictionary of Dress*, 2 vols., London, 1876.

———— "Extravaganza and Spectacle," *Temple Bar*, III (1861), 524-32.

———— *The Extravaganzas of J. R. Planché, 1825-1871*, ed. T. F. D. Croker and S. Tucker, 5 vols., London, 1879.

———— *History of British Costume*, London, 1834.

———— *The Recollections and Reflections of J. R. Planché: A Professional Autobiography*, 2 vols., London, 1872.

Pollock, W. H., "A Glance at the Stage," *The National Review*, V (July 1885), 646-51.

Purdom, Charles Benjamin, *Harley Granville Barker, Man of the Theatre, Dramatist, and Scholar*, London, 1955.

Quinn, Arthur H., *A History of the American Drama from the Civil War to the Present Day*, New York, 1937.

———— ed., *Representative American Plays*, 6th ed. rev., New York, 1938.

Rattray, Robert Fleming, *Bernard Shaw: A Chronicle*, London, 1951.

Rede, Leman Thomas, *The Guide to the Stage . . . Founded on and partly taken from Leman Rede's Book*, London and New York, 1872.

———— *The Road to the Stage; or, The Performer's Preceptor*, London, 1827.

Riding, George A., "The Candida Secret," *The Spectator*, 185 (17 November 1950), 506.

Robertson, Thomas William, *The Principal Dramatic Works*, 2 vols., London, 1889.

Rowell, George, ed., *Nineteenth Century Plays*, The World's Classics, London and New York, 1953.

———— *The Victorian Theatre; A Survey*, London, 1956.

St. James's Theatre, London, *Notes on Granville Barker's Productions at the St. James's Theatre, Sept. 1st, 1913, with a few portraits* [London, 1913].

Saunders' News-letter, History of the Theatre Royal, Dublin, Reprinted with Additions, Dublin, 1870.

Scott, Robert Lee, *Bernard Shaw's Rhetorical Drama: A Study of Rhetoric and Poetic in Selected Plays,* diss., U. of Illinois, 1955, University Microfilms.

Scribe, Eugène, *Théâtre,* 20 vols., Paris, 1856.

Shaw, George Bernard, *Advice to a Young Critic and Other Letters,* ed. E. J. West, New York, 1955.

———— "Art Corner," *Our Corner,* V-VII (June 1885-September 1886).

———— "Barker's Wild Oats," *Harper's Magazine,* 194 (January 1947), 49-53.

———— *Bernard Shaw and Mrs. Patrick Campbell: Their Correspondence,* ed. Alan Dent, London, 1952.

———— *Bernard Shaw's Letters to Granville Barker,* ed. C. B. Purdom, New York, 1957.

———— "Caesar and Cleopatra," *New Statesman,* I (3 May 1913), 112-13.

———— "A Dramatic Realist to His Critics," *The New Review,* 11 (1894), 56-73.

———— "The Dying Tongue of Great Elizabeth," *The Saturday Review,* 99 (February 1905), 169-71.

———— *Ellen Terry and Bernard Shaw: A Correspondence,* ed. Christopher St. John, New York, 1931.

———— "Fanny's First Play," a letter to the editor, B. W. Findon, signed Flawner Bannel, *Play Pictorial,* 19 (1911), p. 50.

———— "George Bernard Shaw as a Man of Letters," *New York Times,* 5 December 1915, Sec. VI, 6.

———— *How to Become a Musical Critic,* ed. Dan H. Laurence, New York, 1961.

———— *Letters from George Bernard Shaw to Miss Alma Murray (Mrs. Alfred Forman),* [Edinburgh] 1927.

———— "Mr. Shaw on Mr. Shaw," *New York Times,* 12 June 1927, Sec. VII, 1.

———— "Mr. Shaw's Method and Secret," *Daily Chronicle,* 30 April 1898, p. 3.

———— MS letters to Alan S. Downer and reply to a questionnaire, 1947-1948.

———— MS letters to Charlotte Payne Townshend (Mrs. George Bernard Shaw), Sept. 1896 to 4 May 1897, 19 April 1912 to 30 Jan. 1934, British Museum Add. MSS 46505-46506.

Shaw, George Bernard, MS letters to Siegfried Trebitsch, 1902-1950, Berg Collection, New York Public Library.

_____ MS letters to J. E. Vedrenne, 1907, Enthoven Collection, Victoria and Albert Museum.

_____ MS rehearsal notes for *Arms and the Man, Getting Married,* and *Fanny's First Play*; in the Enthoven Collection, Victoria and Albert Museum.

_____ "Notes to Act I [of *Caesar and Cleopatra*]," typescript, carbon, with MS heading and beginning note in author's hand, unsigned and undated, 2 pp. numbered 27 and 28; in the Berg Collection, New York Public Library.

_____ *On the Rocks: A Political Fantasy in Two Acts by a Fellow of the Royal Society of Literature. First Rough Proof—Unpublished,* Privately Printed, 1933.

_____ *On the Rocks: A Compendium of Contemporary Politics in Two Acts. First Revise after Rehearsal—Unpublished,* Privately Printed, 1933.

_____ "The Play of Ideas," *New Statesman and Nation,* N.S., 39 (6 May 1950), 510-11.

_____ Preface to *Three Plays by Brieux,* New York, 1911.

_____ *The Quintessence of Ibsenism,* London, 1891.

_____ "The Religion of the Pianoforte," *Fortnightly Review,* 61 (1894), 255-66.

_____ "Shakespeare: A Standard Text," *Times Literary Supplement,* 17 March 1921, p. 178.

_____ *Shaw on Theatre,* ed. E. J. West, New York, 1958.

_____ "Shaw's Rules for Directors," *Theatre Arts,* 33 (August 1949), 6-11.

_____ "Some Unpublished Letters of George Bernard Shaw," ed. Julian Park, *University of Buffalo Studies,* 16 (September 1939), 115-30.

_____ Standard Edition of the Works of Bernard Shaw, 37 vols., London, 1930-1950.

_____ "Sullivan, Shakespear, and Shaw," *Atlantic Monthly,* 181 (March 1948), 56-58.

_____ "The Theatre Today and Yesterday according to George Bernard Shaw, in answer to questions asked by Roy Nash," *Manchester Evening News,* 6 December 1938.

_____ "Trials of a Military Dramatist," *Review of the Week,* I (4 November 1899), 8-9.

_____ "What George Bernard Shaw Looks Forward To: Every

Irish Town Its Municipal Theatre," *Bristol Evening Post*, 3 December 1946, p. 2.

———— "What the Films May Do to the Drama," *Metropolitan*, 42 (May 1915), 23, 54.

———— WIDOWERS' HOUSES. A Didactic Realistic Play in Three Acts. [Holograph MS with note in Shaw's script:] "First two acts written 1885. First part of 3rd act probably in 1890. Second part in 1892—finished 1st August: pp. 83, 84 & 85 added 20/10/92." Berg Collection, New York Public Library.

———— *Widowers' Houses: A Comedy By G. Bernard Shaw, First Acted at the Independent Theatre in London*, ed. J. T. Grein, Independent Theatre Series of Plays, Number One, London, 1893.

Siddons, Henry, *Practical Illustrations of Rhetorical Gesture and Action, Adapted to the English Drama from a Work on the Same Subject by M. Engel*, London, 1807.

Sillard, Robert M., *Barry Sullivan and His Contemporaries*, 2 vols., London, 1901.

S[pence], E. F., "The Stage from the Stalls," *The Sketch*, 9 November 1904, p. 122.

Spencer, Terrence J., *The Dramatic Principles of George Bernard Shaw*, diss., Stanford, 1957, University Microfilms.

Spiller, Robert E., Thorp, Willard, et al., *Literary History of the United States*, 3 vols., New York, 1948.

Stanton, Stephen S., ed., *Camille and Other Plays*, New York, 1957.

Stevenson, Robert Louis, *Works*, ed. Sir Edmund Gosse, Pentland Edition, 20 vols., 1906-1907.

Sullivan, Herbert, and Flower, Newman, *Sir Arthur Sullivan, His Life, Letters, and Diaries*, New York, 1927.

Taylor, Tom, *Historical Dramas*, London, 1877.

Tennyson, Alfred, Baron Tennyson, *Works*, ed. Hallam Tennyson, 10 vols., 1907-1913.

Times (London), 29 October 1873, and 2 September 1913.

Tomlins, Frederic Guest, *A Brief View of the English Drama, from the Earliest Period to the Present Time*, London, 1840.

Trevelyan, George Macaulay, *British History in the Nineteenth Century*, London, 1927.

Vanbrugh, Irene, *To Tell My Story*, London, 1948.

Walkley, Arthur Bingham, "Arms and the Man," *The Speaker*, IX (28 March 1894), 471-72.

———— *Drama and Life*, New York, 1908.

Who's Who in the Theatre, ed. John Parker, 8th ed., London, 1936.

Wilde, Oscar, *The Plays of Oscar Wilde*, 4 vols., Boston and London, 1905-1920.

Wilson, Albert Edward, *King Panto; The Story of Pantomime*, New York, 1935.

Wilson, Edmund, "Bernard Shaw at Eighty," *Eight Essays*, New York, 1950.

Winter, William, *Life and Art of Richard Mansfield, with Selections from His Letters*, 2 vols., New York, 1910.

Young, Stark, *Immortal Shadows; A Book of Dramatic Criticism*, New York, 1948.

INDEX

Abbey Theatre, Dublin, 288
à Beckett, Gilbert Arthur, 391, 395-97
"Absalom and Achitophel" (Dryden), 377
Achurch, Janet, 144, 441
acting, requirements of Shaw's plays, 59, 95-96, 116-18; Prince of Wales style, 94-97; rhetorical style, 95-106; "classical," 114-15; "idiosyncratic," 115; and drama of the passions, 431-34; actor's bond with playwright, 437
Adelphi Theatre, London, 80, 82-83; acting style, 97-98, 184, 328
Admiral Guinea (Stevenson and Henley), 316-17
Admirable Bashville (Shaw), 387n
adventure melodrama, 206-215
Aeschylus, 84
After Dark (Boucicault), 26n
Aïda (Verdi), 49
Ainley, Henry, 110
Aladdin (Barrett and Harris), 333
Albery, James, 14, 16, 74-75, 242, 249, 400, 403, 424
Alfred the Great (Marylebone pantomime), 328
allegory, 185, 223. *See also* representative personages
All's Well That Ends Well (Shakespeare), 31
All That Glitters Is Not Gold (T. and J. M. Morton), 72, 162, 165n, 174-75
American melodrama, 220-22
Amoroso, King of Little Britain (Planché), 387
Anderson, Mary Antoinette, 340-41
Androcles and the Lion (S. Planché), 330
Androcles and the Lion (Shaw), revision of Barker production, 108, 113, 123, 161; and farce, 245-47; genre associations, 324-26; and Christmas pantomime, 326-34; and Christian melodrama, 334-48, 380

Angel of the Attic (T. Morton), 192
Annajanska, the Bolshevik Empress (Shaw), 113
Antony and Cleopatra (Shakespeare), 359
Apple Cart (Shaw), 50, 55, 246, 314n; as extravaganza, 378, 380, 383, 391, 399-403, 406, 407, 439
Arabian Nights, 330, 423
Archer, William, 71, 85-86, 126; and *Widowers' Houses*, 162-63, 191, 235, 242-43, 315, 324, 326, 337-38, 378; letter to, 255; and *Arms* controversy, 382-83, 385, 433
Aristophanes, 381, 387-88, 393, 409
Aristotle, 315, 413
Arkwright's Wife (Taylor), 350
Arms and the Man (Shaw), 36, 46, 47, 58, 85, 123; as Pleasant Play, 127-28, 134-36, 141, 161, 168; and military romance, 184, 186-94, 222, 269, 378; critical controversy, 381-83, 388
Arrah-na-Pogue (Boucicault), 22, 27n, 197-98, 201, 278, 280
artist figure, in domestic comedy, 226-27; in *Candida*, 231-33; in *How He Lied*, 233; in *Doctor's Dilemma*, 233-38
As Like as Two Peas (Lille), 261-62
Asquith, Herbert Henry, 407
Auberge des Adrets (Antier *et al.*), 215-16
Augier, Emile, 145, 151, 153n, 163
Augustus Does His Bit (Shaw), 243
Aulnoy, Marie Catherine, Comtesse d', 330, 386
Awakened Conscience (W. H. Hunt), 153n
Aynesworth, Allan, 34
Ayrton, Acton Smee, 392

Babes in the Wood (Taylor), 166
Bacchae (Euripides), 304n
Back to Methuselah (Shaw), 31, 33, 57-58, 60-61, 140; and farce, 245-46, 314n, 322; as extravaganza,